PENGUIN BOOKS

Ka Whawhai Tonu Matou
Struggle Without End

Ranginui Walker belongs to the Whakatohea tribe at Opotiki. He is married to Deirdre and has three grown-up children. He was educated at St Peter's Maori College, Auckland Teachers' College and the University of Auckland. He taught in primary schools in Northland and Auckland, and lectured at Auckland Teachers' College for five years before taking up a temporary post in Maori Studies at Auckland University in 1967.

From 1970 Dr Walker worked for fifteen years in Continuing Education before taking up his present post as Associate Professor in Maori Studies. He has published numerous papers on Maori education, Maori activism and Maori politics as well as his 'Korero' in the *New Zealand Listener*. In public life Dr Walker was chairman of the Auckland District Maori Council for fifteen years and a member of the New Zealand Maori Council for twenty years and is a council member of the Auckland College of Education and was also a foundation member of the World Council of Indigenous People.

Ka Whawhai Tonu Matou

Struggle Without End

Ranginui Walker

PENGUIN BOOKS

PENGUIN BOOKS

Penguin Books (NZ) Ltd, 182–190 Wairau Road, Auckland 10, New Zealand
Penguin Books Ltd, 27 Wrights Lane, London W8 5TZ, England
Viking Penguin Inc., 40 West 23rd Street, New York, New York 10010, USA
Penguin Books Australia Ltd, 487 Maroondah Highway, Ringwood, Australia 3134
Penguin Books Canada Ltd, 2801 John Street, Markham, Ontario, Canada L3R 1B4

Penguin Books Ltd, Registered Offices: Harmondsworth, Middlesex, England

First published 1990
5 7 9 10 8 6 4

Editorial services Michael Gifkins and Associates
Designed by Richard King
Typeset by Typocrafters Ltd
Printed in Hong Kong

CONTENTS

Preface   7

Introduction   9

1   *Mythology*   11

2   *Te Hekenga o Nga Waka*   24

3   *Nga Korero o Nehera*   44

4   *Nga Tikanga Maori*   63

5   *Tauiwi*   78

6   *Takahi Mana*   98

7   *Ka Whawhai Tonu Matou*   117

8   *Te Ana o te Raiona*   135

9   *Nga Pou o te Iwi*   160

10   *Mana Maori Motuhake*   186

11   *Nga Totohe ki Tauiwi*   220

12   *Ma te Ture te Ture e Patu*   248

Epilogue   248

Appendices   289

Glossary   295

References   300

Bibliography   317

Index   325

CONTENTS

Preface   7

Introduction   9

1 *Mythology*   11

2 *The Canoe Migrations*   24

3 *The History of Ancient Times*   44

4 *Maori Customs*   63

5 *Foreigners*   78

6 *Over-riding Mana*   98

7 *We Shall Fight Forever*   117

8 *The Lion's Den*   135

9 *The Leaders of the People*   160

10 *Maori Sovereignty*   186

11 *The Struggle Against the Foreigners*   220

12 *Only the Law Can Defeat the Law*   248

Epilogue   248

Appendices   289

Glossary   295

References   300

Bibliography   317

Index   325

PREFACE

This book is a distillation of forty years' experience as a teacher, academic and participant in the dynamic field of cultural politics. By education and professional training I was an upwardly mobile member of mainstream society. I held conservative views, I had security and a comfortable life. My teaching experience spanned primary and secondary schools, a technical institute, teachers' college, continuing education and university undergraduates. My only ambition was to do well in my profession and to benefit my family. I was an intensely shy and private person with no aspirations to politics or public life. But I was also Maori. I inhabited a dual world of two social and cultural landscapes. As long as those two landscapes were kept discrete, I could shuttle back and forth between the two with ease as a bicultural person. For the first twenty years my career goals were achieved on schedule. Then, in 1970, my life changed as career and community involvements put me at the interface of cultural politics between Maori and Pakeha.

Late in 1969 Peta Awatere and Matiu Te Hau invited me to become secretary of the Auckland District Maori Council, and in the new year I took up an appointment in Continuing Education at Auckland University. These posts put me in the unique position of delivering knowledge to Pakeha about Maori and making the resources of the university available to the Maori in their struggle against the Pakeha monopoly of power and resources. My work in the Maori Council put me in contact with urban-born Maori who railed openly and vehemently against monocultural Pakeha dominance and Maori subjection. That was the beginning of my own awakening and my involvement in the Maori struggle. This book is about that struggle in both its historic and contemporary contexts.

I am grateful to my wife Deirdre, my staunchest supporter and confidante in the experiences that brought this book to fruition. My warmest thanks go to my colleagues Jane McRae, who proof-read the manuscript; Jan Kelly, who did the maps; Judith Binney, who checked the historic chapters; and Rangimarie Rawiri, who helped me with the rudiments of computer management and word-processing skills.

7

Finally, I wish to thank my mother Wairata, to whom this book is dedicated. She taught me the meaning of love for family, kinsfolk and humanity.

This book has been written for a New Zealand audience of Maori and Pakeha. Since many Maori words have entered common usage, the usual practice of italicising them in the text has not been followed **Nor** has vowel length been marked by macrons. This latter departure from linguistic practice was taken to facilitate editing and typesetting. For the serious student of language, H. W. Williams's *A Dictionary of the Maori Language* is recommended for indication of vowel length.

Ranginui Walker
Auckland 1990

INTRODUCTION

The colonisation of New Zealand by the British during the era of European expansionism in the nineteenth century was a historic process predicated on assumptions of racial, religious, cultural and technological superiority. The Maori had lived in isolation for a thousand years when the advance party of colonisation, the navigators, whalers, sealers and traders, came upon them late in the eighteenth century. These first visitors were welcomed by the people of the land for the cornucopia of material goods they brought with them from the factories of industrial England. Economic welcome, trade and sexual congress were the equalisers in Maori New Zealand for the first forty years of European contact.

In 1814 the missionaries arrived bearing the cross in one hand and the Bible in the other as justification for their mission of converting the Maori from heathenism to Christianity and savagery to civilisation. This glorified mission masked the insidious nature of their cultural invasion. They railed against the sacred icons of the Maori as works of the Devil and systematically undermined their myths and spiritual beliefs to replace them with their own.

After the missionaries, the settlers of the New Zealand Company and Captain William Hobson came to annex the country as another jewel to add to the Crown of the British Empire. Like his predecessors, the Governor cloaked his mission with words of false generosity to win acceptance of his governorship from the chiefs. He came in the name of Queen Victoria, not to take land but to protect and guarantee under treaty the rights of the chiefs and tribes to their lands, homes and treasured possessions.

Once the Governor and his successors were established, they systematically set about acquiring Maori land, expropriating Maori resources and making them available to white settlers. The colonial techniques to achieve European ends included taking advantage of tribal divisions to divide and rule, flattery of chiefs to give them a semblance of consultation while excluding them from political power, and extinguishment of native title to land by 'fair purchase' to extend the Crown's dominion into native districts. Fair purchase in the case of the sparsely populated South Island included the threat of state violence against unwilling sellers.

In the more populous North Island the chiefs organised to resist subjection by the settler government. When the General Assembly met for the first time in 1854, sagacious leaders such as Wiremu Tamihana sought Maori admission into the Assembly. When that was denied, he pressed for a council of chiefs to advise the Governor on Maori policy. When even that level of participation in the administration was denied, Tamihana put his talents to work for the election of a Maori King. His response to the dual world of the colonised and the coloniser was to form a conjoint administration coexisting under the mantle of Queen. The Governor would not countenance coexistence so he made war on the Maori King to assert the sovereignty of the Crown. The settler government took advantage of the conflict by making laws in Parliament, where Maori had no representation, to take land by confiscation, and later by legal artifice through the Native Land Court.

The outcome of colonisation by the turn of the century was impoverishment of the Maori, marginalisation of elders and chiefly authority and a structural relationship of Pakeha dominance and Maori subjection. So total was Pakeha dominance at a time when the Maori population had fallen to its lowest point of 45,549, that the coloniser deluded himself into thinking he had created a unified nation state of one people whereby amalgamation of the races would resolve once and for all the problem of the Maori.

The coloniser had not taken into account the resilience of human nature. The Maori population recovered and grew exponentially within three generations to its present level of over 404,185. This growth was accompanied by a cultural renaissance and a demographic shift of 75 per cent of the Maori population to towns and cities after the Second World War. As portended by the freedom fighters at Orakau that the struggle against an unjust social order would go on forever, the urban Maori have taken up where their forebears left off. This book is about the endless struggle of the Maori for social justice, equality and self-determination, whereby two people can live as coequals in the post-colonial era of the new nation state in the twenty-first century.

CHAPTER 1

Mythology

The mythological origins of Maori society are laid out in three major myth cycles, beginning with the creation myth of Ranginui, the sky father, and Papatuanuku, the earth mother. The second sequence of myths deals with the adventures of the demi-god Maui, who fished up the land and brought many benefits into the world for humankind. The third series of myths deals with the life of Tawhaki, the model of an aristocratic and heroic figure. The stories of mythology are set in the remote past of the fabled Hawaiki homeland somewhere in the trackless wastes of the vast Pacific Ocean. The central characters in the myths are gods, their progeny and their human descendants. The stories are narrated in prose form, with the notion of an evolutionary sequence conveyed by the storyteller linking the main characters through the traditional method of genealogical recital. Inherent in the genealogy of earth and sky, the gods and their human descendants is the notion of evolution and progression.

The Maori divided the phenomenological world into three states of existence which were designated Te Kore (the void), Te Po (the dark), and Te Aomarama (the world of light). Although Te Kore signified space, it contained in its vastness the seeds of the universe and was therefore a state of potential.[1] Te Po was the celestial realm and the domain of gods. This was the source of all mana and tapu. Te Aomarama is the world of light and reality, the dwelling place of humans.

Ranginui and Papatuanuku

The creation myth starts with the sequential recital of the various names for the first state of existence. In the beginning, there was only Te Kore, the great void and emptiness of space. The different qualities of Te Kore were described by a series of adjectives. Thus, Te Kore became Te Kore te whiwhia (the void in which nothing could be obtained), Te Kore te rawea (the void in which nothing could be felt),

Te Kore i ai (the void with nothing in union) and Te Kore te wiwia (the space without boundaries). The number of descriptive names for Te Kore varied from tribe to tribe. Whatever the number and gradations of Kore, they signified the aeons of time during which the primeval matter of the universe came together and generated earth and sky.

Te Po, the second state of existence, also had qualifying adjectives and gradations. Beginning with Te Po, the recital proceeded to Te Po nui (the great night), Te Po roa (the long night), Te Po te kitea (the night in which nothing could be seen), to Te Po uriuri (the dark night), Te Po kerekere (the intense night) and Te Po tangotango (the intensely dark night), to the tenth, the hundredth and the thousandth night.[2] As in Te Kore, these periods of Te Po correspond to aeons of time when the earth came into being. Te Kore and Te Po also signify the emptiness and darkness of the mind. Because there was no light, there was no knowledge. The reason for this state of affairs was the self-generation during Te Kore of the primeval pair Ranginui and Papatuanuku. They were the first cause preventing light from entering the world because of their close marital embrace. The procreative powers of Rangi and Papa brought into being their sons, Tanemahuta, Tangaroa, Tawhirimatea, Tumatauenga, Haumia-tiketike and Rongomatane. The sons, living in a world of darkness between the bodies of Ranginui and Papatuanuku, plotted against their parents to let light into the world. They concluded that their plight of living in a world of darkness and ignorance could be alleviated only by separating their parents, so that Ranginui would become the sky father above them and Papatuanuku would remain with them as their earth mother.[3]

The task of separating earth and sky was accomplished by Tane-mahuta, who prised them apart with his shoulders to the ground and his legs thrusting upwards. Thereafter, one of his names became Tane-te-toko-o-te-rangi, Tane the prop of the heavens. The verity of this name is evident in the great forests of Tane, where the mighty trunks of the totara and kauri trees can be seen soaring upwards to the green canopy overhead and the sky above it.

The separation of earth and sky brought into being Te Aomarama, the world of light. This is the third state of existence, the abode of human beings. The separation was thought to be the first hara, or misdeed, in the story of creation. Letting light into the world brought with it knowledge of good and evil and was the analogue to the biblical tree of knowledge and its forbidden fruit. The binary opposition of good and evil is one of the central themes underlying Maori mythology. The gods played out this theme in their disagreement over the separation of their parents.

In the war of gods which followed the separation, Tawhirimatea, the god of winds, who opposed it, devastated the forests of Tane with winds of hurricane force. Having vanquished Tane, he lashed up mountainous seas over the domain of Tangaroa, driving the descendants of that deity to seek shelter from his wrath. The scattering of the children of Tangaroa brought about a separation of the species, with Ikatere fleeing to the depths of the ocean to become progenitor of fishes, and Tu-te-wehiwehi going inland to establish the reptilian family. Tawhirimatea was unable to vent his wrath on Rongomatane and Haumiatiketike because their mother Papatuanuku hid them from him by thrusting them deep into her bosom. Being untested in the crucible of war, these descendants were cast in passive roles. Haumiatiketike became the deity associated with edible fern roots and other wild and uncultivated plants. Rongomatane became the custodian of the kumara and the god of cultivation and peaceful arts.

Tawhirimatea's assertion of mana over his brothers was incomplete. When he turned his wrath on Tumatauenga, he was unable to vanquish him. Tumatauenga, who was left to stand alone against Tawhirimatea, was angry with his brothers for not supporting him. For this reason he is known by the names Tu-ka-riri (Tu of violent temper), Tu-ka-nguha (Tu of raging fury) and Tu-whakaheke-tangata-ki-te-po (Tu who consigns men to Hades). Tu, as the god of war and ancestor of fierce man encompassed in his names the aggressive characteristics of the warlike nature of human beings.[4]

Tumatauenga sought utu from his brothers for leaving him to face Tawhirimatea alone. First, he attacked the children of Tane and asserted his mana by debasing them and converting them to common use. From trees and vines he fashioned spears and snares to kill and trap Tane's birds. He also made nets and canoes to catch the children of Tangaroa. By his actions of using the children of his brothers as food and common objects, Tumatauenga negated their tapu, thereby making them noa. In this way the basic dichotomy in Maori life between the sacred and profane came into being. Tu's assertion of mana over his brothers was the rationale for the superior position of human beings in the natural order.

The personification of natural phenomena in the Maori pantheon is fundamental to the holistic world-view of the Maori. Papatuanuku was loved as a mother is loved, because the bounty that sprang from her breast nurtured and sustained her children. Humans were conceived of as belonging to the land; as tangata whenua, people of the land. This meant that they were not above nature but were an integral part of it. They were expected to relate to nature in a meaningful way. For instance, trees were not to be cut down wantonly. If a tree was needed for timber, then rituals seeking permission from Tane had to be performed first. Similarly, a fisherman had to return to the sea the first fish he caught as an offering to Tangaroa. The first fruits of the harvest season had to be offered to Rongo, the god of cultivation. It was believed that these practices ensured the bounty of nature would always be abundant.

Maori mythology also preserved a widespread ancient folk memory of a great flood. The genesis of the submergence of the world is found in the personification of other natural phenomena and the recital of their names in a genealogical tabulation similar to Te Kore and Te Po. First came Ua-nui (great rain), Ua-roa (long rain), Ua-whatu (fierce hailstorms), Ua Nganga (light rain) and their many progeny, including mist, heavy dew and light dew.[5] These forms of precipitation were the manifestation of Ranginui's sorrow at being parted from Papatuanuku, whose face far below was a constant reminder of the painful separation. In order to alleviate the discomfort to those on earth, the gods decided to turn Papatuanuku over so that her face would be hidden from her husband. This event is known as Te Hurihanga a Mataaho, the overturning of Mataaho. The youngest of the brothers, Ruaumoko, was still a child at breast at the time, and as the god of volcanoes he was left there to warm and comfort his mother.

The First Human Being

Tane and his brothers, who were the epitome of ira atua, the divine principle, searched the natural world for ira tangata, the human principle. In his restless search, Tane the creator tried his procreative powers on various elements in nature, bringing forth trees, birds and insects. The gods concluded from these results, that ira tangata could not be derived from ira atua. A separate act of creation was needed for human beings. To this end, Tane fashioned Hineahuone, the earth-formed maid, and breathed the life force of his mauri into her mouth and nostrils. Tane cohabited with Hineahuone and brought forth Hinetiitama, the dawn maid. He then cohabited with Hinetiitama, to produce other children.

In due course, Hinetiitama asked Tane about her father. His evasive answer telling her to ask the posts of his house drove her to the inevitable conclusion that her own husband was her father. This discovery appalled Hinetiitama, who fled from Tane in the direction of the underworld of Rarohenga. As she entered the portal to the underworld, she turned to Tane, who had followed her, and bade him farewell, saying, 'Tane, return to our family. I have severed connection with the world of light and now desire to dwell in the world of night.' Thereupon she descended into Rarohenga, where she became Hinenuitepo, the goddess of death. In a creation myth that begins with a single pair, incest in the next generation is inevitable for the establishment of the human line. But that necessity did not absolve the act from moral judgment. Tane's evasive answer to Hinetiitama, and her reaction to the discovery that their relationship was incestuous, suggests there was an innate antipathy to it. The story served to establish and promulgate the incest taboo among the adherents of the myth. Alpers, however, goes too far by suggesting in his book *Maori Myths* that Tane's relationship with Hinetiitama was the first sin.[7] The Arawa scribe Te Rangikaheke, who recorded the story 'Nga Tama a Rangi', as published by Grey in *Nga Mahi a Nga Tupuna*, is quite specific. He states categorically that the first sin was the separation of Rangi and Papa.[8]

Maui the Demi-God

The descendants of Tane and Hineahuone increased until the time of Maui, the most important culture hero in Maori mythology. The significance of Maui as a heroic figure derives as much from the circumstances of his birth as from his many accomplishments. He was a potiki, the last-born of five brothers. In a society where status and succession were based on order of birth, Maui, as a last-born child, was low in the family hierarchy. Furthermore, he had the additional disadvantage of being an aborted child, wrapped up in the topknot of his mother Taranga, and discarded into the sea. Fortunately for Maui, gentle breezes cast him ashore on a clump of seaweed which saved him from drowning. From this inauspicious start in life was derived his name Maui-tikitiki-a-Taranga. The potiki in Maori society was usually an indulged child and tended to be precocious. So it was with Maui. He was quick, intelligent, bold, resourceful, cunning and fearless, epitomising the basic personality structure idealised by Maori society. He was also an arch-trickster who had penchant for deceiving his elders, from which practice is derived his second name Maui-nukurau-tangata. As a heroic figure, Maui served as a model to all teina (junior children) and in particular the last-born, that provided they had the determination and qualities displayed by Maui, they too could succeed in life.

When Maui was rescued from the sea by his ancestor Tama-nui-ki-te-Rangi, he was revived by being suspended over a smoky fire, which in the myth reflected the customary way of reviving drowned persons. In due course, after a sojourn in the celestial realm, Maui returned to earth to join his family. When he appeared in their midst and was challenged, Maui identified himself to his mother as Maui of the top-knot of Taranga. With the revelation of Maui's survival, and the use of the name that exposed her secret abortion, Taranga welcomed her lost child back. She invited him to stand on the ridgepole of his ancestor Hinenuitepo's house.[9] The ridgepole was the metaphor for Maui's line of descent, whereby his membership in the family was validated. Taranga gave him a favoured place in her affections by allowing him to sleep in her bed. But when he awoke in the morning, she was gone. The disappearance of his mother and her reappearance at night caused Maui to wonder about his parents. He decided to search for them. Maui's search for his parents established the parental tie as a fundamental one in Maori society. In a culture where it was customary for visiting chiefs to enter into temporary liaisons with local women, ex-nuptial births were common. The theme of a child such as Maui searching out his father is a recurring one in Maori myth and tradition.

In order to discover where Taranga went, Maui tricked his mother into oversleeping by darkening the room and hiding her clothes. He even spied on her to discover the portal to the passage that led to the nether world where his father lived. Maui's encounter with his parents illustrated an important social convention concerning polite introductions to strangers. Because she was not in her own country, Taranga was not certain that the person before her was Maui and it was impolite to ask him directly. So she approached him carefully and questioned him obliquely, asking whether he came from the north. When he said no, she then proceeded around the points of the compass, nominating east, south, and west and receiving negative answers to each. She finally drew the conclusion that he came from the direction of the breeze that touched her skin and, having identified the place where he lived, she concluded it was indeed Maui. She welcomed him and introduced him to his father.

With the formalities of introduction over, Maui's father Makeatutara performed the tohi ritual of purification over him. The tohi purified Maui of tapu of the unclean type surrounding his birth. It also served as an act of public legitimation by his father. Unfortunately for Maui, Makeatutara made an error in the ritual, which was a bad omen. He knew Maui would be the first human to die and lose immortality for humankind. But the incident is more than just a rationale for death. It is also a cultural statement in the myth for the correct performance of ritual. Errors in recitation of karakia were offensive to the gods and were punishable by misfortune or death.

In his encounters with his other ancestors when seeking knowledge from them, Maui dramatised the ambivalent relationship of tension and indulgence between young and old. His kuia, the female ancestors above him in the line of descent from the gods, were the repositories of knowledge. He had to win knowledge from them for the benefit of humankind, because humans had no knowledge of their own. All knowledge emanated from the gods and their most immediate descendants. But Maui's kuia had primeval forces at their command which could destroy him should he try their patience. Therefore, he had to tread carefully and use all his guile to get the information he wanted. Above all, he had to be patient and persistent to achieve his aims.

Maui began his mission to bring benefits to people on earth by deceiving his blind kuia Murirangawhenua. When he visited her abode, he tried her patience by hiding her food from her. Yet despite that teasing, which could have ended with Murirangawhenua devouring him, Maui was able to placate her. As soon as she recognised her mokopuna, she favoured him by giving into his keeping her enchanted jawbone. Maui used the jawbone as a fabulous weapon to beat the sun and slow its passage across the sky. That exploit gave humans sufficient daylight to go about their work and daily affairs. He also fashioned a fish hook from the jawbone, with which he fished up the land known as Te Ika a Maui. The great fish of Maui is the home of the Maori people in the North Island of New Zealand. Maui's exploits of slowing down the sun and fishing up the land are testament to the special properties of bone for the manufacture of artifacts such as weapons and fish hooks.

In a similar episode to his encounter with Murirangawhenua, Maui obtained the secret of fire from another of his kuia named Mahuika. Maui tricked her into giving up all her fire fingernails and toenails. When he wrested the last one from her and lodged its power to generate fire in selected trees of the forest, he almost lost his life for being too presumptuous. The conflagration of the world that resulted from Mahuika's anger would have destroyed Maui had not

Tawhirimatea heard his prayer and doused the flames with torrential rain. It was a salutary lesson that tampering with primeval forces could destroy the world. Maui dared Mahuika's wrath, and survived to reveal the secret of fire to human beings. Maui is the source of knowledge for the method of generating heat and fire by friction between two pieces of timber from the mahoe, taraire or kaikomako trees.

Maui also invented the strongest twine, cord and ropes, which he used to snare the sun and fish up the land. When Maui's brothers went on a fishing expedition, he outwitted their attempt to leave him behind by rising early and concealing himself in the bilges of the canoe until they were well out to sea. When he asked for bait, they refused him. Undeterred by their refusal, Maui demonstrated his resourcefulness by beating his nose and smearing blood on the hook. So big was the fish Maui caught that he had to chant a powerful incantation, a hiki, to bring it to the surface.[10] Unfortunately, Te Ika a Maui roused the greed of his brothers, who quarrelled over the fish and began hacking at it while Maui was away conducting thanksgiving rituals. Maui's fish, which was in the form of a stingray, writhed in agony in its death throes. That is why the fish today is wrinkled and contorted, otherwise it would have been smooth and flat. The myth not only condemned the cutting of the fish as an offence against the gods, but also taught the need to conduct appropriate rituals of thanksgiving for the gifts of nature. Failure to respect nature brought its own evil consequences. The scribe Te Rangikaheke made the observation that the cutting up of the fish before the rituals were completed was the second evil to come into the world.

On another fishing expedition with his brother-in-law Irawaru, Maui was incensed that Irawaru caught fish and he caught none. When they got back to shore, Maui pursuaded Irawaru to get down on all fours to lift up the outrigger of the canoe on his back, while he pretended to push. While Irawaru was down, Maui leapt on the float and by the power of karakia turned him into a dog. This episode is more than just an origin myth for the dog, as suggested by Alpers in *Maori Myths*. It is true the creation of the dog was a boon, because not only was it a companion, it was also useful for the making of fine cloaks, necklaces, bone instruments as well as for food. But underlying the myth is the caveat that the relationship between brothers-in-law is a capricious and dangerous one. The mythological precedent set by Maui and Irawaru is repeated in subsequent myths and later in the era of traditions.

Maui's final encounter with the goddess of death, Hinenuitepo, as presaged by the ill-omen of his tohi, ended in Maui's defeat. The task Maui hoped to accomplish was to enter Hinenuitepo through her vagina and pluck out her heart. By emerging from her mouth he would have effectively reversed the process of birth and won immortality for himself and the rest of humankind. The task was the most dangerous one Maui had undertaken, since she was equipped with formidable weapons of vaginal teeth made of obsidian. When Maui was only halfway in the birth passage, the ludicrous sight of his legs threshing around outside made the fantail laugh out loud. This woke Hinenuitepo, who crushed Maui to death. The death of Maui, the greatest culture hero in Maori mythology, is the rationale for the death of human beings. Since Maui was unable to defeat death, all humans must be reconciled to its inevitability.

Rupe

After Maui's death, the myth sequence was continued by his brother Rupe, who went in search of his sister Hinauri. Hinauri was so bereft when Maui turned her husband Irawaru into a dog that she tried to commit suicide by throwing herself into the sea, but she was cast up on to strange shore. Rupe's search for Hinauri, like Maui's search for his parents, indicated the primacy of the bond of affection for a female sibling. Rupe extended his search right up to the tenth heaven, the realm of Rehua. There he was welcomed by Rehua. With the formalities over, Rehua undid his topknot and shook out bellbirds and tui which fed on the lice in his hair. Rehua caught the birds and prepared a meal of them for his guest. Rupe was disgusted. The myth evoked revulsion because the head is the most tapu part of the body. The notion of eating food that had been in contact with the head is so repellent that in the customary usages of the Maori it hardly bears contemplation.

On Rupe's second visit to Rehua's courtyard, he found it soiled with children's excrement. His tidying of the marae with wooden scoops and the building of a heketua for the proper disposal of human waste served as a model for the provision of hygienic arrangements in communal life.

Tinirau and his Pet Whale

With the origins of the world and the basic elements of human culture defined by myth, the next myth in the Maui series dealt with human behaviour. The high chief Tinirau, who found Hinauri, took her home and cohabited with her. Tinirau was renowned for having a pet whale, Tutunui, on which he sometimes rode at sea. The tohunga Kae, who performed the tohi ritual for Hinauri and Tinirau's son Tuhuruhuru, was allowed to ride the whale back to his village. When he reached his own shores, Kae and his tribe killed Tutunui and ate him. The killing and eating of the pet whale by the treacherous Kae introduced a basic theme of utu in human affairs. Revenge is correct if there is a just cause. By killing the whale loaned to transport him home, Kae betrayed his host's trust. In the myth Kae was cast in the role of a villain who exhibited the negative characteristics of greed and treachery. Villains deserve to die, and so Kae was marked down for death.

Instead of sending a war party after Kae, which would have alerted the enemy, Tinirau sent a party of women, who put the garrison off its guard. Tinirau's strategy of sending women to kidnap Kae is indicative of how war should be conducted. Cunning and subtlety are to be preferred ahead of direct attack. The women succeeded in their mission and took Kae back to Tinirau's village, where he was killed as utu for Tutunui. But, as in human affairs, the death of Kae did not close the account. Instead, it engendered a vendetta in subsequent generations. The Popohorokewa retaliated by killing Tinirau's son Tuhuruhuru.

Whakatau Potiki

The hero in the last of the Maui series of myths was Whakatau Potiki. It is significant that he, like Maui, was also a junior brother thus reinforcing the example set by Maui. His first task was to avenge the death of his brother Tuwhakararo, who had been killed by the people of Kae. The manner in which Whakatau went about defeating his enemies is a model of military strategy and the conduct of war. Whakatau reviewed his warriors, practised the order of battle, and arranged for the disposition of assault columns, support columns and reserves. He also developed techniques for selecting a cadre of élite warriors to be the cutting edge of his forces. Reconnaissance of enemy territory, the lone exploit, and the capture and interrogation of prisoners to gain information were all part of Whakatau's military repertoire. Even the apparently arbitrary act of cutting out a prisoner's tongue served the purpose of establishing the fundamental principle of denying intelligence to the enemy. Whakatau's lone exploit of spying in enemy territory and even entering their house was a heroic act necessary for the accomplishment of utu. To qualify as a hero one had to do heroic things; in this respect Whakatau served as a model by which subsequent generations could measure the performance of their heroes.

Whakatau's avenging of the death of Tuhuruhuru by defeating in single combat ten of the enemy champions is also instructive of the way in which war should be conducted. War is a dangerous business in which there is a high probability of being killed. Therefore the prudent hero leaves nothing to chance. Whakatau defeated ten men, not because he had the strength of ten but because he devised strategies that ensured he lived and his enemies died. For instance, on a lone expedition to the enemy village he stood offshore in his canoe as local champions challenged him to single combat. Having ascertained that the first challenger was a skilled diver, Whakatau invited him to dive into the water to do battle. While his opponent was submerged, Whakatau poured a calabash of oil on the water to calm the ripples. This enabled him to see his enemy as he approached the canoe from a great depth and despatch him as he surfaced. The second challenger was an expert jumper, so Whakatau invited him to jump from the shore to the canoe to do battle. When his adversary landed in the canoe, Whakatau had a snare waiting for him. He simply pulled it tight, pinioned his opponent's arms, and finished him with his club. In this manner he defeated ten champions as utu for the murder of Tuhuruhuru.

Tawhaki

The Tawhaki sequence of myths begins by reinforcing the theme of the dangerous nature of the brother-in-law relationship. Tawhaki was subjected to a treacherous attack by his brothers-in-law after returning from a fishing expedition. They beat him and left him in a shallow grave, thinking he was dead. He would have died had he not been found by his wife Hinepiripiri, who revived Tawhaki by warming him beside a fire. To build up the fire, she fuelled it with a long length of uncut wood. She was pregnant at the time, and when her child was born she named him Wahieroa, which means long length of wood. This incident set the cultural precedent of naming a child after a significant event close to the time of its birth. In the case of Wahieroa, his name carried the moral imperative to avenge the misdeed of his uncles if his father failed to do it in his own lifetime. Tawhaki, being the heroic figure that he was, destroyed his enemies with mighty floods, which he induced by his power to command the elements.

Tawhaki's father Hema had been killed by the goblin-like Ponaturi, who lived under the water and came ashore to sleep at night in their house, Manawatane. These strange people held Tawhaki's mother captive as the doorkeeper of their house. It was her job to warn the Ponaturi of the onset of dawn so that they could return to their watery abode before sunrise, otherwise they would be killed by the sun's rays. Tawhaki set out to avenge his father and recover his bones as a filial duty. In keeping with the rules of war laid down in the preceding myth, Tawhaki sought information about the Ponaturi from his captive mother. Having learned of the lethal effect of sunlight on this strange tribe, Tawhaki devised an appropriate stategy to defeat them. He simply blocked up the chinks in their house, inducing them to oversleep. Then, when the sun was high in the sky, he destroyed them by letting in the searing rays of sunlight.

Tawhaki's victories spread his fame far and wide, even to the sky, so that the celestial maiden Tangotango came down to earth and visited him nightly. In due course she became pregnant and stayed with Tawhaki. After the birth of their child, Tangtango felt insulted because Tawhaki said the child smelt when he went to perform the tohi ritual for it. Because of the insult, she abandoned Tawhaki and returned to the celestial realm with her child. Tawhaki missed his wife, so he searched for her. In previous myths, Maui had searched for his parents and Rupe for his sister. The searches for loved ones by heroic figures establish the bonds between parents, children, siblings and spouses as the most significant relationships in Maori culture.

On the journey to the hanging vines by which Tawhaki climbed to the celestial realm, his brother Karihi forbade their slaves to look at the sacred citadel of Tongameha. One of them was overcome by curiosity, looked and perished when his eyes were torn out. The myth served to transmit two fundamental tenets in Maori society. Firstly, that the injunctions of superiors must be obeyed, and secondly, that the all-pervading force of tapu carries the ultimate sanction of death.

Tawhaki's lone exploit of climbing up to the heavens on the hanging vines was the first of a series of tests of his love for his wife. He accomplished it, as one would expect of an heroic figure, without too much difficulty. Even more testing for a person of Tawhaki's rank were the humbling experiences he had to endure at the hands of his wife's people. He entered the celestial realm disguised as an old man and came upon his brothers-in-law making a canoe. At the end of the day his brothers-in-law treated him as a slave and made him carry their adzes home. On the way he was accosted by women collecting firewood and they made him carry the wood home as well. These trials were Tawhaki's expiation of his insult to his wife and child. The myth concluded with Tawhaki's reunion with his wife and his performance of the purification rite for their child Arahuta. Thereafter, Tawhaki remained in the celestial realm, where he was semi-deified.

The hero in the last myth of the Tawhaki series was Rata, whose task was to avenge the death of his father Wahieroa at the hands of the demon-like Matukutakotako. Following the canons of military procedure laid down in preceeding myths, Rata went to the entrance to Matukutakotako's lair and sought information about the habits of his enemy from the keeper of the portal. Forearmed with the knowledge that Matukutakotako would detect his presence while dressing his hair at the pool he used as a mirror, Rata decided to attack him while he was in his bathing pool, where the muddy water would not betray him. Rata's defeat of the man-eating Matukutakotako reinforced the precedents set by Whakatau Potiki and Tawhaki that the defeat of powerful enemies is accomplished by devising strategies to attack them at their most vulnerable point.

The myth sequence ends with the story of Rata's canoe. Rata needed a canoe to go on a campaign of war. When he felled a forest giant to make his canoe, he neglected the propitiatory rights to Tane. On his return to the site the next day, the canoe had vanished but the tree was back in its place. After felling the tree again and shaping the canoe, Rata hid himself and waited. In due course the hakuturi, denizens of the forest, the birds, insects and fairies, gathered before the canoe. They reassembled every chip, branch, leaf and twig. When the tree was back in place, Rata leapt out of hiding and remonstrated with them for interfering with his canoe, but in turn he was mortified when they turned on him and upbraided him for his failure to perform the propitiatory rites to Tane before taking the tree for his own use. Rata acknowledged his guilt and was told to come back the next day. When he returned, he was astonished to behold the finest canoe he had ever seen. In essence, the myth of Rata's canoe codified the relationship between human beings and nature. Before natural resources can be appropriated for human use, rituals to the deity presiding over the relevant department of nature must be conducted. Observance of ritual ensured that nature was not treated in a wanton manner.

CHAPTER 2

Te Hekenga o Nga Waka

The Polynesian ancestors of the Maori people had been living in Samoa and Tonga over a thousand years when they began undertaking a series of long ocean voyages of discovery and settlement of islands in the Great Ocean of Kiwa. Beginning around AD 200 the voyagers made their way progressively eastwards to the Marquesas by AD 300, swung north to Hawaii about AD 600 and east to Easter Island.[1] New Zealand was the last to be settled, around AD 800. Within a time frame of 600 years Polynesians had colonised an oceanic environment that was 995 parts water to five parts land. Given the period in human history when this task was accomplished — seven centuries before Columbus dared venture out of sight of land — it was a remarkable achievement.

The maritime prowess of Polynesians was based on the double-hull waka, the precursor of modern multi-hull technology. The genesis of the waka was the simple dugout canoe made from a single tree trunk. The dugout was progressively refined by attaching an outrigger for stability and sails to harness wind power. The addition of planks to the hull to raise its freeboard improved the seaworthiness of the craft. Finally, with the shaping of the hull to counteract drag from the outrigger, and the addition of a steering paddle to maintain course, this type of vessel had reached its design limitations. It was swift and seaworthy enough, but had low carrying capacity. The solution to the limitations of the outrigger was the double hull with deck space between hulls large enough for a cabin. Captain Cook recorded a Tahitian pahi with an impressive length of 108 feet (33.2 metres). Even larger was a drua recorded by the missionary Thomas Williams which was 118 feet (36.3 metres) long and had a beam of 50 feet (15.4 metres).[2] These vessels were capable of speeds up fourteen knots and could cover up to 150 miles a day. Under favourable conditions a thousand miles in ten days was possible. The feasibility of voyages by double-hulled vessels using traditional Polynesian navigation methods has been demonstrated in recent years. In 1980, despite low average speeds of forty to eighty miles a day through the doldrums, the voyage of the *Hokule'a* retracing the ancestral route taken by Hawaiians to Tahiti took just a little over a month.[3] In 1985 the double-hulled *Hawaikinui* made landfall in New Zealand from Tahiti after a passage of eight weeks.

Polynesian Navigation

The maritime achievement of the Polynesians in colonising the Pacific has been both denigrated and romanticised. Because waka were unlike their own vessels, early European observers designated them canoes. The image conjured up by the word canoe — a dugout propelled by paddles — is hardly an accurate rendering of waka such as the drua or pahi. These vessels stocked with provisions, laden with cargo, and carrying up to a hundred passengers were ships in their own right capable of blue-water passages of a thousand miles or more. But because they were different, they were not ships and were therefore consigned to the more primitive status of canoe. The lurid image in the Goldie painting of emaciated Polynesian voyagers arriving in New Zealand further reified European perceptions of Polynesian voyaging as being a rather chancy affair. In his imagination, Goldie probably presumed too much, but of course there were others who were equally presumptuous in the other direction.

Much of the literature up to the 1950s on Polynesian maritime skill was tinged with romanticism. Percy Smith,[4] for instance, wrote: 'They had a very complete knowledge of the heavens and the movement of stars, etc., to all the prominent ones they gave names. In the accounts of the coming of the six canoes to New Zealand in the fourteenth century, we have references to the stars by which they steered.' In similar vein Elsdon Best[5] said, 'They steered their primitive craft by the heavenly bodies, and by the regular roll of the waves before the trade winds.' Similarly, Te Rangihiroa[6] romanticised Polynesians as intrepid mariners pushing eastwards towards the sunrise.

In 1957 Andrew Sharp[7] challenged the romantic view of Polynesian voyaging by resurrecting the drift-voyage theory. Sharp argued that, using the sun, moon and stars to steer their course, Polynesians were capable of voyages of up to 300 miles. Anything beyond that was a drift voyage, brought about by vagaries of weather obscuring stars, unknown set or drift, being blown off course by storms and being unable to reset a course. According to Sharp's argument, the long ocean passage between the western Polynesian islands of Samoa,

Tonga and Rotuma, and the eastern Polynesian islands of Tuamotu, Marquesas and Society Islands was crossed by accidental drift voyages.

In response to Sharp there was a flurry of research and academic publications defending Polynesian navigation skill. The difficulty that Europeans encounter in cross-cultural analysis arises out of their ethnocentric world-view. As a literate people, Europeans face the peculiar difficulty that they must be able to set down on paper — maps, charts and almanacs — what non-literate people might easily read in the sky or carry in their heads. In the end they think the job can be done in no other way.[8]

The most ardent defender of Polynesian maritime skill was David Lewis,[9] who made it his business to find out in detail from surviving practitioners of the art of Polynesian navigation their techniques for setting courses and making landfall. In his writings, Lewis revealed quite a stunning array of techniques used by Micronesian and Polynesian navigators to make a landfall on voyages of discovery and settlement.

From the home island, the direction and existence of new land was readily deduced from the flight path of migratory birds. Suitable landmarks or stone markers set up on the shore then fixed the direction. In the evening, using a star compass that divided the horizon into thirty-two sectors, the priest-navigator took nightly observations of horizon stars that rose in line with the markers indicating the direction to the new land. As each star rose and moved away from the marks, another star rising closest to the bearing of the markers would be selected. In this way the navigator worked out the ara whetu, the star path, to the new land. Celestial navigation was complemented by a broad array of techniques that are most aptly described as the signposts of nature. Knowing how to read those signposts in combination with celestial navigation made landfall predictable and not as haphazard as Sharp suggested by his theory of drift voyages.

One of the signposts in nature that helped in maintaining course was ocean swell. Trade winds, blowing consistently in one direction, influence swell, so the navigator could hold his course, should the stars or sun be obscured, by keeping the angle of his course constant in relation to the swell. Long before land was actually sighted, the observant navigator read other natural signs that indicated its presence. One of the most significant was 'land clouds', which by comparison with clouds over the sea appeared to be stationary to those who could interpret them. High volcanic islands like Hawaii, even though well out of sight, could be 'seen' from a distance of eighty miles by virtue of the cloud standing above them. This phenomenon results from the moisture-laden trade winds being forced to rise up over the mountains. For each ninety-two metres in ascent the temperature drops one degree and the moisture condenses out to billow upwards as clouds high above the mountain peaks.

The low islands of coral atolls were also found by land clouds. These islands are so low, being only a metre or so above sea level and twenty or so metres to the top of the highest palm tree, that they are very difficult to see even within a radius of five to ten miles. They could easily be missed by a navigator who was unable to read the signposts in nature. Yet the Polynesian navigators could 'see' them as far away as thirty to forty miles from the cloud formations above them. The loom of the shallower water of the lagoon, for instance, was reflected off the cloud base above an island. Islands with heavy vegetation gave a darker tinge to the clouds above them while those with white sand gave a brighter sheen. Then there were clouds known as tukemata, a cloud formation like a pair of eyebrows. These were caused by the disturbed airflow over an island.

The presence of land for a navigator in search of it was also indicated by betia, or sea marks. These included an interruption in the swell by land, changes in the colour of the ocean indicating shallower water, seaweed, driftwood, and species of fish found close to land, including dolphins. Experienced navigators after weeks at sea could even smell the presence of land with a favourable breeze at night.

One of the most useful signs indicating the presence of land and its direction was land-roosting seabirds. Birds fly out from their home island in a radius of thirty miles to fish at sea. In the late afternoon the direction to land can be readily deduced from the birds' flight path as they home in to roost. Similarly, in the morning the direction could be confirmed as the birds flew out to fish and feed for the day.

One of the more abstruse methods of finding land involved the bounce-back or return wave. Only the most experienced navigator was capable of detecting the change in the motion of a vessel in response to waves bouncing back from land. The phenomenon of lapa, or flashes of phosphorescent light apparently linked to the bounce-back wave was more readily detected. Both phenomena could indicate the presence and direction of land from as far as thirty or so miles out to sea.

The maritime skill and navigation lore of Polynesians were supplemented by their religious beliefs pertaining to the deity Tangaroa.

Although they chose the time of the year when the weather was favourable to make long ocean voyages, their confidence was boosted by belief that rituals and prayers to Tangaroa would ensure safe passage to their destination. Furthermore, their belief that certain species of shark, whales or dolphins were the embodiment of the spirits of some of their ancestors, which had assumed the role of guardians, strengthened their confidence en route as they appeared at different times to accompany a vessel.

By the second millenium, with the exception of occasional return voyages, Polynesian ocean voyages of discovery and colonisation came to an end. But the seafaring traditions lived on in the cultural symbolism of the waka. In New Zealand, the waka of ancestral forebears took on new meaning as the symbol for tribal identity, territorial ownership and political relations.

The First Settlers

The first canoe migrants from Eastern Polynesia reached New Zealand shores between AD 800 and 900. They arrived in the warm summer month of December when the pohutukawa was in bloom.[10] This gave them five months of warm weather to settle into their new environment, build shelters and become acquainted with local food resources before winter set in. They may well have attempted to plant their tropical food plants, the kumara, gourd, paper mulberry and taro, but they were too late in the season. The first frosts in May or June would have damaged the crops, especially the kumara, a tropical plant which grows best within thirty degrees of the equator.

This setback to crops made the first settlers dependent on hunting, fishing and gathering. Fortunately, the virgin land teemed with fish and bird life that sustained a subsistence economy over the winter months. In the first phase of settlement population density remained low, with people moving about, living in crude shelters and temporary encampments to take advantage of the different resources available in each locality. New Zealand was large enough to accommodate later arrivals on a subsistence economy for at least two hundred years.[11] But as the population was supplemented by subsequent arrivals and natural increase, the subsistence economy made it necessary to disperse around both the North and South Islands.

The only mammals the Polynesians brought to New Zealand were the dog and rat, the first as a pet and the latter as a stowaway. Neither was plentiful enough to provide an adequate supply of animal protein.

However, the forests abounded with bird life. Of particular importance was the moa, a large flightless bird that the ancestors of the Maori
hunted for food.

The smaller species of moa, *Euryapteryx gravis*, which stood 1.7
metres high, was the main quarry of the moa-hunters from one end of
the South Island to the other.[12] *Emeus crassus* was about the same size,
while *Pachyornis elephantus* was 2.3 metres. The largest moa, *Dinornis
maximus*, stood at 3 or 3.7 metres.[13] Although the word moa occurs
in the traditions of both the North and South Island tribes, only a few
of them give any details.

Considering the importance of the moa as a source of food in the
first two hundred years of settlement, Maori traditions concerning the
moa are rather sparse. Its name is the Polynesian word for the
domestic fowl. Because the first settlers did not bring any moa with
them, they applied the name to this wonderful bird that made up for
the absence of the pig.[14] There are only five or six references in Maori
traditions to the moa. An explorer named Ngahue killed a moa at a
place called Wairere and reported to his people at Hawaiki that it was
suitable for food.[15] Another explorer named Ruakapanga also encountered the moa. In time, as the moa became scarce, the hunters may well
have resorted to burning scrub to flush them out. One Maori tradition
alludes to moa being driven into swamps by the fires of Tamatea.[16] In
the Bay of Plenty the ancestor of Ngati Apa was kicked in the leg and
maimed when he killed a pet moa belonging to another tribe. Thereafter he walked with a stoop and was known as Apa-koki.[17] By the time
of Tuhoto Ariki, around 1350, the moa was already the subject of
myth. The last moa that escaped the fires of Tamatea survived ever-
lastingly in a cave guarded by lizards at Whakapunake.[18]

As the number of moa in the North Island declined, the hunters
were forced to move to the cooler South Island to maintain their
subsistence economy. It is likely this move occurred before the successful development of agriculture in the North Island.[19] Although
moa-hunter settlements have been excavated at Ohawe, Tairua, Opito,
Wattle Bay and Motutapu in the North Island, there are more
numerous moa-hunter sites in the South Island, particularly along the
eastern coastline. Some of the settlements in the South Island include
Papatowai, Pounewa, Pleasant River, Waimataitai, Shag River,
Wairau Bar and Moncks Bay. The moa was a grazing bird that
flourished on open grassy plains, low hills and swampy margins. Only
the smaller species lived in the forests. The eastern side of the South
Island, where these conditions occurred together, had the densest

concentration of moa and the habitation sites of the men who hunted them.

The Moa-hunters

There is a uniform pattern in the moa-hunter camp sites of the South Island. Coastal locations were favoured ahead of inland ones. Most of them were located on dry shingle spits or sand dunes adjacent to lagoons or river mouths. Fish and water-fowl abounded in these localities and supplemented the diet of moa meat. The Wairau Bar site excavated by Roger Duff is the archetype of the culture of the people he designated as the moa-hunters. The culture was so named because of the importance of the moa as a source of food and bone material for ornaments in the economy of the people who lived there. The occupation site at Wairau Bar, which is about seven hectares in extent, was well established by 1150.[20] Even at that early period of settlement, the basic dichotomy between the sacred and the profane was marked by the separation of the cooking area from the habitation site. Burial grounds were located on the outer fringe of the habitation site. There was no attempt at concealment of the burials at Wairau, which suggests there was no fear of enemies robbing and and desecrating graves. This is in contrast to later practices, when bones of ancestors were hidden away in secret places to prevent them being converted into fish hooks. The post-burial removal of the skull, which was widely practised in Polynesia, was also practised by the moa-hunters. Moa-hunter graves were oriented on an east-west axis. The orientation of the corpse to the west expressed a common Polynesian concept that the point of departure for spirits of the dead was in this direction.[21]

The use of necklaces for personal adornment was a characteristic feature of moa-hunter culture. Beads were made from bone, ivory and stone. Necklaces of bone reels made from the femur of moa with a centrepiece of a drilled tooth of a sperm whale, or a copy made in stone, were found in association with a number of male burials. This association suggests the reel necklaces were worn by persons of rank. Whale-tooth necklaces of the moa-hunters had a remarkable resemblance to the necklaces of the Moriori of the Chatham Islands.[22]

The adzes of the South Island moa-hunters are distinguished from the North Island ones by having tangs, a cut-away section at the upper end to which the handle was fitted and lashed. This type of adze was widely distributed throughout the Pacific from Hawaii to Pitcairn, Rarotonga, Tokelaus, the Marquesas and the Society Islands. The same type of adze is found on the Chatham Islands. Greenstone did not figure much in moa-hunter artifacts. Only three of the sixty-nine adzes found at Wairau Bar were made of greenstone, and its use for ornaments did not come into vogue until the later period.[23]

It is significant that the small barbless one-piece fish hooks of the moa-hunters were similar to those of the Chatham Islanders. The similarity in the necklaces, adzes and fish hooks suggest a cultural affinity between the South Island and the Moriori of the Chathams. The fishing lures of the moa-hunters were quite distinct from those of a later period. The composite lures consisted of a minnow shank in stone or bone to which was lashed an unbarbed point. These minnow shanks with oval or triangular cross-sections were widely distributed from North Cape to Stewart Island. Over eighty such shanks were found in the Wairau Bar site alone. The lures are copies in bone and stone of pearl-shell lures found at Hane in the Marquesas and at Maupiti and Vaito'otia in the Society Islands. One pearl-shell lure found at Tairua on the Coromandel Peninsula is similar to lures found on Hane in the Marquesas, indicating it was brought to New Zealand by some of the early voyagers from East Polynesia.[24] Harpoon points found in moa-hunter sites are also similar to those of the Marquesas.[25] In the Society Islands, artifacts recovered at Maupiti and Huahine have strong affinities with material from this period of settlement in New Zealand. Burials at Maupiti furnished with grave goods including stone adzes, ornaments and fish hooks were similar to those at Wairau Bar.[26]

Moa-hunter culture in the South Island is defined by type fossils including adzes, fishing gear and ornaments. The prototypes of these artifacts are to be found in Polynesia, the immediate affiliations being with eastern Polynesia, specifically the Society Islands, as the dispersal area. Unfortunately, only durable artifacts made from stone or bone have survived from this first phase of settlement. No evidence has yet been found about their house construction or their woodwork.

The moa-hunters, living under harsh conditions, had a low life expectancy. An analysis of the skeletal remains of forty individuals at the Wairau Bar site indicated that the average age at death was twenty-eight years for men and twenty-nine for women.[27] The oldest individual lived to only forty years of age. A similar pattern of young skeletal remains was found at Castlepoint, Kaikoura, Otago and Motutapu Island. At Motutapu some adults lived up to fifty years of age. The short lifespan was caused by the diet of shellfish and fern-root prematurely wearing down teeth. Once the pulp cavity was reached, infection and dental loss followed. Jaws also became abscessed. Poor nutrition, debilitation and death ensued. Furthermore, women at that time bore only two or three children at the most, so that the population living in widely scattered settlements remained low for at least the first 200 years.

The Second Phase of Settlement

By 1100, the settlements and habitation sites of the early period became stabilised in favourable localities. More substantial houses were built. The wharepuni, the characteristically Maori dwelling with its gable roof and rectangular design, made its appearance in the twelfth century. The internal plan consisted of a hearth down the centre and sleeping places down the sides. The wharepuni had a very small door with the roof and the walls extended beyond the front wall to form a sheltered open porch oriented to catch the sun. This architectural design is not found elsewhere in the Pacific and appears to have been developed in reponse to the colder climate of New Zealand.

The early wharepuni had a length-to-breadth ratio of 1.5 and up to 2 to 1, with the porch taking up a quarter of the length.[28] A site at Palliser Bay indicated that the typical Polynesian settlement pattern found in other islands of the Pacific was well established by the twelfth century. The settlement there consisted of small village at the mouth of a stream with cultivations close by on a sandy coastal platform.[29] Wharepuni at Pouerua in Northland around 1300 were seven metres long and nearly six wide. The superior houses were characterised by a flat open space in front. The space was as wide as the house and varied in length from three-quarters to the full length of the house.[30] These superior houses with the courtyard in front were symbolically the most potent buildings at Pouerua and were probably associated with people of rank.

As the moa-hunters decimated the moa and other species on which their subsistence hunting economy was based, the development and elaboration of horticulture became necessary for survival. The hunting settlements were abandoned for localities suitable for gardening. The first pit dwellings appeared at this time in association with underground food storage pits. The presence of these pits indicates that the settlers had solved the problem of growing some of the Polynesian food plants in the colder climate of their new home. Of particular importance was the kumara, the staple root crop. One key to the problem of growing kumara was the parekereke, a specially made seed-bed lined with straw and overlaid with soil to promote early shooting of the tubers. The shoots were then planted out in spring on mounded earth after the danger from frost was past. The kumara is a very delicate root crop, prone to rot at the slightest sign of cold, damage, bruising or accumulation of moisture. It needed a minimum storage temperature of 13–16°C over the winter months at 80 per cent humidity, otherwise the crop spoiled.[31] This problem was resolved by the development of controlled temperature storage in underground bracken-lined storage pits, which allowed seed tubers to be carried over the winter for the new season planting in spring.

The growing importance of horticulture in the twelfth century marked a watershed between the first settlers, who belong to what Duff refers to as the moa-hunter period of Maori culture, and the later Classic Maori culture that succeeded it. Golson, another archaeologist, refers to the earlier period as Archaic.[32] In the Archaic period of the moa-hunters there is little firm evidence of warfare, but with the development of horticulture and the consequent increase in population, that changed. By 1300, when the population grew to approximately 25,000, cleared fertile garden land became more valuable.[33] From the fourteenth century on, Maori traditions abound with accounts of tribal fights over gardens. It was much easier to dispossess weak neighbours of their gardens than to clear virgin forest. It was at this time that the tribes began building fortifications to defend their territory.

The Rise of Tribalism

Most of what is known of the Archaic period of the moa-hunters has been unearthed by archaeologists. The tribal traditions which date from the fourteenth century have little to say about that earlier period except to record the names of some of the tangata whenua tribes. In the North Island tribes such the Maruiwi, and the multitudes of Taitawaro, Ruatamore and Panenehu,[34] failed to maintain their identity during the tribal wars. It is likely they lost out in the contests over horticultural land and were absorbed by the victors. One tribe that did survive the test of time claimed great antiquity by tracing descent from the culture hero Maui. These people of the Maui Nation[35] on the East Coast region of the North Island assert that their ancestor's canoe lies in a petrified state on Mt Hikurangi. Their modern descendants are the Uepohatu, who live in the shadow of Mt Hikurangi. Another tribe from the Archaic period which survived into historic times were the

Moriori of the Chatham Islands. They probably left the South Island before tribal wars broke out on the mainland to settle in the Chathams. These people became the subject of a false myth of extermination in the twentieth century.

Te Tini-o-Toi

On the east coast, in the Bay of Plenty, one of the early founding ancestors of the proto-Maori period was Toi. His originating ancestor was Tiwakawaka (fantail), the first person to settle the land in ancient times. This origin myth implies that Toi's ancestors had been in New Zealand from the beginning of time. According to Tuhoe and Ngati Awa traditions, Toi lived in a pa named Kaputerangi at Whakatane.[36] The geneaologies of the Ngaiterangi, Tuhoe and Ngati Awa tribes, who claim descent from Toi, range in length from thirteen to twenty-three generations. From the baseline of 1900 when these genealogies were recorded, they would place him somewhere in the thirteenth or fourteenth century,[37] at the time when major population movements were being brought about by economic change. Toi's descendants were known as Te Tini-o-Toi. He was born in New Zealand and was known as Toi te-hua-tahi, Toi the only child. He was also known by the name Toi Kai-rakau, Toi the wood-eater. This latter name, meaning eater of forest products, was bestowed on him by later settlers who introduced horticulture into the Bay of Plenty.[38]

Toi's son Awanuiarangi founded Te Tini-o-Awa, one of the tangata whenua tribes of the Bay of Plenty. The other tangata whenua tribes of the area which were subsequently overlaid by the bearers of horti-culture and fighting pa technology from the north included Nga Potiki, Te Tini o Tuoi, Te Hapuoneone and Marangaranga.[39] To the east the related tangata whenua tribes, which were also absorbed by the later arrivals, included the Ngariki living around Ohiwa, Opotiki, Hawai and Poverty Bay, and Te Wakanui of Opotiki.[40] The last-named tribe was overlaid by the Pananehu and later the Whakatohea in the fifteenth century. This pattern of the displacement of earlier tribes by later ones that emerged in the fourteenth and fifteenth century was repeated in other parts of the country. They will be dealt with later in the tribal traditions.

Kupe the Explorer

The traditions of the tribes on the west coast cite Kupe in the proto-Maori period as a legendary navigator who explored the coastline of

New Zealand around 1325.[41] From his home in Hawaiki, Kupe sailed down the west coast of the North Island bestowing names on physical features such as mountains, hills, reefs and outcrops of rock as he went. There are eleven such names in the North Island. Starting at Whangaroa on the east side of the Northland peninsula is Te Aukanapanapa, the flashing current. In the Hokianga, at the mouth of the Whirinaki River, is Kupe's dog. On the west side of the narrows of the Hokianga Harbour is Kupe's anchor. Kupe gave sixteen names to places in the region of Cook Strait to mark his passing. Some of them include Nga Ra-o-Kupe, the sails of Kupe, Nga Waka-o-Kupe, the vessels of Kupe, Nga Tauari-o-Matahorua, the thwarts of his canoe Matahorua, and Te Kupenga-a-Kupe, Kupe's net. Because he took the passage through Cook Strait, Kupe is credited in the traditions with dividing the North from the South Island in this chant from Te Rauparaha:[42]

Ka tito au	I will sing
Ka tito au	I will sing
Ka tito au ki a Kupe	I will sing of Kupe
Te tangata	The man
Nana i topetope	Who severed
Te whenua	The land
Tu ke Kapiti	Kapiti stands apart
Tu ke Mana	Mana stands apart
Tau ke Arapaoa	So does Arapaoa
Ko nga tohu, tena	Those are the signs,
O taku tipuna	Of my ancestor
O Kupe	Of Kupe
Nana i waka tomene	Who explored
Titapua	Titapua
Ka toroke i au	This land was thrust
te whenua nei.	apart by me.

As he sailed around the coastline, Kupe saw birds, the kokako, or blue wattle crow, and tiwaiwaka, the fantail. There is some doubt as to whether he saw any people on his voyage. When he returned to the North Cape, the Ngapuhi traditions relate that Kupe met up with Nukutawhiti, commander of the *Mamaari* canoe. Kupe told Nukutawhiti that the man he was looking for, Tuputupuwhenua, who was another navigator-explorer, could be found down the west coast of the North Island. Four years after he set out, Kupe left Te Hokianga-nui-a-Kupe, the great departing place of Kupe, for Hawaiki. When he reached home, he spoke to Turi, commander of the *Aotea*, about his discoveries. He instructed him to steer by the rising sun, and he would find a river mouth (the Patea) to the west. Kupe told Turi he would find there a suitable site to build a house on a terrace of the riverbank. Kupe's conversations with Turi and Nukutawhiti, who were commanders of canoes involved in migrations in the fourteenth century, indicate that his exploration of the New Zealand coast took place about 1350.[43]

This basic outline of the traditions concerning Kupe was complicated by Percy Smith, who recorded them and then reinterpreted them to fit what he thought to be a tidy chronological sequence for European consumption. Smith believed some of the stories that there were no people in New Zealand when Kupe explored the west coast of the North Island. But the canoe migrants who went south soon after his voyage found both sides of the North Island well populated. For Smith, this was a dilemma that needed resolving. When he found a Ngapuhi genealogy from Aperahama Taonui with a length of forty-two generations to Kupe, he was elated. He wrote: 'The persistent statements made in Maori traditions to the effect that Kupe found no one living in New Zealand is thus accounted for.'[44]

On the basis of this one genealogy Smith drew the conclusion that there were two persons named Kupe. One Kupe he placed just before the canoe migrations in the fourteenth century, which accords with the traditions. But of the Kupe whose name was connected with so many place-names along the coastline, he wrote: 'I would make the suggestion that Kupe was another name for one of the earlier navigators . . . If this suggestion is allowable then we can understand why Kupe is said to have seen no people.'[45]. This expropriation of knowledge and its transformation from the spoken to the written word is just one of the many facets of colonisation. Peter Buck, who admitted that the genealogies for Kupe were confusing, accepted Smith's hypothesis for two persons named Kupe and the 925 date for Kupe the explorer.[46] The consequence of this expropriation and transformation of knowledge by another culture is that generations of school children, both Maori and Pakeha, have been reared on a diet of misinformation concerning Kupe.

In a scholarly sifting of tribal traditions and genealogies, Simmons debunked Smith's two-Kupe hypothesis and the 925 date for his exploration.[47] On the east coast of the North Island, Toi is recognised as the founding ancestor for the proto-Maori period. Only the Ngati Kahungunu claim Kupe as an ancestor, and their genealogies are no longer than twenty-three generations. Many tribes on the west coast claim Kupe as an ancestor of the proto-Maori period. The Rangitane and Muaupoko genealogies for Kupe vary from twenty to twenty-six generations. The genealogies of the Tainui tribes range from thirteen to twenty-six generations. From this evidence, Simmons concluded that a single genealogy of forty-two generations for Kupe not corroborated by the genealogies of other tribes was unusual. On closer examination he found the genealogy was inflated by the interpolation of the names of gods and myth heroes. Therefore the 925 date for Kupe was false. Instead, an average of twenty generations derived from all tribal genealogies would have placed Kupe in the early fourteenth century.

The Migrations of 1350

The rise of horticulture in the economy of the Maori, the increase in population, the appearance of fortifications around 1300 and their subsequent elaboration and efflorescence, coincide with the traditional accounts of population movements and canoe migrations of people in search of land. Simmons[48] draws the conclusion from his study of tribal genealogies tracing descent from migrating ancestors on the canoes of the fourteenth century, that these traditions refer to the origin of tribes as corporate groups, and their purpose is to validate claims to mana and land.

The tribal traditions refer to Hawaiki as the place of origin of Maori people. The word Hawaiki is simply the generic term for homeland, and in their seafaring history of migration across the Great Ocean of Kiwa, there are for the Maori many Hawaiki along the route all the way back to Samoa and Tonga. But the word Hawaiki is used to refer only to the last homeland and not a specific island. The only time a specific place is named as a point of origin is in this aphorism from Taranaki:[49]

> E kore au e ngaro; te kakano i ruia mai i Rangiatea.
> I shall never perish; the seed sown here from Rangiatea.

Ra'iatea in the Society Islands was thought to be the Hawaiki of Kupe. According to the legend, Kupe observed the annual migration to the south-west of the long-tailed cuckoo. He deduced there was land in that direction and followed the migratory route of the birds to New Zealand. Turi was also thought to have lived in Ra'iatea,[50] and when Kupe returned home, Turi used his sailing directions on the voyage to New Zealand. Kupe's instruction to Turi was to steer to the right of the setting sun, or the moon or Venus on Orongonui, the 28th day of Tatau-ururoa, the month of November.[51]

The citation of Rangiatea as the Hawaiki of some tribes is consistent with the evidence cited earlier of similarities in the material culture of the Marquesas and the Society Islands to artifacts in New Zealand from the Archaic moa-hunter period. The affinities are so strong as to leave little doubt of the close relationship between the first settlers of New Zealand and those islands.[52] But for some tribes the last Hawaiki could just as likely be the Cook Islands as the Marquesas or the Society Islands. Linguistically, the Cook Island dialect is the closest of the Polynesian languages to New Zealand Maori. Although there is not yet sufficient archaeological evidence to demonstrate the cultural affinity, the Cook Islands cannot be ruled out as a source of some of the first settlers of New Zealand.

Hawaiki, then, as the point of origin and last homeland of Maori people outside New Zealand, could have been any one or even several of the islands in Eastern Polynesia. But with the evidence from archaeology demonstrating internal population movements from Northland to less densely populated areas in the south, the last Hawaiki for some of the migrating tribes may well have been within New Zealand. Muriwhenua in Northland, where the kumara would most readily have taken root and land soon become overpopulated, is a likely candidate as the last Hawaiki for the internal migrations.

In view of the occupation of New Zealand for over 400 years by an Archaic Maori culture that is identified by archaeological evidence and not tradition, and the evolution of Classic Maori culture from that earlier period with 1350 as the watershed, there is a need to reassess the canoe traditions that emerged at this time.

Because the maritime tradition of the Polynesians endured as an important folk memory of Maori tribes, the waka in New Zealand became a potent symbol of tribal identity, mana and territory. The Ngati Raukawa chant cited by Buck attests to the cultural significance of that symbolism:[53]

> If thou art asked in the spirit-land
> To recite thy genealogy,
> Thou shalt reply,
> I am but a child,
> A child of little knowledge;
> Yet this have I heard,
> *Tainui, Te Arawa, Mataatua,*
> *Kurahaupo* and *Tokomaru*

These were the canoes of my ancestors
In which they paddled
Across the Great Ocean of Kiwa
Stretched before them.

A modern popular song, 'Nga Waka', cites seven canoes as having brought the ancestors of the Maori to New Zealand. To the five named in the Ngati Raukawa chant, this song adds to the list the names of *Takitimu* and *Aotea*. It is these seven canoes that are thought of as having comprised the 'fleet' migrants of 1350. Buck[54] names other canoes as well, including *Nukutere, Horouta, Mahuhu, Mamaari, Araiteuru* and *Te Mamaru*. In addition he lists the names of seven other canoes for the Taranaki and Whanganui districts that are not so well known. Buck derived his conception of a 'fleet' of canoes from Percy Smith, who wrote of six large sea-going pahi putting out to sea from Ra'iatea in 1350.[55] Subsequent authors, including Best, Buck, Dansey and others, reified the concept of the fleet to the level of dogma so that generations of children have been taught to believe what Simmons has termed 'the great New Zealand myth'.

Other writers before Smith in the mid-nineteenth century who tended to think of the Maori canoe traditions in a collective manner were Horatio Hale, Dieffenbach, Shortland and Taylor. But it was Percy Smith who was guilty of truncating the tribal genealogies by averaging them out and establishing 1350 as the date of the so-called 'fleet'. The concept of a fleet of canoes is just another example of the expropriation and transformation of knowledge by the coloniser. Nowhere in the traditions is the claim made of a large number of canoes arriving in New Zealand at the same time.[56] The only validity of 1350 as a date in the prehistory of New Zealand is as a mathematical exercise.

The Moriori Myth

Underlying the myth of the fleet is the two-strata theory for the settlement of New Zealand, which is tinged with overtones of European supremicist notions grounded in Darwinian social evolutionist theory. The point was made as early as 1852 by John Shaw,[57] who thought that there were two races among the Maori. One the 'regular Maori', and the other an 'inferior dark-skinned' people supposed to be the aborigines of the islands. This essentially racist myth was strengthened by Percy Smith when he wrote that the Maori aristocracy preferred to trace their descent from the canoes that formed the 'fleet' in

1350. He thought this last migration was composed of people who were 'more advanced' in ideas and had 'greater warlike powers' than the original inhabitants. He thought the 'purest' descendants of the oldest inhabitants were the tribes of the Urewera, whose different appearance likened them more to the Moriori of the Chatham Islands. Then, without adducing any evidence, he suggested that they were one and the same people.[58]

Smith did not demonstrate any differences in the Maori population, yet with this passage he laid the foundations for yet another false myth to add to the one of the fleet, that the Moriori lived in New Zealand and were overrun by the Maori. A year later the false myth was reinforced by Elsdon Best, who wrote that the original settlers of New Zealand were the Mouriuri, who were described as having flat noses, distended nostrils, bushy hair, dark skin and restless eyes.[59] Best, like Smith, thought the 1350 migrants were a 'more energetic and masterful people' than the earlier inhabitants.[60] Both of them are responsible for promulgating the false myth that the Moriori lived in New Zealand and that they were of Melanesian stock. They also used the terms Mouriuri and Maruiwi as synonyms for Moriori. Buck dismissed the evidence adduced by Smith and Best from the Te Matorohanga school of learning held in 1865 to support their two-strata theory of settlement as being inconsistent. Melanesians characteristically have woolly hair, but these early people were described as having long lank hair. Nor is there any evidence of Melanesian personal and place names in New Zealand. The names of these tribes and their canoes are unequivocally Polynesian.[61]

A more recent critic of the two-strata theory for the settlement of New Zealand was Duff.[62] He argued that the word Moriori was unknown in New Zealand until after the Chatham Islands were discovered in historic times. The words Maori and Moriori did not come into general use until after the 1800s to distinguish the people designated by those terms from Europeans. Duff also indicates that as long ago as 1923, Skinner demonstrated that the people of the Chatham Islands were Polynesians in their physical characteristics with cultural affinities to Eastern Polynesia. Buck was of the view, on the basis of genealogical evidence, that the Moriori were among the early people who settled New Zealand but left soon after to establish themselves in the Chatham Islands.[63]

Duff suggests that Moriori contact with the mainland ceased about the twelfth century.[64] But despite that early isolation from the parent culture, there are enough affinities in the cultural assemblage of the

Moriori to link them to the early culture that Duff identified in his excavation of the Wairau Bar site as the moa-hunter period of Maori culture. The distinctive quadrangular-tanged adze type 1A with poll lugs, which is dispersed from the Society Islands throughout the whole of Polynesia, is found in the Chatham Islands as well as both the North and South Islands.[65] This adze is concrete evidence that the ancestral Moriori culture in the Chathams was an early offshoot of the first Polynesian settlers in New Zealand whose culture evolved at the Wairau Bar site into the moa-hunters identified by Duff. In addition there are fifty-two whale-tooth necklace units made of ivory from the Chatham Islands which closely resemble those of burial No. 2 at Wairau Bar. As well as these affinities with moa-hunter culture, Duff also drew attention to the prevalence of the tangless, rounded, quadrangular-sectioned adze in the Moriori cultural assemblage, together with stone clubs of the patu and wahaika types which it shared in common with Maori culture.

Sutton,[66] one of the more recent analysts of Moriori culture, confirms the general conclusions advanced by Buck and Duff. The Chatham Islands were settled by people from the South Island when the carrying capacity of the hunting, fishing and gathering economy reached its optimum around the twelfth century. There may have been secondary settlement beyond the date advanced by Duff to as late as 1400, but thereafter there was no further contact. The prehistoric population was probably around 2,000 or so. The people subsisted by hunting seals and birds, fishing and gathering shellfish and plant foods. Linguistically, the Moriori language is regarded as a dialect of Maori. Moriori shares with Maori the same basic phonological structure, a high degrees of vocabulary agreement and some shared innovations in vocabulary and syntax.[67] The absence of evidence of carving in Moriori art suggests separation from the parent culture before the development of carving on the mainland.

The discovery of the Chatham Islands by Captain Broughton in 1791 had devastating consequences for the Moriori. European diseases such as measles and influenza reduced the population by a fifth. The extermination of the seals by European hunters cut off the basic food supply of the Moriori causing a further decline in numbers. Then, in 1835, Taranaki tribes displaced by the musket wars of the previous decade invaded the Chathams in search of land for themselves. The Moriori population at that time was estimated at 1,663; the invaders killed a further 226 Moriori. The cumulative impact of these events demoralised the Moriori. The violation of their mana by the Maori and the intrusion of European ideas shattered their morale; they could not cope and perhaps might be said to have 'died of exhaustion'.[68]

The Moriori population declined rapidly after 1835 to 500 in 1840 and to fewer than fifty persons by the turn of the century. The so-called 'last Moriori', Tom Solomon, died in 1933.[69] He was characterised in history books as the last 'full-blooded' Moriori. Despite the apparent demise of the Moriori, the last chapter in the history of these people has yet to be written. Social, political and cultural domination of the Moriori is the root cause of their disappearance, not the loss of 'full blood' as the myth would have us believe. The bloodline of the Moriori continued in the mixed descendants of unions with Maori invaders and European settlers. These descendants had the option of identifying as Moriori, but it would have been unfashionable as a consequence of being overrun, to emphasise or claim Moriori descent. So how many Moriori there are today of mixed descent either in the Chathams or in New Zealand has yet to be determined. In the meantime, the fate of the Moriori on the Chathams has been exploited by the Pakeha coloniser to underpin the false myth that they were exterminated on the mainland by the Maori bearers of a superior culture.

The myth of the Moriori is essentially ideological in the sense of being a false consciousness as a solution in the mind[70] to conflict generated by the coloniser's expropriation of Maori land. According to the myth, the Maori, as a superior and more warlike people, expropriated the land from the Moriori. Therefore Pakeha expropriation of the same land on the basis of their superior civilisation was in accordance with the principle of survival of the fittest. For this reason the false myth of the Moriori has been one of New Zealand's most enduring myths. Pakeha need the myth for the endorsement of colonisation and Pakeha dominance.

The better understanding we now have of New Zealand's pre-history, together with Simmons's debunking of the 'fleet', in no way affects the canoe traditions and the tribal histories that flowed from them. The published accounts of the traditions of Te Arawa, Tainui, Takitimu, Tuwharetoa, Whakatohea and the Taranaki coast are as valid now as they were before they were pushed into the lineal mode of Western chronology and analytical thought by Percy Smith. But they need to be reinterpreted and integrated with the archaeological record and the historical period that followed.

There is no question that the Polynesian ancestors reached New Zealand by ocean-going vessels towards the end of the first millenium. It is probable that many names of those early vessels and crew were not perpetuated as the first settlers struggled to master their new environment. Except for the names of some of the early tribes, the traditions have nothing to say about them. From their cultural assemblage dug up out of the earth we have some knowledge of their economy and social organisation. But with the rapid growth of population in the north brought on by the successful development of horticulture in the twelfth and and thirteenth centuries, tribal wars erupted. The appearance in the archaeological record of fortifications in association with horticulture in the fourteenth century marked the transition from the Archaic to Classic Maori culture. As horticulture spread around the country so did the technology of constructing fortifications. Of the 4,000 to 6,000 pa sites in New Zealand 98 per cent of them are associated with horticultural parts of the country. This is the measure of the difference between the Archaic period of the moa-hunters and the Maori whose culture flourished for the next 500 years into historic times.

CHAPTER 3

Nga Korero o Nehera

Canoe Traditions

Percy Smith's assertion that the ancestors of the Maori arrived in a fleet of canoes in the fourteenth century is readily dismissed as a construct of his imagination by even the most cursory examination of the traditions themselves. Only two of the canoes, the *Arawa* and *Tainui*, are cited as leaving Hawaiki at about the same time. The *Mataatua* arrived in the Bay of Plenty a century later. Some of the legends woven around canoe ancestors to enhance their mana indicated that they were such rugged individualists that co-ordinating sailing times with them would have been difficult. For instance, Tama Te Kapua, the captain of the *Arawa* canoe, perpetrated three acts in Hawaiki that necessitated his hasty departure. First, he roused the ire of Uenuku, high chief of Hawaiki, by his escapade of using stilts to steal breadfruit growing over Uenuku's house. Since the breadfruit was tapu by contagion because it grew over the roof and hence the sacred head of Uenuku, eating it was an insult tantamount to eating the head of the high chief himself. Such an audacious act was punishable by death. In another account, the insult was perpetrated by the family dog digging up and eating matter cast out from Uenuku's carbuncle. This offense was just as grievous, and retribution from Uenuku was expected. In the second incident, Tama Te Kapua sent his compatriot Ruao ashore on a bogus mission to fetch the axe Tutauru left by the window of their house. Tama Te Kapua coveted Ruao's wife and while Ruao was gone, he weighed anchor and left him behind. In the third incident, Tama Te Kapua inveigled Ngatoroirangi, the priest-navigator of the *Tainui*, on board the *Arawa* to perform rituals for a safe journey. As soon as Ngatoroirangi and his wife were aboard, Tama Te Kapua weighed anchor and abducted them both.[1] Under such circumstances, the *Arawa* undoutedly set out alone.

The traditions of the *Aotea* canoe, like those of the *Arawa*, also indicate a hasty departure from Hawaiki.[2] Turi, the captain of the *Aotea*, was a vassal of the paramount chief Uenuku. One year when the tribute to Uenuku from the annual harvest was not up to expectations, Turi's son Potikiroroa was killed by Uenuku's tribe and added to the provisions. Turi's father Rongotea retaliated by killing Uenuku's son Awepotiki and hiding a portion of his heart inside a kumara sent among the first fruits tribute to Uenuku. Such a terrible insult could only be avenged by massive retaliation and bloodshed. To avoid possible extermination, Turi and his people left Hawaiki.

Given the circumstances of conflict with Uenuku, which could have resulted in wars of extermination, it is unlikely that the *Aotea* and the *Arawa* canoes would have been able to co-ordinate their departure times with those of other vessels. The political opportunism displayed by Tama Te Kapua in abducting the high priest Ngatoroirangi to lend mana to his expedition, and his sexual opportunism in the cuckolding of Ruao, would have made collaboration with him well-nigh impossible. Smith's notion of a fleet of ocean-going canoes putting out to sea in line astern from Hawaiki is patently absurd. It is also contradicted by genealogical evidence. Of the fourteen genealogies listed by Simmons for the *Mataatua* canoe, only one is of sufficient length to place it at 1350. The rest range from fourteen to twenty generations.[3] The average of these genealogies places the *Mataatua* at least a century after the *Tainui* and *Arawa* canoes.

The two-strata theory favoured by Smith and Best of a fleet of invaders in the fourteenth century, who with their superior culture displaced the tangata whenua, is not borne out by tradition either. The traditions of canoes making landfall along the New Zealand coastline at different times over several generations all cite the presence of tangata whenua tribes. A canoe-load of migrants including women and children was hardly capable of mounting a war of conquest against well-established people. All the traditions indicate that where crew disembarked at various places they did so without recourse to fighting. They either took up unoccupied land, or joined up with the tangata whenua. The accommodation of migrants by host communities was acknowledged among tribes in the Bay of Plenty by this aphorism:

> Na Toi raua ko Potiki te whenua, na Tuhoe te mana me te rangatiratanga.[4]
> The land belonged to Toi and Potiki, the mana and chieftainship belonged to Tuhoe.

The acknowledgement of mana whenua as belonging to the tangata whenua and chieftainship as coming from canoe migrants also occurred in the interior among the Tuwharetoa confederation of tribes around Lake Taupo. Tuwharetoa, the founding ancestor of the tribe, was an eighth-generation descendant from Ngatoroirangi, the priest-navigator of the *Arawa* canoe. The mana ariki of the tribe was transmitted from Ngatoroirangi to Tuwharetoa. But his line of aboriginal forebears went back seventeen generations to Te Hapuoneone. It was freely acknowledged that Tuwharetoa's mana came from his father's ancestors, while his undisputed right to land came from his aboriginal forebears.[5]

The traditions of the *Tainui* canoe are a good example of amalgamation of canoe migrants with tangata whenua. After making its landfall at Whangaparaoa, the *Tainui* made its way north up the Bay of Plenty into the Waitemata Harbour, where it was dragged across the isthmus to the Manukau Harbour and went out to sea again to put in at various points along the west coast all the way down to Mokau. At different places en route small groups of crewmen disembarked to join local tribes. The tohunga Rakataura settled at Rarotonga (Mt Smart). Riukiuta and others settled at Three Kings. Hoturoa, the captain of the vessel, decided that Tamaki was already overpopulated by the Waiohua tangata whenua, so he and the rest of the crew journeyed on in search of vacant land. Small groups of settlers joining already numerous tangata whenua were hardly conquerors. A *modus vivendi* of peaceful integration had to be arrived at or else expulsion and possibly annihilation would have surely followed. Hoturoa's wife Whakaotirangi, who was the custodian of the basket of seed kumara which she carried from Hawaiki attached to her waist, settled at Pakarikari. There she established her kumara in a garden named Hawaiki. This invaluable gift of horticulture made Whakaotirangi and her husband Hoturoa most welcome settlers in the area. In the meantime, Rakataura left Rarotonga and journeyed south with his wife Kahukeke. After she died on the way, he settled at Te Aroha, so named after the abiding love he had for his wife. None of the traditions of these founding ancestors of the Tainui has them embroiled in wars of conquest.[6]

The *Arawa* canoe, which arrived at Whangaparaoa shortly after the *Tainui*, also journeyed north-west across the Bay of Plenty. Although the captain Tama Te Kapua settled at Moehau (Coromandel), the bulk of his descendants and crew established a beachhead at Maketu, where the canoe landed. There were already strong tribes and fortifications in the area, but despite that, Tama Te Kapua's son Kahumatamomoe settled peacefully among the tangata whenua. It was not until the fourth generation after the *Arawa* landed that the fighting chief Rangitihi emerged and extended the canoe's beachhead inland by conquest of the tangata whenua tribes.[7] Similarly, it was not until the time of Tuwharetoa's sons and grandson Rereao, over 200 years after Ngatoroirangi arrived in the *Arawa*, that the Tuwharetoa tribe extended its foothold at Kawerau inland to Taupo.[8]

The *Mataatua* canoe, which entered the Bay of Plenty a century or more after the *Arawa*, found even more numerous tangata whenua tribes in occupation. Only three ancestors from this vessel are claimed in the descent lines of the Bay of Plenty tribes. They are Toroa the captain, his elder sister Muriwai, and Taneatua. The *Mataatua* was taken north by Puhi together with most of the crew after he quarrelled with Toroa over the use of kumara-planting rituals. The three who stayed behind, together with Toroa's children and their retainers, hardly constituted an invasion. They were in fact integrated peacefully into the local tribes by marriages with tangata whenua spouses. Muriwai's daughter Hinekauia married Tutamure of the Wakanui people at Omarumutu east of Opotiki.[9] Taneatua married Hineahuone, and Toroa's daughter Wairaka married Rangikitua.[10]

The failure of Percy Smith's two-strata theory for the settlement of New Zealand to be supported by traditional, archaeological and linguistic evidence, poses the question of how the canoe traditions of the fourteenth century should be interpreted. Simmons suggests an interpretation that is more compatible with the evidence.[11] The original Polynesian ancestors of the Maori who settled New Zealand and the tangata whenua tribes they established between 900 and 1350 no longer exist. They were overlaid by the dynamics of population increase brought on by the efflorescence of horticulture, endemic warfare and the formation of new groups. Eventually, overpopulation in the north led to a series of internal migrations to more sparsely settled areas in the south. The canoe traditions correspond to this period and are interpreted by Simmons as validating charters for the mana, chieftainship, and territorial claims to land of the new corporate groups that emerged after 1350. Invariably the canoes cite Hawaiki as their point of origin and the last homeland for many of them was more than likely in the overcrowded region of Northland, particularly Muriwhenua in the region of Kaitaia. The routes taken by the canoes are to the south, with some back-tracking north along the coast in search of vacant land. The use of totara trees and greenstone adzes in the construction of canoes for the migrations indicate that the *Arawa* and *Tainui* were built in New Zealand.[12] The *Takitimu* was also fash-

ioned with greenstone adzes.[13] When the *Aotea* was loaded with cargo
in Hawaiki for the voyage in search of a place to live, the provisions
included pukeko and karaka, flora and fauna native to New Zealand,
as well as kumara and rats.[14] The main themes that emerge from the
traditions are a search for vacant land. If there was none available, then
the migrants joined existing tangata whenua groups. In subsequent
generations, when there was no more vacant land, warfare and conquest
was the only way to get it. At that point the lineages of migrant
ancestors became important as legitimating charters for the groups
that emerged after the fourteenth century, and the canoe that was identified with their migration became a political symbol of the new order.

As validating charters for tribal identity and ownership of land, the
canoe traditions follow on in sequence from the three myth complexes
which precede them. In the traditions, heroes from mythology span
the gap between the remote past and the ancestors of the canoes from
whom descent was traced to living persons. The tohunga who crafted
the migratory canoes of *Tainui* and *Arawa* were Rata, Wahieroa and
others.[15] That traditions are the sequel to myths is evident in the
repetition of themes from mythology in the behaviour of founding
ancestors. The traditions of the Arawa tribes, for instance, portray
their ancestor Tama Te Kapua as an heroic figure with personality
characteristics similar to those of the legendary Maui. Like Maui, he
was a trickster who was bold, cunning, assertive, and utterly ruthless
in his pursuit of mana. His lone exploit of rescuing his brother
Whakaturia from being slowly asphyxiated by smoke as he hung in the
rafters of Uenuku's house for stealing breadfruit was a deed worthy of
a mythic hero. But as a mere mortal he also exhibited human failing
in his seduction of Ngatoroirangi's wife and the cuckolding of Ruao.
However, he paid for both of these indiscretions when Ngatoroirangi
punished him by threatening to destroy the *Arawa*. Then, when the
vessel landed at Maketu, waiting to meet him was Ruao, who defeated
him in single combat but spared his life only to insult him. As with
Maui the demi-god, success was tempered by defeat. But from the
point of view of his descendants, he was revered as a founding ancestor
for his success rather than his defeats.

Ngatoroirangi, the founding ancestor of the Tuwharetoa tribe, was
an even more formidable character of mythic stature. With his power
to command the elements he asserted his mana over Tama Te Kapua
for seducing his wife Kearoa by almost sinking the *Arawa* with a
mighty whirlpool. But when he heard the fearful and anguished cries
of women and children, he relented at the last moment.[16]

The theme of the dangerous nature of the brother-in-law relationship made explicit in the Maui and Tawhaki myths is also repeated in the canoe traditions. The Atiawa tribes assert Kupe killed his brother-in-law Hoturapa and stole his wife Kuramarotini. The tribes of the Hokianga also mention Kupe stealing Hoturapa's wife. One version has Kupe taking his brother-in-law fishing. When their anchor got stuck Kupe persuaded Hoturapa to dive down and free it. He then cut the rope, sailed away and left Hoturapa to drown.[17]

This same theme of brother-in-law enmity was played out also between Ngatoroirangi and Manaia.[18] Manaia cursed his wife Kuiwai for not cooking his food properly. When Ngatoroirangi heard of the curse, he travelled back to Hawaiki to punish his brother-in-law. In his battles with Manaia, Ngatoroirangi emulated the canons of Maori warfare laid down in mythology by Whakatau Potiki. He carried out reconnaissance of enemy territory, spied on them to discover their plans, and devised a strategy to defeat them. He and his men had overheard Manaia's tohunga praying to their gods to deliver their enemy into the hangi they had prepared for them. After they had gone, Manaia instructed his men to beat their noses until the blood flowed. Smearing their bodies liberally with blood, they lay in the hangi with their weapons concealed beneath them. In due course Manaia's people returned to see their prayers had been answered. They were taken completely by surprise when the apparently dead men rose up and attacked them. Manaia's forces were routed, but as so often happens in warfare, Manaia escaped to fight again another day.

Some time after he had moved from the mainland to live on the island of Motiti, Ngatoroirangi awoke one morning to find a flotilla of canoes standing offshore under the command of Manaia. Knowing they had Ngatoroirangi surrounded, the enemy took their time sailing around the island taunting him. In the afternoon, Ngatoroirangi suggested that the battle be joined the next morning. After the fleet had anchored for the night, he communed with his god and by the power of incantation raised a mighty storm that overwhelmed his enemies. All that was washed ashore after the multitudes of Tangaroa had done their work were the fingernails of the victims.[19]

The battles of Ihumotomotokia, Bloodied-noses, and Maikukutea, Fingernails, are epic stories which may have their genesis in real events but, by the poetic licence of the storyteller's art, were embellished to the level of legend. As canoe ancestors, the stories of the exploits of Tama Te Kapua and Ngatoroirangi serve to enhance their mana and consequently that of their descendants and tribes of the

Arawa and the Tuwharetoa confederations.

The concern of the traditions with mana and the assertion of prior rights of discovery are extensively portrayed in tribal stories. When the *Arawa* arrived at Whangaparaoa in the eastern Bay of Plenty, Tama Te Kapua came upon a stranded whale with a rope tied to it signifying ownership. He realised it belonged to *Tainui*. Undeterred by this turn of events, Tama Te Kapua had a shrine built on shore to prove the *Arawa* had arrived first. An old-looking rope was attached to the whale beneath that of the *Tainui* and buried in the sand. When the *Tainui* returned Tama Te Kapua showed the crew his shrine and rope as proof the *Arawa* had arrived first. The *Tainui* did not contest the claim and sailed off.[20] Later, as the *Arawa* sailed up the Bay of Plenty to Maketu, the chiefs exercised the power to claim land by prior right of discovery under the custom of taunaha or tapatapa whenua.[21] Tama Te Kapua bespoke Maketu Point for his descendants, saying, 'That point is the bridge of my nose.' This was a notional claim to mana whenua which had to be validated by settlement. Tama Te Kapua's son Kahumatamomoe exercised that right by settling at Maketu with his followers but Tama Te Kapua went on to Moehau on the Coromandel Peninsula, where he died and was buried on the mountain.

When Ngatoroirangi and Tia, another ancestor from the *Arawa*, went inland to explore, they competed against each other in claiming the land. Ngatoroirangi went inland via the Tarawera River and then on to Taupo, where he stirred up clouds of dust in the water as he claimed ownership. The dusty water flowed down the Waikato River, where it was seen by Tia. He knew immediately that someone had beaten him, so named that place Atiamuri, Tia who came after. But when Tia got to the lake himself, he had the satisfaction of naming it Taupo-nui-a-Tia, the great cloak of Tia, after a formation on a cliff which resembled a cloak. Other names which mark Tia's exploration include the Aratiatia Rapids, which he likened to the stairway of Tia, and Te Horohoro-nuinga-a-Tia, the large swallowing of Tia. This latter name arose out of the need for Tia to swallow cooked food in a whakanoa rite to remove the tapu which had contaminated him when he touched the dead body of a tangata whenua person.

In the meantime, as he continued his exploration, Ngatoroirangi had climbed Mt Tauhara, where he installed his god Ikatere as a guardian of ownership. But when he climbed Tongariro as a vantage point from which to bespeak the land, he was challenged by a tangata whenua named Hapeketuarangi. Ngatoroirangi destroyed him by invoking

Ruaumoko, the god of volcanoes, who spilt dense sulphurous clouds out of the mountain. As he climbed higher, he almost perished with cold so he called on his ancestors to send volcanic fire from Hawaiki to warm him. As it travelled from Hawaiki, the fire emerged at Whakaari (White Island), Rotorua, and Taupo. Near Tongariro, where the cold southerly wind chilled his bones, Ngatoroirangi cast one of his sacred ara stones down on the ground and a burning volcano appeared. Before he returned to the coast, he planted his personal god Rongomai at Taupo as protector of his descendants.[22] The deeds of Ngatoroirangi are clearly those of a legendary figure who was more than halfway to being elevated to the realm of heroes of mythology such as Maui, Tawhaki and Rata. What the Tuwharetoa traditions indicate is that the mana of the tribe came from the canoe ancestor Ngatoroirangi. His exploration of the interior staked out a nominal claim to the lands of Taupo when he surveyed them from the summit of Tongariro. But it was left to his descendants, the sons of Tuwharetoa, to assert that claim over the tangata whenua tribes when they took over Taupo 200 years later.

The *Takitimu* canoe after leaving Hawaiki made its first stop at Awanui on the west coast of Northland. There some of the crew disembarked and went across to live at Kaitaia. As with the other vessels, there was no mention about invasion and warfare. After rounding North Cape, *Takitimu* sailed on to Tauranga, where Tamatea-mai-tawhiti settled and married a descendant of Toi. The *Takitimu* continued under the command of Tahu down the east coast. The tohunga Ruawharo left the vessel at Nukutaurua and settled at Te Papa. At Wairarapa, more of the crew disembarked under the leadership of the tohunga Tupai. Finally Tahu-potiki took the vessel to the South Island, where it entered the Arahura River and was petrified on a papa ledge. Tahu became established in the South Island as the eponymous ancestor of the Ngai Tahu.[23]

The canoe traditions for *Tokomaru* and *Kurahaupo* are not as detailed as those for *Tainui*, *Te Arawa*, *Mataatua*, and *Takitimu*. The *Tokomaru*, commanded by Manaia, made its landfall on the east coast in the Bay of Plenty. It sailed north around the North Cape and down the west coast to the Tongaporutu River. Manaia and his people settled at Tongaporutu where his descendants are the Ngati Tama hapu.[24]

The *Kurahaupo*, which was wrecked at Rangitahua, was commanded by Moungaroa. He and his crew transferred to the *Mataatua*. On arrival in the Bay of Plenty, Moungaroa and his people travelled overland to Whanganui-a-Tara and up the west coast to the Wairau Stream near Oakura. According to some traditions, the *Kurahaupo* was repaired and sailed on by Ruatea to the North Cape. Ruatea sailed south to Cape Kidnappers where some crew disembarked. Some settled at Cook Strait to become the Ngati Apa tribe of Rangitikei.[25]

The sparseness of the traditions for *Tokomaru* and *Kurahaupo* is because of the lack of ancestral descent lines from them.[26] Ancestors on these vessels were probably assimilated by the host communities which accepted them, from Taranaki through to Whanganui, Manawatu, Horowhenua and Rangitikei. But despite that, the canoes are retained in these areas as symbols of tribal identity and federation in relation to other areas with strong canoe traditions.

The traditions of the *Aotea* canoe, like those of the *Tokomaru* and *Kurahaupo*, are also shrouded with uncertainty. The vessel landed north of Kawhia, but ended up in the harbour of Raglan, which was originally named Aotea after the canoe. But the crew left the area on foot, travelling south along the coast searching for the Patea River, which was described by Kupe to Turi. There Turi found the river terrace on the south bank alluded to by Kupe as the ideal site for his house.[27] Turi's son Turangaimua was a warrior chief who campaigned as far north as Tamaki and across to Hawke's Bay. He was the only migrant who on landing engaged immediately in warfare against the tangata whenua. Although he conquered ten tangata whenua tribes on these expeditions, he did not consolidate at any one place. When Turangaimua was killed in the Ruahine Ranges, Turi was so bereft by the loss of his son that he disappeared. It is said his spirit returned to Hawaiki.

The uncertainty of the *Aotea* migrants in the area where they landed is exemplified by the story of Tamaahua, who settled south of the Oakura River. One day his loincloth fell off and exposed his circumcised penis to his aboriginal wives, whose people did not practise circumcision. Because they laughed at him, Tamaahua left the area and sailed away to Hawaiki. Both Turi and Tamaahua clearly failed to stamp their mana among the host tribes that received them, and so when they encountered difficulties, they withdrew. Another new settler who did the same was Ngarue. He married Urutekaraka from Kawhia. But because his wife's people taunted him for being landless, he left the district and went to Waitara. It was not until well after the arrival of the *Aotea* that the mana whenua of the tribes claiming descent from that vessel was established around 1600. But it was done so without reference to Turi.[28]

The traditions of the Ngati Porou tribes on the East Coast have several origin stories. The most fabulous is the story of the founding ancestor Paikea arriving from Hawaiki on the back of a whale. Another group claim descent from Maui as Te-Iwi-Pohatu-o-Maui, the stone-age people of Maui. These people, now known as Uepohatu, say Maui's canoe, on which their ancestors came, lies in a petrified state on Mt Hikurangi. The *Nukutere* canoe under the command of Te Whironui put in at Opape, east of Opotiki, almost 200 years before the *Mataatua* arrived. The crew that settled there under Tauturangi established the Te Wakanui people.[29] The canoe journeyed around the East Cape to the mouth of the Waiapu River. Te Whironui built a pa on a headland beside a small lake near Te-Wai-o-ue Stream. It was in the lake where the villagers bathed that Paikea came upon Te Whironui's daughter Huturangi when he arrived. Paikea married Huturangi and from that union, four generations later, came Porourangi, the eponymous ancestor of the Ngati Porou tribes.[30] The *Horouta* canoe, under the command of Pawa, arrived not long after the *Nukutere*. The priest-navigator Kiwa went ashore at Turanganui-a-Kiwa (Poverty Bay) to lay claim to the area by planting the mauri of his people transported there from Hawaiki. Pawa explored the area and named the river he found Te-Wai-o-Pawa. He also named the prominent headland in the bay Te-Kuri-o-Pawa. The names placed on the land by Kiwa and Pawa verify to the descendants of these early explorers the part played by their ancestors in the settlement of the East Coast region. Although Pawa, like Turi, was thought to have returned to Hawaiki, his daughter and people remained at Turanga. The mana ariki of the tribes in the area was transmitted from Hineakua down seven generations to Ruapani, the recognised paramount chief of the Turanganui district.[31]

Although there are a number of canoes associated with the Northland tribes, such as *Mataatua, Mamaari, Mahuhu* and *Nga Toki-o-Matawhaorua*, the canoe traditions are not so clearly defined as for some areas. This is because none of the tribes in the North, with perhaps the exception of Ngati Kahu, have had a corporate identity for any longer than twelve generations.[32] This late definition of identity was probably related to the state of flux in tribal relations owing to overcrowding in the Far North. Population pressure and wars over garden land could only be alleviated by forcing small groups to migrate south in search of land. Furthermore, the canoe traditions are about people moving in among tangata whenua in less crowded areas to establish new tribes from the resulting amalgamation. So the North was characterised by an outflow rather than an inflow of migrants.

The *Mataatua* of course was an exception. When Puhi quarrelled with his older brother Toroa, he left Whakatane and returned north to search for a place to settle. According to one version, he had the *Mataatua* portaged across Tamaki to the Manukau and travelled up the west coast to Hokianga. From there he crossed overland to the Kerikeri inlet. Another version had Puhi sailing directly up the east coast to Whangarei. There he was warned off by Manaia, who told him he was in danger of being killed in the manner of a canoe being pounded on the shore by the thundering waves of Taiharuru. Puhi wisely continued up the coast to Ngunguru, Tutukaka, Matapouri and Whananaki. Although food was abundant in these places, he did not stay, as those areas were well populated. Puhi went on to Whangaruru then Cape Brett. His journey ended past the Bay of Islands at Takou Bay, where he and his crew settled.[33] Puhi was exceptional in being able to settle in the North at a time when others were being forced out. Those exceptional qualities founded the powerful Ngapuhi tribes that dominated the North from the sixteenth century into historic times.

One migrant who was clearly forced out of the North in the fifteenth century was Tamatea, father of Kahungunu. After being driven out for poaching on the birding reserves of others, he went by canoe on an expedition in search of land. After circumnavigating New Zealand in a voyage that covered 3,000 miles, Tamatea returned for his family. The people at Mangonui, who were impressed by his feat, named him Tamatea-pokai-whenua to commemorate his circumnavigation. They tried to persuade him to stay, but Tamatea refused, saying, 'He rangai maomao ka taka ki tua o Nukutaurua e kore a muri e hokia.' He likened his migration to a shoal of maomao which, once past Nukutaurua, a rock at the entrance of the harbour, would not return.[34] The aphorism aptly expressed the general trend of groups of people leaving the area by canoe never to return. The widespread Ngati Awa were driven out of the North about the same time as Tamatea. The last known group to be forced out were the Ngati Whatua, who moved southwards some time in the seventeenth century to fill up the vacant spaces left by Ngati Awa. Although Ngati Whatua claim ancient descent from Tumutumu-whenua in the Far North, it was not until they established themselves at Kaipara and conquered the Tamaki isthmus around 1750 that they became clearly established as a powerful corporate group.

In view of the deeply rooted tradition of Polynesian ocean voyaging, and the significance of the canoe as a symbol of identity, the names of some of the original migratory canoes from the Pacific may well have been used for the canoes of the internal migration. The two traditions of the original canoes and the internal migrations could have been confused and the internal migrations reified by Percy Smith into a migration from outside New Zealand. Simmons draws the conclusion that 'the overland and partly seaborne migration from Muriwhenua to Taranaki, East Coast, Bay of Plenty and Coromandel of Awa and related groups is fairly definitely established by the pattern of tradition. The Hawaiki of the *Arawa*, *Tainui* and *Aotea* canoes is more than likely in Northland as well.'[35]

Mana Whenua

After the initial resettlement of migrants through claiming of unoccupied land or amalgamation with existing groups in the south, the traditions abound with accounts of tribal wars which spanned a period of almost 500 years. Theses wars were the means by which tribes defined their political relations and territorial boundaries.

In the case of the Arawa confederation of tribes, it was not till the fourth generation from Tama Te Kapua in the time of Rangitihi that the Arawa people moved inland from Maketu up the Kaituna River. The importance of Rangitihi as a founding ancestor was attributable to his four marriages, which produced seven sons who assisted him in the conquest of the interior and the consolidation of their hold on the Rotorua lakes district. Indeed, it was not until the time of his grandson Rangiteaorere, around 1500, that the conquest of Mokoia was achieved. Rangitihi and his son Tuhourangi are commemorated as two of the hapu of the Arawa confederation. One of Rangitihi's grandsons, Pikiao, also became an eponymous ancestor of a hapu that occupied the lands around Lake Rotoiti. The Ngati Whakaue hapu held the west shore of Lake Rotorua, while Ngati Rangiwehiwehi held land from Awahou towards Mourea. Ngati Rangiteaorere and Uenukukopako owned the territory from Mourea in a south-west direction around Lake Rotorua to Owhatiura. Ngati Tuhourangi and other sections occupied the land between Owhatiura in the east and Kawaha Point in the west. Stafford's account of Te Arawa traditions is as much about the petty inter-hapu fights in the definition of these territories as they are of Rangitihi's displacement of tangata whenua tribes.[36]

Tuwharetoa, the eponymous ancestor of the Tuwharetoa confederation of tribes, married a tangata whenua woman named

Paekitawhiti. This first marriage produced a daughter called Maniawharepu, the female ariki tapairu line of the tribe. The second child of this marriage was Rongomaitengangana, the aho ariki (chiefly line) of Tuwharetoa. His second marriage to Waitahanui of Ngai Tai produced eight children and another five children came from his third marriage. He also fathered Tutanekai in an illicit liaison with his cousin Rangiuru at Rotorua. Originally Tuwharetoa and his people lived at Kawerau. But after a severe defeat at the hands of the Maruiwi who settled amongst them, Tuwharetoa's sons drove out the Maruiwi and pursued them into the interior. This brought them into conflict with other tangata whenua tribes. On the excuse of avenging the curse of Hinekaharoa of the Ngati Kurapoto, Tuwharetoa's grandson Rereao and his uncle Rakeipoho led a war party to Taupo. Rereao mistook Ngati Hotu for Ngati Kurapoto, inflicting a defeat on them and other sections of their people. In the meantime Rakeipoho defeated Ngati Kurapoto and peace was made. After the two war parties joined up, Rereao learned he had attacked the wrong people so he concluded a peace with Ngati Hotu. The chieftainess Hineuru was given in marriage to Paepaetehe, the Ngati Hotu chief, to cement the peace. A few years later Ngati Hotu planned revenge by attempting to kill Hineuru's three brothers. A timely warning by Hineuru enabled them to escape. Tuwharetoa responded by invading and inflicting a series of defeats on Ngati Hotu. With the death of Paepaetehe, Ngati Hotu power was shattered and Tuwharetoa were masters of Taupo. Thus, by take raupatu (right of conquest) did Tuwharetoa validate the claim to Taupo lodged on their behalf by the exploration of their ancestor Ngatoroirangi 200 years before.[37]

Kahungunu, the ancestor of the Ngati Kahungunu tribes, was in many ways similar to Tuwharetoa. He had an impeccable pedigree from Tamatea, who circumnavigated the country before settling at Tauranga. Kahungunu was handsome and had enormous appeal to the opposite sex. He left Tauranga in disgrace for greedy and unseemly behaviour. After a sojourn at Opotiki, he made his way to the East Coast, entering into a number of liaisons as he went. Eventually he reached Mahia, where he married the East Coast chieftainess Rongomaiwahine. This marriage produced four children, with the aho ariki descending through his son Kahukuranui. In the next generation Kahukuranui extended his influence by a political marriage to Ruatapuwahine, daughter of Ruapani, the paramount chief of Turanganui. He made another political marriage with Tuteihonga at Otatara (Taradale). Their son Rakeipaaka founded his own hapu and settled at Wairoa. One of Kahungunu's great-grandsons, Taraia, was a warrior chief who in a southward migration won a series of engagements to extend Ngati Kahungunu territory beyond Wairoa to Heretaunga. Perhaps one of the most astute of all leaders was the chief Te Huki, six generations from Kahungunu. He was the key ancestor in the unification of the sub-tribes, not by making war but by making strategic political marriages. The strategy was known as 'Te Kupenga a Huki', the net of Huki, which he set throughout the tribal domain. The plan involved keeping his wives in their home territories and visiting them periodically. The 'floats' of Te Huki's net were set at Heretaunga, Nuhaka, and Turanganui. One of Te Huki's sons married Te Whewhera, a high-ranking woman of the Ngati Rakaipaaka hapu. This union was known as the 'seed-bed of chiefs'. Nine of the seeds from the marriage were placed judiciously about the tribal territory at Heretaunga, Whakaki, Paeroa, Wairoa, Waiau, Kihitu, Ruataniwha and Waihirere.[38]

The initial centre of Tainui settlement was at Kawhia, where the vessel ended its journey. For the first hundred years or so the Tainui settlers built up their numbers and strengthened their position. It was not until the time of Tawhao, seven generations after Hoturoa, that the penetration of the interior was undertaken. There was intense rivalry between Tawhao's sons Turongo and Whatihua over seniority, and their suit for the hand of the chieftainess Ruaputahanga. Turongo's disappointment at losing the contest to his brother was more than assuaged when he married the East Coast chieftainess Mahinarangi. Tawhao wisely decided to separate his sons by dividing his lands between them. The northern lands he gave to Whatihua and land to the south-west to Turongo. The Tainui penetration inland was led by Turongo's grandson Rereahu. He took the country around Tiroa by defeating three local chiefs. His eldest son Te Ihingarangi went to live at Maungatautari and it is from him that the Ngati Haua trace their line of descent. His younger son Maniapoto, whom he favoured, became the founding ancestor of Ngati Maniapoto, who controlled the southern part of Tainui territory. One of the key ancestors in the definition of Tainui boundaries was Hotunui, who left his original residence at Kawhia to live at Hauraki because of a theft that was blamed on him. In due course his son Marutuahu, who was born after he left, grew up and went in search of his father. Marutuahu avenged the insults given to his father by the local tribe by making war on them. Marutuahu went to live at Waitakaruru. His descendants are the Ngati Maru section of the Tainui tribes that occupy the Hauraki district. The heartland of the Waikato was occupied by the Ngati Mahuta people. This tribe, led by the powerful chiefs Wharetipeti and Tapaue, defeated the Te Iranui people and took over their fertile flat lands around Taupiri. In subsequent generations when Ngati Raukawa began to encroach on Ngati Mahuta land from Maungatautari to Horotiu, Raukawa were defeated and driven out.[39]

The Ngati Toa tribe descended from the ancestor Tawhao, who lived on the south side of Kawhia. One of his grandsons, Mango, founded the Ngati Mango sub-tribe which produced the warrior chief Toa Rangatira. This chief and Kawharu became the undisputed masters of Kawhia until Kawharu went north to assist Ngati Whatua in their conquest of Kaipara in the mid-eighteenth century. Eventually, because of border disputes with other strong Waikato clans such as Ngati Mahanga and Ngati Mahuta, Ngati Toa decided to vacate Kawhia. The fighting chief Te Rauparaha led an evacuation known as 'Te heke tahutahu ahi', the migration of lighted fires, of Ngati Toa, Ngati Koata and Ngati Rarua south to Okoki. There they were welcomed as allies by Ngati Mutunga, and given land to cultivate and the pa of Pukewhakamaru.[40]

On the East Coast, four generations after the arrival of Paikea, Porourangi, the founding ancestor of Ngati Porou, was born at Whangara. Porourangi's two sons, Hau and Ueroa, were responsible for the initial extension of the tribal domain from Whangara. Ueroa went south to Turanga while Hau and his followers went north, settling for a time at different places. Eventually Hau extended his claims to land right around the East Cape into the Bay of Plenty as far as Taumata-Apanui near Torere. In later years this last portion of the territorial claim was pushed back to Te Kaha and the land ceded to Te Whanau-a-Apanui. In the next generation Hau's son Poroumata migrated from Whangara, staying for a time at Uawa, then on to Whareponga. There Poroumata was murdered by the local Ngati Ruanuku people. Poroumata's youngest daughter Atakura left the district, got married and went to reside with her husband's people at Opotiki. There she dedicated her second child, Tuwhakairiora, while he was still in the womb, to avenge the death of her father.

In due course Tuwhakairiora grew to manhood and travelled east on his mission of vengeance. At Hicks Bay he married Ruataupare and became the overlord of her tribe, the Ngaituiti. From there Tuwhakairiora launched his campaign around the East Cape, conquering the Ngaituere and other aboriginal tribes before settling his account with Ngati Ruanuku at the battle of Hikutawatawa and taking the fortress of Tokanu. The conquests of Tuwhakairiora moved the centre of Ngati Porou territory from Whangara towards the East Cape. Thereafter Ngati Porou expanded and consolidated their territory in three stages, each defined by physical features on the land. The first phase took in the land from a stream named Paua-o-ruku near Te Araroa and Te-kopu-o-kanae at the mouth of the Waiapu River. The second phase extended the northern boundary to Patetangata, a cone-shaped mountain near Hicks Bay. The southern marker was Tawhiti-o-Pawa, a hillock between Te Puia and Tokomaru Bay. In the third phase the southern boundary was pushed to Toka-a-Taiau in the mouth of the Turanganui River. The northern boundary was held at a rock named Te-toka-a-Kuku at Te Kaha. In the last phase the conquest of the southern sections of Ngati Ruanuku was undertaken by Pakanui, the grandson of Tuwhakairiora's aunt Materoa. But south of the Waipiro Stream he came up against the Wahineiti. Tuwhakairiora assisted Pakanui in the defeat of the Wahineiti at the battle of Rorohukutai on Waipiro Beach. On his return home Tuwhakairiora remarried and established his own hapu. His wife Ruataupare and her people moved to Tuparoa and later Tokomaru Bay, where she established Te Whanau a Ruataupare.[41]

In the Bay of Plenty the first act of Toroa, the commander of the *Mataatua*, was to plant the mauri of his people in the new land. To this end a manuka post was set up on a mound on the bank of the Whakatane River where the prow of the vessel came to rest. That place is known as Te Manuka-tutahi, the lone manuka, prow of *Mataatua*. After planting the mauri, the task of housebuilding and gardening was undertaken. It was at this time that Toroa quarrelled with his younger brother, Puhi, who withdrew and went north with the *Mataatua*. Toroa's daughter Wairaka married a tangata whenua named Rangiki-tua. From this union came Tamatea, who married Paewhiti. Their children, Ueimua, Tanemoeahi and Tuhoe Potiki, were known as the 'terrible three of Paewhiti'. As ferocious warriors they gained a reputation which was celebrated in the aphorism 'he iti na Tuhoe e kata te po', a small section of Tuhoe gives delight to Hades. These men settled at Ruatoki and gradually extended their influence over tangata whenua tribes to Opouriao. They pushed their coastal boundary as far as Waiwherowhero creek.

In a fraternal fight Tuhoe Potiki and Tanemoeahi killed their senior, Ueimua. As a consequence of this, Ueimua's son Irataketake moved to Whakatane with the Ngati Awa. Because of Irataketake's continued harassment with his Ngati Awa allies, Tuhoe Potiki, his brothers and others left the district. Tuhoe Potiki's younger son, Karatehe, remained in the district at Waihoru pa, where he established his own hapu, Ngati Karatehe. His other son, Mura-kareke, settled at Putauaki (Mt Edgecumbe). In his old age Mura-kareke burnt himself when he was sleeping by the fire. Because it was his penis that suffered the pain, the incident is commemorated by the name Urewera for the mountain domain of the Tuhoe. The feud between Ngati Awa and Ngati Karatehe continued in the next generation, with the latter moving to other places for a time before consolidating themselves at Ruatoki. Their descendants are the Ngati Koura hapu.[42]

The Tini-o-Awa tribes, against which Tuhoe fought for so long to define their own identity, were the descendants of Awanuiarangi, the son of Toi. The descendants of these people known today as Ngati Awa are linked in to the Mataatua traditions through Toroa's son Ruaihonga and his brother Taneatua. Taneatua married Hine Mataora of the Nga Potiki hapu of the tangata whenua. He was the priest-explorer of the *Mataatua* who journeyed inland up the Whakatane River and bestowed names on the landscape as he went, thereby asserting his mana over the land. His exploration took him as far as the summit of the Huiarau Range. At various points of the journey, he planted puhi (plumes) from the bow of the *Mataatua* to denote his canoe's mana whenua. He lived for a time at Purakau before finally settling at Otara-hioi (Taneatua).

Ngati Awa held the valuable coastal strip at Whakatane. Their feud with Tuhoe lasted over 200 years. Eventually their relentless pressure forced Tuhoe to retire inland from Ruatoki to Ruatahuna, which became the heartland of Tuhoe territory. The last decisive battle between Ngati Awa and Tuhoe was fought at Te Kaunga in 1823 on a ridge above the Tauranga River. With a two-to-one numerical superiority and the advantage of twenty muskets, Tuhoe inflicted a severe defeat on Ngati Awa. Thereafter Ngati Awa was more circumspect towards Tuhoe. The victory at Te Kaunga gave Tuhoe confidence to come down from their mountain fastness to live at Ruatoki and Waimana. Minor skirmishes continued until the chiefs Tikitu of Ngati Awa and Piki of Tuhoe called a truce. The two conferred on the future of their tribes and decided to close the tatau pounamu, the greenstone door of peace between them. Other sections continued fighting for a time until Ngati Awa called a hui at Te Teko to negotiate a fuller ratification of the peace by all hapu of both tribes.[43]

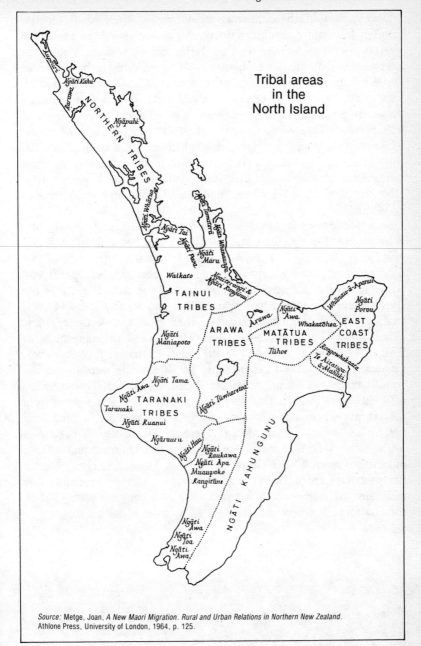

Tribal areas
in the
North Island

Source: Metge, Joan, *A New Maori Migration. Rural and Urban Relations in Northern New Zealand.*
Athlone Press, University of London, 1964, p. 125.

One section of the *Mataatua* canoe was established at Opotiki through Muriwai's daughter Hineikauia, who married the aboriginal warrior chief Tutamure of the Pane Nehu and Te Wakanui people. In later generations the descendants of this union came to be known as the Whakatohea. The Ngaitai of Torere continually encroached on Pane Nehu territory at Opape, Waiaua and Tirohanga. Eventually they were pushed back to Torere, and it was Tutamure who fixed the hills between Torere and Opape as the boundary between the tribes. The evolution from Pane Nehu to Whakatohea was a gradual process. In the time of Upokohapa, six generations from Tutamure, the Pane Nehu name was no longer identified with the fertile Waiaua valley. However, sections survived in the forested hill country of the interior at Whitikau.

Some sections drifted to Otara, where they were finally absorbed by Whakatohea. But the Whakatohea identity was not defined until 200 years after the arrival of the *Mataatua*. It was the emergence of two descent lines, from Muriwai through the marriage of Pakihi and Korokaihau, that forged Whakatohea as a tribe in control of the fertile river valleys of Opotiki and Waiaua. On the western edge of their territory, Whakatohea had to secure their land against their Tuhoe neighbours. The immediate adversary was Te Whakatane hapu of Tuhoe, which was connected to the Ngati Ira hapu of Whakatohea. Gradually, over several generations, Te Whakatane were forced out and Whakatohea's boundary defined at Ohiwa Harbour. The traditions of Whakatohea indicate that they are a people of ancient descent from the tangata whenua tribes that were in possession of the land long before the arrival of the *Mataatua* canoe. Essentially, Whakatohea evolved out of Te Wakanui, Pane Nehu and others for mutual defence of territory against Ngai Tai in the east and Tuhoe and Ngati Awa in the west. Descent lines from canoe ancestors were a convenient way of linking up hapu whose fortunes were in a constant state of flux, thereby forging a new and stronger identity as Whakatohea.[44]

CHAPTER 4

Nga Tikanga Maori

The Whanau

The basic social unit in Maori society was the whanau, an extended family which included three generations. At its head were the kaumatua and kuia, the male and female elders of the group. They were the storehouses of knowledge, the minders and mentors of children. Their adult sons and daughters, together with their spouses and children made up the whanau so that it may have numbered up to twenty or thirty people. The whanau, depending on size, occupied one or several sleeping houses, known as wharepuni. Large whanau had their own compound in the papakainga, or village settlement. If they lived in a fortified pa, the whanau occupied its own clearly defined space. Cooking and eating was done outdoors at a kauta, because taking food into the sanctity of the sleeping place was a violation of tapu. The main function of the whanau was the procreation and nurture of children. In the absence of parents engaged in gardening or other activities related to the food quest, all other adults in the vicinity were *in loco parentis*. This meant that in the whanau children were used to receiving care and affection from many people besides their parents. In fact, as mokopuna they were probably more influenced by their grandparents, the kaumatua and kuia, in their upbringing. In the security of the whanau the loss of a parent by death or desertion was not such a traumatic matter. The whanau also looked after its own aged or debilitated members. The old people were not only revered for their wisdom but also valued for their own contribution in minding the young and performing tasks useful to the livelihood of the group. Light tasks, such as rolling twine, weaving or the time-consuming task of grinding an adze could be done to an advanced age. The whanau provided its own workforce for its subsistence activities in hunting, fishing and gathering of wild plant foods. It was self-sufficient in most matters except defence, a fact of existence recognised in the aphorism that 'a house which stands alone is food for fire'.[1]

The Hapu

As a whanau expanded over succeeding generations it acquired the status of a hapu, or sub-tribe. But achievement of hapu status was not automatic. The conditions under which identity as a hapu was recognised included the emergence of a leader with mana derived from founding ancestors through his or her whakapapa, skill in diplomacy, ability to strengthen the identity of the hapu by political marriages, and fighting prowess. A combination of these factors defined a hapu's identity as a land-holding political entity. Once territorial control of the hapu's turangawaewae or standing in relation to other hapu was confirmed, then the name of the founding leader was adopted as the name of the hapu. Although most hapu names were preceded by a clan prefix such as Ngati, Nga, Ngai, Aitanga (people or descendants of), the word whanau was also used to designate a sub-tribe indicating the hapu's derivation from an extended family such as Te Whanau a Apanui, or Te Whanau a Ruataupare.

Children whose parents belonged to different hapu could claim membership in two hapu, but in practice, identification with the hapu of residence was much stronger. The other hapu did, however, exist as an alternative place of residence or even refuge should the need arise.

Hapu ranged in size from 200 to 300 people. Several small related hapu might occupy a single pa, while a larger hapu may have had a whole pa to itself. At first the chief and his house symbolised the hapu, but in time the wharenui or large carved ancestral house, replaced the chief's house as the enduring symbol.

The hapu was the main political unit that controlled a defined stretch of tribal territory. Ideally, the territory would have a sea frontage with particular inshore fisheries such as shellfish beds being the property of a hapu. Inland tribes made similar claims of ownership over stretches of streams, rivers and lakes. The hapu undertook all the major tasks necessary for group survival. The members co-operated in large-scale fishing operations, major land-use projects such as building fortifications, and the production of major capital assets like canoes and meeting houses. The viability of a hapu was dependent on its capability of holding and defending its territory against others. Therefore, one of its major political functions was defence and the maintenance of alliances with other related hapu of the tribe. When a hapu got too large it became unstable and a section would split off, usually under the leadership of a teina, or junior brother of the chief, who, with his followers, established his own whanau and eventually hapu.[2]

The Iwi

The largest effective political grouping was the iwi, or tribe. The iwi was composed of related hapu from a common ancestor. Canoe ancestors, or one of their descendants who had great mana, were used as points of reference for the definition of iwi identity. Although the hapu of an iwi were not above quarrelling and even fighting with one another, generally they stayed on amicable terms and co-operated with each other in defence of tribal territory against other tribes. The chiefs of the component hapu units of an iwi regarded themselves as coequals, although there was a hierarchy in terms of tuakana and teina relationships of senior and junior descent. Some large iwi confederations on the East Coast, at Taupo and in the Waikato developed the concept of a paramount chief to integrate the iwi into a more cohesive political unit in relation to other tribes. The iwi was at its most effective in defending tribal territory against enemy tribes.[3]

The largest social grouping of Maori society was the waka, comprised of a loose confederation of tribes based on the ancestral canoes of the fourteenth century. The tribes of waka confederations usually occupied contiguous territory, such as Te Arawa at Rotorua and Tuwharetoa at Taupo. But that was not always the case. Ngaiterangi at Tauranga were separated at Maketu by Te Arawa from the co-tribes of their waka at Whakatane, Opotiki and Maungapohatu. The waka was only a very loose ideological bond. The iwi of a waka, like the sub-tribes of a tribe, often fought each other. But should tribes from other waka invade their domain, the waka bond would be used to form an alliance against the intruders.[4]

Social Rank

Internally, hapu and iwi were stratified into three classes: rangatira (chiefs), tutua (commoners) and taurekareka (slaves). Rank and leadership were based on seniority of descent from founding ancestors. At the head of the rangatira class was the ariki, who was the first-born in the senior male line. His teina, or junior brothers, were the rangatira. An ariki was respected for the qualities of tapu, mana, ihi and wehi (awesome power) which he inherited from his ancestors. However, these qualities could be increased by prowess in war, wise rule and generous behaviour to his people. On the other hand, they could easily be diminished by mean behaviour or unwise rule. A first-born female in the senior line was known as an ariki tapairu. She had certain ceremonial functions attached to her high rank as well as being the custodian of some rituals. Like the ariki, she was an extremely tapu person and was accorded the respect that one would associate with a princess or a queen. In some instances, a chief's daughter was also accorded the status of a puhi maiden, a virgin princess. Her virtue was guarded day and night by female attendants. This made her more desirable as a bride when her father sought a political alliance with a powerful chief. Young men of rank often went on expeditions to pay court to a puhi. The traditions are full of accounts of young men who succeeded in winning a puhi and being revered as founding ancestors. One of the most famous of such unions was that between Turongo of the Waikato confederation of tribes and Mahinarangi of the East Coast tribes. However, occasionally headstrong women escaped betrothal by eloping with a lover of their choice, as happened in the case of Hinemoa and Tutanekai of the Arawa confederation of tribes.

The tutua, or commoner class, were all other members of the hapu who theoretically could claim descent from the founding ancestor. But because they were of junior descent lines that diverged away from the senior line in succeeding generations, they were to all intents and purposes not chiefs and therefore were commoners. This divergence from the main line meant that junior members of a hapu had a tendency to split off and start their own hapu.

The taurekareka were slaves taken into captivity after defeat in war. They lived with their masters and did the menial tasks of cooking, paddling canoes, fetching wood and water, or acted as arms bearers in war. They were not restricted physically, because more often than not they chose not to run away. This was because their own hapu preferred to regard them as dead rather than attempting to rescue them. The children of slaves taken as wives, husbands or concubines by their masters were born free members of the hapu. Slaves were also known as mokai, or pets, because of the services they rendered their masters. They were also valued for their productive capacity and ability to add to the wealth of a chief. Slaves who lost the goodwill of their masters were likely to be killed at any time and consumed.[5]

The Tohunga

In addition to the three main classes there was a fourth class of specialists, known as tohunga. This was the generic term for an expert in the various fields of human endeavour. There were different grades of tohunga depending on their specialty. At one level were the artisans and artists such as the tohunga tarai waka (canoe-builder), tohunga hanga whare, (house-builder), tohunga ta moko (tattooist) and tohunga whakairo (carver). Some families tended to specialise in one or more of these fields. At another level were the tohunga ahurewa (high priests) and tohunga makutu (shaman). These tohunga were trained in their own whare wananga (schools of learning). The highest grade of tohunga was the tohunga ahurewa, who was trained in a whare wananga that met in the winter months over a period of up to seven years. The curriculum included astronomy, genealogy, faith-healing and a large repertoire of chants and karakia for planting, felling trees, building houses and canoes, making war, healing the sick and fare-welling the dead. The tohunga ahurewa also had to learn the arts of white magic, to command the elements and call up supernatural forces. Graduates of this school had to pass difficult tests such as blasting the mauri (life force) of a plant or tree, or killing a bird in flight by the power of karakia alone.

Tohunga makutu were the counterparts of tohunga ahurewa. They trained in a lower grade school known as the whare maire (house of black arts). They were often rejects from the whare wananga. Tohunga makutu were greatly feared for their ability to makutu, that is, cast spells to make people sick or to kill them. Despite the fear of tohunga makutu, they were tolerated as a necessary evil, one of the elements for controlling human behaviour.[6]

Social control in Maori society was maintained by an interlocking system of rank, mana, utu, and spiritual beliefs pertaining to tapu, mauri and makutu. The Tawhaki myth laid down the axiom that the injunctions of superiors must be obeyed under pain of death. It also taught that the penalty for breaking the law of tapu was death. Tapu was a spiritual force which emanated from the celestial realm of the gods. It had three dimensions of sacredness, prohibition and unclean-liness. All three kinds of tapu had to be treated with great care. Objects that had no tapu attached to them were noa (common or profane) and could be handled freely. Tapu in the sacred sense applied to people of rank, places of worship and ancestral houses. Tapu in the pro-hibited sense applied to pursuits such as carving. Women and children were prohibited by tapu from going near tohunga whakairo while they were at work. Tapu in the unclean sense applied to menstrual blood, which prevented women from gardening or other pursuits connected with food. Similarly, the tohunga ta moko was in a state of tapu in the unclean sense because of the blood that flowed from the practice of his craft. He was prohibited from touching food himself and had to be fed by an attendant.[7]

Tapu

Tapu was an all-pervasive force that touched many facets of Maori life. Personal tapu enhanced the dignity of the individual. The higher the rank, the greater the personal tapu. The most sacred part of a person was the head. Articles of toilet, such as combs which came in contact with the head or head dress, were tapu by contagion. It was a breach of tapu to put such things where food was prepared. Sickness, death and urupa (cemeteries) were tapu in the unclean sense. The tapu pertaining to death and cemeteries had to be ritually removed by washing hands before resuming normal activities. Sacred precincts known as wahi tapu included mountains, tuahu (places of worship), caves and hollow trees where bones were deposited, and wai tapu, the sacred waters where people bathed to cure illness. One of the most useful applications of tapu in controlling human behaviour was as a sanction to the institution of a rahui. The rahui was a prohibition to institute a closed season on some valued natural resource such as the forest or sea to allow bird and fish life to recover. A rahui was also imposed in the event of death by drowning over a defined area where it occurred. The time the rahui remained in force depended on how soon the body was recovered. No one dared transgress a rahui under penalty of death.[8]

The power of tapu to control behaviour derived from spiritual beliefs concerning human nature. Maori believed in a tripartite division of human beings into tinana (body), mauri (life force), and wairua (spirit). It was thought that the spirit could leave the body at will during the experience of a dream and return again. But death ensued if the mauri left the body. If a person became ill, it was thought to be the mauri that was not well. It was believed that there were evil spirits waiting to attack a person's mauri, but they were kept at bay by benevolent protection of the gods. If one offended the gods by breaking the laws of tapu, the gods withdrew their protection. The person then sickened and died if the offence was a serious one.

The power of makutu worked in the same way. If a person gave some serious offence to another, such as committing adultery, the aggrieved party could seek utu by enlisting the services of a tohunga makutu. Besides casting a spell, the tohunga put up a signpost indicating to the selected victim that a makutu was on him. On coming across the sign the victim's mauri would be startled. The physical response triggered by fear pumped adrenalin into the blood stream sending the heart leaping, and the pulse racing was thought to be the mauri coming under the influence of the makutu. The victim became withdrawn, sickened and, in serious cases, died. But the power of the shaman was not irrevocable; a makutu could be countered by the tohunga ahurewa.

Beliefs concerning the principle of the mauri were not confined to human beings. It was thought all living things possessed a mauri. If crops did not flourish or fish were not plentiful, it was because their mauri was weak. The tohunga resolved the problem by concentrating the mauri of a valued resource, such as the kumara, in a durable symbol in the form of a suitably shaped stone. He then prayed over the mauri to strengthen it and to assure fertility and abundance. The mauri was hidden away so that enemies could not blast it with black magic. These practices concerning the mauri were aimed at controlling unpredictable natural forces. Each valued resource, such as the sea, forest and gardens, were imbued with mauri. Even a pa, as a living organism, had its own mauri for the well-being of its inhabitants.[9]

Utu

The mediation of social control by rank, tapu and spiritual beliefs was supplemented by the principle of utu. There were several dimensions to the meaning of utu. At its simplest level, utu meant equivalence or payment. Gift-giving to others, in the form of garden produce or fish from a successful expedition, was a widely practised custom in Maori society that cemented social ties. But the gift set up imbalance between the recipient and the giver. At some later date, equivalence was restored when the recipient gave a return gift after a successful hunt or food-foraging expedition. In this case, gift-giving and utu mediated warm and enduring social relations of mutual support.

At a more serious level, utu meant compensation for some injury. The misdemeanour of adultery, for instance, disturbed social relations for which the aggrieved party sought compensation. If the compensation was not given voluntarily, then it was sought by the custom of a taua muru. This was a raiding party which wiped out the offence by plundering the goods of the offender. Sometimes physical punishment was meted out as well. The most serious level of utu was revenge against other hapu or iwi for past defeats or encroachment on territory. Infidelity of a wife or harsh treatment of a wife by her husband if they were of different hapu were offences that called for utu by making war. This is why brothers-in-law were considered as potential enemies. Utu between sub-tribes and tribes by making war was one way of regulating their relationships concerning territory and rights over the reproductive power of women. That these were the major 'take', or causes, of war, is emphasised in the proverb that 'women and land are the reasons why men perish'.[10]

Whenua

Maori attachment to land is rooted in mythology, tradition and the long history of tribal wars. Mythology conceived the earth as Papatuanuku, the earth mother, from whose bosom sprang plants, birds, animals and fish for human sustenance. Therefore the earth was loved as a mother is loved. The eternal nature of the earth in relation to man's brief life span is encapsulated in the aphorism 'man perishes but land remains'. When man dies, he is thought of as returning to the bosom of the earth mother, where he is met by his ancestor Hinenuitepo.

The maritime traditions of ancestral voyages of discovery and settlement of new lands is one of the deeply rooted sentiments of Maori attachment to land. That sentiment was amplified by traditions of generations of occupation of dwelling places, tilling of garden lands and fighting to defend them against others. Tribal wars served to demarcate territorial boundaries. The bones of buried ancestors, and blood spilt in the defence of territory, hallowed the land as a gift from the ancestors to their descendants and future generations. Each generation was bonded to the land at birth by the custom of planting the afterbirth, also known as whenua, in the land. When a child's pito (umbilical cord) was cut and buried with the afterbirth in the land, it was known as an iho whenua. The iho is the core, the centre portion of the cord which is between the child and the whenua, symbolising the connection to the land. The iho whenua of a child of rank was marked by the planting of a tree. The tree was named as the iho whenua of that child and signified ownership as well as connection to the land. The iho whenua was cited in any disputes over territory.

The turangawaewae, the standing and identity of a people, was defined by their territory. In time the territorial boundary marks of prominent physical features such as mountains, rivers, lakes, streams or distinctive landforms, came to symbolise the chief and his tribe. That symbolism was expressed in sayings and figures of speech in oratory on the marae. The following are some of the widely known aphorisms in the repertoire of an orator wanting to pay tribute to a host tribe:

Ko Tongariro te maunga, ko Taupo te moana, ko Te Heuheu te tangata.
Tongariro is the mountain, Taupo is the sea, and Te Heuheu is the man.

Ko Hikurangi te maunga, ko Waiapu te awa, ko Porourangi te tangata.
Hikurangi is the mountain, Waiapu is the river and Porourangi is the man.

Waikato taniwha rau, he piko, he taniwha.
Waikato of a hundred monsters, on every bend is a monster.

Warfare

Crossing the territorial boundaries of another tribe was fraught with danger, not only because of past hostilities but because of dangers from local demons and guardian spirits called kaitiaki. These had to be placated by rites of entry known as uruuru whenua. War parties, known as taua, tried to advance into enemy territory unobserved so as to maintain the element of surprise. Maori defensive positions were so well chosen to take advantage of natural landforms, and reinforced with palisades, ring ditches and fighting stages, that they were difficult to take with weapons of the stone age. The basic strategies for taking a pa relied on surprise attacks, feint assaults and mock retreats to lure the defenders out into the open. Traditions abound with accounts of pa that had never been taken by storm or siege eventually falling to cunning, sagacity and trickery on the part of the attackers. The strategies of deception were as many and varied as the human imagination could devise. They included disguise, impersonation and the use of decoys. Occasionally however, pa were taken by brute force, especially when the attackers were led by a chief with exceptional courage or physical prowess. But the preference in the conduct of war was to rely on subtlety instead of force.

The basic tenets of Maori warfare, as laid down in mythology and practised in the tribal wars of traditional times, were simple but effective. They revolved around respect for the prowess of the enemy, discovering his strength, neutralising it and attacking him at his weak point. Vayda[11] offers some interesting observations on the frequency of fighting among tribes. Because there was a strict account kept of debit and credit with enemies, there was always some tribe in arrears with another. When one group was defeated, it retired from the field to its hinterland or mountain fastness, where it kept its ahi ka (domestic fires) alight on its land, thus keeping its title to the land warm while it built up its strength. When a tribe felt strong enough, it would drive out its enemies and reoccupy habitation sites. The defeat of the invaders set up another cycle of revenge and counter-revenge. Thus Vayda defined peace as 'a temporary absence of hostilities which were liable to be renewed as soon as the defeated tribe were prepared to square its account'. Therefore, tribes had to be always on the alert to fight, although being ready to fight was not, as Vayda whimsically remarks, the same thing as fighting. There were long periods when there was no fighting.

It is difficult to gauge the casualty rate in tribal wars conducted with no projectile weapons such as throwing spears and bows and arrows. The main weapons were short and long clubs used in close-quarter fighting. Therefore, where combat occurred in the open, the losing side could easily retreat and make off by scattering in different directions. Another difficulty in assessing the mortality rate in warfare was the tendency to exaggerate victories. Traditional accounts of battles often claimed the enemy were exterminated to a man, or only one survivor escaped to tell the tale. On the other hand the traditions also cite stories of chiefs stopping pursuit of fleeing enemies because it was not considered proper to exterminate opponents to whom one was related. However, that same convention did not stop them from cannibal feasting on the fish of Tumatauenga. Eating an enemy was more than a symbolic ingestion of mana. It was the ultimate debasement to be passed through the alimentary canal and emerge as excrement.

One of the recognised titles to land was whenua raupatu, land taken by conquest. But the land had to be occupied for a long time for the title to become permanent. It was not an easy title to maintain because a precondition was a series of victories over most if not all the related hapu in a tribe. Maori warfare was more characterised by one tribe attacking an enemy and returning to their own territory. However, when one group was displaced by a more powerful tribe, the dispossessed group looked for land elsewhere by displacing another group weaker than themselves.

Just as there were recognised customs for the conduct of war, there were also conventions for making peace. The first step was for the side losing a battle to ask for peace. The exchange of weapons to cement the peace was known as the tatau pounamu (greenstone door). But the tatau pounamu was recognised as a male peace which could be abrogated by either party when it suited them. A more enduring peace was a woman's peace, where women were exchanged with the victors. The marriages secured a peace that was more enduring than that involving only an exchange of weapons.

Wero

Since tribal wars were endemic for almost 500 years, the approach of any sizeable party of people from another hapu or iwi was always a matter of concern. The tangata whenua had to determine whether the visitors were hostile or friendly. The sentry, on sighting a party of strangers approaching, alerted the inhabitants of the pa, who prepared to receive or repel them. The rituals of encounter determined how the tangata whenua responded to the strangers. A warrior sallied forth from the safety of the pa to challenge the visitors with a wero, which consisted of a highly ritualised display of weaponry with the taiaha, the favourite longstaff weapon in single combat. During the whole of his performance as he advanced, the warrior faced his adversaries and kept his eyes on them. Should anyone break ranks to intercept him, the warrior had to be ready to defend himself or to turn and flee back to the safety of the pa. If the visitors were hostile, it was considered a good omen if they could kill the challenger before he made it back to the pa. To this end the visitors designated the fastest runner in their ranks to try to catch him. Because of this danger, the challenger had to be fleet-footed as well as a skilled exponent of the taiaha. If the visitors came in peace and the challenger got right up to them without being threatened, he placed a dart before them. When the visitors picked up the dart, the challenger turned and led them into the pa. Even so, the challenger kept his eyes over his shoulder in case of treachery until they were inside the courtyard.

The Welcome

As visitors entered the marae, the courtyard in front of the ancestral house of the chief, they were welcomed by the high-pitched karanga (call) of a kuia. The reason for the first voice to be raised in welcome being that of a woman was because of her power to negate tapu and evil spiritual influences. Visitors from afar came as waewae tapu (strangers with sacred feet), and with them came the accompanying spirits of their own ancestors. The tapu and spirits that came with the guests had to be neutralised in case they conflicted with those of the tangata whenua, and so the woman's voice was the first step in the process that allowed the guests to come closer. On entering, a kaumatua among the visitors recited a waerea, a chant, to counter any negative spiritual influences among the host tribe. The manuhiri (guests) maintained a spatial separation from the tangata whenua by stopping short of crossing the marae. At that point both paid homage to their mutual dead, while the kuia keened their sorrow for the departed with the haunting melodic tangi. After a while the hosts signalled the guests to come forward and be seated on the marae, thereby diminishing the distance between them. The kaumatua then made their mihi (formal speeches of welcome). After the visitors replied with their whaikorero, the distance between visitors and hosts was closed at a signal from the latter for the guests to come forward and hongi (press noses).

The sharing of food which followed was the final negation of the alien tapu of the guests. The manuhiri and the tangata whenua were then able to intermingle freely.[12] But as a precaution against some possible negative spiritual influences being retained among the visitors, a female figure was carved on the door lintel of the guesthouse. Any residual spirits and tapu were discharged and negated by mana wahine, that is the dual generative and destructive power of the female sex. This binary opposition in the female genitals is conceptualised as te whare o te tangata (the house of men) and te whare o aitua (the house of death). The womb and the female sex are the house that both created and destroyed the culture hero Maui.

Tangihanga

The death of an important person was one occasion when the tribes and sub-tribes came together in unity and peace to farewell the dead. After death, the body of a deceased person was dressed in its finest cloak, the hair oiled and decked with feathers, and the face smeared with red ochre. The body was usually trussed in the sitting position and placed on view in the porch of the house. Among some tribes a special platform, and in some cases a rough shelter, was built for the deceased to lie in state. The chief mourners, who were usually the closest female kin of the deceased, kept vigil over the corpse until burial. It was their duty to wail for the deceased and the collective dead of the tribe as each party of visitors arrived to pay their last respects. The mourners also expressed their grief by singing well-known dirges and laments. Although it was often stated in the orations and farewell speeches that death was requited by a liberal flow of tears and mucus, women sometimes lacerated their bosoms with flakes of obsidian as an expression of grief. The women also wore wreaths of kawakawa leaves on their heads as a symbol of mourning.

In reply to the speeches of welcome to the tangi, it was not unusual for speakers on behalf of the visitors to address their remarks directly to the deceased person as if he were still alive. The orators used elaborate figures of speech, likening the dead person to the broken horn of the crescent moon, or the fall of the shelter-giving totara tree in the great forest of Tane. As each orator finished eulogising the dead person, they bade him farewell and exhorted him to traverse the broad pathway of Tane to Hawaiki-nui, Hawaiki-roa, Hawaiki-pamamao, the gathering place of spirits. It was only at this separation between the living and the dead that the orators turned to their hosts and thanked them formally for their welcome. For the duration of a tangi the visitors were housed and fed by the host tribe. In traditional times, a tangi may have gone on for up to two and even three weeks. In Maori thought, death was regarded as a gradual process. That is why poroporoaki (farewell speeches) were made directly to the deceased. Death was not final until the onset of physical decay. When the body was buried, the tangi concluded with a hakari, the funeral feast of farewell to the dead.

Hahunga

Although the burial was in some cases the final disposal of the body, the custom of exhumation known as hahunga was widely practised. The hahunga was a matter of prestige and appears to have been practised mainly with people of rank. There was a public assembly on the marae to welcome the exhumed bones back. Speeches of welcome were made to the bones of the deceased, who were mentioned by name. They were eulogised and farewelled for the last time and the bones then deposited in a secret place where they could not be disturbed. The bones of chiefs were enclosed in carved burial chests and hidden in caves or hollow trees. The effigy on the burial chest was made to look horrific in the dim light of a cave so as to frighten off stray intruders. Like the tangi, the hahunga concluded with a feast.

The customary practices of the Maori surrounding the tangi were seen by Oppenheim[13] as a significant cultural expression of the Maori's reaction to death. In traditional times, the full-scale tangi appears to have been reserved for people of the highest prestige and it marked the beginning of the process of adjustment to a change in social relations. The death of a chief left vacant a power position that had to be filled. There was a danger that rivalry for the position between surviving chiefs would cause factions and the splitting-up of a hapu under different leaders. According to Oppenheim, the tangi was a mechanism for continuity. Firstly, it promoted unity in bereavement. Secondly, if the chief had already nominated his successor before his death the tangi facilitated the recognition of the new chief by all who attended. However, where no successor had been nominated, the chief who took the initiatives for conducting and controlling the arrangements for the tangi usually emerged as the recognised natural leader. The hahunga gave final notice of the chief's death and the fact that succession had been established. It was only when the new chief was secure in his position that he initiated the hahunga for his predecessor. The political effect of the hahunga was to bring the group together and validate the succession of the new chief by associating him with the relics of the dead chief. The hahunga feast was an important element in the recognition and legitimation of the chief's mana because not only was he responsible for its organisation, but he was also its main provider.

Hakari

The institution of the hakari, whether for a tangi, hahunga, wedding or inter-tribal feast, was symbolic of chiefly and tribal mana. The feast reflected deeply held values related to food, power and prestige. Throughout the year, except for the summer months, the food quest pre-empted a good deal of time and energy. Because of the seasonal nature of natural resources and gardening produce, food had to be accumulated for future use during winter months. To this end, whitebait, fish, eels, sharks, pipi and potted pigeons were preserved by cooking, smoking or sun-drying, and storage pits were filled with kumara. Only the accumulation of surplus above daily needs enabled a chief and his people to provide for the various feasts that occurred throughout the year.

When guests from other tribes attended a hakari, the reputation of the hosts rose or fell according to their ability to be lavish with food. Each tribe strove to provide the best of the local delicacies for visitors. Coastal tribes fed their guests with kaimoana (seafood) such as fish, shellfish, crayfish and edible seaweed. Inland tribes fed their guests on eels, freshwater crayfish and shellfish, and above all, potted birds. Food, as a major symbol for the expression of tribal mana, was put on large display stages at feasts given between hapu or between tribes. Some of these food stages recorded in historic times were up to twenty-five metres in height, five metres wide and sixty metres long. The aim was to impress visitors with a veritable mountain of food. Quantities of food recorded at intertribal feasts were stupendous. Firth[14] cites a feast given by Te Wherowhero at Remuera in 1844 where the provisions included six large albatrosses, nineteen calabashes of shark oil, several tonnes of fish, 20,000 dried eels, great quantities of pigs, and baskets of potatoes. Any food that was left over was gifted to the guests as they departed. At one feast at Ohaeawai in 1831, Firth noted that 3,000 bushels of kumara were given away as presents. Feasts and gift-giving on this scale were more than an expression of generosity. They were also expressions of incurred reciprocal obligations and political relations.

Generosity with food as a cardinal value also cemented internal relations within a hapu. Firth[15] noted that aristocratic birth by itself was not sufficient to maintain the position of a chief, he had to be generous to his own people as well as outsiders to maintain their respect and loyalty. The institutions of polygamy and slavery enabled the chief to accumulate wealth by way of food and manufactured articles. Certain chiefly prerogatives such as gifts of first fruits by his people, or a share in the catch from a successful individual hunting expedition, added to the chief's store of wealth. From this store he initiated gift exchanges with his own people. A faithful follower was rewarded with a gift of choice food from the chief's store or a fine mat. The follower became more obliged to the chief and reciprocated in kind, often with an even larger counter-gift. The chief had several such exchange relationships going at the same time, so that his wealth was in constant circulation among his people. By acting as a distributing agent for wealth, rather than accumulating it for personal aggrandisement, the chief strengthened his mana and maintained the loyalty and cohesiveness of his people.

CHAPTER 5

Tauiwi

Coming of the Pakeha

The Maori people had been in occupation of New Zealand for at least
800 years when the first European ship arrived under the captaincy
of Abel Tasman in 1642. The tribes in the South Island gave him a
hostile reception, killing four of his men, so he left the country with
an unfavourable impression. A whole century passed before another
European, James Cook, visited the country again in 1769. As a consequence of Cook's reports on the large seal colonies in the south and
the big stands of native timber in both main islands, seal-hunters
began operating out of Dusky Sound in 1792, and, two years later,
traders were taking timber out of the Hauraki Gulf.[1] After 1807,
whaling ships from the major maritime nations of France, America,
Norway and Spain and the East India Company visited New Zealand
shores.

Tribes in favourable locations prospered by supplying ships with
pork, potatoes, sweetcorn, fish and cargoes of flax and timber. Besides
the system of barter, the Maori also became accustomed to trading
with cash. As the competition for whales escalated, visiting whalers
began establishing shore stations. Tribes wanting to take advantage of
European whaling skills readily made grants of land to whalers to
establish such stations. In accordance with the customary practices for
cementing alliances of this nature, women of high status were married
to sea captains and station managers to confirm the deals. Other
reciprocal rights were also arranged. These included participation in
the whaling industry as crewmen, harpoonists, recovery teams to bring
whales ashore for processing and the right to help process the whales.
Most of the shore stations were in the South Island, but there were
some in the North Island as well, the most notable being at Te Kaha
on the East Coast.[2] Although there were occasional conflicts arising
out of European transgression of tribal customs, this early period of
foreign contact was characterised by economic welcome. On his first

visit Cook found the Maori willingly offered fish for trade, but not their prized cloaks, weapons and ornaments.

When Cook visited Queen Charlotte Sound on his second voyage in 1773, he found the Maori readily bartered cloaks, tools and weapons for nails, hatchets and cloth. Some tribes even crossed Cook Strait to trade with him. On another visit the following year the population had been augmented by people who were actually manufacturing artifacts for trade.[3] At this time Cook introduced the potato into New Zealand. The potato had a profound effect on Maori life. It was hardier than the kumara and had a wider growing range. After the turn of the century, the potato became the staple food, with the kumara being elevated to the status of delicacy or luxury food. Although Cook introduced the pig along with the potato, it was not until others reintroduced the animal after 1800 that it flourished in New Zealand. The pig was a boon as a ready source of animal protein to replace the long-extinct moa. Paintings of early houses by Augustus Earle show them with open porches. But as pigs had free range in the villages and wandered into houses, a beam known as a paepae was erected across the porch to keep them out. Pigs and potatoes became important items of trade in the provisioning of visiting ships. Blankets, hatchets, knives, guns and hoop-iron, which could be made into chisels and cutting tools, were sought-after items of trade. The whalers, sealers and traders were the advance guard of colonisation. Barter and trade are universal human pursuits which have their own dynamic for the achievement of equivalence and satisfaction between trading partners. Maori chiefs went to great lengths to cement trading relationships with Europeans, even to the extent of encouraging ship-jumpers and ex-convicts to settle among them. They were given land and wives to bind them into the tribe on whose behalf they acted as intermediaries in trade with visiting ships. These new settlers provided the first infusion of European genes into the Maori population. The children of these mixed unions were much admired for their fair skin and generally handsome appearance.

Mate Pakeha

Economic welcome and free trade were boundless in this first phase of contact. By the 1830s nothing was sacrosanct. The Maori, who had no alcoholic beverages of their own, took to drinking the Pakeha's rum and waipiro (stinking water). In 1836, when 151 whaling ships visited the Bay of Islands,[4] drinking and prostitution were rife. One of the unforseen side-effects of contact was the introduction of contagious diseases from Europe. The most coherent picture of Maori health in prehistoric times is drawn by Houghton.[5] Apparently the Maori did not suffer from the common infectious ailments such as measles, rubella, chicken pox, influenza and scarlet fever. These diseases were filtered out along the Polynesian migratory routes across the Pacific because they needed a population of 50,000 to sustain them. A few canoe-loads leaving home islands every two or three generations was not sufficient to sustain such diseases. But the absence of these contagious diseases meant that the Maori had no immunity to them. In 1790 and again in 1810, influenza epidemics swept the Tamaki isthmus, debilitating Ngati Whatua's hold on the pa of Maungakiekie and Maungawhau. Eventually the latter was abandoned because it was thought to have been invaded by an evil spirit.[6]

The Maori did not have a germ theory of illness. The literature on Maori medical practice is rather sparse, but what there is suggests that the Maori had a theory of illness based on spiritual causation, which Best[7] dismissed as 'superstitious mummery'. Given the fact that they could not see the microbes that their European trading partners were bringing into the country, their attribution of influenza epidemics to the spiritual causes of mate Maori (Maori sickness) was the only rational response open to them. Abandoning a pa because of 'spiritual invasion' indicated an appreciation of cause and effect that would have at least ameliorated the impact of epidemics.

Sexual liaison with sailors from visiting ships was another matter. It introduced venereal disease, which could not be controlled by simply abandoning a pa. Houghton[8] suggests that gonorrhoea rather than syphilis was implicated in sterility and a decline in population. It was these unseen bacterial invaders that softened up the Maori population for the human invasion that lay ahead.

As more Europeans arrived, there was a rise in the number and virulence of epidemics. There were further epidemics in the 1820s and even worse ones in the 1830s including measles, influenza, smallpox and tuberculosis. To the Maori people, it seemed they died while Europeans lived. By 1840 the Maori population had been reduced by 40 per cent as a consequence of diseases and the tribal wars fought with muskets in the 1820s.[9] Stannard notes that in other islands and countries around the Pacific rim, a 90 per cent collapse of indigenous populations was not unusual as a consequence of European diseases. He revised James King's 1778 estimate of the Hawaiian population upwards from 400,000 to 800,000. By 1890, introduced diseases had reduced that population down to 40,000. It is significant that the Maori population fell almost to the same level, 45,000, by the turn of the century. Stannard postulates a 75 per cent population collapse for the Maori over the course of the nineteenth century.[10] We will not know how catastrophic was that collapse until we have studies such as Stannard's on the pre-European numbers in New Zealand before the arrival of vessels with disease-riddled sailors.

The Missionaries

In 1814 Samuel Marsden arrived in the Bay of Islands to introduce Christianity into New Zealand. On Marsden's advice to the Church Missionary Society the first mission station was established at Rangihoua, where he had preached the first sermon. The mission was under the patronage of the chief Ruatara, but it did not flourish because the terrain was too steep. Marsden also made the mistake of advising the Church Missionary Society to send out a carpenter, a blacksmith and a ropemaker to get the mission going when a farmer would have been more useful in getting the mission self-sufficient in producing its own food.[11] Consequently the missionaries were dependent on the Maori for food, which they traded for iron tools and muskets. Missionary trade in muskets was common by 1818.[12] The primary source of muskets was whaling ships, and dependence on Maori goodwill drove Kendall, the missionary school teacher, to act as a go-between to get them. His involvement in the musket trade earned him the displeasure of Marsden, his superior.

Eventually a second mission station was established, at Kerikeri under the protective mana of Hongi Hika in 1819. Hongi protected the missionaries because he hoped that their presence would attract more ships to the Bay of Islands, thereby increasing his chances for trade.[13] The missionary blacksmiths were also useful to him for repairing the muskets he had already managed to acquire and was using in tribal wars. When Marsden prohibited missionaries from trading in muskets or even repairing them, Hongi determined to acquire his own. In 1820 he travelled to England with Kendall, ostensibly to work at Cambridge on a Maori dictionary and grammar. Both men had their own hidden agendas. Kendall sought ordination so that he could gain independence from Marsden's control, while Hongi sought muskets.[14] On their return to Sydney the numerous presents that had been given to Hongi by royalty were sold and a supply of muskets was purchased. Hongi invited two chiefs, Te

Hinaki and Te Horeta, who were in Sydney, to accompany him back
to the Bay of Islands and indulged himself in a conspicuous display
of his new power by laying his muskets in front of them. He signalled
his intentions of making war on his guests and other tribes by naming
each musket after past defeats of Ngapuhi. One musket was named
Kai-a-te-karoro (food for seagulls), the battle in which Ngapuhi were
severely mauled by Ngati Whatua in 1807. Others were named Te
Wai Whariki, Wai-kohu and Te Ringa-huruhuru, and each designated
musket was intended to avenge those past defeats.[15] Te Hinaki and Te
Horeta returned to their respective homes knowing that Hongi would
come after them in due course to exact utu.

The Musket Wars

In 1821 Hongi began the musket wars, taking tribal warfare to an
unprecedented level in the history of New Zealand. The musket upset
the balance of power between tribes. The tribes in the North, sensing
their advantage, flocked to join Hongi's campaign in anticipation of
certain victory and the spoils of war. His war party of over 2,000 men,
armed with a thousand muskets as well as their traditional weapons,
set out from the Bay of Islands in September to attack Te Hinaki's pa
Mokoia on the Tamaki isthmus. Some accounts claim the war party
numbered upwards of 3,000 men.[16] Allowing for exaggeration, compared with traditional warfare, where a taua usually numbered around
140 men, this was war on a grand scale. The largest war parties until
Hongi's campaign had been that led by Te Morenga to the East Coast
in 1817 with 400 men and another the following year when a combined
Ngati Paoa and Ngapuhi force of 900 men attacked Ngati Porou at
Hicks Bay.

One effect of the musket wars was an increase in the casualty rate.
After the battle at Hicks Bay, one Ngapuhi canoe returned to the Bay
of Islands with seventy heads of slain enemies. Hongi's attack on
Mokoia at Tamaki and Mauinaina Pa on the other side of the estuary
brought even higher casualties. Ngati Paoa lost 300 men. As a consequence of killing on this scale, Tamaki was deserted as the survivors
abandoned the bones that littered the plain and sought refuge among
their Tainui kin. That same year Hongi took the Ngati Maru strong-
hold of Te Totara at Thames, killing sixty people and taking 2,000
prisoners.

Hongi added two other major victories to his reputation as a warrior
chief by defeating the Waikato tribes at the battle of Matakitaki in

1822 and the Arawa tribes the following year at the battle of Mokoia Island. Nearer home, he defeated Ngati Whatua in 1825 at the battle of Te Ika a Ranganui, which took place near Kaiwaka. The Ngati Whatua chief Apihai Te Kawau, who went north from Waitemata with reinforcements, met the survivors of the battle fleeing south, whereupon he retreated up the Waikato to Pukewhau on the Waipa River. Thereafter Ngati Whatua lived in fear of Ngapuhi guns. Kaipara and Waitemata were virtually deserted. Apihai Te Kawau lived for a time with the Ngapuhi border tribes that were friendly to him at Mahurangi. But at intervals he visited his lands at Waitemata to maintain his domestic fires, thereby keeping his title to the land warm.

Hongi's campaigns disrupted Maori society by precipitating a deadly arms race among the tribes. Although Hongi did not occupy the lands of the people he had defeated, the tribes concluded that muskets were essential for their survival. Guns and ammunition had to be purchased at any price.[17] The chief article of barter was dressed flax fibre. Cultivations were neglected as whole tribes were mobilised to cut and dress flax. The exchange rate was between five and eight hundredweight of fibre for one musket. People even moved to live temporarily in the swamps to speed up the work, with disastrous consequences for their health. Inland tribes such as Tuhoe were unable to participate directly in the musket trade, so they sent trading parties to the Waikato and Thames to obtain muskets. The going price was five slaves for one musket. These slaves were put to work by their new masters to cut and dress more flax. One item traders wanted for sale as curiosities in Europe was smoked heads. It was customary in Maori society to preserve the heads of enemies as objects of derision. These they readily traded for muskets. But when the supply dwindled, chiefs resorted to tattooing slaves, killing them and selling their heads. The heads of chiefs taken in war now took on new meaning as booty to trade for European goods, which is why missionaries observed canoes returning to the Bay of Islands laden with heads from their forays to the south.

In response to the killing power of the new weapons, the Maori developed the gunfighter's pa, which was to stand them in good stead in later years against the Imperial Army of the British colonists. Hilltop fortifications were abandoned and new types of defence systems built on level ground where there was no cover for the enemy. The gunfighter's pa had only two stockades. The outer one was simply a screen designed to impede the charge of an assault force at close range to the defenders. Behind the inner stockade, through which the defenders fired their own weapons, was a trench and firing parapet. Later innovations included flanking angles to provide enfilade fire against attackers who made it to the main stockade, and bundles of green flax were used to deaden the fall of enemy shot.[18]

Despite this ingenuity in countering the new weapons, the musket wars debilitated Maori society. The population, which had been estimated by Cook at 100,000 and by others as high as 200,000, went into decline.[19] Disease, warfare and lowered food production all took their toll. The musket was no respecter of rank, and chiefs were just as likely to be brought low by a commoner armed with a musket as anyone else. The mighty Hongi himself died of a gunshot wound inflicted in a tribal fight near Mangamuka in 1827. Once other tribes acquired muskets, the aggressors, too, began to take unacceptable casualties. In 1832 a Ngapuhi expedition of 3,000 warriors once again raided the Waikato. There was no major engagement, and the expedition killed only forty people. But the Waikato forces followed the Ngapuhi on their return North and attacked them at Tawa-tawhiti near Kawau Island. On this occasion it was the Ngapuhi raiders who suffered great slaughter.[20] Eventually the tribes tired of the blood-letting and longed for surcease. Men no longer rushed to join war parties for excitement and plunder. The Ngapuhi lost 20 per cent of their warriors in the musket wars. By 1836 recruitment of warriors was down. War parties, which had numbered up to 800 men, fell to 300 or so.[21]

The Peacemakers

The Reverend Henry Williams was appalled by the tribal blood-letting of the musket wars. He put a stop to the missionaries selling muskets and intervened to save lives when he could. In 1828 he saved the life of Pango, a captive Arawa chief, by taking him from the Bay of Islands back to Tauranga. Increasingly as the tribes wanted peace, they turned to the missionaries as peacemakers. Their position as independent negotiators between tribes was facilitated by the establishment of their own agricultural base in 1830 at the new mission station at Waimate. The acquisition of their own ship, the *Herald*, and later the *Active*, enabled them to trade with other tribes. This economic independence raised the mana of the missionaries in the eyes of the Maori. On one of his return visits to the Bay of Islands, Marsden himself joined Williams in negotiating a peace between two warring tribes.[22] Early in 1832 Williams accompanied Titore's expedition to Tauranga in his schooner the *Active* in the hope of mitigating some of the horrors of tribal warfare.[23] His crowning achievement was the negotiation of peace between Waikato and Ngapuhi at Otahuhu in 1836. That same year one of the last great battles of the East Coast, named Te-Toka-a-Kuku, was fought at Te Kaha. As a consequence of missionary teaching, Tumata-a-kura, one of the Ngati Porou chiefs in the attacking party, agreed to participate in the battle only on the condition that there would be no cannibalism.[24]

Unlike the traders, who were motivated only by commercial gain, the missionaries were the cutting edge of colonisation. Their mission was to convert the Maori from heathenism to Christianity and from barbarism to civilisation. Underlying this mission were ethnocentric attitudes of racial and cultural superiority. Colenso, the missionary printer, thought Maori gods were nothing but 'imaginary beings'. The Catholic Bishop Pompallier thought that Maori were 'infidel New Zealanders'. The Reverend Robert Maunsell referred to Maori waiata as 'filthy and debasing', and Williams wrote that Maori were 'governed by the Prince of Darkness'.[25] Driven by such attitudes, the missionaries were the advance party of cultural invasion. Their immediate goal was to replace the spiritual beliefs of the Maori with their own. Such an agenda of cultural invasions in Paulo Freire's analysis was based on 'a parochial view of reality, a static perception of the world, and the imposition of one world view upon another. It implies the superiority of the invader and the inferiority of those who are invaded.'[26]

The assumed superiority of the incoming Europeans was built into the institutions of the new society. The first such institutions to be transplanted and take root in New Zealand were the mission schools. They taught only the standard subjects of the English school curriculum, namely English, arithmetic, reading, writing, and catechism. One redeeming feature was that teaching was done in the Maori language. The teacher Kendall compiled the first booklet in Maori, *A Korao no New Zealand*, in an attempt to compose some lessons for the instruction of the natives.[27] When the first scriptures were translated and printed in Maori in 1827, the people demonstrated keen interest in literacy. Adults as well as children arrived at the mission schools for lessons.[28] Soon chiefs in remote parts of the country were asking for missionary teachers to bring the boon of literacy to their tribes. The Maori readily learned the symbolling system of the written word since it was easily seen as an extension of their own symbolling system in the art of carving. Mission-trained Maori became the new men who carried their message of written language into tribal villages in advance of their European mentors. By the time the Reverend William Williams went to Poverty Bay in 1840 to establish a new mission station, he found there people who could already read and write. Similarly, the Reverend Johannes Riemenschneider was surprised on his arrival in Taranaki in 1846 to be greeted by a young man named Te Whiti who could recite whole passages of scripture from memory.[29]

Besides formal schooling, missionaries taught the useful crafts of carpentry, domestic management and agriculture. At first they made few converts while they were under the patronage of the chiefs who were using them for their own purposes. But by the 1830s, when they became economically independent and influential as teachers of new knowledge as well as peacemakers, whole tribes began converting to Christianity. Besides, the new God of the Pakeha was more appealing because it seemed his Pakeha followers were blessed with greater power and wealth than the Maori in the form of ships, weapons and an amazing quantity of goods.[30]

While the musket wars were physically debilitating, conversion to Christianity led to further erosion of Maori culture and power. The missionaries condemned polygamy, slavery, the tohunga and tapu,[31] the institutions that buttressed social control and the power of chiefs. Without slaves and wives to produce wealth for them, the mana of chiefs was diminished. The missionaries also attacked the sacred symbols of the tribe by emasculating ancestral carvings of their genitals, an act that portended the cultural and human emasculation to come. The most celebrated ancestor to suffer the indignity of losing his famous penis was Kahungunu. When the master carver Pine Taiapa was asked to carve a replacement, he demurred on the grounds it was better for the carving to remain as it was for the world to see what the missionaries had done. The missionary practice of condemning carvings of ancestors depicting sex organs as 'erotic, sinful and evil' continued into the modern era of the 1940s when the building of carved houses was revived.[32] In the North, the first point of contact and missionary influence, many of the sacred songs and chants of that part of the country were displaced by hymns.

The central motif in the carved ancestral houses of a tribe was the tiki, the human form. The symbolism of carvings incorporated themes of mythology, creation and the descent of humans from the gods through myth heroes down to founding ancestors. Both male and female genitals were prominently displayed to express fertility. Nor was it uncommon to depict in carving male and female figures copulating. The concern with fertility was also expressed verbally in the aphorism 'I shall never disappear the seed brought thither from Rangiatea'. This concern was heightened by harsh living conditions in New Zealand, where the average life expectancy was thirty-one years and women bore few children. Consequently, fertility, procreation and continuity of the human line were central themes in artistic expression. The emasculation of carvings which symbolised these concerns of Maori culture was like a thrust to the jugular by the cultural invader. The missionaries knew that destruction of the sacred symbols of Maori society would facilitate their replacement by their own icons.

Although the missionaries were men of God, they were also men of the flesh with an eye for their own terrestial wellbeing. Besides the lands on which mission stations were established, individual missionaries bought substantial estates for themselves and their descendants. Some of the largest estates claimed between 1814 and 1838 belonged to George Clarke (7,600 hectares), Henry Williams (8,800 hectares) and Richard Taylor (20,000 hectares). Out of thirty-five missionaries cited by John Grace,[33] only thirteen did not indulge in land-buying. Some of these were Robert Maunsell, William Colenso, and Octavius Hadfield.

From the outset, missionaries were concerned over the conduct of Europeans who had settled in New Zealand. Of particular concern were the ex-convicts and ship-jumpers who had thrown their lot in with the Maori. Although their numbers were small, about 150 in 1830, their behaviour was an embarrassment to the missionaries. They were also scandalised by the drunkenness, debauchery and licentious behaviour of sailors at the settlement of Kororareka. While the merchants and traders in the main regulated their behaviour towards the Maori in as much as profit could be made by trading with them, some were quite unscrupulous in their pursuit of profit. One of these was Captain Stewart, who in 1830 aided the warrior chief Te Rauparaha in the massacre of his enemies at Akaroa in return for a cargo of flax. This involvement of a British national in a petty tribal war was a stain on the British escutcheon and a reproach to the Government's failure to control the behaviour of British people in the raw frontier of New Zealand.

Declaration of Independence

Under missionary guidance, thirteen leading chiefs in the North petitioned the king of England to provide some form of control over

British nationals in New Zealand and protection from the possibility of other foreign intervention. A token gesture was made to the request by the appointment of James Busby as British Resident. Although Busby had no power to enforce law and order, he symbolised an official British presence in the country and the initial step towards formal annexation. As a consequence of the impounding in Sydney of a New Zealand-built ship for not flying an ensign, the master of the vessel was forced to fly a Maori mat from the masthead before it was allowed to sail. In response to that event, one of Busby's first official acts, in 1834, was to convene a meeting of twenty-five chiefs in front of his residence at Waitangi to select a flag for their country. The meeting concluded with a ceremony hoisting the chosen flag beside the Union Jack, an act signifying recognition of Maori sovereignty over New Zealand.

In October 1835, Busby convened a more significant meeting at Waitangi of thirty-four chiefs from Northland down to the Hauraki Gulf to sign a declaration of confederation and independence. This move was designed to neutralise his rival Thomas McDonnell in the Hokianga and the pretensions of a Frenchman, Baron de Thierry, who intended to settle on land he had bought at Hokianga and proclaim himself king. In the first clause of the declaration, the chiefs declared New Zealand to be an independent state under the name of the United Tribes of New Zealand. The second clause said:

> All sovereign power and authority within the territories of the United Tribes of New Zealand is hereby declared to reside entirely and exclusively in their collective capacity, who also declare that they will not permit any legislative authority separate from themselves in their collective capacity to exist, nor any function of Government to be exercised within the said territories, unless by persons appointed by them, and acting under the authority of laws regularly enacted by them in Congress assembled.[34]

The translation of the first part of this clause pertaining to the nature and seat of sovereignty gives some insight into how Busby dealt with the concept in relation to Maori equivalents. He rendered it as 'Ko te kingitanga ko te mana i te whenua', meaning the king is the sovereign power of the land. Clearly, he and Henry Williams, who assisted him, equated the word mana with sovereignty and power, a point that was to become significant under the Treaty of Waitangi five years later. A copy of the declaration was sent to the King of England with an expression of thanks for his recognition of their flag.

The tribes agreed under the declaration to meet once a year at Waitangi to make laws for the preservation of peace and the regulation of trade. However, few chiefs attended, as notions of Maori nationalism were alien to tribal society. In 1836 tribal fighting continued as before, with chiefs complying with Pakeha concepts of law and order only if it suited their purposes. Busby concluded that the diffusion of authority among tribal chiefs who were fiercely independent, made it impossible to create a central administration through them. By 1837 the missionaries also concluded that the chiefs were not ready to govern the country as a whole. The next year, when settler numbers had increased to a thousand and it was clear further settlement was inevitable, the missionaries George Clarke and Henry Williams called for British intervention and asked for a governor with military power to back his authority. By 1839 another thousand Europeans had settled in New Zealand and land speculation in a free market, unregulated by law or a central administration, was creating new tensions as some tribes realised they had surrendered too much for too little. But mounting pressure from metropolitan society was now irreversible.

The situation was aggravated by plans of the New Zealand Associ-ation, which formed a company to promote systematic colonisation of the country. The Company was headed by the rakish rogue Edward Gibbon Wakefield, who was benignly designated the 'father of New Zealand' in the sanitised school history book *Our Nation's Story*. Wakefield's theory of colonisation was based on the capitalist principle of 'buy cheap, sell dear'. Capital to buy cheap land in New Zealand was to be subscribed by the English upper-class land-owners and merchants. The idea was to replicate in the new land the vertical profile of the English class structure. In theory, the junior sons of the gentry would migrate to New Zealand to become the landholders. After the land had been purchased, surplus capital would be used to assist the working classes to migrate and provide the necessary labour as agricultural labourers, and as artisans such as wheelwrights, shoe-makers, blacksmiths and carpenters. They were induced to migrate by the promise of employment on the land or, failing that, employment by the Company. One tenth of the Company's land purchases was to be reserved for Maori chiefs as the landholders and their people as the workers. Wakefield sensed that unemployment, low wages and the grim living conditions of industrial England were threatening social stability. Therefore he believed that England could 'ease her discon-tents by exporting large numbers of the discontented'.[35] In 1839 the Company learned that annexation of New Zealand was imminent, so it sent Colonel William Wakefield out in the *Tory* to buy land while the price was still cheap and before the establishment of an official administration that would regulate and control the price of land.

Although moves had been set in train earlier in response to missionary appeals for intervention by the British Government, New Zealand was not annexed until 14 January 1840 by Order in Council as a colony of New South Wales. Captain Hobson, who was despatched in HMS *Herald* to carry out the Order, arrived in the Bay of Islands on 29 January. Lord Normanby's instructions to Hobson acknowledged New Zealand as a sovereign state even though it consisted of numerous independent tribes with only the confederation of northern tribes having any semblance of a larger polity. Hobson was instructed to obtain the surrender of that sovereignty to the British Crown by the free and intelligent consent of the 'natives'. They had to be persuaded that the sacrifice of their national independence would bring the benefits of British protection, law and citizenship. The instructions specified that Hobson was to treat for sovereignty over the whole or part of the islands that the natives were willing to cede. He was warned that they might feel distrustful or humiliated by British encroachment, but these impediments he had to overcome by mildness, justice and the sincerity of his intercourse with the aborigines. If necessary, he was to engage their consent by presents and other pecuniary arrangements. Once sovereignty was obtained, Hobson was to contract with the chiefs for the sale or cession of lands to the Crown only. Thereafter he was to issue a proclamation that all land titles would emanate from Crown grants. Hobson's first duty as the official protector of the aborigines was to confine his acquisition of land for British settlers to districts the 'natives' could alienate without distress to themselves. It was on the basis of these instructions that the Treaty of Waitangi was drawn up and subsequently signed on 6 February 1840.

The Treaty of Waitangi

The most penetrating critique in recent times of the drafting and signing of the Treaty was made by Ruth Ross.[36] According to Ross, Hobson made some notes for the Treaty based on his instructions. From those notes, Busby and two officers from HMS *Herald* drew up the first draft of the Treaty, which Hobson corrected on 3 February. The first draft was translated by Henry Williams while Hobson spent more time revising the document. The outcome of these combined efforts was four English versions and a translation into Maori which matched none of them. The English version from which the translation was made has yet to be found. Consequently, the official English version of the Treaty lodged with the Colonial Office does not match the Maori version which the chiefs of New Zealand signed (see Appendix 1 for the Maori and English texts).

The purpose of the Treaty embodied in the first article was the cession of chiefly sovereignty over New Zealand to the Queen of England. That is made absolutely clear in the English version, which reads:

> The Chiefs of the Confederation of the United Tribes of New Zealand, and the separate and independent Chiefs who have not become members of the Confederation, cede to Her Majesty the Queen of England, absolutely and without reservation, all the rights and powers of Sovereignty which the said Confederation or Individual Chiefs respectively exercise or possess, or may be supposed to exercise or to possess, over their respective Territories as the sole Sovereigns thereof.

But the Maori version does not accomplish that purpose because its meaning was obscured by Henry Williams whose translation (see Appendix 1), when retranslated back into English, reads:

> The Chiefs of the Confederation, and all the Chiefs not in that Confederation, cede absolutely to the Queen of England forever the complete Governance of their lands.

Ross blames the Protestant missionaries Henry Williams and his son Edward for translating sovereignty as kawanatanga (governance) instead of the word mana, which was used in the 1835 Declaration of Independence. The word kawanatanga did not convey to the Maori a precise definition of sovereignty.[37] Had the word mana been used, no Maori would have had any doubt what was being ceded. So, says Ross, 'was the Williams translation of sovereignty political rather than meaningful? Did they, knowing the chiefs would never sign away their mana to the Queen, deliberately eschew the use of this word and this concept in their translation?'[38] Although the question is rhetorical, Ross left it unresolved. Williams was not a disinterested party. He and other missionaries had a vested interest in ensuring that the Treaty was signed because of their substantial landholdings. They owned their lands at the pleasure of the chiefs, which might be withdrawn at any time. Therefore, besides their publicly proclaimed desire for law and order, the prospect of gaining secure title in fee simple from the Crown provided them with a strong personal incentive to ensure that the Treaty was signed.

The use of the word kawanatanga poses other difficulties. It is derived from a transliteration of governor into kawana, which, with the addition of the suffix tanga, becomes governance. Although some northern chiefs had met a governor in New South Wales, there was no model or referent for a governor in New Zealand, and we can only imagine what the chiefs thought they were conceding to such a person. Sir William Martin wrote what he thought the chiefs had ceded twenty years after the Treaty was signed:[39]

> The rights which the Natives recognised as belonging thenceforward to the Crown were such rights as were necessary for the Government of the country and for the establishment of the new system. We called them 'sovereignty'; the Natives called them 'kawanatanga', 'Governorship' . . . To the new and unknown office they conceded such powers, to them unknown, as might be necessary for its due exercise.

But as Ross points out, it was not the 'natives' who called this unknown thing kawanatanga, but the Protestant missionaries. Their fudging of the meaning of the first article was not redeemed by their more faithful but inaccurate treatment of the second article, which protected Maori rights. This article states:

> Her Majesty the Queen of England confirms and guarantees to the Chiefs and Tribes of New Zealand, and to the respective families and individuals thereof, the full, exclusive, and undisturbed possession of their Lands and Estates, Forests, Fisheries, and other properties which they may collectively or individually possess, so long as it is their wish and desire to retain the same in their possession; But the Chiefs of the United Tribes and the Individual Chiefs yield to Her Majesty the exclusive right of Preemption over such lands as the proprietors thereof may be disposed to alienate, at such prices as may be agreed upon between the respective Proprietors and and persons appointed by Her Majesty to treat with them in that behalf.

From this retranslation of the Maori version of the second article back into English, discrepancies are clearly evident:

> The Queen of England confirms and guarantees to the Chiefs, to the Tribes, and to all the people of New Zealand, the absolute Chieftainship of their lands, of their homes and all their treasured possessions. But the Chiefs of the Confederation, and all other chiefs, cede to the Queen the right to purchase over such lands as the proprietors are disposed to alienate at such prices agreed to by them and the purchaser appointed by the Queen on her behalf.

Forests and fisheries are left out of the Maori version. Although these might be subsumed under the general rubric of treasured possessions, this omission is an indication of the lack of precision in the drafting and translation of the Treaty. But the primary consideration of this article is the meaning it conveyed to the chiefs. By this article the Queen guaranteed the tribes 'tino rangatiratanga', the absolute chieftainship, over their lands, homes and treasured possessions. Tino rangatiratanga was a much closer approximation to sovereignty than kawanatanga.[40] The word rangatiratanga is a missionary neologism derived from rangatira (chief), which, with the addition of the suffix tanga, becomes chieftainship. Now the guarantee of chieftainship is in effect a guarantee of sovereignty, because an inseparable component of chieftainship is mana whenua. Without land a chief's mana and that of his people is negated. The chiefs are likely to have understood the second clause of the Treaty as a confirmation of their own sovereign rights in return for a limited concession of power in kawanatanga.[41]

The question arises as to who was sovereign over New Zealand. The British Crown claimed sovereignty on the basis of the English version of the Treaty. But that was not the version signed by the chiefs. The Treaty of Waitangi they signed confirmed their own sovereignty while ceding the right to establish a governor in New Zealand to the Crown. A governor is in effect a satrap, who, according to the Oxford dictionary, is the holder of provincial governorship; he was a subordinate ruler, or a colonial governor. In New Zealand's case, he governed at the behest and on behalf of the chiefs. In view of the fact that Governor Hobson had no power to enforce his will, and gunboat diplomacy was distinctly unfashionable among the humanitarians in England, Hobson governed by the acquiescence of the chiefs. In effect, the chiefs were his sovereigns. But subsequent to the signing of the Treaty, the Pakeha behaved towards the Maori on the assumption they held sovereignty, while Maori responded in the belief that they had never surrendered it.

The third article of the Treaty, which was the least contentious, said:

> In consideration thereof, Her Majesty the Queen of England extends to the Natives of New Zealand Her Royal protection, and imparts to them all the Rights and Privileges of British subjects.

The translation of the Maori version back into English states:

> This (the third clause) is in consideration of the acknowledgement of the Queen's Governance. The Queen of England will protect all the maori people of New Zealand. They will be given all the rights equal to those of the people of England.

Again, in this clause, it is clear that the Queen's governance was acknowledged, not her mana. This clause is also interesting for its use of the word maori. Prior to the advent of Europeans, Maori people had no single term for themselves. People were distinguished from one another by their tribal names. But with the coming of the whalers, sealers and traders, the word Pakeha was used to designate the strangers. The word is derived from pakepakeha or pakehakeha, which are defined in Williams's *Dictionary* as 'imaginary beings resembling men, with fair skins'. The word maori means normal, usual or ordinary, which through usage has become capitalised to refer to the Maori people collectively. Prior to the third article of the Treaty, Maori people had been variously referred to as New Zealanders, natives and aborigines. Thus the Treaty of Waitangi is the first official document to cite the Maori people as the indigenous people of New Zealand.

On 30 January 1840, Captain Hobson sent out a circular inviting chiefs of the confederation and independent chiefs as far south as Hauraki, to attend a meeting at Waitangi on 5 February to discuss the Treaty of Waitangi. When the chiefs assembled, Hobson addressed them and offered the protection of Great Britain. He read out the English version of the Treaty while Henry Williams gave the translated version. Busby also spoke, assuring the chiefs that the Governor came not to take land but to guarantee their possession of it. Despite the obscure meaning of the Treaty, several chiefs sought reassurance by speaking out against it. Chiefs like Te Kemara, Rewa and Moka opposed the Governor's presence if it meant that their status would be relegated to below that of the Governor. Rewa told the Governor bluntly to return to his own country. He even issued a prophetic warning that those who signed the Treaty would be 'reduced to the condition of slaves and compelled to break stones on the roads'.[42] They also made accusations of sharp practices in land dealing by a number of Pakeha including missionaries. In rebuttal, Williams denied having robbed the Maori of land. In arguing that he wanted land titles to be examined by a commissioner, he ingenuously revealed his motivation for urging the Treaty on the Maori when he said he wanted an investigation because he had a large family of eleven children for whom he had to make provision. The influential Ngati Hine chief Kawiti suspected that something more than kawanatanga was at stake. Since the missionaries had not expressed any desire for temporal power, he invited them to stay, while telling the Governor to return to his own country.

While some chiefs opposed the Treaty, others such as Hone Heke, who were under missionary tutelage, spoke in favour, likening the Treaty to the word of God. But the most persuasive supporter of the Treaty was Tamati Waka Nene, who, in the rhetorical style of the orator on the marae, addressed his fellow chiefs, saying:

> Friends! Whose potatoes do we eat? Whose were our blankets? These spears (holding up his taiaha) are laid aside. What has the Ngapuhi now? The Pakeha's gun, his shot, his powder. Many of his children are our children.[43]

Nene concluded by asking the Governor to remain as both judge and peacemaker, and indicated that he would sign the Treaty. His elder brother Patuone endorsed what had been said and also urged the Governor to stay and avert a possible takeover by the French. The discussion ended at 4 p.m., with the chiefs asking for time to consider the matter among themselves. The meeting was adjourned until 7 February and a quantity of tobacco was handed out, but no food. The customs of Maori hospitality obliged any chief who convened a hui to feed his guests well. Governor Hobson, who claimed high office on behalf of the Crown, had fallen short of that social obligation. It was an inauspicious but symbolic start to a relationship that was supposed to be of mutual benefit. Some chiefs signified they would go home rather than wait around hungry for another day.

The missionaries were afraid that the chiefs would drift off before signing the Treaty so they advanced the meeting to the 6th February. When they arrived at 9.30 a.m., between three and four hundred people were waiting in front of Busby's residence. By 11 a.m. there was still no sign of the Governor; no one had thought to inform him that the meeting had been put forward a day. When two officers came ashore at noon, they immediately went back and fetched Hobson. He was so bustled by the affair that he hurried ashore without changing into his uniform. The only symbol of his high office he wore that day was his naval headgear.[44] Pictures of the signing with Hobson resplendent in his uniform are part of the myth-making surrounding the Treaty.

As soon as Hobson was seated, he announced he was ready to take signatures. Henry Williams read the Treaty again and invited the chiefs to come forward. No one moved. The missionary printer William Colenso queried Hobson as to whether the natives understood what they were being asked to sign. He insisted they ought to understand it in order to make it legal. Hobson exonerated himself, saying it was no fault of his if they did not understand it, they had heard it read by Mr Williams. Busby tried to mollify Colenso by quoting what Hone Heke said the previous day, that 'the native mind could not comprehend these things they must trust to the advice of the missionaries'. Colenso was equal to this evasion, saying that he put the responsibility on the missionaries to explain the Treaty in all its bearings in case there was a reaction and they would be blamed.[45] The impasse was broken by Busby, who hit upon the idea of calling chiefs by name to come forward. Hone Heke was called first and the signing commenced. Of the forty-three chiefs who signed that day, twenty-three belonged to the Confederation of United Tribes, while the rest came from other tribes. One of the latter was Iwikau the younger brother of Te Heuheu, the paramount chief of Taupo. He was at Waitemata on a musket-buying expedition when Hobson's emissary arrived with the invitation to attend the meeting at Waitangi. As each chief signed, Hobson shook hands, saying, 'He iwi tahi tatou' (We are one people), thereby laying down the ideology of assimilation that was to dominate colonial policy well into the twentieth century. Each chief who signed the Treaty was given two blankets and some tobacco.

Since the real meaning of the Treaty was concealed by imprecise translation, grave doubts arise as to whether the chiefs signed with their 'free and intelligent consent'. Furthermore, the association of Treaty signing with gratuities raises the question whether the chiefs were prompted as much by cupidity as by the promised benefits of British protection. Iwikau, for one, thought he had done well securing two blankets by the simple act of putting his mark on the Treaty. At subsequent signings other chiefs exhibited mercenary motives. One was Te Rauparaha, who signed twice when the Treaty was hawked around the country by the missionaries and Hobson's other emissaries. One chief at Tauranga said, 'Pay us first and we will write afterwards.' Another said, 'Put money in my left hand and I will write with my right hand.'[46] For chiefs of this disposition, the Treaty was nothing more than a commercial transaction, the exchange of their signatures for Pakeha goods. But what they thought they gave and what the coloniser claimed, were separated by an abyss that was to have cataclysmic consequences for the Maori people. The chiefs were not to know that nation-building in the new world during the era of European expansionism was predicated on the destruction of first nations. By their acquiescence in the Treaty, the chiefs opened the way to replicate among their own people the colonial experience of African tribes and the Indians of the American continent.

Extensive efforts were made in the collection of signatures for the

A pataka treasure house of the old world.

Paramount chief Te Heuheu Tukino of Tuwharetoa facing the new world, which his father rejected by not signing the Treaty of Waitangi.
Alexander Turnbull Library

Hauhau freedom fighters taken prisoner in 1866 at Wearoa Pa near Wanganui and held in captivity on board ship.
Alexander Turnbull Library, Harding/Denton coll.

Te Whai a te Motu, symbol of Te Kooti's struggle against Pakeha domination.
S. M. Mead

King Tawhiao on a visit to Auckland in 1882.
Auckland Institute and Museum, E. Pulman photographer

Signing of the deed of sale for Wairarapa land processed through the Native Land Court in 1896. Sir James Carroll is seated at the table holding a tewhatewha. Note the absence of carving on the house.
Alexander Turnbull Library

Impoverished victims of the expropriation of land in Wanganui.
Auckland Institute and Museum

The dispossessed were reduced to digging for a living in the gumfields of Northland and Coromandel.
Alexander Turnbull Library, Northwood coll.

Apirana Ngata, the first Maori graduate to put his talents to work for the cultural renaissance.
Alexander Turnbull Library

June 1920, first meeting of one of the Maori councils in the Takitimu district of Hawke's Bay. The councils were given low-level, non-political duties to uplift the Maori people.
Alexander Turnbull Library

Rua Kenana, who built the 'City of God' at Maungapohatu, meeting with the Prime Minister, Sir Joseph Ward, at Whakatane in 1908.
Alexander Turnbull Library

Wiremu Tahupotiki Ratana, the 'mouthpiece' of God, turned his church into a political force.
Alexander Turnbull Library

A typical classroom of a Native school for the domestication of Maori as housemaids and workers.

A Maori concert party, the non-threatening image that Pakeha prefer to hold of their countrymen.
Alexander Turnbull Library, Hall/Raine coll.

Princess Te Puea Herangi, who rebuilt the capital of the King Movement, Turangawaewae Marae at Ngaruawahia.
Auckland Public Library

Piri Poutapu and Waka Kereama, master carvers from the Rotorua school of carving, with a door lintel which marked the beginning of the cultural renaissance, 1928.

Treaty in all parts of the country. But despite an impressive final total of 540 signatures,[47] there were some notable gaps. Two paramount chiefs, Te Wherowhero of the Tainui tribes and Te Heuheu of the Tuwharetoa confederation, did not sign. Although the meaning of the Treaty was disguised by the word governance, Te Heuheu intuitively understood its true intent. On Iwikau's return to Taupo he repudiated what he had done, saying:[48]

> I will not agree to the mana of a strange people being placed over this land. Though every chief in the island consent to it, yet I will not. I will consent to neither your act nor your goods. As for these blankets, burn them.

As a consequence of Te Heuheu's denunciation of the Treaty, chiefs of the Arawa confederation of tribes in the Lakes district and the Ngaiterangi chiefs at Tauranga refused to sign. Nor did the paramount chief of the East Coast, Te Kani-a-Takirau, sign. Ideologically, the word of these ariki placed the populous centres of the North Island outside the Treaty. But the authority of these chiefs was subverted by the process of collecting and aggregating signatures from other chiefs in exchange for gratuities. Thus the coloniser initiated the process of undermining the authority structures of Maori society by the application of his own principle of majority rule. On 21 May, Hobson proclaimed sovereignty over the North Island on the basis of the Treaty of Waitangi. But he did not wait for the return of his emissaries with signatures collected in the south. Instead, he proclaimed sovereignty over the South Island on the basis that it was *terra nullius*, thereby ignoring the existence of the Ngai Tahu. Only the arrogance born of metropolitan society and the colonising ethos of the British Empire was capable of such self-deception, which was hardly excused by the desire to beat the imminent arrival of the French at Akaroa. But even greater deceptions lay ahead over the next 150 years.

CHAPTER 6

Takahi Mana

The Treaty of Waitangi is the legitimate source of constitutional government in New Zealand. It provided the British Crown with a tenuous beachhead on New Zealand soil, which Belich characterised as 'nominal sovereignty',[1] compared with substantive sovereignty. The Maori outnumbered the Pakeha, who purported to govern them, by thirty to one, and it was clear from their understanding of the Treaty that they had not conceded substantive sovereignty. Nopera Panakareao's much-quoted statement when he signed the Treaty at Kaitaia that 'the shadow of the land goes to the Queen but the substance remains with us' was probably the widely held view the chiefs had of the Treaty. This complied with notional but not substantive sovereignty. Orange[2] sees the Treaty as giving only partial entitlement of the country to the British, but in the international arena it was sufficient to ward off other potential claimants such as France. The problem facing Governor Hobson and his successors was to consolidate sovereignty and gradually extend their control into native districts until the whole country was brought under the dominion of the Crown.

Acquisition, control and, ultimately, expropriation of land were the key factors in the consolidation of sovereignty. The first two were built into the Crown's right of pre-emption to the purchase of land under Article 2 of the Treaty, which Hobson construed as sole right of purchase. Expropriation was to come later with political domination. The process began with the issuing of the Royal Charter for the colony to Hobson in November 1840. The charter gave the Governor power to survey the whole of New Zealand and divide it up into districts, counties, towns, townships, and parishes. Reserves were to be set aside for roads, town sites, churches and schools. None of these matters were envisaged by the chiefs who signed the Treaty, nor were they privy to them, otherwise Hobson's governorship might have been short-lived. The charter also instructed the Governor to make grants of 'waste land' to private persons for their use, or to corporate bodies in trust for public use. Since there was no waste land in New Zealand, the instruction can only be construed to mean Maori land. Not even the proviso in the charter excepting land actually occupied by the Maori altered that intent, since the Maori did not recognise a category called waste land in the tribal domain. The charter declared all waste and uncleared land to be Crown land, which was to be sold at a uniform price per acre to European settlers. These instructions breached the Treaty in spirit, and it was only a matter of time before the Treaty was breached in fact. In the meantime, all pre-Treaty land purchases by Pakeha settlers and the New Zealand Company were investigated by the Land Commissioner, William Spain. Most claims, including those of the missionaries, were reduced in size by the Commissioner. Spain found only a fraction of the eight million hectares bought by the New Zealand Company were fairly purchased. But at the the Company's New Plymouth settlement he gave them a generous award of 24,000 acres. The area had been depopulated during the musket wars and so Spain felt the award would not be an imposition on the Maori people. This opinion was overruled by Governor FitzRoy because it neglected the rights of the Te Atiawa owners who were living elsewhere at the time and signified their intention to return.[3] He reduced the award to 1,400 hectares. This constricting of the settlement caused Pakeha resentment in the years ahead, especially when Maori in the following decade decided to oppose land selling.

The Maori Economy

The preamble in the Treaty of Waitangi legitimised the transmigration of settlers from the United Kingdom. At first this one-way flow of Pakeha was acceptable to the Maori because it brought increased trade and material benefits. The Maori were quick to adapt their communal tribal organisation and economic production to take advantage of trading opportunities presented by the new arrivals. The first fifteen years after the Treaty saw a period of economic expansion and prosperity for many tribes, especially those close to Pakeha markets.

In February 1840, Governor Hobson sailed to the Hauraki Gulf to collect signatures for the Treaty. There he was welcomed at Waitemata by the Ngati Whatua chief Apihai Te Kawau. Te Kawau facilitated the confirmation of Hobson's administration by offering for sale 1,200 hectares on which the city of Auckland was established. The shift of the seat of government from Russell to Auckland allowed Ngati Whatua to reoccupy their lands at Orakei under the shelter of

Pax Britannica. The traditional name for the land is Tamaki-makau-rau, Tamaki of a thousand lovers. It was so named because it was the most desirable piece of real estate in New Zealand with its two harbours, fertile soil and numerous volcanic cones for fortifications.

Auckland immediately became a flourishing centre of commercial activity. Within a year of Hobson's purchase, for an outlay of £200, an auction of 119 town lots of 17.6 hectares realised £24,300. Speculators who bought these town lots subdivided and resold them to incoming settlers at 200 and even 300 per cent profit.[4] The prosperity formerly enjoyed by the Bay of Islands shifted to Waitemata. Tribes around Hauraki Gulf headed for the Auckland markets in canoes and sailing vessels laden with produce to service the population of 2,000. They provided large quantities of fruit, pumpkins, maize, potatoes, kumara, pigs and fish. In a single year, 1,792 canoes transported into the Auckland Harbour 1,400 baskets of onions, 1,700 baskets of maize, 1,200 baskets of peaches, and tonnes of firewood, fish, pigs and kauri gum.[5] Tribes around the Tamaki isthmus sold thousands of kits of oysters annually through the ports of Auckland and Onehunga right up to 1858.[6] Tribes from as far afield as Te Whaiti and Ruatahuna brought produce to Auckland in order to acquire manufactured goods. Tribes in the south benefited financially from proximity to Pakeha in the New Zealand Company settlements. As early as 1842 a bank manager in Wellington estimated Maori wealth to be upwards of £150,000. Much of this was invested later in the decade in ploughs, carts and mills. The tribes at Motueka near the Nelson settlement in 1850 harvested 400 hectares of wheat. Those at Waitara, near the New Plymouth settlement, also prospered. They owned 150 horses, 300 cattle, forty carts, thirty-five ploughs, twenty pairs of harrows and a small fleet of ships. The Ngai Tahu people in the South Island took up farming in the 1840s not only to improve their own food supply but also to produce a cash surplus to buy equipment and stock.[8] In 1850, when the Canterbury settlers arrived at Lyttelton, the tribes of that district supplied them with potatoes, corn, turnips and melons. The Ngai Tahu also operated their own sailing vessels to trade up and down the coast.

Prosperity encouraged the tribes to invest their profits in the purchase of capital goods such as flour mills to grind their own corn and ships to transport their produce to markets. These two items were as much symbols of tribal mana and prestige as the hallmarks of economic enterprise. Capital for the purchase of mills and ships was subscribed by members of a tribe in much the same way as one would buy shares in a company. One-pound shares were well within the range of individual whanau. Tribes with a shortfall of cash negotiated loans through the Governor. The first Maori water-powered mill was built at Aotea in 1846.[9] Over the next fourteen years tribes in the Waikato, Taranaki, Wanganui, Hawke's Bay, Bay of Plenty and Coromandel regions built forty-nine flour mills. These were constructed by Maori labour supervised by Pakeha millwrights at costs that varied between £200 and £500.

Ownership of coastal vessels was even more extensive than flour mills. In 1846 the tribes at Opotiki and Whakatane owned three coastal vessels. Three years later there were forty-three Maori-owned vessels averaging up to twenty tonnes operating out of the Bay of Plenty. Twenty of these were owned by the Arawa tribes. At that time there were already forty-three Maori vessels in Auckland.[10] Some of these vessels had a displacement of up to sixty tonnes. Although Lady Martin[11] noted that capital for the purchase of ships was raised by traditional co-operative effort, such as tribal ohu cutting and scraping flax, tribes were not averse to borrowing money. Northland tribes, for example, borrowed £1,700 from the Governor to purchase ships. Maori economic success was clearly evident in their domination of coastal trade up to 1855.[12] The areas encompassed by their shipping operations in the North Island included Wanganui, Manawatu, Taranaki, Hawke's Bay, Poverty Bay, Waikato, Bay of Plenty and Northland. Within fifteen years of having signed the Treaty of Waitangi, the tribes had successfully developed their own economic infrastructure. They were the primary producers of agricultural produce, the millers of flour and the transporters of their own products to the markets. Their dream of achieving progress through sharing their country with the Pakeha under the Treaty was apparently coming to fruition.

Response to Pakeha Transgression of Mana

Although Maori tribes were progressing while Pakeha settlers struggled to establish themselves, there were early portents of the dangers that lay ahead for the Maori. Organised settlement by the New Zealand Company made Maori and Pakeha competitors for land. The Maori owned it and the Pakeha wanted it. At the Company settlement of Nelson, Captain Arthur Wakefield attempted to assert ownership of lands at Wairau. The claim was disputed by the warrior chief Te Rauparaha in 1843. But instead of waiting for the matter to be settled by Commissioner Spain, Wakefield tried to bluff Te Rauparaha into backing down by a show of force with a posse of forty-six settlers armed with defective muskets. He also enlisted the backing of the police magistrate to give some semblance of legitimacy to his actions.

According to Saunders' account of the affray at Wairau, the men were untrained, ill-disciplined and badly led.[13] One of the defective muskets went off while the posse was crossing the Tua Marina stream and the raw recruits panicked and starting firing. The killing of Te Rangihaeata's wife in this first volley forced Te Rauparaha and his men to defend themselves. Being more skilled in the arts of war, Te Rauparaha easily won the day, which culminated in the death of nineteen Pakeha. Because some of the men were killed after they had surrendered, the affray is generally referred to in Pakeha history books as the 'Wairau massacre'. Te Rauparaha's response to Magistrate Thompson's plea to spare his life puts the issue in the cultural context of the Maori. 'A little while ago I wished to talk with you in a friendly manner, and you would not; now you say save me, I will not save you. It is not our custom in war to save the chiefs of our enemies. We do not consider our victory complete unless we kill the chiefs of our opponents.' The other reason for the killing of prisoners was the exaction of utu, blood vengeance for Te Rangihaeata's wife. As a consequence of what happened at Tua Marina, Pakeha settlers felt insecure. They realised they were powerless to defend themselves, and the land was not there for the taking from a warrior race born to fighting. When Governor FitzRoy arrived to replace Hobson, he admitted an impulse on his part to punish Te Rauparaha for the killing. But after conducting an inquiry, he decided the settlers were at fault. In any case, he did not have the resources or power to enforce his will over Te Rauparaha.

While Hone Heke admitted signing the Treaty in ignorance at the behest of the missionaries, that incomprehension soon changed as the Governor began to assert his mana in ways assumed but not stated by the Treaty. The imposition of customs duties to provide revenue to pay for his administration was one of the powers of kawanatanga, but it brought free trade to an end in the Bay of Islands. Furthermore, the Governor and his administration were in financial straits. Under the Crown right of pre-emption, land sales slowed down because the Governor did not have the financial resources to exercise the Crown's prerogative. Initially, revenue from land sales was £69,400, a large portion of this coming from the £200 invested in the purchase and sale of land at Waitemata. A windfall of that kind could not be repeated.

By 1842 revenue from land sales had dropped to £1,300, and the following year the Governor was dependent on a grant in aid from Britain of £7,545 to pay his civil service. Chiefly revenue dried up as land sales slowed and ships were driven to other ports to avoid customs.

The true meaning of the innocent act of putting a mark on a piece of paper became clear to Heke. He saw the flagstaff above the town of Russell as the symbol of his discontent. So in a political act symbolising his disaffection with the Governor, Heke felled the flagpole and confiscated the customs signal balls. He could have felled the Governor instead, but he did not, which is just as well. Unlike the Americans, who have a tradition burned into the psyche of their nation of assassinating presidents, New Zealanders have the relatively harmless one of felling flagpoles. The flagpole was re-erected and twice felled again. On the fourth occasion Kororareka was evacuated. The town fell into the hands of Heke and Kawiti, who sacked and burned it.

Governor FitzRoy sent to Sydney for troops to bring Heke to heel. The older chiefs tried to dissuade the Governor by putting the matter into perspective when they counselled 'it was not worthwhile to shed blood about a bit of wood'.[14] This sage advice was not accepted. The troops arrived in June 1845 under the command of Colonel Despard and marched inland after Heke. At the Battle of Ohaeawai, where he was soundly beaten by Heke, Despard lost 107 men, approximately a quarter of his force. FitzRoy's failure to discipline Heke, combined with criticism over his exoneration of Te Rauparaha, and the financial weakness of his administration, culminated in his recall. The Colonial Office replaced him with the best man in its service, Governor George Grey, who had proved himself an able administrator as Governor of South Australia.

Force as an Instrument of Colonisation

Governor Grey as the hit-man of colonisation heralded the extension of Pakeha power into Maori districts. Unlike his predecessor FitzRoy, Grey had sufficient funds to buy up Maori land. He also introduced enough military force to subdue Heke and pacify the North. Grey reduced expenditure by 60 per cent, raised £22,000 within the colony, and obtained £36,000 from the Imperial Government. The war with Heke was brought to a quick end at the Battle of Ruapekapeka in 1846. While Heke was engaged elsewhere, the seventy-year-old Kawiti conducted the defence of the pa. The events surrounding the battle at Ruapekapeka appear to have been shrouded in myth-making and self-seeking propaganda which have only recently been stripped away by Belich.[15] The pa had been bombarded for two weeks by mortars and artillery when Heke arrived to reinforce the garrison. At that time small breaches were opening up in the palisades and Heke advised abandonment of the position. Kupapa scouts reported that the pa appeared to be deserted. As soldiers moved in to occupy it, they came under fire from a rearguard of a dozen men led by Kawiti, who fled outside followed by soldiers. A heavy engagement occurred for three hours with soldiers inside the pa and Heke and Kawiti's forces outside. The engagement was then broken off.

Despard reported that Ruapekapeka was taken by assault, while Grey proclaimed a brilliant victory. After the discomfiture of British arms at Wairau and Ohaeawai, the news was most welcome and readily believed. But in order to explain having taken the pa without vanquishing and killing more than a handful of defenders, the myth of the pa being taken while the defenders were at worship on the Sunday was widely adopted. In reality, it was only chance that prevented the Pakeha troops from being mauled again by Heke. Having taken the decision to abandon the pa, Heke's alternative plan was to lure the soldiers into an ambush outside it. Kawiti and his men were the decoys. The plan misfired when it was thought Kawiti had been captured. Kawiti's men stopped retreating in order to extricate him. Too late they discovered it was not necessary, so they did battle with the soldiers for a time then left the field. Having tested the strength and fire power of the enemy, and satisfied his own sense of honour in relation to the Governor, Heke made peace.

This was not done without a sense of levity on the part of Heke. FitzRoy, the previous Governor, had put a bounty of £100 on his head, which Heke likened to the Governor's buying him like a pig instead of taking him by military prowess. For this reason his token of peace to Grey was a large pig.[16] The mediator in peace-making was Waka Nene, who advised the Governor against confiscating Heke and Kawiti's lands, on the assurance that they would not disturb the peace again. Thus was the North pacified and the authority of the Governor recognised in that part of the country. Some twelve years later, after both Heke and Kawiti died, Kawiti's son and 400 Ngapuhi men cut a fine spar from the forest and re-erected the flagstaff as a symbolic gesture of goodwill to the Governor.

With peace established in the North, Grey turned his attention to the south. There he arrested the aged Te Rauparaha and detained him on HMS *Calliope* without charges being brought. Te Rauparaha was seventy-seven years of age at the time and hardly a military threat to the Governor. But by acting decisively, albeit illegally, Grey demonstrated there was a new power in the land. It was implicitly understood that the arrest was delayed utu for Wairau. The political effect was the assertion of mana by Grey over Te Rauparaha, thus spreading the mantle of sovereignty to the southern portion of the North Island. Eventually Te Rauparaha was released at the behest of Te Wherowhero and Waka Nene, with their assurance that he would not cause any disruption to the progress of the colony. Grey moved even more decisively in extending the beachhead of the New Zealand Company settlement at Wellington up into the Hutt Valley. The rights of Te Rangihaeata and his people who resisted settlement were ignored. Grey simply declared martial law, drove them out and pacified the area by the technique learned from the Romans of building roads and a series of blockhouses.

Asserting mana over troublesome chiefs by a show of force was one thing. With Te Wherowhero and Waka Nene, Grey moved more circumspectly. He made a show of consulting them and rewarding them with gratuities. Grey needed their co-operation to maintain the peace because he did not have enough military personnel to defend Auckland as well as the widely separated settlements of the New Zealand Company. For their part, the chiefs regarded the Governor's confidence in them as the right and proper exercise of their rangatiratanga as guaranteed by the Treaty of Waitangi.

Takeover of Mana Whenua

With settlers flooding in and clamouring for land, Grey moved decisively to try and meet the demand. Both his predecessors, Hobson and FitzRoy, took seriously their first duty to protect the rights of the Maori from settler land-hunger. In observance of the guarantee of possession of the land, Hobson had appointed 'Protectors of Aborigines'. Their job was to oversee the purchase of land that Maori people could alienate without inconvenience to themselves, in accordance with Hobson's instructions. The protectors' established procedures for the purchase of land included identification of tribal owners, their territorial boundaries, and gaining consensual agreement from the chief and his tribe to validate sales. For Grey, the protectors were an impediment to rapid acquisition of land and the extension of the

Crown's control into native districts. Land not actually occupied or cultivated by tribes was to be treated as 'wasteland' to be purchased by the Crown for settlers. Grey's first move was to abolish the protectors and to replace them with new officials, whose job was to speed up land purchase. These officials were designated 'Commissioners for the Extinguishment of Native Land Claims by Fair Purchase'. Large-scale land buying by the commissioners became the means by which notional sovereignty under the Treaty was converted into substantive sovereignty over the whole of the South Island and a quarter of the North Island.

Apart from the New Zealand Company purchase of Nelson, and the Otago Block, which was purchased in 1844, the whole of the South Island was bought up in six large blocks by the commissioners between 1846 and 1860. Three smaller blocks were bought at Banks Peninsula in the same period. But Stewart Island was not bought until 1863 (for £6,000). The total cost of eliminating Maori ownership of the South Island and Stewart Island was £14,800.[17] The tribes that agreed to these vast land alienations did so under the proviso of the principle laid down by the New Zealand Company that one-tenth of all lands purchased would be reserved to them. The purchase of the Otakou Block by the government agent Symonds on behalf of the New Zealand Company was contingent on the understanding that the Governor would mark off the 'tenths' reserved to Ngai Tahu. This promise was not honoured. The tenths were transmuted to four hectares a head by Governor Grey's instructions to his commissioners.

In 1848 Governor Grey himself initiated negotiations with Ngai Tahu for the purchase of the Canterbury Block, a vast area of eight million hectares for £2,000. A verbal agreement to the sale was made by Ngai Tahu chiefs on the condition that adequate reserves would be set aside for the use of their people. Grey then appointed Tacy Kemp to negotiate the details of the sale. Commissioner Kemp was not scrupulous in discharging his task. The boundaries of the purchase were not properly defined, and he bullied the chiefs into submission by threatening to pay Ngati Toa who, under Te Rauparaha, had defeated Ngai Tahu in the musket wars. He even threatened to use troops to drive them out if they did not acquiesce to the sale. The promised reserves, which Ngai Tahu understood to be 'tenths', were diminished in Kemp's deed of sale to their cultivations and dwelling places with an unspecified area of reserve land to be set aside by the Governor after the land had been surveyed.[18] Grey appointed Walter Mantell to establish the reserves. Following Grey's instructions, Commissioner

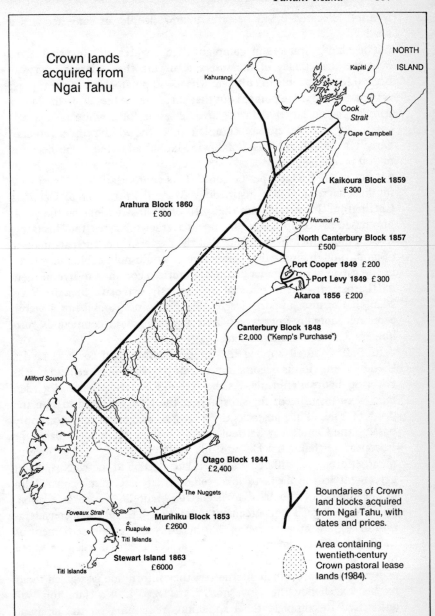

Crown lands
acquired from
Ngai Tahu

NORTH
ISLAND

Kapiti

Kahurangi

Cook
Strait

Cape Campbell

Kaikoura Block 1859
£300

Arahura Block 1860
£300

Hurunui R.

North Canterbury Block 1857
£500

Port Cooper 1849 £200
Port Levy 1849 £300
Akaroa 1856 £200

Canterbury Block 1848
£2,000 ("Kemp's Purchase")

Milford Sound

Otago Block 1844
£2,400

The Nuggets

Foveaux Strait

Ruapuke
Titi Islands

Murihiku Block 1853
£2600

Stewart Island 1863
£6000

Titi Islands

Boundaries of Crown
land blocks acquired
from Ngai Tahu, with
dates and prices.

Area containing
twentieth-century
Crown pastoral lease
lands (1984).

Source: Evison, Harry C., *Ngai Tahu Land Rights and Crown Pastoral Lease Lands in the South Island of New Zealand.*
Ngai Tahu Maori Trust Board, 1987, p. 8.

Mantell allocated 2,543 hectares to 637 people, or four hectares a head.[19]

The chief Tiramorehu complained to Lieutenant Governor Eyre over the inadequacy of the reserves, urging that a larger area was needed for his people to cultivate wheat and potatoes, and to rear pigs, cattle and sheep. He pointed out that since the area set aside for Maori people was no larger than the area set aside for a white man's residence, 'we shall never cease complaining to the white people who may hereafter come here'.[20] At Tuahiwi, Mantell allocated 1,056 hectares to 200 people, and at Moeraki 200 hectares to eighty-seven people, an average of 4.4 hectares per person.[21] This expropriation of Maori land for Pakeha settlers was justified by Mantell in a letter to Octavius Carrington: 'In carrying out the spirit of my instructions on the block purchased by Kemp, I allocated on an average ten acres [four hectares] to each individual, in the belief that the ownership of such an amount of land, though ample for their support, would not enable the natives in the capacity of large landed proprietors to continue to live in their old barbarism on the rents of an uselessly extensive domain.'[22] In Mantell's terms, support clearly meant subsistence and not a viable economic domain from which Maori people could compete as runholders against Pakeha settlers.

In 1849 Mantell applied the same principles and coercive tactics used by Kemp in his negotiations for the purchase of three land blocks covering Banks Peninsula. As the reserves of residential and garden land were insufficient for subsistence, the chiefs refused to sign the deed of sale. This obstacle the Government overcame by simply passing the Canterbury Settlement Act, making the land available for European settlement.[23] Despite this unilateral move by the Government, efforts were still being made as late as 1856 to coerce Ngai Tahu agreement to the de facto takeover of Akaroa. Commissioner John Grant Johnson, who tried to negotiate Mantell's award at Akaroa, failed to get Ngai Tahu agreement to relinquish the block in consideration of a grant of a reserve of 200 hectares and a cash settlement of £150. Johnson commented on the Ngai Tahu refusal when he wrote to his superior saying they 'would rather incur the risk of being dispossessed by force which alternative, they inform me was given them by his Excellency the Governor'.[24] In 1857 J. W. Hamilton was authorised to complete the transactions remaining on the lands at Akaroa and Kaiapoi. In his communication on the matter to his superior, the purchase agent openly expressed his misgivings. Only two years previously an area of 12,000 hectares in the block for which he was negotiating had been sold for £15,000: 'Recollecting this fact I should feel that I had made myself party to a gross fraud practised upon the Maoris in agreeing now to give only £200 for the land which we have already sold at such a very different price.'[25] Although Hamilton was obviously a man of conscience, driven by unbridled colonial power his misgivings amounted to nothing. In the end he rationalised his complicity in government exploitation of Ngai Tahu on the grounds that the land was valueless to them. But the value of the reserves left to them would be enhanced by Pakeha settlement on the lands from which they had been parted. The validity of that rationale does not stand up in the light of subsequent events.

Maori reserve lands, with the exception of lands under occupation and cultivation, were controlled and administered by the land commissioners under the Native Reserves Act 1856. The report of the trustees in 1857 indicates that the owners had no say as to the disposition of their assets. Town sections in Nelson were let for terms of up to twenty-one years at nominal rents. But as the values of sections increased, the trustees proposed, with the sanction of Government, to sell them and invest the money to yield considerable annual revenue to the trust.[26] But the real purpose of the proposed sale was to divest Maori of their tribal patrimony. The trustees reported that they had received applications to purchase the freehold of the leased lands and went on to say that Maori 'should be placed in all respects on the same footing with respect to public lands as Europeans than that they should remain a distinct class with distinct holdings'. Although the 'wastelands' of the South Island had been expropriated by what passed for sales, it was clear from this early report that the reserved lands were not safe from alienation.

The feat of Kemp and Mantell in purchasing vast areas of land in the South Island at nominal prices was matched by Commissioner James Mackay in his purchases of the Kaikoura and Arahura Blocks. Like his colleagues, he also took pride in having granted Maori precipitous and worthless areas of reserve lands. With the sale of Stewart Island in 1863, Ngai Tahu were virtually landless. At the time that Ngai Tahu lands were being alienated, squatters from Australia introduced sheep grazing as a more lucrative pursuit than agriculture. The prosperity in the decades ahead was based on pastoralism. As a landless peasantry Ngai Tahu were unable to participate in that prosperity as settlers flooded into Otago and Canterbury. By 1852 the Otago Association had introduced 2,000 settlers. In Canterbury the Anglican settlement of John Robert Godley brought out 1,512 migrants in eight ships. The settlement soon prospered so that by 1853 it had an exportable surplus of produce. Between 1856 and 1860 the population of Canterbury rose from 6,200 to 15,750.[27] Governor Grey's policy of ignoring Article 2 of the Treaty of Waitangi and Lord Normanby's original instruction to Hobson to purchase only land that the natives could alienate without discomfort or inconvenience to themselves, had impoverished Ngai Tahu. Grey in this instance was clearly the author of colonial dispossession, the very process that the humanitarians did not want repeated in New Zealand. It was all very well for the men at home to propose, but in the final analysis it was the men on the ground who disposed. For the time being, that man was Grey.

Pupuri Whenua

While acquisition of land in the South Island by coercive tactics and broken promises against a handful of tribesmen was readily accomplished, it was a different matter in the more populous North Island. There was greater inertia to overcome, and so colonial spoliation took a little longer. At first the chiefs were willing sellers of land as a means of acquiring material goods brought into the country from metropolitan England. At Whangaruru two chiefs offered to sell a block of land to buy a schooner. At Waitemata the chief Rewiti offered land for £400, four horses, saddles, bridles, 100 blankets, four tents, two casks of tobacco, two boats, ten cloaks, two boxes of candles, one cedar box, ten blue trousers, five bags of flour and five bags of sugar. In the Far North Nopera Panakareao offered land at Maunganui for £8,000, fifty-nine guns, 200 casks of powder, 1,308 articles of dress, twenty bales of blankets, and two casks of tobacco.[28] These applications to sell land occurred before 1845 but were not taken up because the financial resources were not available for the Governor to take advantage of them.

As the city of Auckland flourished, so its perimeter expanded progressively outwards by the purchase of thousands of hectares of land at Mt Smart, Manukau, Maungarei (Mt Wellington), Ramarama, Waiau and Pukekohe. Ponui Island, covering 1,710 hectares, was bought in 1853 from Ngati Paoa for £100. These increments to the Auckland province amounted to 60,401 hectares for a cost of £3,172.[29]

At the time Governor Grey was expanding Auckland boundaries, the country became self-governing under the New Zealand Constitution Act 1852. The Constitution established six provincial councils, a General Assembly, and an Upper House nominated by the Crown. The vote for the General Assembly was based on a small property qualification of freehold land to the value of £50, or leasehold land of £10 in town and £5 in the country. This property qualification effectively disenfranchised most Maori people whose land was still in customary tribal title. The Pakeha population at the time was 30,000, approximately half that of the Maori. When the General Assembly met in 1854, a white minority government was effectively installed in power. The only safeguard for Maori rights was the Governor, who controlled Native Affairs until 1864. This institutionalisation of racism at the inception of democracy in New Zealand was the root cause of the conflict between Maori and Pakeha in the North Island and the colonial spoliation which followed. The first order of business was the struggle to transfer power from the Governor to the Cabinet of Ministers. With the liquidation of the New Zealand Company and the takeover of its assets, the Assembly turned its attention to the purchase of Maori land. Donald McLean, Secretary of the Land Purchase Department, assured the House that he would complete the purchase of the North Island in eight years.[31]

McLean underestimated growing Maori awareness of colonisation by transmigration of surplus population from the United Kingdom. At Wellington one chief, on seeing ships disgorge settlers by the hundred, sat down on the beach and wept. Another chief likened the Maori to a seagull sitting on a reef, who, when the tide came in, would have no place to rest his feet. With no means of asserting an immigration policy over a Parliament in which they had no place, Maori opposition to the endless stream of settlers crystallised around an emerging sense of Maori nationalism. Tribal runanga held meetings at Taranaki, Rotorua and other parts of the country to discuss kotahitanga, unification of tribes.[32] From these meetings emerged the idea of pupuri whenua, withholding land from sale as a means of controlling and slowing down settlement. But in order to bind tribes effectively to the policy of withholding land from the Pakeha, the idea of putting the mana whenua of all tribes under a single person in the office of a Maori king was discussed. Even as these ideas were being generated, sagacious chiefs like Wiremu Tamihana of the Ngati Haua tribe urged Maori admission into mainstream politics.

In 1855 Tamihana sought Maori membership in the House of Representatives. Although he got no encouragement, Tamihana persisted. Two years later he went to Auckland seeking an audience with the Governor to persuade him to establish a Council of Chiefs as a Maori policy-making body to advise the Governor. The provision for this form of home rule was incorporated in Section 71 of the New Zealand Constitution. But the autocratic Governor Grey, who supervised the election of the provincial councils and the General Assembly before departing the scene at the end of 1853, ignored it. While he was at the Native Office, Tamihana was kept waiting as Pakeha who came after him were served first. This insult to his chiefly dignity led to his withdrawal from making further overtures to the Pakeha. Tamihana then turned his considerable talents to the difficult task of electing a Maori king. The crown had already been rejected by the paramount chiefs Te Kani a Takirau of the East Coast and Te Heuheu of Taupo. The Ngapuhi chiefs in the North had also declined the invitation from a Waikato deputation to support the King Movement.[33] The Hawke's Bay chiefs did not support the movement either, nor did the chiefs of Taranaki.

Tamihana was not dismayed by the lack of unity. Early in 1857 he wrote to all the Waikato tribes proposing the aged paramount chief Te Wherowhero as king. In April a meeting was held at Rangiriri, where Tamihana stated he wanted a king to provide law and order. He felt the Governor had neglected to provide it in Maori districts, and bloodletting continued as before. Te Heuheu also spoke at that meeting, citing grievances against the Pakeha as sufficient reason for separation of the races. These included indignities suffered by chiefs from lower-class whites, the debauching of Maori women, the trade in liquor and the Pakeha's habit of calling them 'bloody Maoris'.[34] There was some substance to Tamihana's criticism of the Governor's failure to provide law and order. For the first twenty years government revenue was spent on Pakeha settlements. Some of the most populous tribal districts, such as Hokianga, Kaipara, Taupo and the East Cape, had no resident magistrates. But the grievances of the chiefs were symptoms of a deeper failing on the part of the Governor to fulfil the guarantee of rangatiratanga under the Treaty by the inclusion of the chiefs in the machinery of state. The chiefs had no alternative but to establish their own institutions to protect their land.

Te Wherowhero was installed as the Maori king at Ngaruawahia in April 1858, and he adopted the title Potatau I. The tribes present proclaimed him saying, 'Stand thou, o King Potatau Te Wherowhero, as a mana for man; for the land; to stop the flow of blood, to hold the peace between one man and another, between one chief and another chief. The King and the Queen to be joined in concord.'[35] Potatau then proclaimed the boundary separating his authority from that of the

Governor, saying, 'Let Maungatautari be our boundary. Do not encroach on this side. Likewise I am not to set foot on that side.' What Potatau envisaged was a conjoint administration with the King ruling in territory still under Maori customary title while the Governor ruled on lands acquired by the Crown. The King's emblem, Te Paki o Matariki, the widespread calm of the Pleiades, proclaimed peaceful coexistence, while the motto 'Mana Motuhake' signified Maori independence and self-determination. That same year the Pakeha population of 59,000 surpassed the Maori population of 56,000,[36] a fact that was not lost on either race as relationships between them became more polarised over the Pakeha desire to possess the land and Maori determination to retain what remained. Even before numerical superiority had been attained, the Auckland Provincial Council anticipated expanding its territory into the fertile lands of the Waikato. The kingdom of Potatau was in grave danger.

Eventually, it was the resentment which had festered for years among the 2,500 settlers on the original 1,400 hectares awarded to the New Zealand Company at New Plymouth that touched off the Land Wars. They saw no reason why 4,000 Maori in Taranaki should be allowed to own 800,000 hectares. In one of his dispatches Governor Gore Browne wrote that the Maori had far more lands than they needed and the Europeans were determined to get them '*recte si possint, si non quocunque modo*', correctly if possible, if not then by any means.[37] Wiremu Kingi, who had reoccupied his tribal lands at Waitara, steadfastly resisted pressure from Donald McLean to sell his land. Governor Browne, who was not as well versed in Maori affairs as his predecessor, readily believed rumours that Maori wanting to sell land were being intimidated by a pupuri whenua land league. Early in 1859 he announced that any individual who wished to sell land would be able to sell as an individual without the consent of chiefs. This radical departure from standard practice of gaining the consensus of tribe was wrong. The original proponent of this idea was the Taranaki land purchase commissioner, J. C. Richmond, who urged the necessity to secure Waitara lands for a township. Richmond suggested cutting through the impasse at Waitara by individualisation of Maori land. The Governor's announcement to this effect allowed a minor chief named Teira to go against the authority of his senior, Wiremu Kingi. This undermining of Kingi's rangatiratanga contravened Article 2 of the Treaty and it was the consummate application of the colonial strategy of divide and rule. The Governor accepted Teira's offer to sell the Pekapeka Block at Waitara and agreed to partition the land. Kingi had no alternative but to assert his right by preparing to defend his land.

The Taranaki Land War

Matters came to a head at Waitara in 1860. When the survey began, Kingi sent out old men and women to disrupt it by pulling out the survey pegs, but they were not arrested. Richmond, who was now Provincial Superintendent, declared the aim was 'not to convict a parcel of women and old men of a misdemeanour but to provoke the chiefs to fight . . . to bring the contumacy of the natives up to the point of actual defiance of the Government, i.e., High Treason.'[38] The morality of provoking an unjust war was set aside by Richmond's supremacist notions of European superiority over Maori, whom he was wont to dismiss in private as 'niggers'. In February, Governor Browne declared martial law as the 'means' by which the colonising power would have its way. Waitara was occupied by troops and Kingi's pa Te Kohia attacked without success. Wiremu Kingi, who had not supported the election of a king, then sought an alliance with the King Movement. The Kingitanga responded by sending a party of volunteers to assist him. In June an attacking force of 350 troops was repulsed at Puketakauere. The Battle of Puketakauere, like that at Ohaeawai, was one of the three most decisive defeats suffered by Imperial troops in New Zealand.[39] It was an omen that a warrior race trained for warfare should not be taken lightly. The British were thrown on the defensive and, fearing an attack on New Plymouth, evacuated non-combatants.

The Governor knew that the Imperial Army was not capable of fighting a general uprising of the tribes. As the situation in Taranaki deteriorated, he decided to test tribal opinion. He then convened a meeting of 200 chiefs at Kohimarama in July 1860, ostensibly to discuss the Treaty of Waitangi. Wiremu Kingi, whom the Governor was attempting to isolate, was not invited. Nor was the Maori King. The rangatiratanga of chiefs who were obstacles to acquisition of land was set aside again by the well-tried colonial strategy of divide and rule.

At the opening of the meeting the Governor restated the humanitarian ideals embodied in the Treaty and expatiated on how well treated Maori were. The Treaty was their promissory note of racial equality. At the same time he issued a veiled threat, referring to the 7000 fresh troops that had landed in Taranaki from Australia. Any act violating allegiance to the Crown would negate the rights of British citizenship under the Treaty.

The implications were not lost on the chiefs. Tamihana Te Rauparaha urged affirmation of the Treaty 'as a cover for our heads'. At the end of the first week Donald McLean again emphasised the protective promise of the Treaty as being relevant to all tribes, not just Ngapuhi. The conference went on for four weeks as McLean sought to fathom the Maori mind, whether those present would side with Wiremu Kingi or the Maori King in the event of war. The month-long discussions culminated in a fuller understanding of the meaning of the Treaty by the southern chiefs. In the last week Paora Tuhaere proposed that the Treaty should be endorsed by the Kohimarama Conference as a 'fuller ratification'. The resolution passed in the final session of the conference stated:[40]

> That this conference takes cognisance of the fact that the several chiefs, members thereof are pledged to each other to do nothing inconsistent with their declared recognition of the Queen's sovereignty, and the union of the two races, also to discountenance all proceedings tending to a breach of the covenant here solemnly entered into by them.[40]

Likening the Treaty to a covenant added spiritual overtones that in the religiosity of the Maori made it even more morally binding than the original signing of their ancestors. The Maori were too trusting. There was no reciprocal promise extracted from the Governor to abide by the Treaty. But the Maori affirmation of the Treaty at Kohimarama gave the Government the endorsement it wanted. As the Taranaki war dragged on indecisively, with reinforcements from the Waikato assisting Wiremu Kingi, the Governor issued an ultimatum in May the following year demanding the King Movement submit to the sovereignty of the Queen. It was the act of a desperate man. The army had failed to deliver him a decisive victory; the war was at a stalemate. The Ngati Ruanuku occupied European land at Tataraimaka which they refused to give up until Waitara was returned. The King's Council replied by declaring their policy. They would not sell any more land to the Government, and they would end their neutrality if Kingi's lands at Waitara were subject to survey.

Governor Browne's days were numbered. One hundred and seventy chiefs from the East Coast had petitioned the Queen for a commission of inquiry. They wrote: 'Mother do not listen to the false reports which, perhaps, are sent to you. They are false. Know then that the quarrel relates to the land only. We think it desirable that you should appoint a judge for this quarrel that it may be put an end to.'[41] Bishop

Selwyn also argued the right of the Maori for a tribunal to investigate the dispute, but he was ignored.

The Chief Justice, Sir William Martin, wrote a pamphlet on the Taranaki Question. He argued that it was not lawful for the Government to use force in a civil question without the authority of a judicial tribunal. In the Taranaki dispute no tribunal was consulted and no authority to use force issued.[42] Sir William Martin went so far as to remind the Government of its obligations under the Treaty of Waitangi. He argued that Maori were subjects of the Crown and had to be dealt with as such because the Treaty of Waitangi guaranteed them all the rights and privileges of British subjects. No judicial inquiry was held. In the historic process of colonisation of the indigenous people, cupidity and land-hunger suspended the moral judgment of the Government. For his part, the Governor was remiss in the discharge of his fiduciary obligations as the remaining constitutional protector of Maori rights under the Treaty, simply because he allowed himself to be misled by his advisors. The traditions of British justice did not apply to Maori because the coloniser resorted to pseudo-speciation, the mental process whereby the humanity of the intended victim of exploitation was denied. At the outbreak of the war the *Taranaki Herald* wrote: 'We are at liberty at any time and place to do our best to extirpate them as [we should] any other animals of a wild and ferocious nature. Their lives and land are forfeit.'[43] These sanguine words could only have been uttered by settlers who knew full well that they had the might of the British Empire to back them. They were not wrong. For the second time the colony was in trouble. Governor Browne, like FitzRoy, was removed and Grey returned in September 1861 for his second term of office.

CHAPTER 7

Ka Whawhai Tonu Matou

When he returned to New Zealand for his second term, Governor Grey did not have the freedom to act swiftly as he had on his first tour of duty. He had to contend with a Cabinet of Ministers bent on exercising their powers of 'Responsible Government', especially in the control of Maori affairs. Control in this area would facilitate access to Maori land and its transfer to settlers. As early as 1856, Whitaker, Searle and Richmond sent a memorandum to Governor Gore Browne stating their desire to exercise control over the officers of Native Affairs so that as 'Responsible Ministers' they could advise His Excellency. They were opposed to the Governor taking advice from the chiefs, as that would in their view create an 'independent establishment' which excluded themselves, the advisors appointed by the Constitution.[1] The thought never occurred to them that the power they sought excluded the chiefs, who were their equivalents in the tribal polities of the Maori. But the Governor was equally determined as the ministers that Maori affairs would remain an Imperial responsibility. He appointed Donald McLean Secretary of Native Affairs and soon after formalised the Secretary's office into a kind of government department.[2] But ministers got their way by restricting money they voted to Native Affairs to purposes they approved.

For Grey, the situation had changed irrevocably. Beside the ministers, there was Donald McLean, whom he had appointed Chief Land Purchase Commissioner and who was now Secretary of Native Affairs as well. This combination of roles was a disaster for the Maori people because the department's policy was driven by McLean's primary role as Land Purchase Commissioner. In pursuit of that goal he was not above manipulating a situation to achieve his ends. As Secretary of Native Affairs he should have advised Governor Browne that his decision to buy Teira's land at Waitara as individual property was wrong. He did not, and so he was just as culpable as the Governor and his ministers for precipitating the Taranaki war, which Grey had to deal with. The suspension of hostilities by a truce earlier in the year before he arrived at least gave Grey time to resume the reins of power and generate policies that might retrieve the situation. To this end he managed to get the ministers to give him a free hand in Native Affairs.

Home Rule through Runanga

Governor Grey's task was made more difficult by the fact that his influence with the chiefs had diminished compared to his first term. They distrusted him because they remembered how he had exercised a pre-emptive strike against Te Rangihaeata and arrested Te Rauparaha without cause. The chiefs Tamati Waka Nene and Te Wherowhero whom he had consulted in the past were dead, thus exposing the fragility of his system of personal rule. He had left no official mechanism for the exercise of rangatiratanga in the government of the country. Belatedly he set about repairing that deficiency by establishing a system of district runanga. The plan envisaged twenty districts, each under a Pakeha commissioner. The runanga were to deal with parochial issues such as cattle trespass, sanitation, land disputes, alcohol, roads and schools, and to make recommendations on appropriate laws pertaining to these matters to the Governor.[3] Members of the runanga were to be paid a small salary to act as magistrates in their own areas.

The runanga were partially successful in the North, where the tribes were relatively homogeneous. But elsewhere their application was flawed by their imposition over the existing structure of chiefly rank, and the drawing up of districts without reference to tribal boundaries. This failing was derived from the colonial mind-set, whereby the colonisers deemed it their right to decide on behalf of the colonised how they should be governed. Chiefs who were invited to join runanga regarded it as their right to be there to exercise their rangatiratanga. But chiefs who were left out ignored or disparaged the runanga. This failure to govern and administer in terms of the guarantee of rangatiratanga under Article 2 of the Treaty of Waitangi was to bedevil Maori policy well into the next century. In the south there was no hope of uniting former enemy tribes such as Te Arawa, Ngati Awa and Ngaiterangi into a single runanga.[4]

In territories under the influence of the King Movement, there was suspicion that Grey's plan was an attempt to undermine the King by enmeshing his followers as auxiliaries in the Governor's service.[5] Indeed, John Gorst's appointment as magistrate in the Waikato was seen as an attempt to erode the position of the Maori King.[6] Despite a resolution by the King's council that they would adopt the Governor's plan and work for the common good if he allowed the King and his flag to stand, there was no move on the part of the Governor to accommodate that proposal. Grey prejudiced his own plans at the outset when he went to Taupiri in December 1861 to meet with the Waikato chiefs. There he made it clear that he expected the chiefs to come under his administration. When he was asked directly his views on the King, Grey said, 'I do not care about him; but I think it is a thing that will lead to trouble. It will be stopped by such means as I have adopted, and will die out.'[7] Early in 1863 the Governor repeated his opposition to the King when he said to Tamihana, 'I shall not fight against him with the sword, but I shall dig around him till he falls of his own accord.'[8] Digging around the King meant seducing chiefs away from him by paying those who worked for the Governor's runanga. Grey's institutions could have succeeded if they had been worked through the King's organisation and not conceived as an anti-King device.[9] Grey had misjudged the depth of commitment to the Maori King in the Waikato as the symbol of emerging Maori nationalism.

Although he denied he would use the sword against the King, Governor Grey made preparations for war by building a military road south towards the heartland of the Waikato. The chiefs in the King Movement responded by warning Grey that if the road crossed the Mangatawhiri River, they would regard it as a violation of their territory and therefore a cause for war. They also declared they would support Wiremu Kingi in the dispute at Waitara.

In March 1863 Grey moved to settle the Taranaki question by sending in troops to reoccupy Tataraimaka while at the same time conducting an inquiry into Waitara. His despatch to the Duke of Newcastle concluded that 'the Natives are in the main right in their allegations regarding the Waitara purchase, and that it ought not to be gone on with'.[10] He expressed the hope that his 'Responsible Advisers' would adopt his opinion and act upon it. But they were too dilatory. In the meantime Rewi Maniapoto, the warrior chief of the Ngati Maniapoto tribe within the King Movement, sent word to the people in Taranaki to reopen the fighting in view of the Government's occupation of Tataraimaka without settling Waitara first. The truce in Taranaki ended on 4 May with a skirmish in which nine soldiers were killed at Oakura near Tataraimaka. A month later General Cameron won a slightly larger skirmish with 870 troops defeating a party of warriors at Katikara.[11] This win was grossly exaggerated as the opposing force numbered only fifty warriors of whom twenty-four were killed. But it was sufficient for public consumption as a victory in the Taranaki war. In effect, Grey ended the conflict, in a campaign where the army was unable to pin down the enemy and deliver a decisive victory. He renounced the Waitara purchase on 11 May. This enabled him to withdraw most of the troops and send them north to Auckland in preparation for an invasion of the Waikato.

Invasion of Waikato

Grey's attempt at extending the Crown's dominion over the Waikato by drawing the tribes into his system of indirect rule did not accomplish his primary objective. But it did give him time to redirect his military strength from Taranaki to the Waikato to remove the King as the major obstacle to colonisation of the central portion of the North Island. Grey pursued both a 'peace policy' and a 'war policy' simultaneously, knowing full well that assertion of sovereignty would ultimately have to be accomplished by force of arms. It is difficult to avoid the conclusion that Grey planned the Waikato war well in advance.[12] An invasion of the Waikato had already been mooted as early as April 1861 by the Attorney-General, Frederick Whitaker, to Governor Browne. Whitaker and his partner Thomas Russell, who founded the Bank of New Zealand, had plans for agricultural investment in the Waikato. These two were the prime movers in the abolition of the Crown monopoly in the purchase of land and were responsible for formulating the policy of confiscating large areas of Maori land. As Cabinet ministers they secured a loan through their own bank of £3 million in 1863 for 'defence purposes' and stood to profit from the promotion of an invasion of the Waikato. As Minister of Defence, Russell himself supervised the spending of the loan.[13]

Grey justified his invasion of the Waikato to the Imperial Government on the grounds of conducting a punitive expedition against Rewi Maniapoto for his part in the Taranaki campaign. He also tried to compose a proclamation of war to the Waikato people that would satisfy the designs of the Government on Waikato land without drawing criticism from the Aborigines Protection Society in England.[14] Before the proclamation was issued, General Cameron's forces invaded the Waikato on 12 July 1863. By the time the General Assembly met in October, unfounded rumour of a Maori invasion of Auckland was used to justify the pre-emptive strike by the Imperial Army. Whitaker characterised it as a 'struggle for the possession of

Auckland'. The Governor declared that the Waikato tribes planned 'indiscriminate slaughter' of the Europeans. The ministers claimed that Parliament would be justified in adopting measures of 'exceptional severity' to rid the colony of such a menace.[15] This self-seeking propaganda was reinforced by the papers of the day indulging in jingoistic rhetoric. The *Southern Cross* characterised the Waikato people as 'blood-thirsty murderers', saying, 'there is only one way of meeting this, and that is by confiscation and the sword . . . the natives have forced it upon us . . . At the very least large tracts of their lands must be the penalty.'[16] Thus was an unjust war, which ran counter to the promises entered into by the Crown under Articles 2 and 3 of the Treaty of Waitangi, rationalised and moral conscience suspended. The Governor, politicians and the press, working in concert, prepared the social climate which silenced men of conscience while the General Assembly passed repressive legislation.

The ground for the introduction of oppressive legislation was carefully prepared by the 'Responsible Ministers', who, within three weeks of the invasion of Waikato, sent Governor Grey a memorandum signed by Alfred Domett.[17] The ministers argued that the Waikato, the most powerful tribe in New Zealand, aimed to drive out or destroy the Europeans and establish a native kingdom. The security of the colony demanded that their aggression needed to be punished by a decisive and conclusive end to the war. They proposed the introduction of an armed population from the goldfields of Australia and Otago to be located on land taken from the 'enemy'. Governor Grey's despatch to the Duke of Newcastle a month later set out the details of the plan.[18] It envisaged bringing in 5,000 men as military settlers on twenty-hectare blocks taken from tribes 'now in arms against the Government'. The imputation of rebellion was made even more explicit by Grey's unfounded claim that 'the chiefs of Waikato having in so unprovoked a manner caused Europeans to be murdered, and having planned a wholesale destruction of some of the European settlements, it will be necessary now to take efficient steps for the permanent security of the country'. These included the making of roads throughout the land to connect the military settlements, thus allowing for the rapid deployment of the military forces, and thereby keeping the peace by holding the tribes in awe.

Grey ensured he would gain Imperial concurrence to the plan to confiscate land by concluding that he could devise no other plan that would ensure peace and security in the colony. In a subsequent memorandum he was careful to minimise the effect of confiscation so as to allay potential misgivings in the Colonial Office.[19] He argued that since there were only 3,355 natives residing on the fertile lands of the Waikato, to leave to these natives 200,000 hectares when they cultivated only 6,000 hectares was more than they needed. It was, he said, three times more per head compared to what was to be given to military settlers. The estimated cost of Grey's scheme was £3.5 million. This amount was to be borrowed against 'an Estate so rich in undeveloped resources' that it was 'not only prudent but the simple duty' of those who had the management of it to proceed with development. The loan, of which £1 million was set aside for the cost of the war and the balance to bring in settlers and build roads, was 'to be paid for out of the proceeds of the lands of the tribes at open war with us' wrote Grey to his Imperial masters.[20] This was the supreme irony of the situation of the Waikato tribes. They were to pay for the settlement and development of their lands by its expropriation in a war for the extension of the Crown's sovereignty into their territory, and the achievement of the predatory designs of capitalist investors like Russell and Whitaker.

Legislative steps needed to implement Grey's plan were passed by Parliament. The first measure was the Suppression of Rebellion Act promoted by Russell, the Minister of Defence. The Act gave ministers power to detain without trial persons believed to be taking part in rebellion, and to delegate to military courts power to imprison or kill without proclamation of martial law. The second measure was the New Zealand Settlements Act 1863, which gave the ministers power to confiscate the whole of any district where a considerable number of natives 'were believed to be in rebellion'.

For Grey, the primary purpose for the invasion of the Waikato was the assertion of his mana and the Crown's sovereignty by toppling the King. For the Government it was a war to take land by conquest, thinly disguised by the veneer of law-making in a Parliament where Maori people had no representation. At the time that this conquest was undertaken, the Crown had acquired by purchase only 2.8 million hectares of land in the North Island. The Waikato was the testing ground to see whether the 7.6 million hectares still in Maori ownership could be wrested from them by force for Pakeha settlement.

General Cameron's invasion of the Waikato was hampered by forest terrain, ambushes and minor harassing attacks on his supply lines. The fluid guerrilla tactics adopted by the Maori made it difficult to end the war quickly by a single decisive victory. As he advanced, Cameron was forced to secure the ground behind him by patrols, escorts and redoubts, which tied up three-quarters of his forces.[21] The logistics of keeping his supply and communication lines open blunted his capacity to attack. It took Cameron four months before he attacked the first major Waikato defence line at Meremere, held by a garrison of 1,500 men. According to Saunders' account of the Battle of Mere-mere,[22] Cameron halted when he saw the defences of the pa and demanded more military matériel. The Government willingly sup-plied it in expectation of a decisive triumph of British arms over the natives. It took 1,500 cart-horses, at a cost of £100 each, over three months to bring up the extra equipment and provisions for his army, which had swollen to 8,000 men. On 31 October, Cameron positioned an assault party of 612 men to attack the pa from the rear and another to attack from the flank. For fifteen weeks the defenders observed these elaborate preparations from the safety of their fort, knowing full well what the enemy was doing. Having put Cameron to all that trouble, they thwarted his desire for victory by simply abandoning the pa and escaping by canoe up the Maramarua and Whangamarino creeks. The next day 500 troops took possession of the pa, which con-sisted of trenches and rifle pits extending over forty hectares. These holes in the ground, intrinsically worthless to their owners, were expensively purchased by the Crown at a cost of £500,000.

The Battle of Rangiriri

After retreating from Meremere, the Waikato tribes under the leader-ship of Wiremu Tamihana of the Ngati Haua dug in at Rangiriri only twenty kilometres up river. There, 500 men were given the impossible task of defending a front of 1,000 metres from an integrated series of rifle pits, trenches and a central redoubt between the Waikato River and Lake Waikare. On 20 November, Cameron advanced on them with four gunboats, two Armstrong guns, and 1,300 men.[23] The line was easily breached by the attackers. The defenders responded by con-centrating their defence in the central redoubt. The low silhouette of the redoubt made it look disarmingly innocuous, but it had a wide deep ditch and a high parapet. Its terraces had double and even triple firing lines, and inside were deep artillery-proof bunkers.[24]

The redoubt was the key to the defence system of Rangiriri. Once inside it, the defenders were much more formidable. They repulsed three assaults, inflicting 110 casualties on the British. The troops spent a miserable night feeling disheartened at their heavy losses and failure to take the redoubt. But in effect, the battle was over. Fortifications like Rangiriri and Meremere were not provisioned for long sieges. During the night some of the leaders, including Tamihana, slipped away under escort in an organised evacuation. The next morning the remaining 183 occupants of the redoubt hoisted a white flag of truce, expecting to talk terms with Cameron. But instead, the troops tumbled into their trenches, shook hands and mingled with them. When the general arrived twenty minutes later, it was too late to talk. He demanded the surrender of the defenders' arms, to which the remaining chiefs agreed. Belich concludes that the British, and General Cameron in particular, took unscrupulous advantage of the flag of truce, one of the most widely recognised conventions of war, to claim a victory by unconditional surrender.[25]

The defenders lost only thirty-six warriors and five women and children at Rangiriri. Their gallant defence of their position in repelling an Imperial army deserved a better fate than to be treated as a defeat by the coloniser's propaganda. But the real blow to the Waikato was the loss of 180 men who were taken into captivity. This they could ill afford in a conflict against an Imperial standing army that both outnumbered and outgunned them.

After Rangiriri, Wiremu Tamihana sought to end the war. He sent his mere to Cameron as a token of peace and arranged for the occupation of Ngaruawahia, the King's capital, without resistance. But having embarked on a mission of conquest, the 'Responsible Ministers' were determined to continue the war.[26] The troops were ordered to advance into the upper reaches of the Waikato. The Waikato tribes were forced again to defend their territory, at the Paterangi line, just forty kilometres south of Ngaruawahia. The defences consisted of four large fortifications blocking the advance towards Rangiaowhia, the agricultural heartland of the King Movement. The Paterangi line was ready in January 1864, and manned by a garrison of 2,000 men.[27] This was a much more formidable obstacle than Rangiriri. General Cameron decided it could not be taken by assault, so he bypassed it and advanced on Rangiaowhia. This settlement was a secure area behind the Paterangi line where non-combatants had been sent. On Sunday morning, 21 February 1864, while the people of the village were at church, the Forest Rangers and the 65th Regiment mounted an attack.[28] Rifle fire pinned down the congregation inside and the house was set alight. All inside perished, including two daughters of the Arawa chief Kereopa Te Rau.[29] Kereopa subsequently sought fierce vengeance for this atrocity of war.

After they were bypassed by Cameron's army, the garrison of the

Paterangi line disbanded to return to their homes. The strategic position was as indecisive as when the Waikato war began. The Waikato strength was still intact though dispersed, and the army, for all its numerical superiority and firepower, had not delivered the crushing victory expected by the 'Responsible Ministers'. In the meantime Governor Grey received a communication from the Aborigines Protection Society, expressing concern at the turn of events in the colony. The society urged Grey to accept overtures of peace from the natives and expressed alarm at proposals to confiscate land, as it would 'shut the door to any possibility of settlement of the difficulty except by the sword'. The society warned, 'We can conceive of no surer means of adding fuel to the flames of war; of extending the area of disaffection; and of making the Natives fight with a madness of despair, than a policy of confiscation.'[30]

The reply of the 'Responsible Ministers' signed by William Fox bears mute testimony to the truism that the first casualty in war is truth itself. The ministers denied the tribes had asked for peace. They argued that the tribes believed they could drive the Europeans out of the country and begin the war by a desperate attack upon Auckland. They accused Tamihana, the leader of the 'rebels', of writing in his own hand his determination to carry the war to the utmost extremity, not even sparing unarmed persons. The ministers claimed:[31]

> Acting in this spirit, the Maori threw themselves into the heart of the settled districts of the Province of Auckland, murdering and destroying the settlers within 17 miles [27 kilometres] of the town . . . So sudden was their onslaught, and so completely did they succeed in getting possession of the country close around Auckland, that it was not until after the fall of Rangiriri, five months at least after the struggle commenced that they were driven back and routed out of the wooded ranges.

This memorandum was signed by Fox on 5 May, a month after the war in the Waikato had ended at the Battle of Orakau.

The Battle of Orakau

After the occupation of Rangiaowhia, Rewi Maniapoto and his people decided to continue the struggle in defence of their tribal lands. On his way north to confer with Tamihana on strategy, he met up with Tuhoe and Ngati Raukawa warriors withdrawing from Paterangi. These men persuaded Rewi to fight the British at Orakau, otherwise they would have carried their weapons and ammunition a long way for nothing.[32] Against his better judgment, Rewi dug in with them at Orakau. The site of the fort had no escape route and could easily be surrounded. As a place to challenge the British, Orakau was a trap. Rewi knew it when he warned his allies that if they insisted on making a stand there, they would die and he alone would live. On 20 March, Brigadier General Carey surrounded Orakau with 1,000 men.

With reinforcements bringing his strength up to 2,000, Carey was emboldened enough to chance his arm against the 300 defenders inside the redoubt. Before General Cameron arrived, Carey mounted three frontal assaults on Orakau. They were all repulsed. When Cameron arrived to take command, he sent a messenger to the defenders calling on them to surrender. The defiant response came back: 'Ka whawhai tonu ahau ki a koe, ake, ake, ake.' I shall fight you forever, and ever, and ever.[33] When the battle was renewed, the defenders were in dire straits. They were short of both water and ammunition and were reduced to firing sharpened sticks and peach stones. Despite these difficulties, they repulsed a further two assaults.

Late in the afternoon of 2 April, the third day of the siege, the garrison abandoned Orakau and broke through the encircling troops. This remarkable military feat was accomplished by the warriors forming a solid body with their women, children and chiefs in the centre. The warriors fought their way through the weakest point of the cordon of soldiers and then split up to escape through the swamps. It was at this stage that they suffered their heaviest casualties at the hands of the Forest Rangers who hunted them down. There were eighty Maori killed and forty wounded. The British lost sixteen men killed and and fifty-three wounded, some mortally.[34] The Maori saw Orakau as a defeat, but for the British, it was not the crushing victory they had anticipated. Rewi and at least half of his men had escaped.

Although the lower Waikato was occupied, the rest of the country was not about to submit. Ngati Maniapoto and their allies Ngati Haua and Ngati Raukawa simply regrouped behind another defence line known as the aukati, the closed boundary which indicated their readiness to resist further invasion. The strong fortifications behind the aukati meant that subjugation of the tribes by military conquest was no nearer to resolution than when the campaign began. Land behind the aukati remained native territory and subsequently came to be known as the King Country.

Cameron turned his attention to the Bay of Plenty tribes, particularly Ngaiterangi, who had assisted the Waikato people in their resistance to the British. The extension of Pakeha control into the King

Country was postponed for another time when more subtle colonial techniques could be brought to bear.

The Battle of Gate Pa

On 21 April, General Cameron moved his headquarters to Tauranga to direct the attack a week later against 230 warriors of the Ngaiterangi tribe who had entrenched themselves at Pukehinahina, otherwise known as Gate Pa. This pa was a deceptively innocuous-looking trap sited on a neck of land 300 metres wide and surrounded by tidal swamps.[35] From external observation its defences were not insurmountable, but the pa was honeycombed with numerous small anti-artillery bunkers and covered walkways.

Cameron had at his disposal 1,700 troops. But before committing them to assault the pa he subjected it to heavy artillery bombardment with one 110-pound Armstrong gun, two 40-pound Armstrongs, two 6-pound Armstrongs, two 24-pound Howitzers, two 200 mm mortars, and six coharu mortars.[36] After a breach had been made in the defences, Cameron presumed that the rain of lead and shrapnel had debilitated the garrison enough for the pa to be taken by storm. That was his one mistake in what had hitherto been a meticulously prepared battle plan. Only fifteen defenders had been killed by all that firepower; the rest sat out the bombardment in the safety of their underground bunkers. The assault party of 300 men supported by 500 in reserve made it to the centre of the redoubt against only light resistance from the defenders, but at that point they were in the killing ground carefully prepared for them by the chief Rawiri Puhirake. Suddenly the earth erupted with fire from around them and under their feet as the defenders opened up at point-blank range from their underground bunkers. A hundred men were killed in this cauldron of fire, and with no chance to retaliate against an enemy they could not see, the survivors fled in disarray, much to the chagrin of their general. This defeat of an Imperial army at the hands of natives whom Europeans disdained as an inferior race was preordained by the conduct of Maori warfare.[37] In their prosecution of the New Zealand Wars, the British showed they had not profited from their adverse experiences at the battles of Ohaeawai in the North, Puketakauere in Taranaki and Rangiriri in the Waikato.

Belich[38] attributed the ability of the tribes to resist a standing army, which over the course of the conflict involved 18,000 troops, to the flexibility of their military strategy. Earthwork fortresses had no intrinsic value; each was constructed for a one-off battle and then abandoned. After a battle, warriors returned home to their tribes to attend to their domestic affairs. In the meantime a new fortified position was prepared and fresh warriors moved in to invite the British to attack them. They obliged time after time, sustaining losses yet believing they were making progress as they took fortresses evacuated by the defenders who lived to fight another day. British faith in the efficacy of heavy artillery, the strategy of bombardment and the *coup de main* by frontal assault was not blunted by their experiences. That faith, combined with belief in their own superiority, led them to their defeat at Gate Pa. The canons of Maori warfare threaded through Maori myth, traditions and history ordained their victory at the outset. The basic principles, although simple, provide a coherent philosophy of war that seems to have been singularly lacking on the British side. The enemy has the capacity to kill, therefore show him the respect that is his due by discovering his strength and neutralising it. Thereafter the battle plan was arranged to maximise survival for the defenders and death for the enemy. The invention of earthworks, trenches, covered walkways and bomb-proof shelters provided those conditions. British reliance on numerical superiority, and a willingness to take casualties in storming an objective, was such a crude and transparent tactic, that time and again Maori leaders were able to thwart them by their more subtle approach to the arts of war.[39]

For Cameron, the defeat at Gate Pa was a salutary experience. He realised that continuance of the campaign against strong Maori fortifications was a futile exercise in expending the lives of British soldiers to acquire land for the Government. He abandoned the campaign and withdrew the bulk of his forces to Auckland, leaving Colonel Greer and a small occupationary force to hold the line at Tauranga.[40] The defeat was equally unpalatable for Governor Grey, who was caught between the punitive demands of the Government to confiscate large areas of land to pay for the war, and the Imperial Government's insistence that British troops should be used only for the defence and security of settlers.[41] Furthermore, the Secretary of State for the Colonies, Edward Cardwell, attempted to dissuade Grey from confiscating land. Instead he suggested that the defeated chiefs be persuaded to make voluntary cessions of land as part of the process of peace-making.[42] This combination of factors disposed Grey to discuss peace negotiations with neutral tribes.

Grey's task of making peace with honour was facilitated by the defeat of Ngaiterangi at Te Ranga in June, when Colonel Greer attacked them before they completed digging their fortifications. Although the British lost fifty-two men killed and wounded to Ngaiterangi's sixty-eight killed and twenty-seven wounded, Te Ranga was promulgated as a victory that made amends for the discomfiture of British arms at Gate Pa. Peace was made on terms that were acceptable to Ngaiterangi — a cession of a quarter of their lands — otherwise they were quite capable of continuing resistance. Thus was the Waikato war officially brought to an end. But against Cardwell's advice to abandon confiscation under the 1863 Settlements Act, Grey and his ministers proceeded with the confiscations.

The injustices that provoked the Land Wars were not readily forgotten, especially when the tribes that defended their lands were penalised by confiscations as well. Over 1.2 million hectares of land were confiscated in Taranaki, Tauranga, Waikato and the Bay of Plenty. The end result was the extension of the Crown's hegemony into these districts, but the rest of the country remained unconquered. The tribes still held 6.4 million hectares of land in the North Island to the Crown's acquisitions of 2.8 million hectares by purchase and 1.2 million hectares by confiscation. Only 640,000 hectares was actually taken at the time of the confiscation; the rest was returned to the owners and 'purchased' later at the barrel of the gun.

For the Pakeha, the Maori had proved to be a much more formidable military obstacle to the acquisition of land by conquest than anticipated. With the confinement of British troops to a defensive role, the Government was incapable of taking those lands by military means. Other, more sophisticated methods than the blunt instrument of war had to be devised to get those remaining hectares. For Governor Grey, the Land Wars served the egotistical purpose of asserting his dominion over the Maori King by smashing his military power and nationalistic claim to be coequal with the Governor. But confiscation of 360,000 hectares of fertile Waikato land was a much more serious blow to the King than military defeat. It crippled the Waikato people for the next sixty years, and for twenty years after the war King Tawhiao lived in exile among his Maniapoto kin.[43] For a time he looked in hope towards the new prophets that arose to continue the struggle without end as promulgated by the battle cry at Orakau: that the Maori would fight on forever and ever and ever.

The Prophets

Loss of mana, military invasion, and loss of land by creeping confiscation were the most obvious effects of colonisation. In order to counter the inroads that the Pakeha had made by surveying the land and inserting military settlers there, prophets arose as new leaders to unify the tribes against their common oppressor. Unity across tribal divisions was to be achieved through the mystical power of religion. The first religious cult that portended the collision between the two cultures of Maori and Pakeha was the cult of Papahurihia, which emerged in the Hokianga area in the 1830s. The cult worshipped Te Atua Wera, the Fiery God, and designated its followers as Hurai, or Jews.[44] The cult was anti-missionary. Its identification with Jews indicated that Papahurihia saw the Maori as having more in common with the Israelites than with their Protestant religious mentors.

The first overtly anti-Pakeha religious cult, founded by the prophet Te Ua Haumene, arose in Taranaki, where the Land Wars began. Te Ua had fought beside Wiremu Kingi in the war and realised that something more than military prowess was needed to counter a standing army with superior numbers and weapons. Te Ua gained a reputation as a man of mana when the wreck of the *Lord Worsley* was attributed to his mystical powers of makutu. He communed with his god, Te Atua Pai Marire, the Lord Good and Peaceful, and claimed visitations from the Angel Gabriel, who revealed a vision of Te Ua surrounded by all the tribes. The vision symbolised Te Ua's mission of unification, and his cult, known as Pai Marire (Good and Peaceful), signified the new relationship between tribes. Converts worshipped around a Niu Pole, rigged like the mast of a ship, and expected to be endowed with the gift of tongues and knowledge of science. Followers of the cult were promised that when every tribe was converted and unification achieved, the Pakeha would be conquered. They were also promised immunity to Pakeha bullets if they went into battle crying 'Hapa Pai Marire Hau! Hau!'[45] It was from this battle cry that the Hauhau cult derived its common name. The cult initiated a new kind of guerrilla warfare, which the Secretary of State for Colonial Affairs had warned would be the consequence of confiscation.

The Hauhau Struggle

The Hauhau rebellion began on 6 April 1864, when a company of the 57th Regiment was ambushed. Seven soldiers were killed and twelve wounded. This minor success was taken as a sign that the new religion had divine favour. Among the dead was Captain Lloyd, whose head was smoke-dried and exhibited from village to village to aid the work of recruitment to the Hauhau cause. People flocked to join the new movement and five extra prophets were appointed to speed up the work. One of these was Kereopa Te Rau, who had lost his family at Rangiaowhia. Kereopa blamed missionary complicity in the massacre of women and children at Rangiaowhia, and so he and his followers sought utu against missionaries. In March 1865, when Kereopa and his men reached Opotiki, they captured the Anglican missioner Carl Volkner.

The Hauhau charged Volkner with spying for the Governor, found him guilty then executed him.[46] When Patara arrived a few days later, he too conducted a court against Grace, another missionary held captive by the Hauhau. Although Patara expressed anger against soldiers, clergymen and Englishmen, Grace was not harmed.[47] As a German who had converted from the Lutheran to the Anglican faith and come out to New Zealand, Volkner expressed his insecurity in his adopted country by ingratiating himself with Governor Grey and keeping him informed on Maori activities in his parish. Volkner's execution was correct according to the recognised conventions of war. Despite that, the execution provided the Government with an excuse to exact a rapacious penalty against the Whakatohea tribe. Kereopa was subsequently apprehended and executed along with the local chief Mokomoko, whose rope had been used in the hanging of Volkner. But two lives for one was not sufficient. It mattered not that the perpetrators of Volkner's execution came from elsewhere, the Whakatohea bore the additional unwarranted penalty of confiscation of 69,200 hectares of their land for military settlers.[48]

The most able of the Hauhau military strategists was the Ngati Ruanui chief Titokowaru of Taranaki. At first he tried to resist confiscation by peaceful means, but eventually, as more and more land was taken for settlers, Titokowaru was forced to defend what remained. Titokowaru's fortress was at Te Ngutu o Te Manu, in a forested area of southern Taranaki just north of Waingongoro River. From there, with a small force of eighty men, he conducted a harassing hit-and-run guerrilla campaign against the colonists. Titokowaru's strategy was to goad the Armed Constabulary of the colonial forces into attacking him on his own ground. This they did on 7 September 1868 and were soundly defeated at the Battle of Te Ngutu o te Manu. This battle was not only the death of Von Tempsky, it was also the end of Colonel McDonnell's reputation as the most able commander in the colonists' forces.[49] The defeat coincided with the reading of the financial statement in the House that revenue from confiscated land amounted to only £11,929, while the claims and charges on the land amounted to £54,410.[50] Yet despite the clear evidence that the cost of waging war to acquire land by confiscation was not a sound policy, the Government persisted with it.

In November, Titokowaru defeated McDonnell's successor, Colonel Whitmore, at the battle of Moturoa. Again, the same tactic was used of enticing the enemy to attack him on a battleground of his own choosing, with his pa as the objective used to decoy the enemy into the killing ground. Titokowaru's success affirmed his mana as a new leader, and recruits from other Ngati Ruanui hapu raised his fighting force from the original eighty of his own hapu to 400.[51] Farms were abandoned and a siege mentality fell over the town of Wanganui. Titokowaru was the nightmare realisation of the worst fears of the colonists: the possibility of defeat at the hand of the natives followed by abandonment of the colony.

Te Kooti — Prophet and Freedom Fighter

After the execution of Volkner at Opotiki, the Hauhau rebellion against colonial oppression spread to the East Coast. There, in an engagement at Poverty Bay, Te Kooti Arikirangi Te Turuki, who fought on the government side, was wrongly denounced by one of his opponents as a Hauhau sympathiser. Te Kooti was arrested, detained without trial and shipped off to be imprisoned on the Chatham Islands. On arrival there in 1866 along with 272 prisoners, Te Kooti was reputedly ill and spitting blood, an advanced sign of the deadly illness of tuberculosis. He was put in an isolation hut where he was expected to die. Instead he effected a miraculous recovery. He arose, walked out of his hut and it burst into flame. He announced that the spirit had spoken to him, saying, 'Rise! come forth! you are spared to be made well, to be the founder of a new church and religion, to be the salvation of the Maori people and to release them from bondage.'[52]

The allusion to the Israelites was not lost on the prisoners. They accepted Te Kooti's revelations and the teachings of his Ringatu faith because he held out hope against despair. In July 1868 Te Kooti and his followers overcame their guards and escaped back to the mainland on the captured supply ship *Rifleman*. He landed at Poverty Bay with 163 men, sixty-four women and seventy-one children. Although Te Kooti wanted to live in peace, he was cast in the role of outlaw as government troops pursued him in the longest manhunt in the history of New Zealand, known as 'Te Whai a Te Motu', the Pursuit of the

Island. In the first month after he landed, Te Kooti fought three successful engagements against his pursuers as he made his way inland from Poverty Bay to the safety of the high country. The most important of these fights was against Colonel Whitmore at the Ruakituri River. Although Whitmore's casualties were light, five dead and six wounded, his forced withdrawal was seen as a defeat.[53] But on the west coast the strategic position of the Pakeha had become precarious after Titokowaru's victory at Te Ngutu o te Manu. An overture of peace was made to Te Kooti, which he rejected.[54] For the time being, Te Kooti was left alone as the troops were withdrawn from the East Coast to concentrate on Titikowaru.

Te Kooti's success emboldened him to announce his prophetic mission of struggle against Pakeha domination. He told his followers, 'If you are all strong in faith, God will give the Pakeha and Government into our hands . . . Turanga (Poverty Bay) will be given to us to dwell in.'[55] The hunt for Te Kooti had been instigated by Captain Reginald Biggs, commander of the military settlement built on Te Kooti's ancestral land at Matawhero. Te Kooti went on the offensive on 9 November and attacked Matawhero. In this battle twenty Maori and thirty-four Pakeha were killed, including Biggs. One of the Maori killed was the chief Paratene, who had forced Te Kooti onto the boat as a prisoner for the Chatham Islands.[56] The raid on Matawhero, ostensibly presented as a struggle for liberation, was clearly one of utu against Te Kooti's persecutors.

Thereafter the manhunt for Te Kooti was taken up in earnest. He took refuge in the rugged forest lands of the Urewera, from where he conducted sporadic raids on the East Coast and the Bay of Plenty. The emergence of the new prophet and his exploits spread Te Kooti's fame throughout the land. Recruits from disgruntled tribes augmented his freedom fighters. The mountain dwellers of Tuhoe supported Te Kooti, many of them converting to his Ringatu Church.

Te Kooti suffered a setback to his mana when he was defeated and forced to evacuate his pa at Ngatapa by Colonel Whitmore in January 1869. His Tuhoe supporters were invaded at Maungapohatu and their crops destroyed. Although he suffered another defeat at Te Porere redoubt, beside Mt Tongariro, in October, he eluded his pursuers. A legend took hold around Te Kooti that he had a charmed life. The pursuit and the retaliatory raids continued throughout the following year, but always, it seemed, Te Kooti had advance knowledge of his pursuers. By 1871 the pursuers were getting closer, and Major Ropata Wahawaha, the kupapa auxiliary who dogged Te Kooti's footsteps for three years, built a redoubt at Ruatahuna, the heartland of the prophet's Tuhoe sympathisers. Te Kooti's freedom of movement was hampered further by the rigging of telegraph lines around the Urewera. In 1872 he resorted to the King Country, the last bastion of free Maori land. But the King Country, too, was hemmed in by redoubts and military posts. Battle weary and tired of the chase, Te Kooti on his own admission in 1874 decided to live in peace. After twelve long years the fighting had ended. King Tawhiao made peace with the Government in 1881, and Te Kooti was pardoned in 1883.

Although Te Kooti's war continued to 1872, his defeat at Ngatapa early in 1869 had adverse consequences for Titokowaru's campaign. Colonel Whitmore returned from the East Coast to the Whanganui theatre of war, where he was able to concentrate a force of 1,753 men against Titokowaru, who withdrew from engaging them at his fortification of Taurangaika. His forces dispersed and, like Te Kooti, he became a hunted man. Belich[57] attributes Titokowaru's decline to adultery with the wife of one of his chiefly allies, by which act he defiled his mana tapu, the spiritual source of his prowess in war, and lost the moral support of his warriors. For this reason they deserted him in the hour of battle, an apt fulfilment of the saying 'women and land are the reasons why men perish'. Despite the reverse of his fortunes, Titokowaru was too sagacious to be caught by the hunters, whom he deterred by occasional ambushes. In the end, as he recovered some of his supporters and showed every indication of being able to continue the struggle, he too, was left in peace. Titokowaru had won his battles against the Pakeha, but not the war. All told, the Hauhau had fought 130 engagements against the Pakeha over eight years before it became clear that the clash between the cultures could not be resolved by armed resistance. The wars had ended, but not the struggle.

CHAPTER 8

Te Ana o te Raiona

The colonists were convinced they would ultimately triumph in the New Zealand Wars until they suffered reverses against Te Kooti and Titokowaru in 1868. It was only then that they were assailed with doubt and there was talk of abandoning the colony or sending to Mother England for help. Consequently, when Titokowaru was harried into hiding after Taurangaika and decided to live in peace, the Government left him alone, as he gave every indication that he was capable of continuing armed struggle if it was forced on him. Similarly, when Te Kooti retired from the field, he too was left alone. There was no thought of demanding unconditional surrender as had been the case when the Imperial Army was fighting the war in Waikato on their behalf. But on the original assumption of ultimate victory, Parliament enacted laws that would reap the fruits of triumph even as the war of attrition was taking its toll on the colony as well as wearing the freedom fighters down.

The Native Land Court

The primary objective for which the war had been waged was the assertion of sovereignty and acquisition of land. A more successful instrument for the achievement of both these aims over the 6.4 million hectares still in Maori possession was devised in the institution of the Native Land Court. The first step in its establishment was the Native Land Act 1862. This Act abolished the Crown right of pre-emption and made provision for a Native Land Court to decide the ownership of Maori lands. The aim of the court as defined in the Act was to identify the owners of tribal land and transform communally owned land held under customary title into individual title cognisable in English law, so that Maori ownership would become 'assimilated into British law'.[1] Thus was the ideology of one people enunciated by Hobson, defined as assimilation and incorporated into statute. Since land is the very basis of identity as tangata whenua, this law was to

135

have the most destructive and alienating effect on Maori people.

There was nothing Maori about the Native Land Court, since it was designed for Pakeha purposes of freeing up Maori land from collective ownership and making it available to individual settlers. The court was not constituted until the passing of the Native Land Act 1865 and in the following year the first Chief Judge of the Land Court, Francis Fenton, set 1840 as the time when tribal boundaries became fixed. The 'owners' were then expected to apply to the court for a hearing to grant them 'ownership' in the form of a certificate of title for that which they already owned. But the real purpose of the measure was to facilitate the purchase of land and its sale to settlers. It was so successful that within thirty years four million hectares had been acquired. Transmigration of surplus population from the United Kingdom to take up the land increased the Pakeha population from 100,000 to 600,000 between 1861 and 1881.[2] This attainment of absolute numerical superiority brought about the political subjection of the Maori and their progressive dehumanisation by the displacement of their culture through the power of the state.

The Native Land Court polarised Maori society into hoko whenua and pupuri whenua factions. As long as Maori land was retained under customary title, it was secure from alienation. But as soon as one member of a hapu broke ranks and applied to the court for a hearing to award a Crown grant of ownership over part or whole of the tribal domain, then there was nothing the rest of the tribe could do to stave off the court by asserting the tribe's mana whenua. If other members of the tribe did not appear at the hearing they could lose out by the land being awarded to those who forced the court hearing against their wishes. The problem for the pupuri whenua was compounded by the law confining the court to name no more than ten persons on a certificate of title. From the tribe's point of view, those named on a court order were trustees. But the certificates of title and Crown grants showed them as absolute owners with power to alienate, because the Land Transfer Act, through which all titles were registered, did not permit the notation of trusts on the register.[3] The Native Land Act 1867, which attempted to correct the ten-owner rule by listing the names of other 'owners' on the reverse side of the certificate, made no difference. Nor did the Native Land Act 1873, which replaced the certificate with a memorial of ownership, improve the situation. The basic thrust of the legislation remained; that is, to treat those listed as individual owners with power to alienate. Claimants who appeared before the court had to prove their claim by citing traditional evidence, including ancestral right, whakapapa, conquest, boundaries, names of battle grounds, urupa, habitation sites and cultivations. As a consequence, the minutes of the Native Land Court are a rich record of traditions and tribal history.

With the removal of the Crown right of pre-emption, and the destruction of tribal mana by the power of the court to determine the retention or disposal of Maori land, land sharks, speculators and government land-purchase officers moved in to buy the land as soon as 'owners' got certificates of title. The system was so open to corrupt practices that twenty years after the court was instituted, W. L. Reesa Cour was moved to comment on the morality of Pakeha making laws in which Maori had no say. He concluded that 'the records of Maori land transactions will make the cheeks of our children burn with shame for many generations'.[4] In Hawke's Bay, for instance, the Heretaunga Block was obtained by speculators advancing credit, fostering debts, suborning influential chiefs with bribes and threatening law suits for non-payment of debts. The block was reputedly sold for £21,000, but only £3,000 was ever paid to the owners in cash. The rest went to the storekeepers who had supplied the clothing, food and liquor on credit against the sale of the land.[5]

Obtaining a Crown grant was a costly affair to both hoko whenua and pupuri whenua alike. Once a court hearing was forced, then charges against the land began to accumulate. These included credit advanced to support the claimants while attending court sittings in towns away from their homes, court costs, lawyers' fees and, when partition orders were granted, survey costs as well. The only way that these debts could be paid was by the sale of land. If owners were not satisfied with the court orders, they had recourse to the Supreme Court, where the costs accumulated at an exponential rate. Sorrenson[6] cited one case that went four times before the Native Land Court and four times to the Supreme Court over a fifteen-year period at a cost of £18,000 to the owners. Selling land was usually the only option for clearing a debt of this magnitude.

One of the unresolved contradictions of capitalism is the cycle of boom and depression. The decade of 1880 was one of depression, and the politicians' panacea to unemployment was 'back to the land' — Maori land, especially lands locked away in the King Country. The tribes in the upper Waikato had held out against land sales for ten years after the Land Wars. By 1880 their resistance and isolation were broken down, and there was an indecent scramble before the Native Land Court at Cambridge as the law pitted brothers, sisters, families and hapu against each other. Storekeepers at Cambridge collaborated with purchase 'rings' of speculators and lawyers who used the court sittings to 'harvest' the money advanced by purchasers. With the loans expended in the buying of sugar, flour and clothing, the purchasers were better able to force a sale of land by demanding payment. Even the purchase agent James Mackay in the Thames Valley participated in this nefarious practice of fostering debts to secure government interests. So did J. C. Young, the agent at Tauranga.[7] Although Maori leaders knew their birthright was being prostituted, there was little they could do about it. Parliament was the den of lions where laws were designed to achieve Pakeha aims. The laws were made to settle as many Pakehas on the land as could be accommodated, even those without money. To this end, various types of tenure were instituted, including deferred payment, lease in perpetuity, and lease with right of purchase. Maori reserved lands which came under government control with the passing of the Native Reserves Act 1864 were used for this purpose.

Pakeha Control of Maori Reserves

Of the original reserved lands known as the 'tenths' from the purchases of Wakefield's New Zealand Company, only 9,080 hectares remain. These reserves at Greymouth, Nelson, Motueka, Wellington and Palmerston North were valued at £1,059,935 in 1960. In Taranaki, the West Coast Settlement Reserves valued at £1 million amounted to 28,640 hectares. The Maori townships established by the Native Townships Act 1895 at Tokaanu, Te Kuiti, and Otorohonga comprised 80 hectares, worth another £1 million. Other reserves exempted from purchase amounted to a further 600 hectares worth another £1 million.[9] Most of these reserves, totalling 38,400 hectares, were all leased by land purchase commissioners in the first instance to Pakeha settlers in perpetuity at peppercorn rentals. They were for a time administered by the Public Trustee, who handed them over to the Maori Trustee when that office was established under the Native Trustee Act 1920. The status of the Maori Trustee is unique in that besides the functions of trustee of Maori assets and normal estate administration, he is also general factotum under the Maori Affairs Act and related legislation.

As a consequence of the state arrogating to itself power over Maori reserved lands, Maori people had no say in their control and administration. This meant that the state, which served the interests of the settlers, did so at the expense of Maori people, who were treated as if they were incompetent state wards. In 1902, for instance, all the Taranaki reserved lands were administered under the West Coast Settlement Reserves Act 1892. The 23,313 hectares that remained, with a capital value of $4,085,450, brought in rent of $183,365 which represented a return of only 4.5 per cent on capital value. The situation was even worse on the township reserves of Palmerston North which brought in a return of only 1.68 per cent. On the Rotorua township reserves of eight hectares, the return was $5,706, yet the rates the city council earned off that same land was almost four times as much, at $21,206. Leases on land were traded on the open market at inflated prices that brought no return to the beneficial owners under existing laws. The value of the land on which the Granville Flats stood in Wellington, for instance, was $150,000. The annual rent was only $340, yet the lease was sold on the open market for $19,000.[10] The Maori Trustee could have bought the lease and negotiated a more realistic rental, but did not. The designation Maori Trustee is a misnomer, because, like its predecessor the Public Trustee, it perpetuated an exploitive regime from the colonial period established by the land commissioners.

By the turn of the century all the best land had been alienated, and only two million hectares remained in Maori ownership. Pakeha desire to acquire those lands was not sated by the 24.4 million hectares they already had. Parliament continued to pass laws to get the rest. Land 'not required or suitable for occupation by the Maori owners' was placed under land councils by the Land Settlement Act 1904. Pakeha determined what was 'suitable', because Maori opinion was not represented on the councils. Then came two pieces of legislation designed to mop up the remnants of Maori land. The first was the Maori Affairs Act 1953, under which the Department of Maori Affairs became a land-purchase agent for the Government. The Maori Trustee had power to purchase Maori land deemed to be 'uneconomic' or land that was not being developed according to Pakeha standards. The second and more draconian measure was the Maori Affairs Amendment Act 1967, which gave the Maori Trustee compulsory power to purchase 'uneconomic' interests in Maori land of under £50. To this end, a conversion fund was established for the Maori Trustee to use. The Act also decreed that Maori land held by fewer than four owners lost its designation as Maori land and had to be registered in the Land Transfer Office in the same status as European land. The statutes cited here do not exhaust the plethora of laws that Parliament passed on Maori land to the bewilderment and detriment of

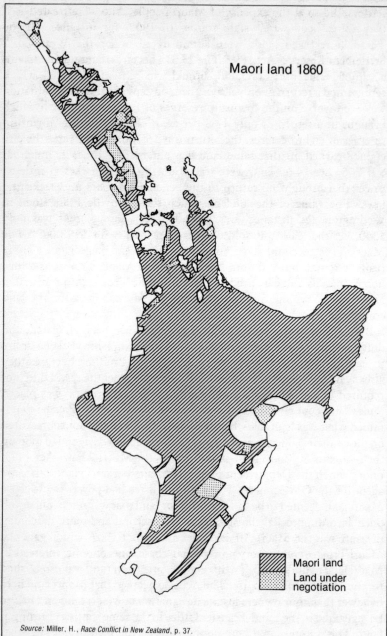

Maori land 1860

Maori land
Land under negotiation

Source: Miller, H., *Race Conflict in New Zealand*, p. 37.

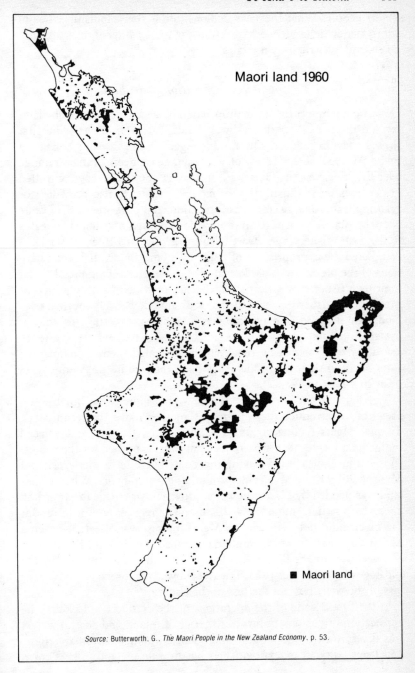

Maori land 1960

■ Maori land

Source: Butterworth. G.. *The Maori People in the New Zealand Economy*. p. 53.

Maori people. What the laws demonstrate is the colonising ethos of white men which reduced Maori to being mere wards of the state with no control over their own affairs.

Government Expropriation of Fisheries

Government moves for the expropriation of land were matched by laws for the takeover of both freshwater and marine fisheries. The first fisheries law introduced without due regard to the Crown's obligation under Article 2 of the Treaty of Waitangi, guaranteeing rangatiratanga over fisheries, was the Oyster Fisheries Act 1866. The law controlled oyster beds by the institution of closed seasons. It also provided for granting leases over oyster beds for commercial purposes. Three years later the Act was amended to provide for granting of 'exclusive' leases to the oyster fishery of Stewart Island. The Oyster Fisheries Act 1892 completed the expropriation of fisheries by making explicit the intentions of the preceding Acts. It excluded Maori from commercial use of their own fisheries. Section 14 of the Act provided for recognition of Maori oyster fisheries where they took oysters exclusively for their own food, but it could also prescribe regulations preventing the sale of oysters from their own beds. The law then recognised only a subsistence use of oyster fisheries by the Maori and denied them a commercial component in their use, which they had exercised in the twenty years prior to the Land Wars.[11]

The Salmon and Trout Act 1867, which allowed acclimatisation societies to introduce these fish, was another move that eroded traditional Maori fishing rights. The introduced fish ate or displaced indigenous species that were traditional sources of food for the Maori. Monocultural bias in lawmaking that contributed to further erosion of Maori fishing rights was evident in other developments. When settler land was flooded by Maori eel weirs, provision was made for awarding damages to settlers under the Williamson Compensation Act 1868. But the inverse did not hold when a Maori interest was affected. When a Maori won a case for compensation against a Pakeha for the destruction of an eel weir by the flotation of logs, the decision was nullified by the Floatage of Timber Act 1873. The Act allowed for compensation for the loss of the weir, but not the loss of the fishery.[12]

In the first decade of the operations of the Native Land Court, the application of customary law to fisheries of inland and coastal waters was determined by the court, which ruled whether customary rights had been retained or extinguished by the sale of land. The Crown removed that jurisdiction from the court, and therefore the recognition of customary fishing rights as guaranteed under the Treaty of Waitangi, by the Harbours Act 1878. This Act negated any assertion by Maori claimants that the Crown's rights under common law were subject to customary rights, an assertion already evident in the Fish Protection Act 1877. It made a ritual bow to the Treaty of Waitangi under Section 8, which provided that nothing in that Act was to affect any of the provisions of the Treaty of Waitangi or to take away any Maori rights to any fishery secured by it. Thereafter every provision in the Act contravened the Treaty.[13]

The power of Parliament to make laws to expropriate Maori land and fisheries guaranteed to the Maori by the Crown under the Treaty of Waitangi emanated from Pakeha domination of political power. Soon after the establishment of the General Assembly under the New Zealand Constitution Act 1852, Pakeha concern over maintaining political dominance became evident. Late in 1855 Wiremu Tamihana had suggested that Maori leaders should be admitted to the House of Representatives.[14] This just claim for Maori participation in the democratic process was neutralised by arbitrary authoritarian rule. In 1858 the House sought a ruling from the Imperial Government under Sections 7 and 42 of the Constitution as to whether Maori possession of land or property not derived under title from the Crown qualified them as voters. The memorandum sent by James Richmond noted that a Maori population of 56,000 posed a grave danger and inconvenience to the government of the country should men 'destitute of political knowledge' and 'ignorant of the language' in which English laws are written be given the franchise.[15] Opposition was expressed to an 'admixture of a Native constituency' with that of the European, '. . . for a Native constituency implies, Native representatives; and what greater debasement of the House can be conceived, than the occupation of seats in it by men raised, as yet, but one step above barbarism'.[16] Richmond asserted that 'the natives have a natural right, not to vote, but to be well governed' — by Europeans. These overtly racist views were in the next decade translated into action and institutionalised in Parliament. The New Zealand Government got the ruling it sought from the Imperial Government that property held in common by tribes did not qualify them as voters. For the next nine years Maori were excluded from Parliament, enabling it to wage a racist war on its brown citizens unchallenged by a dissenting voice. But back in England a storm of criticism was raised by the Aborigines Protection Society urging the Imperial Government to recognise the Maori King and return confiscated lands to the Maori. The humanitarians also suggested the establishment of an independent Maori Council to control Native Affairs.[17]

Token Maori Representation

The 'Responsible Ministers' of the colonial Government had opposed Governor Browne consulting a council of chiefs because they wanted to direct Maori policy. Their position had not changed after the Waikato war because they knew an independent Maori Council would oppose their own policies for the alienation of Maori land. In order to allay the criticisms of the humanitarians, and to avert possible intervention by the Colonial Office, Donald McLean, Secretary for Native Affairs, introduced the Maori Representation Act 1867. When McLean introduced the measure into Parliament, he argued that without some form of Maori presence in the House, the Maori interest was likely to be forgotten. This sudden expression of concern for the Maori interest from a man who had overridden it in the past does not conform with his behaviour prior to the wars. When McLean was under pressure to secure land for settlers, it was to the settler interest that he gave priority. He resorted to taking shortcuts in some of his land purchases by consulting only one or two chiefs, ignoring pupuri whenua, or at best gaining agreement from only a minority of owners. His most obvious failure to abide by the Maori interest at Waitara, as expressed by Wiremu Kingi, had precipitated the Taranaki war.

It might be readily assumed from McLean's promotion of Maori representation in Parliament that full equality was being granted. The measure was in effect only a token gesture designed to keep Maori under political subjection. The Act limited the number of Maori representatives to four in a House of over seventy members. The Maori population at that time was 56,000, compared with the Pakeha population of 171,009. On a population basis Maori were entitled to twenty seats. A minority as large as that would have been a severe challenge to the Pakeha balance of power in the House.[18] South Island members were critical of the Bill. A gold rush had increased the population of the South Island and justified an additional three seats there. Maori representation nullified this gain because the Bill proposed three Maori members for the North Island and only one for the South. Furthermore, the Bill proposed that Maori seats be held by Europeans. James Richmond countered opposition to the Bill by arguing that Maori representation, because of its 'exceptional character', was not the same as the ordinary franchise. He exhorted the South Islanders to press the 'exceptional character' of the seats to a point that excluded from them all except persons of the native race.[19]

Eventually the South Island members agreed to support the Maori Representation Bill, provided the seats were restricted to Maori. Both Richmond and the South Island members had such a low opinion of Maori that they were prepared to concede their admission to the House because in their view it provided the least disturbance to the status quo. This institutionalisation of racism by legislation is one of the contradictions of New Zealand society. The contradiction is resolved by the ideology of 'one people'. But because this ideology is a false consciousness, a solution in the mind only, the contradiction remains to be perpetuated in other ways. Maori representation was envisaged as only a temporary measure for five years, but in 1876 it was extended indefinitely. The secret ballot, which was applied in European electorates in 1870, was not introduced to Maori electorates until 1937. The 'exceptional character' of Maori electorates was also manifest in the lack of provision for electoral rolls until 1949, and the holding of elections for Maori electorates right up to 1950 on the day before the General Election. Compulsory registration of Maori for electoral purposes was not introduced until 1956, over twenty years after it had been applied to European electorates.[20]

The most discriminatory measure of all in the application of the law to Maori representation is its exclusion from the provisions for revision under the Electoral Representation Commission. Since 1887 the boundaries of European electorates have been subject to regular revision by the commission. Every five years, when the growth in population has been determined by the census, the size and number of European electorates is revised. A new seat is created for each increment of 30,000 to the population. Despite the increase of the Maori population at the 1986 census to 404,778, Maori representation has been held down to four seats. Although the provisions for Maori representation have been included in the Electoral Act 1956, Maori seats are not entrenched as is the case with European seats. Maori representation in Parliament exists at the pleasure of the Pakeha majority, since it can be amended at any time or repealed altogether. These differences between Maori and Pakeha representation in Parliament are a legacy from the colonial past which perpetuate social and political inequalities into the post-colonial era. They indicate that white New Zealanders are very much still captives of their own past, despite protestations that exploitive or oppressive behaviour belong in the last century and not the enlightened present.

Although colonisation was driven by economic forces, which impelled imperial powers such as Great Britain to expropriate the land and resources of indigenous people, its implementation was underpinned by assumptions of cultural superiority. Colonial domination was justified by the 'civilising' mission of the coloniser. For this reason the process of colonisation is total, in that it involved cultural invasion and colonisation of the minds of the invaded as well. In fulfilling an historic mission, the coloniser had few options in the treatment of the invaded: extermination of the indigenous population, or subjection by force or assimilation. The influence of the liberals, humanitarians and specifically the Aborigines Protection Society in England ruled out extermination. Beginning with the missionaries, the founding fathers of the new nation state were therefore committed to the policy of assimilation. To this end, the missionaries, and later the state, used education as an instrument of cultural invasion.

Schools for Assimilation

The aim of the mission schools was to teach only the standard subjects of the English school curriculum, thereby anglicising their pupils. Subjects taught included reading, writing, arithmetic and English, as well as catechism. Initially the mission schools did their teaching in the Maori language. But when Governor Grey arrived, he diverted them from that sound pedagogical practice with his 1847 Education Ordinance subsidising the mission schools, and insisting that instruction be conducted in English. It was also his expressed hope that the schools would take the children away from the 'demoralising influences of their villages', thereby 'speedily assimilating the Maori to the habits and usages of the European'.[21]

In 1867 William Rolleston reported to the Minister of Native Affairs, James Richmond, on the progress of thirteen Native schools run by the Anglican, Catholic and Wesleyan Churches. He noted that the schools succeeded originally in spreading throughout the country knowledge of reading and writing in the Maori language in a 'short time and at trifling cost'. But he was critical of their role in carrying out the Government's aims. They had not justified the financial support given them as the means of breaking through the 'communism of the Maori pa' because no general system of primary or village schools had been established by the churches. He also criticised the schools for emphasising religious instruction ahead of other subjects, especially English. He recommended that government assistance be contingent on inspection and attainment of results in teaching subjects of the English school curriculum. He also recommended that natives in any district who formed a school committee, and wanted a school on land they set aside for the purpose, be subsidised on the amount they were prepared to expend on establishing a school.[22]

Rolleston's report on the failure of the mission schools to assimilate the Maori gave the state the opportunity to assume responsibility for education and carry the campaign of cultural invasion itself right to the heart of Maori communities. The 1867 Native Schools Act established a new but discrete policy of education provision for Maori people. Maori tribes wanting a school in their area provided the Government with the land. They were also expected to raise half of the teachers' salaries, but with economic hardship visited on them as a consequence of social disruption by the Land Wars, this obligation was beyond them. The state assumed complete responsibility for the cost of the schools.

The Native schools were at first administered by the Department of Native Affairs and then transferred to the Education Department in 1879. The Inspector of Native Schools drew up a Native School Code in 1880. Initially, teachers were expected to have some knowledge of the Maori language, which was to be used only in the junior classes to induct new entrants into school routines, and as an aid to teaching English. But because the aims of Native schools were alien and incongruent with life in Maori communities, progress was slow. Poor English was blamed as the cause. In 1905 the Inspector of Native Schools instructed teachers to encourage children to speak only English in school playgrounds. This instruction was translated into a general prohibition of the Maori language within school precincts. For the next five decades the prohibition was in some instances enforced by corporal punishment. The damaging aspect of this practice lay not in corporal punishment *per se*, but in the psychological effect on an individual's sense of identity and personal worth.

Schooling demanded cultural surrender, or at the very least suppression of one's language and identity. Instead of education being embraced as a process of growth and development, it became an arena of cultural conflict.[23]

In 1900 over 90 per cent of new entrants at primary school spoke Maori as their first language. By 1960 white dominance and the policy of suppression had taken their toll: only 26 per cent of young children spoke Maori.[24] By 1979 the Maori language had retreated to the point where it was thought it would die out unless something was done to save it.[25]

The Struggle for Autonomy

While Maori were rendered powerless by the parliamentary system of the coloniser, they were not supine. Their cultural resilience enabled them to continue the struggle for the assertion of their identity as tangata whenua. When Wiremu Tamihana realised that Maori were not going to be admitted into Parliament, he turned his talents and political skills to the election of a Maori king. Tamihana did not see this move as being in conflict with the Crown. He envisaged a conjoint administration, with the King presiding over Maori land and the Queen over Crown lands. Tamihana's model of two sticks in the ground, one representing the Maori King, and the other the Governor, with a third stick across them representing the law of God and the Queen,[26] was a succinct model of his vision of a bicultural nation under a conjoint administration. That vision, though denied by the Governor, was doggedly pursued by Maori leaders over the next century into the modern era.

Although the chiefs who had participated in the Kohimarama Conference in 1860 had been manipulated by McLean and the Governor into affirming their allegiance to the Queen and disassociating themselves from the Maori King and Wiremu Kingi, they were satisfied with the conference. For the first time they felt their rangatiratanga under the covenant of the Treaty of Waitangi was accorded its proper place in the governance of the country. Accordingly, at the conclusion of the conference they thanked the Governor for granting them the 'great boon' of a runanga, whereby they could express their views and propose measures for the settlement of difficulties. The chiefs requested that the runanga be established on a permanent basis.[27] This desire was thwarted by the Land Wars. But as the dust settled from the conflict, the chiefs wrote to McLean in 1869 asking for another Kohimarama Conference. The Ngati Whatua chief Paora Tuhaere supported the request from Tamihana Te Rauparaha, saying that had the runanga been continued, none of the disturbances in the land would have taken place.[28] This is a charmingly ingenuous attribution of moral integrity to the intentions of a colonial government bent on assertion of hegemony as evidenced by its refusal of further consultations with the chiefs.

Paora Tuhaere's request for a revival of the Kohimarama runanga was made at a time when there were already four Maori members in the House. Tuhaere and his fellow chiefs were not satisfied with the system of Maori representation because it was introduced without reference to them and had serious shortcomings. Consequently, Maori interest at the inception of the seats was minimal. The Department of Native Affairs made no attempt to involve people in the selection of candidates, and so the elections were a farce. In Northern Maori, Frederick Russell, a man of mixed ancestry, was the only candidate and was elected unopposed. Tuhaere refused to endorse him because a Ngapuhi MP might put the Ngati Whatua in a false position in the House. On the East Coast an open poll was held of thirty-four hands for Tareha and thirty-three for Karaitiana Takamoana. In Western Maori there was only one candidate, Mete Kingi Paetahi, who was disqualified on a technicality and had to have his position validated by special legislation. In Southern Maori a low poll of 8 per cent put a man named Patterson into the House.[29] Because they had been excluded at the outset from Parliament, and Maori representation foisted on them without their involvement or consent, the chiefs were still intent on maintaining their mana and pursuing their own models of political development.

The emerging sense of national consciousness arising out of the pupuri whenua and Kotahitanga Movement prior to the Land Wars did not die out with Pakeha dominance and the implementation of strategies through the Native Land Court for the alienation of land. Initially, many chiefs such as Wiremu Tamihana resorted to the court to secure Crown grants on their tribal lands. By July 1867 Chief Judge F. D. Fenton reported to Richmond that he had issued thirteen court orders on 225,600 hectares, most of it belonging to Ngati Haua. Because a number of chiefs were willing `sellers, the price of land became depressed. Walter Kukutai, for instance, was reduced to offering a block of 16,000 hectares of prime land in the Waikato at five shillings instead of £1 an acre.[30] Poorer land in the North went down to a shilling an acre. Judge Frederick Maning commented to Fenton on the effect of individual title in the Far North in transforming the natives from barbarism to civilisation. In some places natives had hired Europeans to erect expensive fences. Maning cited two farms that had not only been fenced and grassed but stocked as well with 200 sheep. He also cited instances of natives building bigger and better houses as an example of the transformation.[31] These 'benefits' were achieved not by productive effort as had been the case prior to the Land Wars, but by selling land.

While the judges expressed overly optimistic views on the benign effects of the Native Land Court, others were not so enamoured of its work. In July 1869 the Hawke's Bay chief and Member for Eastern Maori, Karaitiana Takamoana, tabled a submission in the General Assembly criticising the court. He pointed out that it was open to abuse by admission of false claims to land. He argued that the law was faulty in recording only ten names on a Crown grant from a hundred claimants. The rest were wrongly dispossessed by the law. Another fault, he wrote, is 'the European invites the man to whom the Crown grant belongs to drink spirits, and that the Maori then says, "I have no money." Then the European says, "Your money is your Crown grant:' your land is [your money]." I look upon this as a cruelty to the Maoris so that they may cease to have any land.' Takamoana roundly condemned the law granting individuals the power to alienate as a 'lame system', a 'regulation which destroys men'.[32]

Takamoana was not the only critic of the Native Land Court. Paora Tuhaere wrote to McLean recommending that the employment of lawyers by claimants in the court be barred because they were ignorant of Maori custom and an unnecessary expense. He also condemned the use of interpreters who were worse than the lawyers because they prompted witnesses as to what to say, and often advised them to make false statements. Tuhaere was very conscious that one of the results of court orders was a subsequent rise in land sales. In his view insufficient land was being reserved by the court as inalienable. Accordingly, he recommended that from 20 to 200 hectares should be reserved for every man, woman, and child, depending on the size of their block, to ensure that Maori would not become landless. But the request was ignored. The scenario of dispossession in the South Island was now being repeated in the North Island.

In 1870 Wi Te Wheoro, a chief of the Lower Waikato, wrote to Colonel Theodore Haultain asking that lawyers be barred from the Land Court and complaining that interpreters taught Maori to 'trump up stories' that were at variance with the facts. He also complained that native assessors were useless because they sat on the bench like 'blocks of wood'. When the Native Land Court was first established, Te Wheoro saw the danger and wrote to the Government requesting that Waikato lands be left outside its jurisdiction. When Te Wheoro sat as an assessor, he was confirmed in his original view and recommended that the court be abolished. He proposed that it be replaced by a Maori runanga of seven members to determine titles to Maori land and for the district magistrates to confirm their decisions. The attempts of these leaders to safeguard the Maori interest made little difference as the work of the court continued. Consequently Te Wheoro resigned, saying, 'I was an assessor and have sat on seven courts, but now I have sent in my resignation. I have always been opposed to the court from the very commencement. It is a pity that the Maori were not consulted before the Act was brought into the General Assembly.'[33]

Clearly, Maori leaders knew they were being destroyed by laws enacted in the den of lions where they were powerless and reduced to making recommendations to the lawmakers from the outside. They were treated as being less than human by the power-brokers of the colonists because their opinions counted for nothing. Freire[34] argues that although dehumanisation as a concomitant of colonisation is a concrete historical fact, it is not a given destiny, but the result of an unjust social order engendered by violence in the oppressor. The oppressed are dehumanised by the colonial experience, by the loss of their land, their fisheries and the loss of their language through cultural invasion. But the great humanistic task of the oppressed is to recover their stolen humanity; to liberate themselves and to liberate their oppressors as well. This profound thought from Freire expresses the innate desire of the human spirit to be free, to achieve self-realisation. The Maori leaders at Orakau had indicated that they were prepared to struggle forever for freedom, for their cultural integrity as tangata whenua. Post-war leaders such as Tuhaere, Te Wheoro and Takamoana continued the struggle in their own way, by a rational appeal to the coloniser's sense of justice and fair play. But unbridled power is not necessarily rational or fair. The coloniser once embarked on a policy of exploitation is committed. There is no turning back, because 'the oppressors do not perceive their monopoly of having more as a privilege which dehumanises others and themselves. They cannot see that, in the egoistic pursuit of having as a possessing class, they suffocate in their own possessions and no longer are; they merely have.'[35]

The only way that the colonisers can exculpate themselves is in the hope that the natives will do the decent thing and die out, or if they survive, become assimilated. But assimilation is not a real option, because the coloniser as the oppressing class has created a dichotomy of white dominance and brown subjection. In creating that dichotomy, the coloniser thinks he has created a unified society. The illusion of national unity is maintained by the ideology of one people. But the oppressed know, as did the Maori leaders, that they must struggle for their liberation, and a basic component in that struggle is their own consciousness of themselves as an exploited class defined on the basis of ethnicity. For this reason, racism is an artifice of colonisation and not a construct of class. The victims of racial oppression are the new underclass to emerge from the colonial experience. To break out of this underclass encirclement, Maori informed their own political consciousness by entering into a dialogue with others. To this end, the institution of the marae and the political structures of the tribes were admirably suited.

The Tribal Assemblies

Maori leaders turned to the runanga system of tribal and inter-tribal meetings that had formed Kotahitanga and the King Movement to discuss their plight and develop responses to Pakeha dominance in the post-war period. In 1875 the Ngapuhi tribes opened the Tiriti o Waitangi Marae as a potent symbol of the significance of the Treaty, and as a place where the tribes could gather annually on the anniversary of its signing to discuss grievances arising out of Pakeha infractions of it. Maori leaders knew that Parliament was the source of their afflictions. In 1875 the Arawa chief Wiremu Maihi Te Rangikaheke, confidant of Sir George Grey and a court assessor, petitioned Parliament for an increase of Maori members in the House to twenty-six. The following year he endorsed proposals raised in the House by Karaitiana Takamoana, that in view of the refusal, perhaps it would be better for the Maori members to withdraw from Parliament and a Maori Parliament be established by petition to Queen Victoria.[36]

One of the most trenchant criticisms made against Maori representation came from Hone Kotuku of Waikato. In December 1875 he wrote to the Maori newspaper *Te Wananga* saying when Governor Grey waged war in the open, the enemy could be seen and each man had the power to defend himself. But in the post-war years, where the sword was sheathed in its scabbard, the sword of steel was replaced by the sword of deceit because public opinion was against naked aggression and confiscation. Instead, political power was used to override the rights of the Maori people. This was accomplished by limiting Maori members in the House to four and stultifying their right to act for the good of the people. Only two of the members, Karaitiana and Taiaroa, maintained their integrity. The other two 'whose mouths have been filled with cash' were like 'tame parrots'. Kotuku identified Donald McLean, who introduced Maori representation, as 'a man of deceit

and duplicity'. When the petition seeking an increase of Maori membership in the House was put before McLean, 'the man most learned in
matters appertaining to the Maori people', he responded in a
patronising manner. He said the Government was thinking that 'the
Maori children might be sent to school and the English language
taught to them, when they would be fit to take a position in the
Parliament'.[37]

It was against this background of Pakeha domination that the tribes
came together. One of the first large inter-tribal meetings took place
in March 1876 at Waiohiki on the East Coast. There were 1,200
representatives present from the East Coast and Bay of Plenty tribes
as far north as Thames and from the interior Lakes district. The west
coast tribes were represented from Wellington as far north as Raglan.
Henare Tomoana pointed out to the meeting that the tribes set up a
king to unite the people. That move ended in disaster, he said, 'on
account of our ignorance, and our being strange to such work'. Henare
Matua identified the divisiveness among the people brought on by
spurious claims before the Native Land Court as the major evil of the
day. He proposed that the court should be reconstituted. An astute
comment on Maori representation in Parliament was made by Renata
Kawepo, who argued that the reason why the Government allowed
Maori members into Parliament was to sanction Government actions.
Should an act of Government be condemned by the public then they
could point to the Maori members who agreed to it on behalf of the
people.[38]

In June 1876 another large Kotahitanga inter-tribal meeting took
place at Pakowhai on the East Coast. Besides the Ngati Porou and
Kahungunu tribes from the East Cape down to the Wairarapa, there
were representatives from Ngati Awa at Whakatane, Ngai Tahu from
the South Island, and Tuwharetoa and Te Arawa from the Lakes
district. From Patea on the west coast came Ngati Apa, Ngati Matepu,
Ngati Upokoiri, and Ngati Tama. The chairman of the meeting,
Henare Matua, blamed the 'laws of the world' for the evils that had
befallen the Maori. But despite that, he urged the meeting to adhere
to Christian worship and declare obedience to the Queen. He indicated
that the purpose of the hui was kotahitanga, achievement of unity, and
the establishment of an organisation to promote the hui as an annual
event.[39] The meeting decided to call for the repeal of the Maori
Representation Act and its replacement by a statute 'giving the Maori
people the same number of members in accordance with the number
of the population, as that given to the Europeans in proportion to the

European population'.[40] The repeal of the Native Land Act 1867, which instituted the Native Land Court, was also sought by the hui. In the far North, the Ngapuhi tribes of Kotahitanga were also organising and drawing similar conclusions. Hone Mohi Tawhai wrote to Hori Taiawhio of Tuhourangi saying that Ngapuhi had agreed that the Native Land Court should be abolished and Maori land retained under customary law. He urged that the contents of his letter be widely publicised among the tribes.[41]

The tribes assembled again in March 1877 at Omahu in Hawke's Bay. There were 200 chiefs present as well as women. The hui confirmed the resolutions of the previous year and condemned the evil laws by which 'wicked Pakehas have been enabled to plunder the Maori of their lands in Hawke's Bay and elsewhere'. It was decided to petition Parliament to incorporate Maori proposals into the new Native Land Act at the next session of the House. In addition, the hui wanted an amendment whereby the full consent of a chief and his tribe was necessary before their land came under the jurisdiction of the Land Court. The view was also expressed that the Government should not enter Native Districts uninvited to pester Maori to alienate their land. Fears about local government emerged as well in the suggestion that tribes should refrain from voting in county council elections in case it be used as a reason for levying rates on Maori land.[42]

The concerns expressed by the tribal runanga on the East Coast were also articulated at similar meetings in the North. One of the more significant of these was a hui convened at Orakei in February 1879 by Paora Tuhaere. There were 300 representatives in attendance from Ngati Whatua, Ngapuhi, Rarawa and the Tainui tribes of Ngati Paoa and Ngati Te Ata. Tuhaere linked his hui with the Kohimarama Conference of 1860 by naming the hall built for the occasion Kohimarama.[43] In his opening address Tuhaere expressed the view that Maori members of Parliament should be selected by runanga such as the one convened at Orakei. In Maori thinking, only selection by a runanga could be considered a true election. He also read out the Treaty of Waitangi and the resolutions of the covenant made at Kohimarama for confirmation by the assembly and as a starting point for discussions. On the third day of the meeting he asserted that when the Queen established her authority over the island, she did not, under the Treaty, deprive the chiefs of their mana. The Treaty of Waitangi left the rights of the soil to the chiefs and their fisheries as well. In the course of the discussions one of the chiefs, Eruera, contended that the Native Land Court and the system of Crown grants were in effect a denial of mana. Waata Tipa complained about the introduction of oyster laws. He heard people now had to have licences to gather oysters. Because laws of this nature were being introduced without Maori knowledge or consent, Pairama proposed that 'new laws be made for the welfare of both races'. He argued that 'the chiefs should meet to inaugurate a new state of things so that we may establish a Parliament for our children'.

On the fifth day of the Orakei hui, Apihai Te Kawau returned to the subject of fisheries. He asserted his aboriginal title and property rights to the sea saying, 'It was only the land I gave over to the Pakeha. The sea I never gave. Therefore the sea belongs to me. Some of my goods are there. I consider the pipi and fish are my goods. I have always considered them my goods up to the present time.' Consequently the assembly passed resolutions asserting Maori property rights over fisheries including shark nurseries, flounder and eel fisheries, pipi beds, rock oysters, mussels, paua, kina and scallops. Other legislation prohibiting rights of access to traditional resources, or restricting access by the issuance of licences to take them, resulted in a resolution asserting tribal mana to take ducks, godwits, pigeons and tui. The hui also called for the abolition of the Native Land Court and surveys of Maori land, and the right for runanga to control Maori land. The runanga also wanted power to grant or disallow access to road boards over Maori land.[44] The discussions at Orakei and previous tribal assemblies indicate not only concern over the erosion of Maori rights but also an attempt to define those rights in terms of rangatiratanga as guaranteed by the Treaty of Waitangi. But it was to no avail, since the Government paid no heed to the recommendations of the hui, thereby undermining the authority of the chiefs and rendering them impotent.

Although the Government did not promote Paora Tuhaere's hui, it gave tacit support by the attendance of John Bryce and other government officials. The Prime Minister, Sir George Grey, who was still encountering resistance to his plans from King Tawhiao, hoped to use Tuhaere and other chiefs to conciliate with the recalcitrant King.[45] Tawhiao refused to recognise the legality of the confiscation of Waikato lands and kept insisting on their return. At three meetings in May and June of 1876, he pressed Donald McLean, Minister of Native Affairs, for the return of Waikato. But McLean took refuge in the decisions of previous governments, saying that the matter was out of his hands. Instead, he offered the possibility of the return of some small portion of Crown lands not yet purchased by settlers.

The only lands McLean made a commitment to return were the ancestral burial grounds asked for by Tawhiao at Te Mata-o-tu-tonga, Pukerimu, and Tangirau.[46] Subsequently, Grey met with Tawhiao in May 1878 at Hikurangi. There Tawhiao made explicit his demand by putting a stake in the ground to represent the Mangatawhiri creek. He insisted that the Europeans should withdraw to the opposite side and he and the other chiefs would manage their side. Grey replied it was impossible to return the Waikato but tried to buy him off by offering him an annual grant of £500 for his district, to disburse and use as he saw fit. He also repeated McLean's offer of a return of Crown lands not sold to settlers on the western side of the Waikato and Waipa Rivers. He offered an additional 200 hectares of land at Ngaruawahia so Tawhiao could be close to the grave of his father Potatau. Tawhiao and his advisors knew this was a paltry offer in settlement of their claim. Although they did not reject it outright, they said they would consider it. Then, in what amounted to a statement in expiation of what he had done, Grey said, 'The land is filling with Europeans in every direction; and I am desirous to see you all in a position of safety before I die. I shall be very glad to see the position of the people whom I have loved for so many years made quite secure and safe. I have grown old. In my youth I knew your fathers, and now before I die I should like to see their descendants safe.'[47]

Whether or not Grey was contrite is a moot point, because as a student of Maori culture he well knew the persuasive and binding effect of ohaki, the final testament of a dying chief. But the prevarication of Tawhiao and his advisors, who knew that acceptance of Grey's offer meant relinquishing their claim to the Waikato, was misunderstood by the Pakeha. On 14 May the *New Zealander* reported that settlers in all parts of the Waikato were jubilant over the prospects of a near and satisfactory settlement of the differences which had hitherto existed between the two races. Tawhiao had other ideas. Like the tribes in the Kotahitanga Movement, his own tribal assemblies had drawn up similar policies calling for abolition of the Native Land Court, prohibition of surveys on Maori land, and suspension of prospecting for gold. Granting lands for school reserves was also opposed. The Kingitanga and Kotahitanga had similar policies, but the two movements were on parallel tracks with no junction to bring them together.

The Prophet of Passive Resistance

During the post-war years, while the Waikato tribes were reviving the political base of the King Movement and the tribes outside it were forging the Kotahitanga Movement, a new prophet arose in Taranaki preaching a message of peace and separation of the races. Te Whiti had come to his pacifist views after seeing the futility of five years of fighting against an Imperial army in Taranaki and Waikato. He and his followers built the model village of Parihaka on the downlands west of Mt Taranaki. There he preached the new message of pacifism and separation of the races, saying:[48]

> Lay down your weapons. Be wise . . . Though the whites exterminate the trunk they cannot pull out the roots. Avoid all sale and lease of land. Permit no European to cross the border of this our last free Maoriland. We want no roads or schools from them. Let them do with their land what they will.

It was just as well Te Whiti had the charisma and mana not only to persuade his followers to accept the policy of pacifism, but to convince them to adhere to it in the face of extreme provocation and violence from the state. At issue were the lands on the west coast confiscated by the Government in 1865. Settlement on confiscated land north of the Waingongoro River was delayed by Titokowaru's resistance in 1868. No attempt was made at that time to settle the Waimate Plains extending northward to Stoney River. Thereafter the tribes resumed occupation of their villages and cultivations under the impression that the Government had abandoned the confiscation. In 1872, as the Government attempted to extend the road around the west coast, Te Whiti stopped it in his territory. He also stopped the extension of the telegraph line designed to link Taranaki with the rest of the colony. For years Te Whiti obstructed the erection of the Cape Egmont lighthouse. In the end the Government used the Armed Constabulary to erect the light, a portent of what was to come in the use of state force to extend its hegemony into Maori areas.

Eventually, Sir George Grey's Government, in the words of John Bryce, moved to effect a 'final solution' to the settlement of the west coast.[49] In 1878 the Government commenced the survey of the Waimate Plains so settlers could move in. In February 1879, as the survey of the confiscated lands proceeded right through the cultivations of the aged warrior chief Titokowaru without reserves being set aside, Te Whiti opposed it with his new policy of passive resistance. In May, Te Whiti sent out men who ploughed up the land of Pakeha farmers to demonstrate Maori opposition to progressive confiscation of their lands[50] for the benefit of Pakeha settlers. The Government responded by jailing the ploughmen. Some were jailed for a year and others held indefinitely without trial under the Maori Prisoners Trial Act 1879, which was hurried through Parliament to give some semblance of legality to Government actions.

The following year Te Whiti opposed the advance of the west coast road around the mountain. The road was driven right through the fences and cultivations of his settlement. He sent out his people to rebuild the fences across the road; the fence builders, like the ploughmen, were dragged off to gaol. The gaols in New Plymouth and Wellington bulged with Maori prisoners, 200 ploughmen and 216 fencers. But because their offences were trivial, and to have charged them in court for ploughing and fencing would have been 'ridiculous', John Bryce, Minister of Native Affairs and Defence, suspended *habeas corpus*. He did so, he claimed, on grounds of extreme emergency because 'the peace of the country hung upon a slender thread'.[51] Scaremongering and disinformation prepared the social climate for state oppression, the course on which Bryce, under the guiding hand of the Prime Minister, Sir George Grey, had embarked.

Te Whiti's continuance of the struggle against colonial spoliation by passive resistance cost the Government £5,600 a month for the ploughmen alone. By 1880 the estimates of the cost of the collision with Te Whiti had passed £1 million, while the value of the land acquired was worth only £750,000.[52] Te Whiti's attempt at a *modus vivendi* with the colonising regime by pacifist separation of the races elicited a violent response from the coloniser. The Government decided, on the recommendation of the West Coast Commission, to confiscate most of the Waimate Plains and 12,400 hectares of the 22,400-hectare Parihaka Block.[53] Te Whiti was an obstacle to the Government's plans and so the full weight of state power was brought to bear against him. The Governor, Sir Arthur Gordon, had grave misgivings over the Crown's moral right to enforce in 1881 confiscation made in 1865. As the Queen's representative and guardian of Maori rights under the Treaty of Waitangi, he would have made his opposition known to the Government and raised the possibility of blocking legislation by withholding his signature. Unfortunately for Te Whiti and his people, the Governor left the country in September on a visit to Fiji. Before he returned in November, the Executive Council was called together while the anti-Maori Justice James Prendergast was still Acting Governor, and a proclamation was issued giving Te Whiti fourteen days to accept the Government's decision on Parihaka lands. When the deadline passed, the proclamation was enforced on 5

November 1881 by John Bryce, Minister of Native Affairs, who led an armed constabulary of 1,500 men into Parihaka. This overreaction by a show of state force against 2,200 unarmed people sitting passively in a dense mass on their marae was calculated to intimidate Maori throughout the land.[54] Te Whiti and Tohu were arrested, the people dispersed, and their houses pillaged and destroyed over the following two weeks.[55] The two prophets were jailed indefinitely by the Government introducing special legislation to detain them under the West Coast Peace Preservation Bill.[56] They were sent to the South Island for a time and eventually released in March 1883. Although Parihaka was rebuilt, without the land its former prosperity was gone. But Te Whiti's struggle was not in vain. Every year on 5 November his followers and their descendants commemorated the pahua by assembling at Parihaka and holding a ritual feast in memory of the prophets and the invasion of Parihaka. Te Whiti, like Rewi Maniapoto, became a symbol of the endless struggle of the Maori people against Pakeha subjection. The struggle in the warrior tradition was symbolised by the freedom fighters Rewi Maniapoto, Te Kooti and Titokowaru. But Te Whiti became the new symbol of the struggle in the creative tradition of pacifism which predated Gandhi's stand against British imperialism by seventy years.

CHAPTER 9

Nga Pou o te Iwi

The First Deputation of Chiefs

The tribal runanga in the decade after the Land Wars clarified the plight of the Maori people as a consequence of colonisation. One more large assembly was held at Waitangi in March 1881 before a course of action was decided. The discussions at these numerous tribal and inter-tribal forums concluded that the Treaty of Waitangi was not at fault. Chiefly mana had not been surrendered to the Crown. The change in Maori fortunes was due to infractions of the Treaty by the New Zealand Government and not the Crown, therefore appeal had to be made to the source of the Treaty, the Crown itself. The following year a deputation of northern chiefs travelled to England to lay their grievances before the Queen. The deputation comprised Parore Te Awha, Hare Hongi Hika, Maihi Paraone Kawiti, Kingi Hori Kira, Mangonui Rewa, Hirini Taiwhanga, Wiremu Puhi Te Hihi, and Hakena Parore.

The deputation was met by Lord Kimberley, Secretary of State for the Colonies, who received their petition on behalf of the Queen. The petition summarised the historical events following the signing of the Treaty of Waitangi. The petitioners stated that the chiefs entered into a compact with England in 1840 to become their protector in preference to other countries. Because of ignorance of some tribes, including Hone Heke, the flagstaff at Kororareka was cut down. But, the chiefs pointed out, there was no blood on the flagstaff, so it was not necessary to raise armies to fight Heke. Had the chiefs been consulted, the war in the North could have been avoided. Then in 1860 the Governor himself, without just cause, drove Wiremu Kingi off his land at Waitara, which renewed the shedding of both European and Maori blood. Some Europeans said Kingi was wrong in opposing the Governor; had he appealed to the Supreme Court, the Government's actions would have been condemned. Thereafter the Taranaki people accepted that opinion and did not oppose the Government when it sent an army to Parihaka to 'enkindle Maori strife', giving them an excuse to confiscate more land.

Governor Grey was sent back to New Zealand in 1862 to settle matters, whereupon he rushed off to Taranaki and gave instructions to make roads in Maori territory, which brought about a war and the slaying of many of both races. In 1863 the war was carried into Waikato territory, and Maori were unaware of any reason why war had been made on the Waikato. The Waikato had formed a land league to preserve their mana whenua, a principle which is embodied in the Treaty. The Waikato had no desire to fight; the desire instead came from the Governor and his council. When the Waikato were over-powered, the army went forth and engendered strife at Tauranga, Te Awa o te Atua, Whakatane, Ohiwa, Opotiki, Turanganui, Ahuriri, Whanganui, Waimate and various other places. The motive behind the perpetrators of these deeds was to confiscate Maori land and to 'trample under the soles of their feet the Treaty of Waitangi'. In 1881 armies were sent to Parihaka to capture innocent men, to imprison them, sieze their property and their money, destroy their crops, break down their houses and commit other injustices. 'We pored over the Treaty of Waitangi to find the grounds on which these evil proceedings of the Government of New Zealand rested, but we could find none.'

The petitioners asked for a Royal Commission to 'abrogate the evil laws affecting the Maori people, and to establish a Maori Parliament, which shall hold in check the European authorities who are endeavouring to set aside the Treaty of Waitangi; to put a bridle on the mouth of Ministers for Native Affairs who may act as Ministers have done at Parihaka'. The petitioners urged the commission to restore wrongly confiscated Maori land 'according to the provisions of the Treaty of Waitangi; and to draw forth from beneath the many unauthorised acts of the New Zealand Parliament the concealed treaty that it may now assert its own dignity'.

As a potent reminder of the Treaty, the petitioners informed the Queen that they had built a house of assembly at Waitangi in 1881. There the articles of the Treaty of Waitangi had been engraved on a stone memorial as a symbolic reminder of the enduring nature of the Treaty. Two invitations had been sent to the Governor to unveil the Treaty memorial, but they had been declined. Perhaps his refusal arose out of the fact that Europeans had disregarded the principles of the Treaty. The petition also cited the laws enacted by Parliament in contravention of the Treaty. These included the Native Land Acts of

1862, 1865 and 1873, which did not have Maori assent, and the Immigration and Public Works Acts. The petition summarised nine Maori grievances as terms of reference for a commission of inquiry.[1]

1. The greed of the New Zealand Company, which caused conflict at Wairau.
2. The war against Te Rangihaeata in 1842–3, and unlawful execution of his followers.
3. The war in the North against Heke and Kawiti.
4. The divisive fight between Te Hapuku and Te Moananui caused by government land buying in 1848.
5. The war against Wiremu Kingi at Waitara.
6. The Waikato war in 1863.
7. The tribal fight among Ngati Tautahi in which four people were killed because of corrupt land-buying practices by government agents, who expended £700,000 in the process.
8. The imprisonment of 200 of Te Whiti's men in 1879.
9. The imprisonment of Te Whiti in 1881. The deputation concluded by asking for the release of Te Whiti.

Lord Kimberley told the chiefs that it was not the duty of the Colonial Office to advise the Queen in reference to local matters like their petition. The management of land in New Zealand was absolutely in the hands of the New Zealand Government, and the Queen was advised by the ministers of the colony in such matters. But, said Lord Kimberley, having received the petition, he would transmit it to the colonial Government, which had power to decide on whether or not there ought to be a Royal Commission.

The New Zealand Prime Minister, Frederick Whitaker, responded to Lord Kimberley by dismissing the petition to the Queen on the grounds that few Maori knew of it. Hirini Taiwhanga was belittled as 'not a man of any rank' and of 'no importance beyond what he has gained in consequence of his abilities and education'. Taiwhanga was also denigrated for his failings as a surveyor and schoolteacher. The first six 'wrongs' listed in the petition were blamed on the Imperial Government, as they occurred before the settlers took over responsible government of the colony. As to the unauthorised laws overriding the Treaty, they were 'enabling and not restrictive'. The Native Land Acts were rationalised as relieving the Maori owners from the monopoly held by Government, and enabling them to sell their lands to whomsoever they pleased. With the exception of land confiscated because of 'rebellion', the Government denied taking Maori land, otherwise the land had been acquired from 'willing sellers'.[2] This self-seeking manipulation of the facts by the New Zealand Government, and its power to deny a commission of inquiry into its own wrongdoing, is consistent with its behaviour as a colonising regime. Lord Kimberley's washing his hands of the whole affair like Pontius Pilate indicated not only compliance with manipulation of the metropolis by a raw colonial outpost, but moral turpitude as well. Truth and justice as abstract principles became victims of the corrupting influence of unbridled power.

King Tawhiao's Deputation to England

Maori belief in the righteousness of their cause was not diminished by the failure of the Ngapuhi delegation of chiefs to get royal assent to a commission of inquiry into their grievances. In 1884 King Tawhiao led a second deputation to England. Accompanying him were Wiremu Te Wheoro and Patara Te Tuhi from the Tainui tribes, Topia Turoa, representing the tribes from Taupo to Whanganui, and Hori Ropiha, representing the Ngati Kahungunu people from Hawke's Bay to Wellington. The deputation was received by Lord Derby, Secretary of State for the Colonies.

The chiefs began their petition by professing loyalty to the Crown. Te Wheoro recounted his lifetime of service and co-operation with the colonial administration. First as a magistrate in 1860, then captain of the militia in 1863, and then Native Land Court assessor in 1866. He resigned in 1872 when he became disillusioned with the court. In 1875 he was made a Maori commissioner. From this post he saw more clearly the unfair treatment of Maori people by the Government and resigned four years later. In 1879 he entered Parliament, hoping to get a better deal for Maori people. But when he saw that Maori members were ignored, he realised the Maori were victims of oppression. For this reason he accompanied Tawhiao's deputation to England to lay Maori grievances before the Queen because 'we are weary of laying our grievances before the New Zealand Government'.[3]

Tawhiao's petition accused the New Zealand Government of trampling on the guarantee of chieftainship to lands, forests and fisheries under the Treaty of Waitangi. The grievances included the seizure of Wiremu Kingi's land in Taranaki, and the war and confiscations that followed. When the war was carried to Waikato, even Te Wheoro, who had aided the Government, was cited as a victim of confiscation. He lost 80,000 hectares, of which only a small portion was returned. The petition complained of the injustice against Te Whiti and the refusal of the Government to provide adequate reserve lands for Maori in the North Island. Concern was also expressed over the practices of the Native Land Court, putting only ten names on a certificate of title to tribal lands and making grants only to those who appeared before the court. The rights of those who did not attend were awarded to those who did. The petitioners asked for a Maori Commissioner appointed by the Queen to control the leasing and sale of Maori land. The petition concluded with a request for the appointment of an independent Royal Commissioner from England to investigate the wrongs done in New Zealand.

Lord Derby forwarded the petition to the New Zealand Government. The latter responded in March 1885 with a memorandum insinuating that infractions of the Treaty of Waitangi before 1865 were the responsibility of the Imperial Government. Lord Derby could do no more than express sympathy for Maori in the English Parliament, and promised to 'use its good offices with the Colonial Government with the view of obtaining for the natives all the consideration which can be given them'.[4]

When Tawhiao received Lord Derby's reply, he led another deputation of chiefs in March 1886 to the Governor, seeking his opinion. With him were Paora Tuhaere, Tana Te Waharoa, Te Tihirahi, Te Arai, Te Toko, Wi Parera, Tareha and Te Koroneho. Paora Tuhaere asked the Governor as the Queen's representative responsible for upholding the Treaty in New Zealand what he thought of Lord Derby's despatch asking the Government of New Zealand to protect the Maori nation. The Governor prevaricated, thereby avoiding a debate with men skilled in the oral tradition of the Maori. Instead, he told the chiefs to put their submissions to him in writing. In due course he wrote to them saying that the one fault in the Treaty was the clause giving Maori approval for the sale of land to Europeans. He also stated that he received no information from Lord Derby asking the Government to protect the Maori race. That being the case, replied Tawhiao in July, where in the Treaty was the mana to do away with the rights of the Maori nation given to the Native Land Court? Showing equal facility with the written conventions of the Pakeha, Tawhiao referred the Governor to paragraph 5 of Lord Derby's despatch to the Government, which said: 'If you are not to be advised by the Government of the Queen with regard to the Treaty of Waitangi, which they ceased to superintend, we wish you to ask your Government to protect the Maori race and abide with the laws that are just and honest.'[5]

In April 1886 Tawhiao invited John Ballance, Minister of Native Affairs, to meet with him at his settlement. There he called upon the Minister to suspend the Native Land Court, surveying of land and making roads until some understanding could be reached on these matters. The Minister agreed that they should reach an accord and thereupon attempted to co-opt Tawhiao by inviting him to stand for the Upper House, where money and other things would come his way. Tawhiao countered with the suggestion that a legislative council for all the chiefs of the land should be established, and to this end he would propose a Bill to Parliament. Ballance made his support for Tawhiao's proposal contingent on his acceptance of office in the Upper House. When Tawhiao's petition for the establishment of a legislative council of chiefs reached Parliament, Ballance did not table it because Tawhiao demurred from joining the Upper House.[6]

Despite the failure of Tawhiao's deputation, the Tainui tried again in 1914. Te Rata journeyed to England, where he was given an audience with the King provided he agreed not to raise any contentious issues. Like Tawhiao, he too returned home empty-handed.

The Maori Parliament

During the 1890s the political aspirations of the tribes crystallised into the formation of their own parliamentary institutions. This was their response to the dual world of the coloniser and colonised. The tribal runanga of the Kotahitanga Movement came to focus on the establishment of an independent Maori assembly at an inter-tribal meeting of ninety-six chiefs at Te Tiriti o Waitangi Marae in April 1892. There the decision was made to launch Kotahitanga mo Te Tiriti o Waitangi, the unification of the tribes under the Treaty.[7] By June, 20,934 people from many tribes in both the North and South Islands had signed the kirihipi, the parchment of the covenant of Kotahitanga. The collection of signatures had started in 1888. Although a number of tribes had not signed and the work of unification was incomplete, a sufficient base had been created to launch a Maori Parliament.

The first meeting of the Maori Parliament was held on 14 June 1892 at Waipatu Marae in Heretaunga. It was a grand occasion with a thousand men and women and numerous children attending the hui. Formalities began with Major Keepa Te Rangihiwinui, the former kupapa, standing at a point three chains distant from the marae reciting a karakia. The chiefs of Heretaunga, Wairarapa and other places stood in support of the prayer. They then advanced on to the marae carrying the flag of the Treaty of Waitangi and the kirihipi. With the Treaty of Waitangi and the Bible of God they were welcomed right to the flagpole at the centre of the marae. As they approached the flagpole, the sound of voices was heard singing the National Anthem. The flag was fastened and hoisted to the top of the flagpole. The Reverend Hoani Piwaka led the assembly in prayer, and Henare Tomoana, chairman of the marae committee, then welcomed the tribes, saying, 'Praise to Jehovah the God of Abraham, the God of Isaac, the God of Jacob and who was also the God of our ancestors who led them safely across the seas to these islands where we live. Glory be to Him forever and ever. Friends, chiefs of decision and power, the aristocracy of the tribes of the Maori people of the two islands of Aotearoa, including the South Island; you who have come from the four winds . . . greetings to you all.' He then outlined the four main issues on the agenda: (1) Unification of the tribes; (2) Examination of the Treaty of Waitangi to discover which part of the Treaty deprived Maori people of mana to determine matters pertaining to land; (3) Examination of Section 71 of the New Zealand Constitution Act 1852 to discover whether there was any clause in that law which enabled the Maori people to establish a council for themselves; (4) To ensure that no trouble should arise between the two peoples of New Zealand because of the first three matters. It was intended that only goodness and well-being of the Crown should flourish.

The Maori Parliament consisted of ninety-six members representing eight districts, six in the North Island and two in the South. The first Prime Minister was Hamiora Mangakahia, the Leader of the House was Te Whatahoro, and the Speaker, Henare Tomoana. Raniera Wharerau and Mitai Titore from Ngapuhi and Timoti Te Whiu from Ngai Tahu were ministers. In a speech to the Assembly, Tomoana summarised the reasons for the formation of the Maori Parliament. The aims had been defined at numerous tribal meetings culminating in those at Waitangi, Waiapu, Omahu, Wairarapa and Whanganui in 1888. These meetings had all decided to propose to Parliament that the Maori people themselves devise laws for their own lands. But when the deputation went to Parliament, the fragile unity of purpose disintegrated as different tribes promoted their own issues. Now the aims of the new Maori Parliament were the same as those defined by the many tribal meetings — to deal with the laws oppressing Maori people. The central issues were the weight of laws from the Maori Land Court, laws pertaining to surveys of Maori land, laws pertaining to partition, succession orders and guardianship of children, laws on goldfields and fisheries, the law that established the Public Trustee, laws of the Appeal Court, laws on mortgaging and leasing Maori land, and laws concerning land settlement companies.[8]

In his address to the Assembly, Tomoana justified the establishment of the Maori Parliament by reference to the Treaty of Waitangi and the New Zealand Constitution Act 1852. He explained to the Assembly that the Treaty gave authority for the Queen's Government to be established over New Zealand. Under the Treaty, the chiefs of the Maori people also gave permission for the Queen and her people to live in Aotearoa and Te Waipounamu. But the Treaty, which was confirmed by both parties, recognised as well the mana of the Maori over their lands. He then cited Section 71 of the Constitution Act as the legal basis for the Maori Parliament. This section allowed for the recognition of Native Districts where Maori people could govern themselves according to their own laws and customs provided they did not conflict with laws governing the lives of Europeans.

After a week of deliberations, the Maori Assembly produced a short Bill on the Maori Land Court, its officers and regulations for submission to Parliament. The submission requested Parliament to stop making laws for Maori people and their lands, and petitioned that power be given to the Maori themselves to make laws for the conduct of the Maori people, their lands and possessions.[9] At the end of the first session, the Assembly declared its manifesto. It claimed the right to review all Maori land grievances, including lands unfairly purchased with hoop iron, or illegally acquired by missionaries prior to the Treaty, lands wrongly sold or ceded, and lands confiscated by the Government. Lands in Maori ownership, whether held under Crown grant or papatipu, customary title, would be adjudicated by Maori committees. It also claimed the right to determine ownership of oyster beds, shellfish beds, fisheries, tidal estuaries and other food resources of the Maori. Its review of confiscated lands included Waitara, west coast reserves held by the Public Trustee, lands wrongly acquired by the Government in the South Island, lands taken without reason, and lands taken by unscrupulous companies. The aim of abolishing the Native Land Court was declared along with laws for the purchase or leasing of Maori land. The manifesto also included a policy for Maori land development, especially sheep and cattle farming and general animal husbandry. The entry of young Maori into high-status occupations was also advocated.[10]

The Maori Assembly considered the role of Maori members of Parliament in the House of Representatives. Some chiefs thought the

Maori members were merely tame parrots for the Government. Others urged they be withdrawn, because when oppressive laws were passed against the Maori, it could be claimed by the Pakeha there was Maori acquiescence by their very presence in the House. Some argued that Maori members should come under the direction of the Maori Parliament. But no firm decision was arrived at. However, the northern section of Kotahitanga succeeded in getting its candidate, Hone Heke, elected to Parliament in 1893. That year the second session of the Maori Parliament at Waipatu sought to reconstruct the economic base of the people by initiating a levy of £1 a head from members of Kotahitanga to establish a pool of capital for land improvement, clearing forests, maintaining farms and buying back land from Pakeha or sections in towns. This session concluded with a Bill seeking devolution of authority for the Assembly of Kotahitanga from the House of Representatives.[11]

In 1894 Hone Heke introduced into the House a Native Rights Bill seeking devolution of power to the Maori Parliament. The rationale for the Bill was the declaration of independence in 1835 by the confederation of northern chiefs, the Treaty of Waitangi guaranteeing rangatiratanga, and Section 71 of the New Zealand Constitution Act 1852. But the Bill was thwarted by Pakeha members walking out of the House during the debate, which was adjourned for the want of a quorum. At the fourth session of the Maori Parliament, held at Rotorua in March 1895, the rejection of the Bill was discussed. Mangakahia blamed the Prime Minister for not wanting to sit and listen to the Bill. Wi Pere drew the prophetic conclusion that 'the Bill seeking mana for Maori self-government would not be granted for perhaps as long as thirty years, like the Irish seeking home rule for themselves. After thirty-five years it has not been granted. This Bill will not be granted until all the land has been alienated, whereupon there will be no place left for its application.'[12] Despite that pessimistic prognosis, the Native Rights Bill was sent back to Parliament a second time and rejected in 1896.[13] Although Pakeha dominance was complete, there was no place yet in the heart of the coloniser for magnanimity towards the colonised. Besides, the remnant 2.4 million hectares of Maori land had still to be acquired. Kotahitanga was determined to defend those remaining hectares. But without executive power, it was forced to resort to direct action. The 1895 sitting of the Maori Parliament resolved to mount a boycott of the Native Land Court. Hone Heke and Wi Pere were deputed to go to the court sitting at Maketu to stop it. It was also decided to write letters to those whose claims were pending before the court to withdraw them.[14] Tribes in the King Country, Whanganui, Northland, Coromandel and East Coast withdrew their claims from the court. Although the boycott was not total and lasted for only three months, it slowed the rate of alienation sufficiently to cause concern for the Government.

Tawhiao's Kauhanganui

In the meantime King Tawhiao replicated what Kotahitanga had done by establishing the Kauhanganui, his House of Assembly, at Maungakawa in 1892. After the disappointing result from his visit to England, Tawhiao concluded that Maori grievances would have to be settled by Maori initiatives within New Zealand. When he got no response to his petition to the Minister of Native Affairs to establish a Maori Council of chiefs, he formed the Kauhanganui.[15] In August 1892 Tawhiao reported to the Kauhanganui on his interview with A. J. Cadman, Minister of Native Affairs, who offered him a pension of £225. He accepted it on the Minister's assurance that there was 'no meaning' to be attached to the pension. But he realised he was wrong when he heard Europeans claiming its purpose was to break down the barrier between him and the Government.[16] After he received the first instalment of £56 6 shillings for the first quarter, Tawhiao announced at a meeting of 300 people at Karikari that he had decided to forego the pension. He returned the money in July 1893 with interest of £1 14 shillings.[17]

In 1894 the Kauhanganui declared its policies in addition to previous pronouncements by Tawhiao. The power to lease land of the adherents of the King was under the mana of Tawhiao. The mineral rights to gold, coal, silver, iron and copper on leased lands remained with the King; only grazing rights went to the leaseholder. The tumuaki of the Kauhanganui, Tana Taingakawa Te Waharoa, was designated as having oversight and general supervision of papatupu lands that had not yet been affected by Pakeha laws or the Maori Land Court. Land on which court orders had been made could be re-examined by the Kauhanganui as to their validity on the application of owners. Surveying of land was prohibited without prior discussion with the tribe, the tumuaki and the kingitanga. For lands under Crown grant, permission from Tawhiao and the Kauhanganui had to be sought before any development of the land proceeded. Control of outsiders by marriage intruding into the remnants of Maori land was expressed in a law prohibiting Maori women from marrying Pakeha, or 'half-caste' children from becoming major shareholders in tribal land. But if a woman persisted in marrying a Pakeha, then she would have no mana and would be known as 'a woman who goes in the night'.[18] This pronouncement was a desperate attempt to halt cultural invasion through sexual congress, a reversal within sixty years of the policy of economic welcome to traders and binding them to the tribe through intermarriage.

In May 1894 the Kauhanganui promulgated its manifesto, which was designated 'the Covenant of Kotahitanga of the Maori People of Aotearoa'. This covenant defined the Maori sense of nationhood as the prior discoverers and inhabitants of Aotearoa and Te Waipounamu. It asserted that the land had not been conquered, or sold to any other nation of the world. This meant that Mana Maori Motuhake, discrete Maori sovereignty, remained over the land of their ancestors. This was the source, the wellspring of Maori motuhake law for the promotion and well-being of the people and the generations to come after them.[19]

The Divided House

In their pronouncements, both the Maori Parliament and the Kauhanganui used the code word kotahitanga, unification of the tribes, as the key to achievement of their aspirations. But the problem confronting them was unification of their own bifurcated political efforts. The first attempt to unify the two movements was made in 1892 by Henare Tomoana. When Tawhiao was asked to sign the covenant of Kotahitanga, the Ngapuhi tribes wrote to him stipulating that he left the designation 'king' out of it. Because of that, Tawhiao did not sign.[20] Following the death of Tawhiao in 1894, Kotahitanga made a second attempt to bring the 'child' who had inherited his father's mantle to stand among the chiefly heads of Aotearoa and Te Waipounamu. On 17 May 1895 a deputation of the Maori Parliament consisting of Major Keepa Rangihiwinui, Hamiora Mangakahia and Takarangi Metekingi took a copy of the covenant of Kotahitanga to a meeting of the Kauhanganui at Maungakawa for King Mahuta to sign. The spokesman addressed the young king, quoting one of Tawhiao's aphorisms: 'Kimihia te mea ngaro', search for that which is hidden, an allusion to the usurped sovereignty and well-being of the tribes. That which was lost would be recovered by unification of the Kauhanganui and Kotahitanga. But the kingship would not be submerged in the interest of unity. Tawhiao had also said, 'I would not like the water to spill out from within, but for the water from outside to flow inside.'[21] The deep waters of tribal rivalry from Ngapuhi in the North would not flow south to mingle with the waters of the Waikato. Although the aims of the two movements were congruent, they pursued them separately.

Kotahitanga and the Kauhanganui continued to meet independently into the turn of the century. The closest they came to unity was when a joint deputation waited on the Prime Minister in November 1897. On that occasion Taua Taingakawa Te Waharoa, president of the Kauhanganui, accompanied the leaders of Kotahitanga. He addressed the Prime Minister, professing loyalty to the Queen, recognition of the authority of Parliament, and the common desire of Kotahitanga and the Kauhanganui for devolution of power to them to administer Maori lands, fisheries and other possessions. Should that wish be granted, then the Maori would live in harmony with Pakeha under the rule of law.[22] Although the Native Rights Bill was unsuccessful, and unity between these authentic indigenous political movements not achieved, their efforts were not entirely profitless. Their boycott of the Native Land Court substantiated the trenchant criticisms of land laws made by the Native Land Commission 1891. The commission recommended the establishment of a Native Land Board, with power to manage tribal lands under the direction of Maori committees representing owners. Consequently the Prime Minister Richard Seddon was conciliatory on the question of land.

Seddon agreed that the sale of Maori land should cease as there were only two million hectares left. He proposed instead that the land be leased to settlers, ostensibly to retain it in Maori ownership. When the Maori Parliament met at Papawai in May 1898, Seddon alluded to the political disparity in the representation of Maori people in the General Assembly. He hinted it was the responsibility of the Government to increase Maori representation.[23] Although he did nothing about the latter, Seddon pushed two measures through Parliament designed to mollify the concerns of Kotahitanga and the Kauhanganui. The Maori Councils Act 1900 provided for the election of village councils to attend to local affairs such as sanitation, health, drainage and the provision of pure water supplies. The Native Lands Administration Act 1900 purported to give some small degree of local control over land matters through the establishment of Maori land councils, but the degree of devolution was illusory, since Pakeha members ended up dominating the councils.[24] The councils had power to confirm alienations of native land, administer lands vested in them in trust on behalf of the owners, act in trust on behalf of the owners over land set apart for native settlement, and to control the administration and disposition of native land on the resolution of assembled owners.[25]

These laws, coming at the turn of the century, marked the reduction of the Maori to a powerless minority as a consequence of the colonial experience. Introduced diseases, musket wars, land wars, and disruption of tribal life and economic activities by the operations of the Native Land Court had reduced the population to its lowest point of 45,549.[26] Humanitarians were moved sufficiently by the plight of the passing Maori to 'smooth the pillow of the dying race'.[27] For some Pakeha, extinction by natural attrition was the preferred outcome of the clash between the races. For others, it was assimilation. At the turn of the century it seemed to the Pakeha that the Darwinian law of survival of the fittest was inexorably being played out in New Zealand. But this primordial view did not take into consideration the resilience and adaptability of the Maori.

The 1906 census indicated that the Maori had recovered from the brink of extinction to record an intercensal increase of 10.45 per cent. The greatest intercensal gain of 29.3 per cent was made in 1936, by which time the population had almost doubled to 82,326.[28] The Maori birth rate that year was more than twice that of the Pakeha, at 43.79 per thousand compared with 16.64. But there was a high attrition rate as well. Maori infant mortality in 1940 was almost triple that of the Pakeha, at 87.22 per thousand compared with 30.21.[29] This population recovery posed a new set of problems for the Maori, whose remaining lands were being picked off by Pakeha laws against their wishes. The old chiefly order exemplified by Kotahitanga and the Kauhanganui had tried to ameliorate the effects of colonisation by seeking a limited form of autonomy within the new nation state that dominated their lives. But to no avail. The torch of self-determination they carried in the nineteenth century passed into the hands of new educated leaders.

The New Kotahitanga

The temporary respite in the Government's aggressive thrust to acquire Maori land for Pakeha settlement was mediated from within by the influence of the Minister of Native Affairs, James Carroll, on the Prime Minister, Richard Seddon. As a senior politician of mixed ancestry who identified with the plight of the Maori, Carroll fought a lone battle for many years to delay the alienation of Maori land. His obstructionism to Pakeha designs was dubbed the taihoa policy.[30] To assist him in his campaign to uplift the Maori from the oppression of colonisation, Carroll took under his wing young Apirana Ngata, who had become the first Maori to graduate when he received an MA degree from Canterbury University College in 1894. In 1896 Ngata completed a law degree at Auckland and he was admitted to the bar in 1897.[31] Although Ngata had a promising career ahead of him in an Auckland law office, he gave it up in the interest of his people to serve them in the arena of cultural politics.

Ngata's stepping-stone into public life was the students' association of Te Aute College, the Anglican school where he received his second-ary education. This association was founded in 1891 by the headmaster, John Thornton, who was its secretary. Its president was Archdeacon Samuel Williams. The original title of the organisation was the Associ-ation for the Amelioration of the Condition of the Maori Race. While some of its aims were benevolent, such as the suppression of alcoholism among Maori and the promotion of health, hygiene and scientific knowledge, it also had an underlying agenda of assimilation in the abolition of 'injurious' customs and 'useless' meetings.[32] Thornton also advocated a reduction in gift-giving at weddings and tangihanga, and abandonment of the custom of burying grave goods with deceased persons. Not much came of these ideas until 1897, when the association was reorganised on Maori terms and renamed Kotahitanga mo Te Aute. Thereafter there were two countervailing forces in the move-ment, one advocating adoption of Pakeha values and the other pursuing a Maori agenda. Both sought accommodation between the races and advancement of the Maori.

The new Kotahitanga aimed to use the educated students of Te Aute as a 'machine' and 'hands to do the work' to advance the well-being of the people.[33] In December 1898 Eruera Kawhia and other Ngati Porou chiefs invited the association to meet at Taumata o Mihi in Waiapu. The following year Tamahau Mahupuku hosted the meeting at Papawai in the Wairarapa. It was at this time that Ngata gave up law and became the full-time travelling secretary for Kotahitanga mo Te Aute.[34] In 1900 Wiki Taitoko and Whata Hipango were hosts at Putiki in Whanganui. The support on the part of chiefs for this new organisation grew partly out of a waning of interest in the Maori Parliament. At Putiki, Te Heuheu, the paramount chief of Tuwharetoa, said he was a strong supporter of the old Kotahitanga because he thought there was salvation in it for the Maori, but it was not found. Should the old Kotahitanga cease, then he hoped the new one would flourish.[35]

Ngata saw the old Kotahitanga of the Treaty of Waitangi as the forum of chiefly elders. At Putiki he stated that Te Aute was in the ascendancy while Kotahitanga of Waitangi was declining, but the two would eventually meet in the middle and combine. In the meantime, he said, 'we will be at the feet of the chiefs'.[36] In that position Ngata hoped they would not be trampled on and discouraged but allowed to flourish to become the 'nurturing sap' for generations to come.[37] But the new organisation did not have the same political thrust as its predecessor. There was no talk of seeking devolution of power. Instead, a policy of co-operation within the parameters defined by the state was followed.

The Maori Councils

In recognition of the role Ngata and the Kotahitanga had adopted, they were invited by Government to draft the model by-laws for the new marae councils being established under the Maori Councils Act.[38] The hui at Putiki in 1900 proposed that meeting houses be built with wooden floors fifteen centimetres above ground and have through ventilation, even though making an aperture in the rear wall was a sign of death in Maori custom. But it was felt that Pakeha customs over Maori houses were so widespread that the old laws of tapu were no longer applicable. Lighting fires inside meeting houses was to be prohibited unless a chimney was installed. Alcohol was to be barred from marae. There were to be proper arrangements for the disposal of refuse and the prevention of contamination of water supplies. Marae reserves were to be enclosed by boundary fences capable of keeping out animals and wandering stock. Lying in state for corpses was not to exceed four days, a radical departure from traditional times when corpses were kept for up to three weeks.[39] The marae councils were also expected to discourage large-scale hui and to spread the burden of holding them, so that host marae would not exhaust their provisions. The regulation requiring the marae councils to discourage the 'mis-guided' practices of the tohunga anticipated the Tohunga Suppression Act of 1907. This measure aimed to improve health care, especially for young children, whose illness derived from contagious European diseases rather than mate Maori.

While the stated aims and regulations formulated by the Te Aute Kotahitanga were directed at making adjustments in Maori society to the colonising culture of the Pakeha, there was underlying its aspirations a dual bicultural thrust as well. It advocated that all Maori boarding schools teach the Maori language, and that it also be taught in the constituent colleges of the University of New Zealand.[40] The latter demand was to engage Ngata's energies in a protracted battle over the next five decades. The association also advocated other integrative practices, such as Maori participation in sport, physical education and the training of Maori youth in dairying and horticulture. It is interesting to note that John Thornton advised the association against rugby as being too violent a contact sport, which was likely to cause injuries and rouse the passion and fighting spirit of the Maori.[41] Instead he suggested playing cricket and tennis, because rugby was not a gentleman's game. But cricket never found favour with the Maori. In the years ahead they were to become passionately devoted to rugby, the national sport in which they found ready acceptance on equal terms with the Pakeha.

From the launch pad of the Te Aute Association, Ngata became the organising inspector of the Maori councils in 1902.[42] That year he suggested that the Kotahitanga of Waitangi go into recess. In his view it had achieved its purpose of protecting the remnants of Maori land by wringing from Parliament legislation that brought the land councils into being. He was supported by Carroll, who predicted the demise of Kotahitanga when their desires were embodied in the Maori Councils Act and the Native Lands Administration Act. Carroll advocated 'uniting the adult with the yearling' so that the annual general assembly of the Maori councils replaced the Maori Parliament.[43]

The establishment of the Maori councils in 1900 provided Maui Pomare, who had graduated in medicine the previous year, with an opportunity to enter the arena of cultural politics with Ngata. He was appointed Maori Health Officer under the Public Health Act and Maori Councils Act. He spent his time visiting marae, investigating Maori health, examining water supplies and giving talks on sanitation hygiene and health.[44] Pomare attended the first annual general meeting of the Maori councils, chaired by Ngata in 1902. There his proposal of a hospital for Maori people, staffed by a Maori doctor and nurses, was warmly received. As a mediator between two cultures, Pomare aimed at combining Pakeha medicine with Maori knowledge of illness.[45]

Although the Government appeared to be making progress in Maori policy through the work of Ngata and Pomare, it continued to woo the Maori King. In March 1903 the Prime Minister, Richard Seddon, welcomed Mahuta and a retinue of 150 followers from the Tainui tribes at Government House in Auckland. There he invited Mahuta to join the Legislative Council, with the ulterior motive of appointing

him to the Executive Council. Mahuta, who had endorsed the boundaries for the Waikato council, stated his desire for the two people to
be reconciled. When Mahuta entered Government House to be sworn
in as a member of the Legislative Council, Ngati Maniapoto sang the
derisive song 'Patupatu'. This was their farewell to Mahuta for
abandoning his mana and people by turning to the Pakeha.[46] While
some Waikato elders saw the move as an honour, the Maniapoto
clearly saw it as dishonour. But for Seddon, there was an ulterior
motive. He wanted land for settlers, and he could get Waikato land
only by Mahuta co-operating and putting the land under the jurisdiction of the land councils.[47] Seddon expressed his disappointment that
Mahuta and his people had initially put their lands under the land
councils then withdrew them.

Pakeha domination of the land councils had dashed Maori hopes for
controlling their remaining lands, and they responded by withdrawing
from the jurisdiction of councils. Under pressure from the Opposition
to open up remaining Maori land for settlement, and spurred by racist
criticism in the *New Zealand Herald* denouncing rule by coloured or
native races over British leaseholders, the Government resumed its
former role of facilitating the sale of Maori land to Pakeha settlers.[48]
The first measure was the Maori Land Settlement Act 1905. The
Government replaced the Maori councils with land boards presided
over by Pakeha presidents and majorities. Aggressive government
buying of Maori land was resumed with the establishment of the
Native Land Purchase Board, which had a monopoly in the purchase
of tribal land.[49] The Lands For Settlements Act opened up Maori land
for purchase, which for a short five years were protected by leasing,
because no self-respecting settler wanted a Maori landlord. This turn
of events agitated Maori leaders and roused talk of reviving Kotahitanga
as an independent voice for the people, because the Maori councils
were seen as creatures of Government and therefore unable to criticise
the changes.[50]

Awareness of the progressive alienation of land was accompanied by
awareness of cultural erosion and loss of identity. The editor of
Pipiwharauroa[51] warned against neglect of the Maori tongue. Loss of
language, customs, land and mana would end in assimilation. Even
kaumatua were guilty of 'bastardising' the language. The expression
of the cultural ethos of the Maori through art was also threatened by
extinction. The art of carving, for instance, had all but died out after
the completion by Te Kooti's followers of the meeting house Te
Whai-a-te-Motu at Ruatahuna in 1888. This house, named to commem-

orate the pursuit of Te Kooti by the militia, was the last of the great carved houses built as symbolic statements of resistance to cultural invasion. The house was begun in 1870 at the height of Te Kooti's campaign to recover New Zealand for the Maori. In the following decade, among shattered tribes, meeting houses continued to be built, some with painted decorations only, and others with little or no carving at all. The Te Aute Kotahitanga discussed these cultural transformations and decided to promote a recovery of culture. Rewiti Kohere suggested establishing a Maori craft school. Wi Pere argued that Maori youths should be taught carving and was prepared to endow such a school with 2,000 hectares.[52] But because of the reversal of Government policy on protecting the remnants of Maori land, cultural considerations had to be set aside for the time being. Ngata took up a suggestion advocated by the Rees Commission in 1891 that a policy of Maori land development and settlement was needed.[53] He argued that finance ought to be made available to Maori committees to develop the land themselves. For Ngata, development of the land was the only solution to its retention. It was no good trusting the law or the Government, because 'the word and the law were slippery'.[54] Ngata's views were reinforced by Carroll in an address to Ngati Porou at Waiomatatini in November 1905. He explained that the laws aimed at settlement of 'idle' Maori land. He tried to pursuade them to lease the land, because people, meaning Pakeha, were against 'idle' land or 'lazy people'.[55]

Graduates in Parliament

Ngata's work in the Te Aute Association and the Maori councils provided him with useful experience for his career in politics, especially in the development of policies that would improve the lot of Maori people. Within five years of the establishment of the Maori councils, it was clear from the lack of government funding that there was no future for them. They stuttered on for a further five years and became moribund.[56] But before that happened, Ngata stepped into the arena of national politics. With the support of the Ngati Porou, he won the Eastern Maori seat in 1905 from Wi Pere. In his election speech Ngata signalled a change of direction from the political thrust of the chiefly leaders of Kotahitanga and the Kauhanganui. As an educated man he was going to put his talents to work for the people by participating in mainstream politics. He said, 'It is correct for us to take grievances to Parliament, to tie up our lands lest they become prey to sales . . . my policy is based on my understanding of the law . . . Let us not sit back on the marae of our homes asking for favourable laws from above, below, or wherever it is hidden. Let us pursue all avenues whereby land can be developed by Maori people.'[57]

In January 1906 Ngata addressed the Ngati Porou farming organisation and exhorted them to familiarise themselves with the Crown's laws pertaining to land. Besides studying the statutes they should also discuss the debates in Parliament so that they would be better able to guide and influence members of Parliament. At home, lands had to be secured by development. Where that could not be done, the land should be leased, because the Government would not let land lie 'idle'. The people should take the initiative by marking out the land they wanted to develop, and separating out land they were unable to use and lease it out. But as a realist, Ngata warned Ngati Porou of the danger of the mortgage debt trap as a pathway to development. He said, 'This thing called mortgage, is a junior brother of alienation. If the conditions are wrong, the debt is not paid, the land will go.'[58]

It was at this time that Ngata proposed consolidation of Maori land interests and incorporation of tribal lands as a solution to the problem of multiple ownership and fragmented land titles. The problem had been caused by Maori who gained Crown grants dying intestate. When that happened, the Native Land Court gave succession orders to all the descendants of the deceased. A repetition of the process in the next and succeeding generations meant that the land-holdings were too small to be economically viable. The problem was the direct outcome of the imposition of Pakeha law of individual title over the Maori principle of group ownership of land. Ngata was also conscious of the lack of provision in the law on leases of Maori land for the protection of forests. He thought it was a grave misfortune not to have trees to shelter the land, protect sources of water, and to preserve timber. Even two hectares out of every 100 leased would have been sufficient. The proposal to reserve 5 per cent of forest lands leased out to Pakeha was put to the Minister of Maori Affairs, James Carroll, on the occasion of Seddon's death, but it was not heeded. Ngata's concern was well founded, as severe soil erosion and landslides set in over the lands of the East Coast in the next fifty years.

Although he was in the corridors of power, Ngata kept his connection with the Te Aute Association as a useful source of ideas for the generation of Maori policy. At the association's meeting in 1906 he advocated that the Minister of Maori Affairs record Maori songs and speeches on the 'machines of the Pakeha'.[59] It was resolved also at this hui to press the Government to establish a carving school, so that the

ancestral treasures of carving, weaving and the making of other ornaments would not be lost. The grievances of the Arawa tribes over
the loss of their food resources and livelihood by the Government's
takeover of the lakes in the thermal district of Rotorua were aired at
this meeting. These issues were to be taken up by Ngata in the years
ahead.

In 1907 Ngata sat on the Commission of Inquiry into Maori Land
chaired by Chief Justice Robert Stout. Despite his policy of retaining
Maori land, Ngata had to bow to the inexorable force of the Pakeha
demand for land. Of the 1.2 million hectares investigated as being
suitable for development, the Commission recommended the use of
260,800 hectares for Pakeha settlement.[60] Even when Ngata had a
hand in the formulation of the Native Land Act 1909, he was unable
to stem the tide of alienation. The Native Land Settlement Account,
for instance, was used for the purchase of Maori land for Pakeha settlement and not to help Maori develop their land.[61] The only trade-off
Ngata got was support from Stout for the principle of developing
Maori land. But almost twenty years were to pass before government
finance was made available for Maori land development. The one
comfort that came Ngata's way was the entry of his colleague Dr Peter
Buck into Parliament.

After graduating from medical school in 1905, Buck was appointed
medical officer to the Department of Health. He worked for a time
around Taupo in 1907, and thereafter in Northland, co-operating with
the Maui Pomare in improving Maori health. When Hone Heke, the
Member for Northern Maori, died in 1909, Buck along with Carroll
accompanied the body back to Northland. Hone Heke's mother was
so honoured by the presence of these two men that she promptly
offered her son's 'widow', the vacant seat in Parliament, to the handsome chief from the south. In his election speech Buck made it clear
that he championed Maori rights and expressed the hope that the
Government would listen to the exhortations of the Maori as much
as it did to the Pakeha.[62] For a time Ngata turned his attention to
co-operate with Buck in the promotion of Maori health. He was particularly anxious to have Maori women trained as nurses, an issue that
had been raised by the Te Aute Association meeting in 1907.[63]

Inevitably, Ngata was drawn back to the almost hopeless task of
trying to halt the alienation of what remained of Maori land. In 1911
he tried to consolidate the Maori position by presenting to the acting
Prime Minister, Sir James Carroll, a Maori farming scheme. It was
rejected.[64] The rebuff had tragic consequences. Between 1911 and

1921, almost a million hectares of Maori land were sold.[65] Ngata's consolidation scheme of exchanging small blocks of land among owners to create viable farming units was too slow to counter the speed at which land was being acquired by Pakeha under existing laws. The consolidation of 40,000 hectares on the East Coast by Ngata, although better than nothing, was poor consolation for his efforts. On the west coast, the Taranaki Maori were virtually landless. All that remained there were their reserved lands which were leased out to Pakeha settlers.

In 1911 Maui Pomare entered Parliament for Western Maori. His purpose was to recover 7,200 hectares of tribal lands in Taranaki for which 133 leases held by Pakeha settlers were due to expire.[66] Pomare negotiated the return of the land over a ten-year period. But he made no provision to ensure the land was inalienable, as it was returned into individual ownership. As an educated man, capable of dealing with bureaucracy and the free enterprise system of capitalism, he made the mistake of assuming his tribesmen were able to make their way in it as well. They failed. 'Enmeshed in mortgages, at the mercy of markets, tempted by cash offers to abandon their worries, the inexperienced converts to private enterprise sold out to the Pakeha, and the Pakeha, now having the freehold, now had the land for all time.'[67]

Professional men and university graduates such as Buck, Ngata and Pomare, have been characterised by Paulo Freire as men who have been determined from above by a culture of domination that has constituted them as dual beings.[68] They are bicultural, and being so, are torn by loyalty to the wellspring of their own culture, and connection by occupation to the power-brokers of the colonising culture. Of these men, Ngata was the one most steeped in Maori culture and therefore had no illusions as to his primary allegiance and obligations. Buck became Maori by enculturation late in life. But being a scholarly man, he made it his business to learn the Maori language, customs and traditions, and accordingly, became Ngata's close friend, supporter and confidant in the struggle for Maori rights. Pomare, on the other hand, was moulded by his education at Te Aute College and the American Missionary Medical College in Michigan, where he trained. He took on Anglophile values to such an extent that occasionally in the prosecution of his work as a Native health officer and member of Parliament he alienated himself from his people.

As medical officer, he directed his efforts against the 'demoralisation of the Maori' caused by drunkenness, smoking, gambling, bad sanitation and disease,[69] as if these were inherent in Maori people and not products of social conditions arising out of colonisation. Describing them as 'pest-holes', he destroyed by fire 1,900 abandoned houses that owners had left standing because they were tapu. There was no room in Pomare's scheme of health for the spiritual healing of tohunga, who were banned from practising, along with charlatans and quacks, by the Tohunga Suppression Act 1907. It was Pomare who begged the Government for the measure to abolish the 'demoralising practice of witchcraft'.[70] The statute was to remain in force for over fifty years before it was repealed.

Maori people lived with these forced changes by Pomare, but, inevitably, his Anglophilia led him into an indiscretion against tribal sensitivities. In the course of the First World War, Maori were exempt from conscription but served as volunteers in Te Hokowhitu a Tu, the the Maori Contingent formed by Ngata.[71] One of the first to volunteer in 1914 after he withdrew from politics was Peter Buck. But tribes in the Waikato who had their lands unjustly confiscated refused to volunteer. As the war dragged on, the Military Service Act was extended to Waikato and Maniapoto by Government Proclamation in June 1917. The ariki Te Puea opposed military service and led an anti-conscription movement in the Waikato. Pomare, who was an advocate of conscription and chairman of the Maori Recruiting Board,[72] went to Waikato the following year to persuade the leaders to waive their opposition. There, he was subjected to whakapohane, the contemptuous war dance done with bared buttocks. The climax came in a derisive dance by a woman who exposed her vulva to him in grotesque contortions of contempt.[73] As a 'man of two worlds', Pomare identified too closely with the Pakeha and inevitably ended up offending the people who voted him into power.

The Prophets Return

While the educated élite were attempting accommodation with the Pakeha through mainstream politics, poverty, alienation and a desire for self-determination impelled the Maori to look again for salvation through charismatic leaders. After the turn of the century, two new prophets arose in the Urewera and Whanganui as the modern counterparts to Te Kooti in the east and Te Whiti in the west. They were Rua Kenana and Wiremu Tahupotiki Ratana.

In the closing years of the nineteenth century, the Tuhoe people resisted Pakeha encroachment into Urewera territory by the way of miners, roadmakers and the Government's triangulation survey of their lands. Although their opposition extracted a concession from the Government in the Urewera Native District Reserve Act 1896, covering 260,000 hectares of land,[74] the people feared it would only be a matter of time before the Pakeha had his way with these lands. The conditions were ready made for the rise of Rua Kenana, who, like Moses, came down from Maungapohatu, the sacred mountain of the Tuhoe, and announced his divine mission in 1904 as the chosen one to follow Te Kooti. He practised as a faith-healer and gathered followers. In 1906 he persuaded them to sell their possessions and give up material goods as Christ had done with his disciples. His next move was to sell 16,000 hectares of Tuhoe lands at Maungapohatu and Waimana for £31,000. After paying survey costs of £7,000, the sale realised £24,000 in capital to develop Hiruharama Hou, Rua's New Jerusalem and City of God at Maungapohatu.[75]

By 1908 Rua's community, like Te Whiti's before him, had cleared and farmed 280 hectares of land, brought in stock, planted orchards, built new houses, laid on a pure water supply, set a high standard of hygiene by providing wash-basins, and established by-laws prohibiting horses in the main street of the village.[76] The community functioned to stabilise the life of the people in the rapidly changing world brought on by colonisation and the aggressive thrust of civilisation into the Urewera. But the authorities distrusted Rua as they did Te Whiti. First they persecuted him for evading the dog tax. This measure was an attempt to control the numerous dogs in Maori villages that were thought to be a menace to Pakeha flocks of sheep.[77] Then they prosecuted Rua for supplying liquor to his followers. At that time Maori, unlike Pakeha, were not permitted by law to buy liquor for consumption at home. As a consequence, there was a flourishing sly-grog trade run by Pakeha to supply Maori customers. Rather than let these people prey on his community, Rua bowed to the demand of his adherents and supplied them himself. The racial discrimination built into the Sale of Liquor Act was not lost on Rua, who proclaimed his commitment to 'one law for two people' by the inscription on his flag.[78] For his temerity in challenging an unjust law, Rua was gaoled for three months in 1915. Thereafter he became public enemy number one, as Pakeha hysteria generated by the war led to accusations of Rua being pro-Kaiser, and holding him responsible for Tuhoe not enlisting. Foisting blame on an individual such as Rua for non-enlistment of Tuhoe, indicated Pakeha ignorance of Maori politics and traditions. Tuhoe identified with the Maori King through genealogical ties, Te Kooti's Ringatu faith, and opposition to colonisation as signified by adoption of the term rohe potae for their territory after 1896.

In 1916 the authorities moved forcibly against Rua on the pretext of an old sly-grog charge. But the underlying agenda was Pakeha paranoia, accusations of sedition and assertion of dominance. It was a replay of what had happened to Te Whiti thirty-five years before. Three police contingents of sixty heavily armed men marched on Maungapohatu. Shooting broke out and two men were killed, one of whom was Rua's son. Rua was arrested and taken to prison at Mt Eden. The trial, which lasted forty-seven days, ended in Rua being sentenced to gaol for resisting an arrest for which there was no substantive charge. The trial exhausted the resources of Rua's commune and his movement collapsed. The people had to bear the cost of the police expedition, which came to £900, and legal defence costs of £500. When dust from the confrontation settled, the underlying reason for the assertion of Pakeha control by the use of state force was made manifest by William Herries, Minister of Native Affairs. Herries sought Rua's co-operation to assist him in finding a peaceful way of settling the country without resorting to confiscating land.[79]

Having tried pacifist separation of the races, which evoked as much violence from the state as did guerrilla resistance, the prophets had to find a new direction for self-determination. In 1918 the mantle of prophet leader was assumed by Ratana, who proclaimed himself mangai, the mouthpiece of God. Ratana gained a reputation as a faith-healer to such an extent that even Pakeha referred to him as a 'miracle man'. People flocked from all parts of the country to hear the teachings of the new prophet. Tents and shacks sprang up as the humble beginnings of the community known as Ratana Pa. People healed by Ratana signed the covenant of his church, which renounced belief in tapu and superstitious practices of the past. The covenant professed faith in Jehovah and belief in the Trinity of the Father, Son and Holy Ghost. A major theme underlying the Ratana faith was unity through a pan-Maori ideology superceding tribal affiliations. Unity was symbolised in the name morehu, the survivors of the ancestors from the trauma of colonisation. After a mission to Northland in 1921, Ratana's adherents increased to 19,000. With his church firmly established, Ratana turned his movement into a political force.[80]

In 1924 Ratana led a deputation to England seeking redress of Maori grievances under the Treaty of Waitangi. But under instructions from the Government, the New Zealand High Commissioner blocked Ratana from gaining an audience with the King or even the Prime Minister.[81] Like Tawhiao before him, Ratana returned to New

Zealand determined to seek an internal solution for grievances against the Crown. He turned to politics and made submissions to successive Prime Ministers seeking assistance for his programmes. Rebuffed in turn by Coates, Ward and Forbes, Ratana turned to help from the fledgling Labour Party. In 1932 he met with Harry Holland to negotiate a coalition with Labour. In return for support from 38,000 of his followers, Ratana asked Holland to take up the cause of his people when Labour won the next election. His programme included recognition of the Treaty of Waitangi, mana motuhake, confiscation grievances in Taranaki, Waikato, Tauranga, and Tairawhiti, the Ngai Tahu land claim, and grievances which included Lake Taupo, imposition of rates and taxes, and the payment of gratuities to Maori soldiers. Although the Taranaki claim had been settled by Government with a £5,000 annuity, the tribes were not satisfied. They wanted the confiscated land returned. So did the Waikato, Tauranga and East Coast tribes. Ratana cemented the liaison with Labour by concluding that 'no matter where the tribes go, my friends will be blacksmiths, carpenters and shoemakers. Today, the tribes are allied to you the little people.'[82] Holland agreed to take up the issues raised by Ratana but it was not to be, he died the following year.

After Labour came to power in 1935, Ratana called on the Prime Minister, Michael Joseph Savage, to renew the compact made with the former leader. He placed four symbols before Savage: three huia feathers, a potato and kumara, a piece of greenstone and a broken watch. After greeting the Prime Minister and expressing a desire for unity in the law, Ratana explained the meaning of the symbols to Savage, saying:

The first gifts are the three huia feathers and the vessel that bears them [the feathers were stuck in a potato]. These feathers are the symbol of Maoritanga on this island. If a man is seen wearing this feather, that man will be known to be a Maori. However, this bird is extinct, eaten by your pests and weasels, namely the pests of the Pakeha. The vessel of these feathers is the potato and kumara, however, we have no land to plant these foods. This greenstone is the symbol of Maori mana which I am giving to you. This greenstone treasure is the symbol of the mana of the Maori people, however, in these days the mana is lost. This watch is from my ancestor Te Ratana. That elder was a man who sided with Governor Grey, a man who also sided with Mr Seddon Premier of New Zealand. This is me, the descendant. Today is the first time I have sided with the Government, namely your day [as the Government]. This watch has no glass. Because that old man had no money the glass was not replaced. I also have no money to fix the glass. I pass these gifts into your hands.

He also gave Savage the Ratana pin, Te Tohu o Te Maramatanga, (symbol of enlightenment) saying: 'This pin is the symbol of all Ratana who are in my movement, they number 40,000. This day I place them under your care.' In return, Savage promised to attend to Maori hurts 'in accordance with the spirit of the Treaty of Waitangi', the guarantee of Maori well-being.[83] The meaning of that promise was to be tested in the years that lay ahead. In the meantime the two Maori seats held by the Ratana candidates H. T. Ratana (Western Maori) and Eruera Tirikatene (Southern Maori) were aligned with Labour. The other two seats followed later. Northern Maori was delivered to Labour in 1938, and Eastern Maori in 1943.

CHAPTER 10

Mana Maori Motuhake

E kore te uku e piri ki te rino, ka whitikia e te ra ka ngahoro.
— Te Whiti o Rongomai

The spontaneous recovery of the Maori population from the trauma of colonisation after the turn of the century was matched by a cultural revival. But because the revival began in rural tribal hinterlands, at a time when the Maori were thought to be a subjected and dying race, the colonising Pakeha were not fully aware of the transformation taking place. This was because Maori and Pakeha lived discrete lives. Up to 1926, 90 per cent of Maori people lived in rural communities[1] away from the main centres of Pakeha population. The points of contact between Maori and Pakeha were superficial as the Maori were reduced to selling their labour as bush-fellers, roadmakers, farm workers, and seasonal workers in freezing works and sheep shearing gangs. This accommodation of the Maori to the forces of capitalism enabled Pakeha New Zealanders to promote the ideology of 'one people'. The ideology functioned in the terms of Larrain[2] as a 'distorted solution in the mind' to the contradictions in Maori-Pakeha relations arising out of the historic process of colonisation. The so-called 'Maori Wars' were a distant memory locked away in the nineteenth century. The crushing of the pacifist prophets Te Whiti and Rua Kenana ended any immediate pursuit of Maori sovereignty in the new nation, that claimed for itself a reputation of having the finest race relations in the world.

Essentially, the ideology of one people functioned to hide the relationship of Pakeha dominance and Maori subjection. But because race conflict was a primary element in the definition of the relationship, as much as the imposition of a capitalist mode of production over a tribal people, it is not of the same order as class conflict. The cleavage is much more fundamental in that it is defined in terms of ethnicity instead of class. Proletarianisation of the Maori by expropriation of their resources did not necessarily, as Ratana suggested to the leader of the Labour Party, make the Maori natural allies of the working class. The liaison with Labour was an attempt to find a political niche for Maori people in the new nation, as other niches had been explored by chiefs consorting with the Governor, Kotahitanga and Kauhanga-nui seeking devolution of power, and the educated élite participating in mainstream politics. Underlying these attempts at accommodation was a desire to maintain the integrity of Maori identity and culture in the face of considerable cultural erosion after a century of European contact.

The bastions of cultural conservatism for the Maori were kinship within the tribal polity, the marae and the institution of the tangi. Seasonal and migrant workers returned often to their kainga to be with kin in times of celebration or bereavement. Weddings, tangihanga, twenty-first birthdays and other community events were invariably held at tribal marae. The marae gave a modicum of stability and cultural continuity in the face of Pakeha dominance and assimilationist pressures. Land on which marae and tribal meeting houses are built are Maori Reservations under the Maori Affairs Act, and as such are inalienable. Accordingly, for landless Maori, the marae was their remaining turangawaewae, on which to hang their identity as the indigenous people who once owned the whole of the country. The marae remained as the beachheads from which the Maori launched their cultural revival in the twentieth century. The instigator was Apirana Ngata, who, despite the powerful political forces in the den of lions that were inimical to things Maori, maintained his cultural integrity and stimulated his people to recover their stolen humanity.

As the most able Maori leader of the century, Ngata concentrated much of his talent and energy on development of land as a means of protecting it from alienation. But government pressure to maintain the colonising goal of acquiring Maori land for Pakeha settlement was difficult to resist. Between 1911 and 1921, a million hectares were sold.[3] Thereafter, up to 1929, as Ngata approached the zenith of his political career, the annual rate of alienation of Maori land continued at an average of 29,091 hectares.

In a critical analysis of the role of Maori members of Parliament during the time of Ngata and his colleagues, McClean[4] concluded that on the basic issue of Maori land and its control, they were impotent. They got for the Maori only what the Pakeha members and their constituents permitted. Despite the energy-sapping nature of the unequal contest, Ngata had enough reserves of energy left to promote a Maori cultural renaissance.

Cultural Revival

Ngata focused the Maori cultural revival on the carved meeting house[5] as the symbol of Maori identity, mana and tribal traditions. The carved meeting house, known by the generic terms wharepuni and wharenui, has a long history. The wharepuni, with its characteristic rectangular design, gable roof, and porch at the front opening out on to a courtyard or marae, has been identified in the archaeological record by Pricket[6] at Palliser Bay, and Sutton[7] at Pouerua in Northland. Pricket and Sutton place the date of the development of the superior type of wharepuni which they associate with chiefs at around 1200. These early houses were not large, being up to 7 metres long and 5.8 metres wide. But by the fifteenth century, some houses were large enough to need one or even two central pillars to bear the weight of the ridgepole.[8] The period when wharepuni were decorated with carving is difficult to define with precision. Simmons[9] postulates that the Kaitaia lintel which he dates at 1400, was a roof coaming. That being the case, it would be reasonable to assume that external carvings in the form of tekoteko on the front gable, and carved window and door lintels appeared about the same time. By the time of European contact in the eighteenth century, all the conceptual design elements of the meeting house were present in the chief's wharepuni. One house seen by Cook and Banks at Tolaga Bay was 10 metres long and had all its interior posts carved.

With the introduction of steel tools, the dimensions of the chief's house increased to 13 metres long and 4 metres high. The houses of Te Rangihaeata on Mana Island and Puatia's house at Otawhao, painted by Angas in 1847, are the direct antecedents of the modern meeting house.[10] It was at this time that the master carver Raharuhi Rukupo built Te Hau-ki-Turanga at Manutuke, thirteen kilometres south of Gisborne. Rukupo, who opposed European settlement in Poverty Bay and the teachings of Christianity,[11] built the house as a cultural statement and symbol of mana Maori motuhake. The house, which measures 16.9 metres long and 5.5 metres wide, is the prototype of the modern meeting house and set the standard of decoration for all subsequent houses with its interior and exterior carvings, tukutuku panels and painted kowhaiwhai rafter patterns. The conceptual design of the house functioned to conserve tribal history and genealogy so that they would be transmitted from generation to generation. To this end, Rukupo carved fifteen ancestors at the lower end of the rafters, four on the poupou of the porch, and thirty-one on the interior poupou. The house is also notable for the two pillars supporting the ridgepole. The tiki at the base of the poutokomanawa, the main pillar at the front, is thicker-set than the one at the rear, signifying the ancestor's role as the powerful person holding the house and tribe together. The poutokomanawa is also the symbol for the chief, the living embodiment of the tribal ancestor.

In the decade of the 1850s, as the flow of European settlers increased, large tribal assemblies were held in Taranaki to discuss ways and means of controlling settlement. As a consequence of these assemblies, the wharepuni was scaled up to an unprecedented size not seen by Europeans before. In 1853 the Anglican missionary Richard Taylor found the people at Manawapou building a house measuring 27.6 metres long by 9.2 metres wide.[12] The house, named Taiporo-henui, signified opposition to Pakeha settlement.

During Te Kooti's guerrilla campaign to recover New Zealand for the Maori at the end of the 1860s, he had three large carved houses built for his followers. The first was Tanewhirinaki, built at Waioeka, notable for its polychrome carvings, painted black and white and pink and white. The second house was Te Whai-a-te-Motu, built at Ruata-huna to commemorate the military pursuit of Te Kooti around the island. This house, begun in 1870, was not completed until 1888.[13] The third house, named Te Tokanganui-a-noho, was built at Te Kuiti in 1873 when Te Kooti gave up fighting and retreated behind the aukati, the boundary line of the King Country. These houses were used for meetings, church services and accommodation. But above all, they symbolised the discrete cultural identity of the Maori against cultural invasion by the Pakeha.

After Te Kooti there was a hiatus in the construction of carved houses as Maori fortunes declined towards the end of the century. Tribal houses were still being built, but on a modest scale, or with little or no carving as the art all but died out. For all these reasons, Ngata picked up on the idea generated within the Te Aute Association to revive the art of carving. For years he pressed the Government to support the school of Maori art at Rotorua run by the Ngati Tarawhai master carver Anahata Rahui. But it was not until Ngata became Minister of Maori Affairs that he succeeded in establishing the first School of Maori Arts at Rotorua in 1928.[14] The inaugural tutor of the school was Tene Waitere of Ngati Tarawhai. He was followed by Eramiha Te Kapua. The school trained the master carvers Pine and Hone Taiapa of Ngati Porou, Henare Toka of Ngati Whatua, and Piri Poutapu of Waikato. These men became influential over the next four decades in re-establishing the art of carving meeting houses in their own districts as well as other parts of the country. They were also learned in the karakia and rituals associated with their craft. Piri Poutapu, for instance, taught his students not just the techniques of carving, but also the chants and offerings to appease Tane for felling trees, the ritual for the correct disposal of wood chips, and the prohibitions of tapu pertaining to food and sex during the construction of a house.[15] One of Poutapu's students was the baritone singer Inia Te Wiata, whose carving of a pouihi stands in New Zealand House, London, as a contemporary expression of the cultural renaissance fostered by Ngata.

Ngata had his own ancestral house, named Porourangi, at Waiomatatini moved away from the flood waters of the Waiapu River in 1907. The house, which the master carvers Tamati Ngakaho and Kihiriini Te Umutaapi took twelve years to complete, had been opened in 1888. Everything, including carvings, tukutuku panels and even thatch, was moved, refurbished and erected on the new site. Thereafter, Ngata's name is associated with many carved houses around the country, including Takitimu at Wairoa, Tukaki at Te Kaha, Wahiao at Whakarewarewa, Raukawa at Otaki, Te Poho o Rawiri at Gisborne, and the Treaty Memorial House at Waitangi.[16] The carved churches at Tikitiki on the East Coast and at Putiki in Wanganui also stand as tributes to Ngata's vision, and the work of the master carvers he fostered. Ngata's focus on the carved meeting house coincided with the aims for cultural recovery of the outstanding woman leader of the day, Te Puea Herangi of the Waikato. Her pragmatic approach in community development had uplifted the tribes of the Waikato from the spiritually devastating effects of colonisation and confiscation, and now complemented Ngata's efforts in the political arena.

In 1922 Te Puea re-established a community at Ngaruawahia, the former capital of the King Movement. She chose the symbolic name Turangawaewae (footstool) for the marae that was to play an important part in the development of the Maori people in the years that lay ahead. Money for building a dining hall and accommodation was raised by doing contract work on Pakeha farms in the district.[17] In the evenings Te Puea instituted a programme of teaching action songs, haka, and poi dances to the young people. She turned this programme of cultural recovery to the useful purpose of fund-raising for a meeting house by giving public performances under the concert party named Te Pou o Mangatawhiri. In 1927 Te Puea sought Ngata's assistance for her project by arranging a fund-raising tour of the Ngati Porou territory on the East Coast. The tour raised £1,336, and as a consequence, Ngata suggested the meeting house be named Mahinarangi after the East Coast puhi who married the Waikato ancestor Turongo, thus linking the genealogies of the two tribes.[18] Both Ngata and Te Puea planned the opening of Mahinarangi in March 1929 to be an event on a grand scale to signal the significance of the cultural renaissance. A multi-tribal gathering of 6,000 people attended the opening and witnessed action songs, haka and poi dances.[19] Thereafter, the spread of the cultural renaissance was assured.

Fight for Equity

A characteristic of Ngata's role as a leader was his involvement in a broad spectrum of Maori causes. One of these was the Maori claim to North Island lakes submitted by the tribes of the Arawa Confederation to the Stout-Ngata Native Land Commission in 1907. The tribes asserted ownership over the beds of Lakes Rotorua, Rotoiti, Rotoehu, Rotoma and Rotokakahi. The claim rested on customary rights to take freshwater inanga, crayfish and shellfish for their subsistence. These rights, guaranteed by the Treaty of Waitangi, had been derogated by the Government and the acclimatisation society stocking the lakes with trout, to the detriment of the native species. The claim asserted the viewpoint of indigenous people, that natives were not accustomed to take fish for sport, nor did they take species they did not eat. When the foreign fish ate the indigenous species, the Maori switched to eating the invaders, only to find they were breaking the law if they did not buy a licence to take them. Ngata advised the tribes to go to court. The Court of Appeal decided the tribes could have their claim heard by the Native Land Court. The First World War intervened and the case was held in abeyance until 1920. The Crown sought a compromise, and Ngata, acting as advisor to Te Arawa, assisted them in the formulation of proposals that resulted in the Arawa Lakes Agreement 1922. In exchange for surrendering the fee simple of the lakes to the Crown, the tribes were given forty licences to take trout, and an annuity of £6,000 per annum for the benefit of the tribes and their several hapu, to be administered by the Arawa Trust Board.[20]

Another cause taken up by Ngata was devolution of power from Pakeha to Maori within the hierarchy of the Anglican Church. In 1923 Bishop Ataria visited New Zealand. He was the first Indian bishop, consecrated in the Anglican Cathedral of Calcutta in 1912.

That fact was not lost on the Maori people who were agitating in the Anglican Church for their own bishop.[21] Their desire for mana motu-hake within the Church was analagous to Kotahitanga agitation in the 1890s for devolution of power to the Maori Parliament. The claim was resisted for years by the Church on the grounds there was no Maori suitable for the office.[22] This racist manifestation of the relationship of Pakeha dominance and Maori subjection within the Church was a continuance of the order established by Bishop Selwyn. In the previous century the Bishop refused to ordain Maori ministers no matter how well versed they were in the Bible or church law, because they were not trained in the Greek language, one of the hallmarks of a classical education. Rota Waitoa of Ngati Raukawa, who became a disciple of Bishop Selwyn in 1842, was a victim of the policy. He was refused ordination for ten years before he was made a deacon in 1852.[23] The continuance of the policy, by way of blocking Maori admission to the office of bishop, roused the ire of Rewiti Kohere, who wrote that there was a need to 'teach bishops and Pakehas to be flexible, not to use the Maori as a ladder for the Pakeha to climb into high positions. It is over 100 years since the Pakeha has controlled the Maori church. It is time the Maori ruled himself.'[24] While the Church was prepared to concede the establishment of a post for a Maori bishop, the matter was delayed by a drawn-out debate over whether the first incumbent should be a Pakeha.

The Maori Synod co-opted Ngata to assist the Reverend F. A. Bennett to prosecute the Maori cause with the Church authorities. In Ngata's opinion, the intransigence of the bishops in denying the wishes of the Maori people, if allowed to continue, would cause a breach with the Church in Ngati Porou.[25] He argued that a man conversant with the Maori mind was the only person suitable for the office of Maori bishop.[26] Ngata opposed the proposition that the Maori bishop be a suffragen of the Archbishop, who would head the Maori section of the Church. He also warned the Church of the danger of its Maori members deserting the fold for Ratana's faith, which was taking such a hold on Maori people. But it was not until the first quarter of 1928, when Ngata was given twenty minutes to speak to the General Synod of the Anglican Church, that the Synod was convinced that conceding a Maori bishop in the interest of maintaining its hold on Maori communicants was the lesser of the two evils.[27] The consecration of Bishop Bennett in December 1928 marked a significant step towards the achievement of equality for Maori people within the Anglican Church. But there was still a long way to go. For the

Catholics, it was even longer. Sixty years were to pass before they repeated Ngata's feat with the consecration of Bishop Mariu in 1988.

Another of Ngata's major achievements was the promotion of Maori literature, and a language recovery programme. One of the techniques of cultural invasion practised by the coloniser was to suppress the language of the indigenous people whose lands they were expropriating. After the turn of the century the repressive policy of banning the Maori language from school precincts marked the steady retreat of the language. At first, before the erosion of language became evident, Maori leaders complied with the policy because they did not fully understand the role of an education system in cultural reproduction and its power to implement the official policy of assimilation. Ngata saw English as the means of gaining access to Pakeha culture and its professions. At a conference in 1936 he said that if he were to devise a curriculum for Maori schools, he would make English four out of the five subjects.[28] Three years later Ngata changed his views when he saw the effect schooling had in subverting Maori culture. He believed there was nothing worse than for a person to have Maori features without being able to speak the Maori language.[29] Years later he wrote:[30]

It explains the case of thousands of Maoris, old and young, who entered the schools of this country and passed out, with their minds closed to the culture, which is their inheritance and which lies wounded, slighted and neglected at their very door . . . There are no wise elders to suspend their excursions into the field of Pakeha education, none at least with the power to enforce such a course. But there are Maoris, men and women, who have passed through the Pakeha whare wananga and felt shame at their ignorance of their native culture. They would learn it, if they could, if it were available for study as the culture of the Pakeha has been ordered for them to learn. For such the journey back to the social life of the Maori race is not so far, or so difficult. It is possible to compromise with it as many of us did sixty years ago, to select those elements in it which should be as satisfying and elevating as the art, the crafts, the music and the literature of the Pakeha, while living according to the material standards of the Pakeha and joining with him in the work of the country. It is possible to be bicultural, just as bilingualism is a feature of Maori life today.

Freire's contention that 'knowledge of the alienating culture leads to transforming action resulting in a culture which is being freed from alienation' is borne out by the Maori experience. As one engaged in transforming action, Ngata wrote, in a child's autograph book, this philosophy for transformation towards biculturalism:

Grow tender shoot for the days of your world!
Turn your hands to the tools of the Pakeha for the well-being of your
    body.
Turn your heart to the treasures of your ancestors as a crown for your
    head.
Give your soul unto God the author of all things.

In these oft-quoted lines, Ngata exhorted the Maori to grasp knowledge from the Pakeha world for one's livelihood, while retaining the
treasures of Maori culture for a sense of pride in Maori identity and
spiritual well-being. Ngata himself initiated transforming action to
raise the level of respectability of Maori culture as an academic study.
In 1923 he argued in the House for government support for publication of research into Maori culture. His efforts resulted in the establishment of the Maori Ethnological Research Board.[32] Although the
board was founded to support the work of Elsdon Best, Peter Buck and
H. D. Skinner, Ngata used it also as a useful platform to promote the
study of Maori language. He channelled a request through the board
to the Senate of the University of New Zealand to have Maori
included in the Bachelor of Arts degree on the same basis as foreign
languages such as French, Italian and Spanish. The Senate attempted
to stonewall the request by asking where was the literature to sustain
the teaching of the language as an academic discipline. But after it was
pointed out that the literature existed in Grey's *Nga Moteatea* and *Nga
Mahi a Nga Tupuna*,[33] the Senate conceded and Maori was introduced
into the New Zealand University in 1925.[34] But the actual teaching
of courses did not begin at Auckland University until 1951, and at
Victoria University almost fifteen years later. Having won the point,
Ngata did not rest until the matter was secure. He spent twenty-five
years collecting the poetry, songs, chants, laments and lullabies that
were in the oral repertoire of Maori women and orators on marae
throughout the land. But because of his heavy work schedule, it was
not until 1959 that he published *Nga Moteatea* as an addition to the
literature and his answer to the Senate.

Backlash on Ngata

During the years of the Depression, when he was Minister of Maori
Affairs, Ngata concentrated his energies on expanding his Maori land
development schemes. He deliberately overspent his budget in order
to commit the Government to his programme at a time of financial
stringency. This earned him the displeasure of Treasury. He made

enemies in the civil service when he dismissed two Pakeha supervisors for not being able to get on with Maori communities. He also cut corners in administration. These matters, combined with his influence in Cabinet, generated white backlash. A campaign to destabilise his position was waged in the civil service and the press. Maori land development was denigrated as a 'waste of Pakeha money'; similarly, the Native Department was described as a 'ghastly sink for Pakeha money' which needed to be reorganised to 'get it away from the influence of the natives'.[35] Ngata weathered this first storm by insisting on an inquiry, which exonerated him of wrongdoing. However, his star had reached its zenith. In 1933 the Audit Department found one of Ngata's appointees had falsified accounts and rumours of corruption were rife. In 1934 there followed a Commission of Inquiry into the affairs of the Native Department. The Public Service closed ranks to protect their colleagues in the department. Although Ngata was again exonerated of any wrongdoing, he was blamed for the department's shortcomings and resigned his portfolio.[36] But the loss of ministerial status did not diminish Ngata's ability to influence Government policies behind the scenes; for example, in promoting a Native Housing Act. When war broke out in 1939, Ngata and the other Maori members of Parliament pursuaded the Government to establish a volunteer Maori unit, subsequently known as the 28th Maori Battalion.[37] The valorous deeds of the battalion in the campaigns of North Africa and Italy did much to uplift Maori mana and enhance their sense of citizenship in the nation that emerged in the post-war years.

In the meantime the prophet Ratana had not been idle. After the 1935 election when the two Maori seats he held were aligned with Labour, the liaison appeared to bear fruit with the flurry of legislation in 1938 that ushered in the welfare state. Pensions and family benefits staved off want when the cows dried off in the winter months and contract or seasonal work was hard to find. Maori gratitude was expressed by the delivery of Northern Maori in 1938 and Eastern Maori in 1943 to the Labour fold. Except for a brief interruption in 1963, when Steve Watene, a Mormon, held Eastern Maori, the Ratana-Labour liaison dominated the Maori seats for over forty years. That loyalty to Labour was misplaced because, apart from the general benefits of the welfare state, not a great deal accrued to the Maori people.

Ratana and his followers tried to speed up the improvement of the situation of the Maori by collecting 30,128 signatures on a petition calling for the Treaty of Waitangi to be ratified. The petition was tabled in Parliament in December 1932 by Eruera Tirikatene, Member for Southern Maori. But the petition was held over year after year and its resolution delayed even further by the outbreak of the war. It was not until 1945, thirteen years after it was tabled, that Ratana's petition was dealt with by the Maori Affairs Committee of the House. The committee recommended that in view of the loyal service of Maori volunteers in two world wars, the Treaty of Waitangi should be published as a 'sacred reaffirmation' and be hung in the schools of the Dominion.[38] This response, at the minimal level and little cost to Government, was to characterise future dealings with Maori grievances. It was on par with other reforms with no cost component, such as granting Maori the secret ballot, when Pakeha had it for years, and replacing the pejorative term Native in official usage with Maori.

In 1939 a new impetus was given to the Maori renaissance by the first Young Maori Conference, organised at Auckland University, by Sir Apirana Ngata, Professor H. Belshaw and Dr I. Sutherland. After surveying Maori communities, Belshaw concluded that their problems were not easy to resolve because they were isolated from each other and from the main centres of European population. Since higher education was not readily accessible to Maori, Belshaw thought that making adult education available might stimulate young leaders to take initiatives in community development.[39] In commenting on the economic plight of the people, Belshaw noted that in 1919, of the 1,996,805 hectares of land left in Maori ownership, only 755,280 hectares were actually held by the owners. The rest, comprising 1,241,525 hectares, was held under Pakeha leasehold. The estimated 5,000 farms under the land development schemes established by Ngata, would support only a quarter of the Maori population, which at that time stood at 82,326. Clearly, employment would have to be found elsewhere. In effect, Belshaw anticipated the inevitability of the urban migration of the Maori a decade before it began.[40] In the meantime the good intentions of the young leaders who attended the conference to tackle the economic, educational, health and housing problems that beset their communities were set aside while they went off to war. Some never returned, and the thinned ranks of the young leaders who did come home had to cope with enormous changes attendant upon the demographic shift of 70 per cent of the population to towns and cities in the post-war years.

The Urban Migration

In the decade before the Second World War, 90 per cent of the Maori population was rural. The war acted as a catalyst in stimulating people to abandon rural poverty, and sell their labour for wages in the factories of the urban milieu. The Manpower Act led to the direction of young Maori not eligible for military service to contribute to the war effort by working in essential industries. This meant leaving the papakainga and marae for towns and cities. Young women were put to work in factories or on the land as farm-girls. In 1942 the Maori War Effort Organisation, under the direction of Lieutenant Colonel Hemphill, mobilised tribal committees to raise produce and funds for the war effort.[41]

The Maori Affairs Department responded to army encroachment on its domain by appointing six Maori welfare officers in the main urban centres to care for the moral well-being of young women living away from home. This was the department's first foray into the delivery of a welfare service. After the war, returned servicemen who had acquired skills in the army migrated to towns to seek gainful employment for those skills. Many of them, officers with administrative experience such as Colonel Awatere, Sir Charles Bennett and Sir James Henare, who were former commanders of the Maori Battalion, Major Rangi Royal, Lieutenant Monty Wikiriwhi, Hei Rogers, John Rangihau, Bill Herewini and others, could find employment only within the Department of Maori Affairs. Another group, including Major Harry Lambert, John Waititi, Frank Latimer, George Sutherland and Maurice Bird, entered teacher training. They augmented a group who were admitted under a 'Maori quota' in 1938 and who resumed their training after the war. In this category were Major George Marsden, Matiu Te Hau and John Rogers. Several of these men had attended the Young Maori Conference and filled key leadership positions in the transition of Maori from rural to urban life, as well as providing a breakthrough into the teaching profession.

By 1951, 19 per cent of the Maori population of 115,740 was urban.[42] At the next census it had risen to 24 per cent. The rural tribal hinterlands were being depopulated at the rate of 1 per cent, or 1,600 people per annum. In 1960 the Department of Maori Affairs encouraged this demographic shift with an urban relocation programme. Maori welfare officers exhorted rural families to leave the subsistence economy of the 'pipi beds' by finding them employment and accommodation in urban centres. Over a five-year period the department relocated 399 families. It also assisted 485 families who moved of their own accord.[43] The major reasons for the urban migration were the 'big three' factors of work, money and pleasure.[44] The population recovery, the cultural revival, the deeds of the Maori Battalion, and prowess on the rugby fields, gave the Maori confidence to abandon rural poverty in exchange for a place in the economy of the social mainstream. Marginal and uneconomic incorporations and dairy farms established under Ngata's land development schemes were abandoned for the security of wage labour and a pay cheque that did not dry up with the cows in the winter months. By 1961, of the 298 registered Maori incorporations, over half were inactive, and the number of Maori farmers had fallen to 2,116.[45]

In the early stages of the migration, inner city locations were favoured because they were close to work on the wharves, in factories and the transport industry. In the metropolis of Auckland, for instance, the Maori population concentrated in the decaying inner-city areas of Freemans Bay, Ponsonby and Herne Bay. But as the migration continued unabated, houses were overcrowded. To relieve the pressure, the State Advances Corporation and the Ministry of Works planned and built new housing estates in the 1960s at Otara, Mangere and Te Atatu. Similar estates were built in Wellington at Porirua, the Hutt Valley and Wainuiomata. The concentration of the working class in these housing estates allowed a critical build-up in the density of Maori people, which contradicted the official 'pepper-potting' policy of Maori Affairs. In suburbs like Otara the Maori population was as high as 40 per cent. Densities above 10 per cent facilitated recruitment and mobilisation into groups to deal with the problems of adjusting to urban life.

Urbanisation posed two developmental tasks for migrant Maori. First, they had to adjust to the economic demands of the urban industrial complex. This meant taking permanent employment, coping with a total cash economy in a milieu that had little scope for subsistence activities, and meeting financial commitments by way of rent, time-payment, hire purchase, rates and mortgages. The universal culture of capitalism is what integrates Maori into the social mainstream of Pakeha society. These economic bonds were supplemented by religious affiliations and a shared passion for the national game of rugby. But outside these transactions, Maori and Pakeha lived discrete lives. Ethnicity, cultural difference and the experience of being colonised impelled the Maori to dwell in the dual world of biculturalism or surrender to the Pakeha imperative of assimilation. While some Maori chose assimilation, the vast majority rejected it. That meant commitment to cultural continuity.

Cultural Continuity

Averting assimilation posed the second development task for migrants of transplanting their culture into the urban milieu. In the early stages of urbanisation, migrants maintained contact with their rural roots by occasional visits to their kainga and marae for holidays, weddings, tangi and unveilings of headstones.[46] But gradually, as the migrants became more sure of themselves, they put down roots and planted their culture in new ground. The key to the successful adjustment of the Maori to urban life is voluntary associations.[47] These include Maori sections of orthodox churches, the Maori protest religions of Ringatu and Ratana, culture clubs, sports clubs, family and tribal organisations, benevolent societies, Maori committees, Maori wardens, Maori councils and the Maori Women's Welfare League. The essence of Maori voluntary association is group membership with the common goal of promoting the kaupapa of perpetuating Maori identity, values and culture. In the alien and hostile environment of impersonal cities, kinship bonds were formalised by the formation of family clubs, adoption of a constitution, and election of an executive for the collection of subscriptions and disbursement of funds against the contingencies of illness, unemployment and the underwriting of expenses incurred in returning the bodies of deceased persons to their home marae. Maori church groups functioned as quasi-kin in fostering Maori cultural values through church membership in a multitribal situation. Maori culture clubs were formed to revive and perpetuate interest in singing, action songs, and arts and crafts. At first, culture clubs provided parochial entertainment, but in time, cultural competitions and national festivals were established for secondary school students as well as adults. This strengthened the culture and raised the level of performance to a professional standard. Maori sports clubs to play rugby and basketball or league were organised in places of employment such as freezing works and bus companies to participate in informal Sunday competitions. The emphasis was on recreation rather than competition, and fraternisation afterwards over a beer and hangi food.[48]

One of the most important cultural transplantations into the urban situation is the kinship network built around the primary social units of whanau and hapu. A social survey in 1967 of a hundred Maori dwellings in Otara revealed that the whanau has been replaced by the nuclear family as the household unit. Ninety per cent of the households were founded on the nuclear family.[49] The reason for this is that the nuclear family fits the demands of the industrial system more easily than the extended family. It is not bound to locality, is more mobile, and therefore can be moved more easily to where work can be found. But that does not mean the death of the whanau and larger groupings such as the hapu. On the contrary, they too are transplanted, but in modified form. Whanau with siblings scattered across different suburbs meet frequently at a central place, usually the home of the kaumatua and kuia, or the pakeke of the whanau, for mutual support in times of bereavement, or the formation of family clubs described above, and the celebration of festive occasions.

Urban Marae

One of the bastions of cultural conservatism in the alien environment of the city is the tangi, the mortuary customs for farewelling the dead. The most appropriate place to conduct the rituals of the tangi is the marae, the other bastion and focal point of the culture. Although there were tribal marae engulfed by urban sprawl in Auckland and Wellington, the first wave of pre-war migrants felt they needed a hall or a marae of their own.[50] In any case as the number of urban Maori increased exponentially, tangata whenua marae were unable to cope with the need. In the meantime, the normal life-crises of birth, death and marriage had to be met with what was at hand, the family dwelling. The head of a whanau responded to death by turning the suburban state house into a 'mini-marae'. The living room cleared of furniture served as a meeting house where the body lay in state, and kinfolk and friends came to farewell the dead. A kauta for outdoor cooking met the obligation of extending hospitality to mourners. Tents with trestle tables and benches served as temporary dining halls. Some whanau erected double garages as permanent facilities for their mini-marae. But these were no substitute for the real thing.

For many years in the early stages of the urban migration, communal halls in the city centre served the needs of quasi-tribes such as Ngati Poneke in Wellington and Ngati Akarana in Auckland. But these were only interim solutions. The Maori Community Centre in Auckland, for instance, was not suitable for tangi, and when it was used in 1965 for the lying-in-state of John Waititi, special permission had to be sought from the city council. Because of the need to cater for tangi, related whanau, hapu, tribal and multitribal groups formed urban marae-building associations. Maori congregations in the various churches also focused on establishing marae as a priority in their development plans. Twenty years after the migration began, urban marae sprang up in many towns and cities. In 1965 the first urban marae named after Te Puea was opened in the Auckland suburb of Mangere. Although Te Puea is a traditional kin-based marae, with the tangata whenua of Waikato in control, the marae is available for use to all migrants, whatever their tribal affiliation. The Te Uunga Waka facility, which opened in the same year, is a marae with a difference. The Catholic Church replaced kinship as the unifying principle, bringing Maori of different tribes together as its tangata whenua. Other church-based marae include Te Whaiora at Otara (Catholic) and Tatai Hono (Anglican) in Khyber Pass.

To serve the needs of migrants from different tribes who had nothing in common except residence in the same suburb, a third principle for marae organisation emerged that was secular, multitribal and elective. The most widely known marae of this type is Hoani Waititi Marae at Te Atatu, but there are many others, including Nga Hau E Wha (The Four Winds) at Christchurch, and another with the same name at Pukekohe. The emergence of these three types of urban marae indicate the dynamism of the cultural renaissance started by Ngata with its focus on the meeting house as the symbol of Maori identity. The establishment of the marae-meeting house complex in towns and cities around the country marked the accomplishment of the second development task by migrants: the transplantation of their culture into the urban milieu. With the culture firmly rooted in the new environment, the energy of the cultural renaissance was turned to political action directed at liberating the Maori from Pakeha domination.

The Struggle Against Hegemony

The Maori struggle against Pakeha domination was taken up in the post-war years of the modern era by Maori women. From the time of the First World War, Te Puea had led the fight seeking compensation for the unjust confiscation of Waikato land. The matter had dragged on for years, despite a recommendation by the Sim Commission in 1928 that it be settled. In 1945 Te Puea reopened negotiations with the Government and concluded a settlement the following year.[51] It provided for an annuity of £6,000, which is administered on behalf of the Waikato tribes by the Tainui Trust Board.

Te Puea's leadership grew out of the tribal struggle of the Waikato people to recover their mana from the trauma of colonisation. She was followed by a new wave of Maori women, who, in 1951, established the first national Maori organisation, the Maori Women's Welfare League. The experience of these women in the Maori committees of the Country Women's Institute and the Maori Health League,[52] combined with growing urbanisation, motivated Maori women to establish a forum of their own to articulate Maori needs outside and across the tribal arena. Educated women in particular, like Mira Petricevich, felt constrained by the male prerogative which in some tribes prohibited women from speaking on the marae. With the assistance of Rangi Royal, a Maori welfare officer, the league was launched at a conference in Wellington. A Dominion council was elected with Whina Cooper as president and Mira Petricevich secretary. The first task of the president was to visit all parts of the country to establish branches and district councils.[53] With its foundation established, the league then undertook a survey of Maori housing needs in Auckland. The league's report of overcrowding, and insanitary slum conditions in which migrants were living, put pressure on the Maori Affairs Department to step up its housing programme. The Housing Corporation also had to expedite its plans for the new housing estate in Otara to relieve the pressure in the inner city.

For the next ten years, the annual conferences of the league became an important forum for the expression of Maori views on housing, health, education, welfare, crime, and discrimination in employment and accommodation. The league's resolutions and submissions to Government were taken seriously by government departments.[54] At the parochial level, the league branches assisted needy families with provisions from a 'distress cupboard' when a breadwinner was unemployed, or a father neglected his family. In some cases the league provided clothing, school uniforms and stationery for children of poor families. Members of the league also gave the Housing Corporation advice on setting priorities in the allocation of state houses to the mounting list of applicants seeking relief from overcrowded accommodation. Individual members of the league also budgeted families who got into debt as a consequence of overcommitment to hire purchase and time-payment agreements. In these transactions the league played a vital role in helping people who were not coping well with the adjustment to urban life.[55]

In 1962, when the playcentre movement as an alternative to kindergarten was launched in Maori communities by Lex Grey and Roy

Saunders, the league branches helped establish playcentres on marae all around the country, in public halls and even in their own homes. Prior to this, few Maori received pre-school education because mothers were too shy to participate in kindergarten education, which was seen as the domain of the Pakeha middle class. Playcentre appealed to the Maori because of its philosophy of self-help, parental involvement, and parental participation in control and management. Furthermore, playcentres were touted as analogous to the American 'headstart' programme and would help Maori children bridge the gap in educational achievement between Maori and Pakeha that was iden- tified by the Hunn Report. The report noted there was a 'statistical blackout' of Maori at the higher levels of education where only 0.5 per cent of Maori secondary students made it to the seventh form com- pared with 3.78 per cent of Pakeha.[56] But without adducing any evidence, the report blamed parental apathy for the situation. Maori commitment to the playcentre movement contradicted that widely held view in educational circles. Furthermore, one of the Hunn Report's recommendations for resolving the problem, which was partly attributed to low income and large families, was the establish- ment of a Maori Education Foundation. The Maori Women's Welfare League, in its commitment to education, put its full weight behind the fund-raising activities that launched the foundation.

The Maori Council

In the next decade the initiative in Maori leadership was taken over by the Maori Council. The council had its genesis in the Maori Social and Economic Advancement Act 1945, which gave statutory recog- nition to the tribal committees. The committees were so successful in supporting the war effort that the Government felt they would have an important role in assisting the Maori adjust to the anticipated changes after the war. Under the provisions of the Act, the committees were expected to promote the social, spiritual, cultural, educational and economic advancement of the Maori. In following this wide- ranging brief, the committees were expected to co-operate with government departments, educational authorities and other agencies of the state. There was provision in the Act for committees to appoint Maori wardens, who were charged with supervision of Maori people in public places, halls, bars and on marae so as to ensure the pro- motion of harmony between Maori and Pakeha. The wardens had no power of arrest but could confiscate alcohol in the possession of anyone in the vicinity of a marae or dance hall. In public bars they could ask the barman to stop serving alcohol to any individual who in their opinion was drunk, and they could confiscate the keys of such a person attempting to drive his car. The wardens were issued with a warrant from the Minister of Maori Affairs and a small, undistinguished badge of office. They wore civilian clothing in conducting their duties, but that did not matter; because since they were operating in the context of their hapu or iwi, they were known to the people. They were invariably known by the young as 'Uncle' or 'Aunty' and their word was law. No one, for instance, queried their right to quell unruly and noisy fans in a picture theatre with a cuff over the ear as the cheering reached a crescendo when the cavalry arrived to relieve a besieged fortress. The tribal committees were the base of the structure under the 1945 legislation. Above them were tribal executives and district councils.

As the urban migration gathered momentum, the Government recognised the changing circumstances of the Maori, and abolished tribal committees, replacing them with Maori committees under the Maori Welfare Act 1962. This Act also brought into being the Maori Council, the top tier of a cumbersome four-tiered structure modelled on Pakeha bureaucratic systems. At the parochial level were the Maori committees with defined areas in a town, region or suburb of a city. Committees were grouped into executive areas, and executives were subject to district councils, of which there were eight covering the country. The district councils were based on the boundaries of the Maori Land Court, namely Taitokerau, Waikato, Waiariki, Aotea, Tairawhiti, Ikaroa and Te Waipounamu. The eighth one was the Auckland District Maori Council, which served the urban Maori population. All levels of the structure held triennial elections, culminating in the district councils sending three delegates to the national council, which elects a president. The weakness of the system is that Maori committees are an artificial construct of the bureaucratic mind and did not fit the authentic Maori systems of mobilising people through whanau, hapu, iwi and marae committees. Despite this blemish, with the assistance of Maori welfare officers, the committees were elected, and the Maori Council brought into being. Marae committees generally designated themselves Maori committees to qualify for membership in the council structure. The one incentive to do so was the role assigned to district councils of allocating priority in the disbursement of government subsidies to marae-building projects. When projects proliferated as a consequence of urbanisation, a distinction had to be made between rural and urban subsidies. A larger amount of money was allocated to urban subsidies because of the greater need, and the fact that most rural areas already had marae to serve what was in effect a dwindling population.

Although the rural districts of the Maori Council were inherently tribal, with some paying their levies to the national council out of tribal monies, some tribes were suspicious of the council as a creature of Government. Others suspected the council as a National Party ploy because it was established during the reign of a National Government, to counterbalance the four Maori seats held by Labour. At the inaugural meeting of the council in June 1962, Ralph Hanan, Minister of Maori Affairs, gave some credence to that view when he said that as a Pakeha unlearned in Maori ways, he found it difficult to tell Maori people under his portfolio what to do. Although the four Maori members of Parliament offered guidance when he sought it, a bipartisan approach was not possible when the issues were political in nature. Therefore he felt the need for some assistance. For this reason he responded to the request from Reiwhati Vercoe of the Waiariki District Council to establish the national body. The Minister wondered why it had not been done fifty years previously,[57] which is one of the ironies of history, considering that the chiefs had pressed for such a council for more than a century. In any case, as subsequent events unfolded, Hanan was not at all averse to deciding unilaterally what was good for the Maori, and proceeding to enforce his will against their protestations.

The identification of the Maori Council with the National Government was deepened by the election of its leaders. Its first president, Sir Turi Carroll, the secretary, Henare Ngata, and succeeding presidents, Pei Te Hurinui Jones and the present incumbent Sir Graham Latimer, were all publicly identified members of the National Party. For this reason, the council was jokingly dubbed by one wag as 'Uncle Tom's cabinet'. Although the council hierarchy was of conservative persuasion, it was leavened by members belonging to the Labour Party, and in recent years one Social Crediter. Despite its origins and the differing political affiliations of its members, the deliberations of the council were driven by the same Maori agenda that drove the Welfare League, Ratana, Ngata and his colleagues, the Maori Parliament, Kauhanganui, and the chiefs: the struggle of Maori leaders for the good of the people against the forces of colonisation. Only time would prove how far the council was prepared to push that agenda against the Government.

The Maori Council addressed the same concerns identified by the league, such as the welfare of girls arriving by boat in Lyttelton, the appointment of teachers in Maori culture, migrant youths getting in trouble with the law, rising crime among Maori,[58] the appointment of Maori to government-appointed bodies, and social problems among urban migrants.[59] But where the council differed from the league was its use by Government as a sounding board for pending legislation such as the Adoption Amendment Bill, Juries Amendment Bill, Maori Purposes Bill and Maori Welfare Bill.[60] None of these were particularly contentious and so support was given to the Minister of Maori Affairs. But when it came to land, the council dug in and opposed the Minister when he proposed to lift the restriction of the term of leases on Maori land from fifty to a hundred years. Sir Turi Carroll likened the move to a 'confiscation of a sort'.[61] Henare Ngata said that the council had no intention of being obstructive to proposed legislative changes for Maori land. He reiterated the sentiments of his father, saying change in legislation was not what was needed, but rather a policy of land development and utilisation with a training programme for young Maori with the aim of Maori occupation of Maori land.[62] The main problem was difficulty in raising loans to finance the development of Maori land. The Maori Council would be greatly pleased, said Ngata, if he could help the Minister see Maori land problems through Maori eyes by conducting him on a tour of the East Coast.

Despite the position staked out by the Maori Council, the Government went ahead with its plan to bring 'idle Maori land' into production by rationalising in an authoritarian way the difficulties of dealing with Maori land because of multiple ownership and fragmentation of land holdings into uneconomic units. The Government's solution was set out in the Pritchard-Waetford Report 1965, which proposed raising the classification of 'uneconomic' shares in land from £25 to £100, with the Crown taking over from the Maori Trustee the power of compulsory purchase of such lands and their disposal. To meet the anticipated workload of acquiring Maori land, there was to be an increase in the parliamentary vote to the conversion fund.[63] The report also proposed to change the designation of Maori land held by fewer than four owners to European land. The administration of such lands would pass from the Maori Land Court to the Land Transfer Office.[64]

The Maori Council made two responses to the Pritchard-Waetford Report. In May 1966, under the auspices of the University of Auckland

Extension Department, it convened a conference of academics, fifty-four district council delegates, representatives from five Maori trust boards, the Maori Women's Welfare League, the Federation of Maori Students and the Maori Graduates' Association to consider the report. The result was a thoroughly professional critique, which opposed the £100 conversion proposal and the Crown being the conversion agent. The proposed compulsory change in status of Maori land to European land was also opposed. Instead, it was suggested that such a change should be optional.[65]

In March 1967 the Maori Council itself responded strongly to the Pritchard-Waetford Report in a letter to the Minister. It pointed out the difficulties of Maori land titles were caused by a one-sided (Pakeha) interpretation of Maori custom, which the Maori Land Court set aside in carving up tribal land into a multiplicity of partitions. A five-point proposal was put forward to retrieve the situation. These included an information service on Maori land, guidance on use through trusts, incorporations and other co-operative organisations (which would be better than conversion), advice on farming, a training scheme and, above all, financial provision at reasonable rates to enable Maori use of their own land. The council concluded by condemning the Government's plan as discriminatory against Maori. By cutting across basic property rights, the report departed from the British rules of property applicable to British citizens. Tribal leaders around the country joined with the Maori Council in opposing the incorporation of the Pritchard-Waetford proposals into legislation, but to little effect.

The Government, driven still by the colonising ethos of its predecessors, hardly heeded the sage advice of the wise leaders of the Maori world. It introduced the Maori Affairs Amendment Act 1967 at the end of the parliamentary session. Although the Maori Council and tribal leaders had succeeded in pegging the conversion limit at $50, the basic thrust of the Pritchard-Waetford Report remained: commodification of land, facilitating its acquisition for sale to others who would make it productive, and assimilation. Europeanisation of Maori land, which is the basis of identity as tangata whenua, would resolve once and for all the Maori problem by conjuring it away, and so realise the Pakeha dream of 'one people'. For Maori people, the Act was seen as the 'last land grab' by the Pakeha. In the next decade it triggered the Maori land rights movement, a movement that was to expose to the world at large the inherent contradictions between the colonised and the coloniser in New Zealand society.

Although land was the primary focus of the Maori Council, it was also concerned with problems arising out of urbanisation, particularly educational failure, juvenile delinquency and rising crime. Over 85 per cent of Maori children left secondary school in 1965 without any recognised qualifications.[66] In 1970, there were 9,094 young Maori offenders before the Children's Court. The following year there was an increase to 10,750. The offending rate of Maori boys under sixteen years was 5.1 times the rate of their Pakeha cohorts. For Maori girls, the rate was even higher at 7.4.[67] While these negative statistics were symptoms of family breakdown, loss of traditional constraints of the tribal elders, and alienation as a consquence of colonisation, the end product was the 1970s phenomenon of 'street kids' and urban gangs. Early in 1970 there was a street battle in South Auckland between the Stormtroopers and a Pakeha group, which did not bode well for the future.

The Maori Council became concerned at these manifestations of social breakdown as a consequence of social dislocation and urbanisation. It convened a Young Maori Leaders Conference at Auckland University on the theme of urbanisation. This conference generated over ninety recommendations directed at conserving Maori language and culture, providing assistance to Maori in making adjustment to urban life, educating the Pakeha to become culturally sensitive, and social transformation towards a more equitable relationship between Maori and Pakeha. Suggested transformations included encouraging Maori to stand in local body elections, training for secondary school principals in cultural sensitivity, discontinuance of exploitive and derogatory use of Maori culture in television and other media, revision of history teaching that promulgated bias and sterotypes against Maori, an increase in Maori Studies lecturers at teachers' colleges, the promotion of Maori welfare officers into administration and posts of responsibility, and an increase of Maori representation in Parliament on the same basis as European seats. A workshop devoted solely to Maori language recommended language teaching and maintenance programmes at primary and secondary schools for children whose first language is Maori. It was also recommended that all children who wished should be given the opportunity to study Maori language at secondary school.[68] In effect, the conference provided a unique opportunity for dialogue involving elders, delegates from the Maori Council, the Maori Women's Welfare League, the Maori Health League, Maori incorporations, tribal trust boards, labour unions, students, the Stormtroopers and Maori sections of orthodox churches.

It helped to define in the urban situation the common lot of the Maori as a subjected people. Yet dialogue alone is not sufficient to implement the decisions arrived at, for there is no transformation without action.[69] One action was the submission of the report to the Government. But past experience had shown that governments seldom heeded the considered deliberations of responsible Maori leaders. Young people felt a standing group from the conference was needed to sustain on-going action. Out of their discussions emerged Nga Tamatoa, the young warriors, who were prepared to challenge the conventional wisdom of the Pakeha establishment.

Modern Maori Activists

One of the consequences of urbanisation is increased knowledge of the alienating culture of metropolitan society and its techniques for the maintenance of the structural relationship of Pakeha dominance and Maori subjection. Freire's observation[70] that knowledge of the alienating culture leads to transforming action resulting in a culture that is being freed from alienation, is an apt description of the dynamic of the Maori cultural renaissance. The early portents of modern Maori activism directed at transformation took the form of two newsletters published in Wellington and circulated to selected Maori people in different parts of the country. The first was named *Te Hokioi* after the original Waikato newspaper of Te Tuhi and King Tawhiao. The initial issue of the paper appeared in August 1968 as 'a taiaha of truth' for the Maori nation. The editor declared the paper was prepared to 'publish and be damned'. Telling the truth meant exposure of the pollution of shellfish resources by the aluminium smelter in the South Island, the stripping of the paua beds along the Wairarapa coast by commercial divers, and the commercial exploitation of greenstone in the Arahura Maori Reserve. In publicising these issues and relating them to the Treaty of Waitangi, *Te Hokioi* functioned as a consciousness-raising mechanism that helped to prepare the way for a wide spectrum of Maori people to engage in the practice of social transformation.

The second newsletter, which appeared at the same time as *Te Hokioi*, was published under the acronym *MOOHR* by the Maori Organisation on Human Rights. Like *Te Hokioi*, which aligned the struggle for Maori rights with the class strugggle, *MOOHR* called for unity to organise the downfall of those sections of New Zealand society which oppress and exploit the Maori people. The aims of *MOOHR* were essentially humanist. These included defending human rights, raising consciousness over the erosion of Maori rights by legislation, and opposition to discrimination in housing, employment, sport and politics. *MOOHR* pledged to uphold the Treaty of Waitangi and the Universal Declaration of Human Rights. It advocated the recovery and takeover of Maori resources held by Pakeha, such as the 'tenths' in the South Island and perpetual leases on Maori land, so that the people would not be dependent on government hand-outs. As an advocate of Maori identity and self-determination, *MOOHR* attacked the education system, accusing it of 'cultural murder' for its denial of the Maori language of a rightful place in the schools of the nation. In its August 1971 newsletter, *MOOHR* postulated a continuum of Maori-Pakeha tension by claiming that 'these movements for Maori rights to run Maori affairs will continue so long as Maoris [*sic*] feel oppressed by Pakeha-dominated governments'. These were prophetic words in the years that lay ahead, as the nation approached the sesquicentennial of the signing of the Treaty of Waitangi.

Nga Tamatoa

While *Te Hokioi* and *MOOHR* were the underground expression of rising political consciousness among urban Maori, Nga Tamatoa became its public face. At its inception, there was a division in the movement between radicals, such as John Ohia, Paul Kotara and Ted Nia, and conservative, university-educated students, such as Syd and Hana Jackson, Peter Rikys and Donna Awatere. Initially, it was the radicals, who modelled themselves on the Black Power leaders such as Rap Brown and Stokely Carmichael of the United States, who drew adverse publicity with their rhetoric of brown power, Maori liberation, separate government and even a separate foreign policy. Eventually, however, the conservatives took control of the movement and initiated a series of self-help programmes. Offices were opened in Auckland and Wellington to interview migrants searching for work and to find job placements for them. Members of Tamatoa monitored the courts and gave assistance to Maori offenders needing advice and legal aid. A petition, which collected thousands of signatures, was circulated around the country calling for the inclusion of the Maori language in the education system at the primary as well as at the secondary level. When challenged that there were insufficient teachers to introduce the language nationwide, Tamatoa responded by calling for the establishment of a one-year teacher training scheme for adult native speakers of the language. To demonstrate the feasibility of the scheme, Tamatoa took parties of urban youth to rural marae to learn the language from their elders.

Tamatoa's campaign coincided with the advent of a liberal Minister of Education, Phil Amos, in the third Labour Government. Under his administration, the 'link system' of teaching Maori at primary and secondary schools was introduced in 1974. To support the programme, a one-year teacher training scheme for native speakers was established as well. To strengthen the language programme, Tamatoa introduced a Maori language day, which was taken over by the education system and eventually extended to one week. That the leaders of Tamatoa were so relentless in their language campaign was due to their own incapacity to speak Maori. They felt culturally disadvantaged and cheated by a monocultural education system.

While the leaders of Tamatoa worked within the parameters of the existing social order (for instance, by making their own submissions to the Select Committee on the Race Relations Bill), they were not averse to engaging in radical protest action against perceived institutional racism. When a Pakeha appointee arrived in the Auckland office of Maori Affairs to take up his post as district officer, he was met by a Tamatoa sit-in. Tamatoa asked the embarrassing question why half the employees in the department were Maori, but not one of the nine district officers was Maori.

In 1971 activists in Tamatoa were presented with an irresistible target by the Government's commitment to the celebration of the Treaty of Waitangi as the cornerstone of nationhood. The Treaty, which for so long had been neglected by the Government, was dusted off under the Waitangi Day Act 1960, which declared 6 February a national day of thanksgiving to commemorate the signing of the Treaty. The New Zealand Day Act 1973 changed the name of Waitangi Day and made it a public holiday as well. Pumped-up ceremony was no consolation for unresolved Maori grievances underlying the Treaty. Tamatoa protested by wearing black arm-bands and declaring the celebration a day of mourning for the loss of 25.2 million hectares of Maori land.

Embarrassed by this show of dissent, the Government sought the advice of the Maori Council, which responded with a submission that cited fourteen statutes contravening Article 2 of the Treaty. These ranged from the Public Works Act, to the Mining Act, the Petroleum Act, the Rating Act, and the Town and Country Planning Act.[71] The council also pressed for an amendment to the Town and Country Planning Act, which was incorporated in Section 3(1)(g) of the Act in 1974. Under this amendment, monocultural law for the first time was modified to take cognisance of the culture of the colonised. In matters of national importance, the planning of regional, district and maritime schemes had to take into account the relationship of the Maori people, their culture and traditions with their ancestral land.

The Maori Council's submissions both substantiated and complemented the protest action of Tamatoa. The Government's response was the Treaty of Waitangi Act 1975, which established the Waitangi Tribunal. The functions of the tribunal are to hear Maori grievances, inquire into claims under the Treaty and to make recommendations to Parliament for their settlement. The tribunal was also expected to report on the effect of new legislation referred to it by Parliament on the Treaty. The Minister of Maori Affairs, Matiu Rata, who steered the legislation through the House, hoped to make the tribunal retrospective to 1900, but was unable to do so. The tribunal was limited by Section 6(c) of the Act to hearing claims after the Act came into force. Furthermore, the tribunal had no power to make awards. The power to settle grievances remained with Parliament.

Maori Land Rights Movement

Maori people were not mollified by a tribunal with no substance. The political consciousness forged by newsletters, Tamatoa, and endless dialogue on marae around the country over grievances against the Crown, coalesced into a powerful Maori land rights movement, which in 1975 marched the length of the North Island to Parliament Buildings in Wellington.

The Maori land march movement was launched at a hui, convened by the dowager of the Maori world, Whina Cooper, early in 1975 at Mangere Marae. The driving force of the movement was rising resentment over the relentless alienation and control of the remaining 1.2 million hectares of Maori land by Pakeha laws. The 'last land grab' under the 1967 Maori Affairs Amendment Act was the trigger. But other statutes were implicated as well, such as the Rating Act 1967. The urban migration had left Maori land in rural areas unoccupied. Although not producing income, the land was subject to rates. As unpaid rates accumulated, local bodies sought payment by getting court orders under Section 81 of the Act, enabling them to lease or sell the land. There was only a six-month period after notification for owners to retrieve the situation by paying the rates. Notification of owners who left no forwarding address was difficult. Inevitably, the land was sold to Pakeha farmers. Resentment was also fuelled by the Town and Country Planning Act, which prevented Maori from building houses on their own land because of zoning restrictions. As far as Maori were concerned, ancestral papakainga should have been sufficient reason for allowing them to build where they wanted. The momentum generated by the Maori land rights movement could not be reversed overnight by the amendment of Section 3(1)(g) of the Act, or the repeal of the pernicious clauses in the 1967 Maori Affairs Amendment Act by the Minister, Matiu Rata, in 1974. Besides, there were widespread Maori land grievances of a contemporary nature around the country that caused anger at the parochial level. The tribes concerned sent representatives to the Mangere hui to air their take in a national forum.

The Ngati Wai Land Retention Committee, led by the kaumatua Waipu Peters, condemned the Whangarei District Scheme for designating under the Town and Country Planning Act seven-eighths of public open space and recreational reserves on the one-eighth of Maori land along the coast between the Whangarei Heads and the Whanga-ruru Harbour. Only one-eighth of the designations fell on the seven-eighths of land held by Pakeha. Waipu Peters was so angry that, in the extravagent rhetoric he used to rouse passion in the hui, he threat-ened to shoot any public servant who dared walk on his land to claim it for the state as public open space. Later, another member of the tribe vowed to enter politics to fight the Labour Government. That was the beginning of the political career of Winston Peters. A repre-sentative from the Tuwharetoa complained to the hui over the 'theft' of a 2.8-hectare island of shingle in the Tarawera River by the Ministry of Works for the Tokaanu power project. Another, from Te Arawa, complained against the Ohinemutu Empowering Bill, which sought to take over the ownership of the Maori road through Ohine-mutu village so the city council could maintain it. The Tainui Awhiro delegate complained about Maori land at Raglan taken under the Public Works Act for an emergency airfield during the war. The land, now under the Raglan County Council, had been handed over to the Raglan Golf Club. The tribe wanted it back. Also aired was the long-standing Ngati Maru grievance over the Thames and Coromandel goldfields. In 1867 the Crown negotiated residential site leases for gold miners at 30 shillings per annum for what was thought to be a tem-porary use. Today, dwellings, hotels, motels and businesses flourish on the leases, but the rent remains at $3 per annum. For generations, the leaders of the tribe had sought a rent review or a return of the leases but to no avail.

When Whina Cooper spoke to the assembly, she criticised the Maori Council and the Women's Welfare League for failing to convince the Government over Maori grievances by the process of making submissions. She called for a more dynamic approach and proposed a land march to Parliament. With the endorsement of the hui, she formed the organisation named Te Roopu o te Matakite. The word matakite, which means seers or prophetic visionaries, was carefully chosen for its spiritual meaning. Redolent with the spiritual powers of ancestors, it served as an ideology uniting Maori across tribal differences. After six months of planning, the march, led by a hard core of fifty marchers, set off from Te Hapua in the Far North on 14 September 1975. At the head of the march was the bearer of the pouwhenua, symbol of mana whenua, and standard carrying the Matakite flag. The marchers went under the slogan of 'Not one more acre of Maori land' to be surrendered to the Pakeha.

As the march approached large towns and cities, the numbers swelled as local people joined for a short while to give moral support. The marchers, together with their support vehicles, stopped overnight at twenty-five marae en route all the way down the centre of the North Island. For the hosts on rural marae, the discussions in the meeting house at night, led by Whina Cooper, informed them of the aims of Matakite and the purpose of the march. As a consequence of the land march, Maori people throughout the land were politicised in a unity of purpose to a level unprecedented in modern times, in the endless struggle against colonisation.

On 23 September the ranks of the marchers were swelled by thousands of supporters as they approached Auckland City. The honour of leading the march and bearing the pouwhenua across the Harbour Bridge was given to Joseph Parata Hawke of the Ngati Whatua at Orakei. The sight of the thousands of marchers crossing the bridge, and later, on 13 October, converging on Wellington City, became a media spectacle in the press and on national television. But the spectacle bemused rather than informed the Pakeha about the Maori struggle for justice. Only those in central government had some inkling what was at stake when Joseph Cooper handed over the Memorial of Rights to the Prime Minister, Bill Rowling, on the steps of Parliament.

The memorial sought the protective principle of entrenchment over Maori land, whereby pernicious clauses in the law to take, alienate, designate or confiscate Maori land be repealed and never administered on Maori land now or in the future. The control, retention and management of Maori land was to remain with the Maori people and their descendants in perpetuity. Some months after the land march, the Dannevirke Borough Council put a designation on 24 hectares of Maori land for no more noble purpose than a rubbish tip. The significance of the land march was lost on the Dannevirke borough fathers. Their action was indicative of how deeply entrenched still was the colonial mentality at the level of local government.

At the end of the land march, the participants split into factions. One group established a tent embassy on the steps of Parliament and was promptly disowned by Whina Cooper. Another group went on its own march around the East Coast. It is a testimony to the charisma and mana of Whina Cooper that she had held the movement together for eight months, when it had in its ranks, radicals, activists, trade unionists and the dispossessed. Inevitably, the factionalism detracted from the impact of the march as the breakaway Matakite o Aotearoa attempted to wrest control from Whina Cooper. The irony of the situation was that both factions of Matakite ended up making submissions to the parliamentary Select Committee on Maori Affairs at Mangere Marae in March 1977, the very process for which Whina Cooper had denigrated the Maori Council and the Women's Welfare League. There were no tangible results other than a referral of Matakite's petition and Memorial of Rights to the Government for 'enquiry'.[72] Within twelve months Matakite became moribund, as the dynamic of Maori activism sought expression through other causes.

Bastion Point

Joseph Hawke, a politically uninvolved young man but with fire in his belly, was on a political high during the land march. He had been plucked from obscurity by Whina Cooper and pitched into the heady broth of cultural politics. For two years after the march he was in a state of limbo, looking for a cause without knowing where to find one. At the end of 1977 the National Government presented him with an opportunity when it took steps to implement its plan to subdivide 24 hectares of Crown land at Bastion Point.

As a boy, Joe Hawke witnessed the eviction of his people as 'squatters' and the burning of their houses on the papakainga of their ancestors at Okahu Bay in 1951. The eviction of the Ngati Whatua at Orakei is a sordid tale of colonial oppression of the once proud owners of Tamaki Makaurau, the isthmus of a thousand lovers. The legal machinations by which the Crown gained control of the 280-hectare estate of the Ngati Whatua is a microcosm of the Crown's dealing in tribal land.

After selling the 1,200 hectares on which Auckland City stands to Governor Hobson in 1840, Apihai Te Kawau and his people reoccupied their lands at Orakei under the umbrella of Pax Britannica, safe from Ngapuhi muskets. But as the city expanded, Te Kawau came under pressure to sell more land. In order to safeguard the land for future generations, he obtained a Crown Grant through the Native Land Court in 1869 to 280 hectares of land at Orakei. The grant by Judge Fenton[73] recognised the three hapu of Te Taou, Ngaoho and Te Uringutu as the owners. In 1873 the Native Land Court issued a certificate of title in the name of thirteen persons as trustees of the estate. The title had a rider 'that the land shall be absolutely inalienable' to safeguard the rights of generations to come. That safeguard was as substantial as mist in the noonday sun in the face of Pakeha hunger for land.

The first step towards the alienation of Orakei was taken when the Orakei Native Reserve Act was passed in 1882. This private member's Bill blew away the inalienable clause by allowing for the leasing of land in the Orakei block for up to forty-two years. In 1898 the Native Land Court partitioned the Orakei Block under Section 14 of the Native Land Court Act, and the thirteen trustees were declared 'owners' with power to alienate the tribal estate. So as not to render the Ngati Whatua entirely landless, the court declared 15.6 hectares of the papakainga at Okahu Bay an 'inalienable reserve'. The Stout-Ngata Commission of 1907[74] declared the partition illegal and void because Orakei was communal land, to be preserved as a dwelling place for the remnant of a tribe. But because the so-called owners had made leases and subdivisions under the partition order, the Commission recommended that they be validated under the Validation of Invalid Land Sales Act 1894.

The Auckland City Council, which wanted a share in the carve-up of Orakei, promoted the Orakei Model Suburb Empowering Bill in 1912. The Bill was opposed by the Maori Affairs Committee and was dropped. Not to be outdone, the Government made its move to get hold of the land. The following year Cabinet recommended that the Crown purchase Orakei. It ensured a Crown monopoly to purchase by a series of Orders in Council prohibiting sales to speculators. By 1916, the buying up of Orakei by the government agent J. A. Tole was well advanced. The Crown also confirmed its hold on 4.4 hectares given by the chiefs in 1859 for defence purposes at Bastion Point during the Russian scare, and 3.6 hectares at Takaparawha, by taking them under the Public Works Act. The rationale that the Ngati Whatua were willing sellers, and therefore the authors of their own dispossession, does not bear examination. In a long-running battle to resist the state and save the land, there were eight actions in the Maori Land Court, four in the Supreme Court, two in the Court of Appeal, two in the Compensation Court, six appearances before Commissions or Committees of Inquiry, and fifteen Parliamentary Petitions.[75] In the end the state prevailed. By 1928 all that remained was the papakainga, which the Crown proceeded to buy as well, despite its being inalienable. By 1929 all that was left was 1.2 hectares. One family, sensing the Government was determined to have even that, exchanged its one-third share in the papakainga for 4 hectares on the hill above. But even that was not safe, as it was subsequently taken in 1950 under the Public Works Act for state housing.

The Kennedy Commission of 1939 commented on the irregular conveyancing procedures used by the government agents. Individuals held undivided shares in the land at Orakei, therefore they could not point to a specific area that was actually 'owned', or was to be reserved. No surveys were made at the time of purchase, and so owners were beguiled into thinking the land was intact. Once all the interests were acquired, the Ngati Whatua were deemed to be squatters on Crown land. Their eviction was only a matter of time. The commission effectively prepared the way for the eviction eleven years later, by noting that the papakainga was only 1.2 metres above the high-water mark. Therefore, in the interests of health and sanitation, 'the natives could no longer in such a locality live the free life which they prefer'.[76] The commission failed to sheet home responsibility to the city council for the muddy and insanitary state of the papakainga. In 1912 the sewer line was built along the foreshore of Okahu Bay to the pumping station and outfall. The line was subsequently covered with soil and a road built on top. The road effectively blocked the run-off of stormwater down the gully behind the papakainga, turning it into a quagmire in winter. The last act in this tale of man's inhumanity to man was played out in 1951 when the people were evicted from the papakainga and moved into thirty state houses in Kitemoana Street above, and Reihana Street on the flat. The houses on the papakainga, including the meeting house, were knocked down and burned. Twenty-six years later, the boy who witnessed that burning sought utu by defying the state over the ownership of the land.

In January 1977 the Orakei Maori Action Group led by Joe Hawke occupied the land at Bastion Point to stop the subdivision going ahead. Tents, cooking facilities, caravans and a meeting house were put on the site for the 150 protesters who moved in to support the cause. The local populace opposed to the subdivision helped the protesters by supplying them with food, water and electricity. The trade unions strengthened Joe Hawke's hand by declaring a green ban on Bastion Point. Matakite, members of Tamatoa, Socialist Action, the Socialist Unity Party and the Citizen's Association for Racial Equality added their support as well. With his position considerably strengthened, Hawke demanded the return of all Crown land at Bastion Point, including the Savage Memorial and Takaparawha Reserve, a total of 72 hectares. The Crown, not wanting a direct confrontation, filed an injunction in the Supreme Court to order the squatters to vacate the land.

In the meantime the elders of Ngati Whatua sought a peaceful resolution to the impasse by entering into negotiations with the Government. A deal was struck for the return of 9.2 hectares in lieu of 5.2 hectares for the Battery reserve, and 4 hectares to replace land taken for state houses. The land, including the houses, was to be handed over to a constituted trust board to administer the estate on behalf of the tribe and take responsibility for paying the residue of the development costs of $200,000. The offer from Cabinet of 11.6 hectares, which was spurned by Joe Hawke, was described as a 'handsome remedy' by Justice Speight. The judge ruled that the protesters occupied the land without right, and issued an injunction for their removal. The elders importuned the protesters to come off the Point, but they refused. The battle lines were drawn as the occupation dragged on.

Finally, on 25 May 1978, the occupation was ended after 506 days when the Point was cleared by 600 policemen. During the occupation, Bastion Point, like the land march, was a media event. But the sensational treatment of it tended to bemuse rather than inform the general public as the drama moved to its inexorable climax. The abiding image from the television news clips of the clearance of the Point, is of an earthmoving machine demolishing the makeshift meeting house of the protesters. It left the impression that the rabble-rousers, who had broken the law, had been crushed like beetles underfoot for daring to challenge the power of the state.

Few people drew the conclusion that the Crown had been down that road before against Rua Kenana, Te Whiti and Te Kooti. Fewer still realised that the Maori is not intimidated by power, just as the fighters of a warrior race were not intimidated by the big guns at Orakau or Gate Pa. The indomitable desire of the human spirit for freedom and justice can not be denied by repression. That was the undying message of Rewi Maniapoto: the struggle will go on forever.

CHAPTER 11

Nga Totohe ki Tauiwi

The Neo-Maori Activists

After Bastion Point, the uneasy peace in Maori-Pakeha relations reigned for a year before it was disturbed again by the emergence of a new wave of Maori activists known under such various names as the Waitangi Action Committee (WAC), He Taua, Maori People's Liberation Movement of Aotearoa, and Black Women. These apparently discrete groups were domiciled in Auckland and had a considerable overlap in membership. The political ethos of the groups was based on the liberation struggle against racism, sexism, capitalism and government oppression. The rhetoric of WAC in their newsletters is couched in terms of revolutionary struggle, but their practice for social transformation stopped short of armed struggle. The tactics in their repertoire for change included circulating newsletters, establishing networks with Maori and Pakeha organisations, mounting demonstrations and marches, and challenging politicians in public places. As they gained experience in radical action, they carried their activism to the edge of the law, and when they were arrested for doing so, they challenged in court the veracity of the law and the judicial system itself. Instead of behaving like cowed defendants, they went on the attack by defending themselves, and challenging their accusers face to face.

The radical cutting edge of Maori politics in the decade of the 1980s was the Waitangi Action Committee. The core group consisted of the Harawira family and their cohorts Ben Dalton, Hinengaro Davis, Wiki Tawhara, Hilda Halkyard and Mangu Awarau. WAC was capable of mobilising scores of people from their network for protest activity, including former Tamatoa members such as Syd and Hana Jackson, Donna Awatere and Ripeka Evans. Also in their network were Sharon Hawke, Orakei Action Committee; Terry Dibble, Bastion Point Working Group; Arthur Harawira, Tama Tu, Mitzy Nairn, Auckland Committee on Racism and Discrimination (ACORD); Ana Macfarlane, Pakehas Against Racism Campaign; and the Ponsonby Black Women's Movement. WAC made the Treaty of Waitangi the focal point of their activism. For them, seeking ratification of the Treaty was a delusion, because the cost of reparations to Maori people for their grievances would bankrupt the state. Ratification was therefore thought to be a futile objective, because no government would do it. Instead, they called for a boycott of the Waitangi Day celebrations. Their aim was to escalate opposition to the celebrations until they were stopped. At this time graffiti appeared in public places proclaiming 'The Treaty is a fraud' and denouncing it as 'The Cheaty of Waitangi'.

Within the movement, WAC was also used as a vehicle for the expression of the rising consciousness of black women against the sexism of some black men. The use of the word black by Maori activists was entirely political rather than descriptive in meaning. The activists used it because they saw Maori people being treated as inferior blacks by the dominating white class of New Zealand society.

In 1979 WAC continued the protests at the annual Waitangi Day celebrations that had been started earlier in the decade by Tamatoa. They began with a protest march from Auckland to Waitangi. During the march, the group was penetrated by an undercover Maori policeman posing as a radical. Consequently the police had files on key members of the group. They came to police notice on 1 May, when an ad hoc group of fourteen activists drawn from WAC and their cohorts from related groups raided the Engineering School at Auckland University. Their purpose was to stop the students from parodying the haka. For over twenty years the engineers had staged a mock war dance as part of the annual capping day festivities, and for at least ten years Maori students had tried to stop the performance because they thought it culturally offensive and racist. As early as May 1971, Syd Jackson of Tamatoa wrote to the Auckland University Students' Association requesting that the haka party be disowned. The publicity officer for the AUSA commented in the student newspaper on the move to disown the haka party because it ridiculed Maori people.[1] At the same time, the Student Representative Council condemned the haka party as an idiotic slight against the Maori people. None of these efforts dissuaded the engineering students, who continued to plan for the haka in 1979 after the president of the AUSA wrote to the president of the Engineering Society in October 1978 expressing formal disapproval of the haka party. That was the last warning they failed to heed.

He Taua

The raiding party, which after the event assumed the name of He Taua, the avengers, confronted the engineering students early in the morning while they were practising their stunt. A fracas ensued, the students were assaulted, and their grass skirts torn from them. In less than five minutes of direct action, the gross insult of the haka party was stopped where years of negotiation had failed.

The problem with this form of activism is that the proponents put themselves at risk with the law. Although the raiders escaped unscathed, eleven of them were rounded up within hours and charged with rioting. The *Auckland Star* reported the incident with the bold headline 'Gang Rampage at Varsity . . . Students at Haka Practice Bashed'.[2] Although not one gang patch was in evidence during the raid, no headline could have evoked a more emotive response from the general public. The patch-wearing gang member is the nightmare incarnation of the Pakeha New Zealander's worst fears.

The first gang to come to notice, in 1970, was the Stormtroopers, with their long hair, denim uniforms, back-patches and swastika emblems, which symbolised their alienation from mainstream society. Thereafter other gangs such as Black Power, Headhunters and Mongrel Mob gained publicity as they engaged in fraternal gang raids and battles over territory. As long as their aggression was among themselves, no one was too fussed. But the thought of a gang invading the hallowed cloisters of the university was intolerable. Public outrage fostered by the media demanded retribution. Editors pontificated 'No Place for Violence'.[3] Passive resistance as an activist tactic was one thing, but violence was another. The coloniser knows all too well the potential of violence to achieve social transformation. It was by violence that a tribal society was destroyed in the first instance and the nation state brought into being. It is for that reason that the state has a monopoly on violence, because it is the means by which control and national security are maintained. Control means each class, race and person functioning according to their assigned position in the polity of the nation. The haka party incident was perceived as a threat to control, and the structurally assigned place of Maori subjection to Pakeha power. The press whipped up Pakeha hysteria into a general condemnation of violence.

Prominent Maori leaders, such as Harry Dansey, the Race Relations Conciliator, and his assistant Dr Pita Sharples, came under intense pressure from the media to disavow violence as a tactic, and thereby isolate the offenders as social outcasts. Their comments on the issue were put under the bold headline 'Attack on Students Condemned'. But Dr Sharples' rider to his disavowal of violence — that Maori people would support He Taua's stand against the haka party — was put in small print. It was not until it was reported that the Auckland District Maori Council was providing 'Maori Help for the Haka Attack Group'[4] that it become evident there was anything but a Pakeha view of the incident.

The action of responsible Maori leaders in espousing an unpopular cause in the eyes of the Pakeha majority was a political exercise in the mobilisation of Maori people to counter the overreaction of the Pakeha and the expression of that reaction through the press. Members of He Taua attended the May meeting of the Auckland District Maori Council and explained the reasons for what they did. This strength-ened the hand of the chairman of the council, who argued that the physical violence of He Taua was no worse than the cultural violence of the engineers' haka party. The extent of the cultural insult had become more serious as shifting standards of sexual behaviour encouraged the engineers to 'tattoo' themselves with lipstick, depicting not moko on their bodies, but caricatures of male genitals and sexist obscenities.[5] Even when these disclosures had been made, Maori were accused in various newspapers of being 'immature', 'unable to take a joke', and even 'oversensitive'.[6]

In view of the widespread condemnation in the media of He Taua and its use of violence, the Auckland District Maori Council coun-tered the reaction by putting the issue before the conservative New Zealand Maori Council and soliciting support from all districts. When the obscene nature of the cultural insult was explained, the national body agreed to support He Taua, as did the Maori Women's Welfare League.

During the court hearing, which began on 6 July, Maori elders, the presidents of the Maori Council, Maori Women's Welfare League and the Auckland District Maori Council were present. The parents of the defendants and Maori university students were also in attendance, and a contingent of Maori students from Waikato University travelled to Auckland to attend the trial. This show of Maori solidarity effectively transformed the court by giving it a social context that exemplified the clash between two cultures. Although the dominating mana in the court was that of the judge, the countervailing mana of the Maori people was equally as palpable. When the first witness, a tall, confident male engineering student walked in, the enormity of what he had done hit him when he turned to face the court and was confronted by a sea of serious brown faces.

In the course of the trial the police photographic evidence of bruised and cut engineering students injured in the He Taua raid was irrefutable. Clearly, He Taua had assaulted the students. In response to the charges, the leaders of the group, Hone Harawira and Ben Dalton, conducted their own defence for the express purpose of claiming cultural insult as the cause of their actions against the engineers. The claim was made not in the hope of having it accepted as a defence, or even mitigating factor, because they had been advised it was inadmissible, but to promulgate the political nature of their act. The court was stunned when Dalton challenged a policeman face to face in the witness box whether he saw Dalton's nose bleeding after he had been assaulted in the police station by a policeman. The witness, who up to that point was able to recall events with considerable detail, responded to each question put to him by Dalton with a standard 'I don't recall' reply. The general impression given to the people in court was that this prevaricating reply was an evasion of the truth. It was an awkward moment in the court for the policeman to be accused of wrong-doing, and for the judge, who by the conventions of the judicial system was bound to accept the word of a policeman ahead of that of an accused person.

The turning point in what could have been a dire outcome for the defendants came when Maori elders were called to the witness box. The kaumatua Dick Stirling recounted how in former times anyone who performed the haka in a slovenly manner was chastised. Indeed, an adversary who performed someone else's haka in an insulting manner could be killed. Elizabeth Murchie, president of the Maori Women's Welfare League, likened the haka to a cultural gem. Graham Latimer, president of the Maori Council, recounted how in his travels around marae throughout the country, Maori people expressed support for He Taua. Good character references for the defendants were also given by the principal of Hillary College, Garfield Johnson, and two of his teachers. Evidence that Dalton and his colleagues ran a disco for the youth of Otara to keep them off the streets indicated that they were responsible young leaders in the community and not a gang of thugs as the media had painted them.

Although Judge Blackwood ruled out provocation and cultural insult as a defence, in finding eight members of He Taua guilty, he was acutely aware of the political nature of the case as a clash between two cultures. That awareness was reflected in the sentence the judge gave of periodic detention instead of imprisonment.

The He Taua attack on the engineers' haka party effectively exposed the raw nerve of racism in New Zealand society, which for so long had been concealed by the ideology of Maori and Pakeha as one people living in harmony. The incident precipitated an inquiry by the Race Relations Conciliator and the Human Rights Commission. The commission's first report in 1980, *Racial Harmony in New Zealand*, was a distillation of 306 submissions on the haka party. The submissions were juxtaposed in the report under two categories, View One and View A. View One attempted to maintain the ideology of one people, despite considerable evidence in this group of submissions of entrenched attitudes of racial, social and cultural superiority. The submissions in View A argued for recognition of New Zealand as a bicultural and increasingly multicultural society. The report was extensively quoted in a public soul-searching in the press. Headlines proclaimed 'All Is Not Well on Race Issues',[7] 'After the Haka . . . Whither New Zealand?',[8] 'Search for Harmony'.[9]

A much more extensive report, *Race Against Time*, which appeared two years later, used the same format of the earlier report in its analysis of 500 submissions from individuals and organisations. But this time, there was a sense of urgency in the opening statement of the report:[10]

> We are at a turning point in regard to harmonious race relations . . . The myth of New Zealand as a multicultural utopia is foundering on reality. Since Bastion Point, the Haka Party Incident and the recent disturbances at Waitangi, there has been heightened awareness regarding racial conflict . . . Pakeha New Zealanders cannot understand why, after all these years, ill-feeling is developing and their institutions are under attack.

The Race Relations Conciliator urged the Government to uphold its obligations under the International Convention of United Nations for the Elimination of Racial Discrimination, and to implement the recommendations of his report. Although nothing changed immediately, the cumulative effect of continued activism both by radical and conservative Maori organisations eventually brought about profound social changes in the decade of the eighties, changes that moved the nation into the post-colonial era.

Maranga Mai

The dust had hardly settled a year after the haka party incident when another group of activists disturbed the equanimity of the nation with its dramatisation of Maori grievances in the play *Maranga Mai* performed at Mangere College. Because the play was an open challenge to the ideology of 'one people' and a contradiction of the myth of New Zealand society as a racial utopia, there was an immediate overreaction by authorities from central government down to local bodies. The reaction, as in the case of He Taua, was fostered by sensationalised treatment of the play in the media. Merv Wellington, the Minister of Education, was reputedly so angered by reports about the play that he asked the Manukau City Council to ban the Maranga Mai theatrical review group from all schools in its area. An officer from the Department of Internal Affairs was sent from the capital to investigate the matter. Six complaints were lodged with the police by parents, and there was a suggestion that a complaint would go to the Race Relations Office.[11] The Manukau City Council called for an investigation as well, especially into the part played by its detached youth worker, Brian Lepou, in arranging the performance. The cause of it all was simply a dramatisation of Maori attitudes to Waitangi Day, Bastion Point and land protest activity at Raglan.

The overreaction of the critics was to the power of drama, however amateurishly presented, to raise the level of political consciousness over Maori grievances, as much as to the content of the play. The play was a direct threat to Pakeha definitions of reality and as such became the target of crude attempts to suppress it. But the oblique criticism levelled instead at the use of four-letter words to express emotion over Maori grievances was not sufficient cause to ban the play. Nor was the complaint that the play was racially offensive. The Race Relations Conciliator rejected the complaint under Section 9A of the Race Relations Act that the play incited racial disharmony.[12] Undeterred by the fuss, the Maranga Mai group, which emanated from Mangamuka in Northland, continued performing around the country. The climax was reached when the play was performed at the Beehive theatre, in Parliament Buildings, in September. The sensational headline 'Urban Guerrilla Play Stuns Beehive'[13] encapsulated Pakeha feelings about the play. It was guerrilla theatre and as such was perceived as threatening by conservative members of Parliament. But sensitive liberal members, like Marilyn Waring, admitted to being 'moved' and made to feel 'guilty' after seeing the show, which is the very reason why attempts were made to suppress it.

Eventually, the foment of Maori activism in the seventies culminated in a challenge to Pakeha dominance in mainstream politics as well. The first portent of contemporary disaffection with Pakeha political domination came from a Maori intellectual. In September 1979, Professor Hirini Mead read a paper at the Labour Party Maori Policy Conference advocating a Maori Parliament to fight for political freedom because the dignity of Maori cultural heritage was at stake.[14] The press moved quickly to attack Mead's challenge to Pakeha power by seeking a counter-opinion from a 'respected' conservative Maori leader, Graham Latimer, president of the Maori Council. Latimer obliged by stating that the Maori Parliament which flourished between 1892 and 1902 grew out of disaffection. But in this case he knew of no disenchantment, and he wondered if there was only one disenchanted individual.

Herein lies one of the fundamental problems of the Maori struggle against Pakeha hegemony: the tendency of conservative leaders to side with the dominating class against their own people. Freire makes the observation that such men have been 'determined from above by a culture of domination which has constituted them as dual beings'.[15] The coloniser knows this and uses them to advantage against those who promote revolutionary thought directed towards decolonisation. Latimer's opinion gave the mandate for the editorial headed 'Rites Without Power' in the *New Zealand Herald*.[16] The editorial stood firmly on the ideology of one people by asserting that sovereignty cannot be divided or even easily shared. It dismissed the notion as creating disturbing social divisions that have little place in a small and isolated country such as New Zealand. Both Latimer and the editorial writer had failed to connect Mead's proposal with the land march, Bastion Point, the mounting protest activity at Waitangi, and He Taua.

Mana Motuhake

As the decade of the seventies drew to a close, protest activity started by the radicals spread to mainstream politics with the resignation of Matiu Rata from the Labour Party early in November 1979. Rata portended his resignation by expressing his disenchantment with Pakeha politics when he delivered his Maori policy report in May. He rejected the one-people ideology as an abject failure, saying:

We have, as a people, never felt more let down, more insecure, and more economically and socially deprived than we are today . . . We will no longer tolerate policies which take no account of our language, customs and lifestyle, nor will we continue to accept being governed or administered by anyone who does not understand the way we think or appreciate our values . . . We will master our own affairs, we must command our own destiny, and we want every acre of land wrongfully taken from us back.[17]

The press moved quickly to defend the status quo. The editor of the *Auckland Star* speculated that Rata's new pressure group, Mana Motuhake, could lead to 'social disruptiveness'.[18] The *New Zealand Herald*[19] dismissed Rata's resignation as chagrin because of his demotion to the backbench of the party rather than attributing it to complaints over Labour indifference to Maori needs. Rata, who had spent seventeen years in Parliament under the wing of the Labour Party, went back to the people to seek a mandate for what he had done. At a public meeting in Auckland attended by 250 people, there was a swell of support for Rata from a cross-section of Maori people, young, old, academics, clerics, workers, activists and conservatives. Some urged the formation of a political party, but no resolution was put to the meeting.

Rata then toured the marae of his Northland constituents. His Labour Party branch committees at Te Kao, Mangonui, Hokianga, Kaipara and Whangarei defected with him to become Mana Motuhake branches.[20] But it was not until April 1980 that Rata announced his resignation from Parliament to force a by-election. In the meantime the press continued to denigrate Rata by suggesting that he ran the danger of encouraging separatism and becoming a tool of the radicals.[21] One editor took the opportunity generated by the publicity surrounding Rata to reassert the ideology of one people by attacking the principle of Maori seats as separatist and discriminatory. Without reference to the historical facts, the editor asserted that the original reasons for 'electoral apartheid' were paternalistic and had long since disappeared, and therefore Maori representation should disappear with them.[22]

Undeterred by the adverse press, Rata launched his party at a hui during Easter 1980 at Tira Hou Marae in Auckland. Rata's formal break with his party effectively ended the forty-year Ratana liaison with Labour. For its part, the Labour Party selected an Anglican, Dr Bruce Gregory, to contest the by-election on 7 June. The activists flocked to Rata's support to the extent that on the polling day he was able to put 400 Maori people into the field as scrutineers, to provide transport for voters and to man his election headquarters. But it was not enough to beat the Labour Party machine and the entrenched two-party system of New Zealand. Although the poll was low, Rata's 38 per cent of the vote to Labour's 53 per cent was seen as a 'respectable performance' for a new party and raised the question whether Mana Motuhake would become a political force in New Zealand politics.[23]

Waitangi Action Committee

Early in 1981 the focus of activism moved from Mana Motuhake to the Waitangi Action Committee. WAC was given an additional reason for targeting the Waitangi celebrations with the announcement that Sir Graham Latimer and Dame Whina Cooper were to be invested by the Governor-General at Waitangi National Marae. In January members of WAC attended the Taitokerau District Council hui to express opposition to the investiture. They argued that receiving Pakeha awards on a marae in view of the history of colonisation would be seen by them as a 'provocative act'. They tabled a letter stating their opposition in writing. The district council ignored the deputation and went ahead with the arrangements for the investiture. On the morning of 6 February, WAC sought speaking rights on the marae from their elders, which were granted. All the major elders of the North, including Sir James Henare, were present when the WAC speaker Arthur Harawira got up to address the Governor-General, Sir David Beattie. Echoing the words of his ancestors 141 years previously, Harawira told the Governor-General to 'go away', he was 'not welcome' until he had something 'decent to offer the Maori people'. This blunt statement of opposition to the heir of kawanatanga derived from the Treaty was typical of WAC's hard-nosed approach to social transformation. It was a challenge to the Governor to forsake platitudes and to do something substantive for the people through the power of his office.

During his speech Harawira was supported by thirty or so members of WAC, who were seated in an orderly group on the marae to the right of the meeting house. When Sir Graham Latimer and Dame Whina Cooper walked from the meeting house towards the dais, one of the protesters, Mangu Awarau, misread the cue from his leader and ran prematurely across to the marae. The plan was to stop the investiture by surrounding the dais, but it misfired because Awarau was too impetuous. In the meantime Hone Harawira called on Sir Graham not to embarrass the Maori people by accepting the award, whereupon the rest of WAC got up and chanted 'Shame! Shame! Shame!' as they milled about. Awarau was thrown to the ground by a security guard and police poured into the marae and arrested eight of the protesters.

Again, as in the case of Maranga Mai, media treatment of the event was sensational and exaggerated. According to the *New Zealand Herald*, Waitangi Marae was in an 'uproar' as the police went into action to prevent a 'full-scale riot'.[24] The police also exaggerated in order to rationalise their intervention by saying they went into an 'emergency situation because people's lives were at stake'. The *Auckland Star* claimed Maori activists and police traded punches as they wrestled on the ground of Waitangi Marae.[25] These reports, together with television newsclips showing people milling around in confusion on the marae, defined public perception of the occasion as one of violence instead of non-violent protest. Sir Graham added to that perception by being quoted in the press as saying 'when the fighting started . . .' The portrayal of WAC in a negative light was completed by the Prime Minister, Robert Muldoon, who said that the protesters would become 'outcasts' from Maori society.[26] Sir Graham himself called for a ban on the protesters from future ceremonies at the Waitangi Marae.[27] This portrayal of WAC as a radical fringe group by the authorities and the media was a miscalculation rooted in the ideology of one people. It failed entirely to appreciate the abiding sense of resentment in Maori hearts over land grievances and the political effect of WAC's protest activity in rousing Maori consciousness. But in the meantime, before that consciousness became manifest, they had to bear the brunt of public denouncement and, more importantly, persecution by the law.

The eight defendants were tried in the Kaikohe District Court on 9 October before Judge H. R. H. Paul. When the defendants were asked to plead, their spokesman, Hone Harawira, who had experience defending himself in the He Taua case, stunned the court by taking the offensive. He called on the judge to dismiss the case because the Treaty of Waitangi had not been ratified and therefore the Maori were still a sovereign people over whom the court had no jurisdiction. Although surprised by the challenge, the judge did not deign to debate the issues raised and continued the standard procedure by instructing the clerk of the court to enter a plea of not guilty before asking the next defendant his plea. Undeterred by the relentless grinding of the judicial machine, Harawira returned to the attack. He called on the judge to dismiss the case on the grounds that the police had no substantive charge. He said it was impossible to prepare a defence when the police kept altering the charges they were making from rioting, to inciting a riot, to behaving in a riotous manner. Although surprised by this attack from a different direction, again the judge instructed the clerk to enter a plea of not guilty. Harawira then launched his last attack by moving a dismissal of the case on the grounds that the position of the defendants had been compromised. Some of the defendants who had been earlier imprisoned during the Springbok rugby tour demonstrations had their defence folios confiscated by the police when they were being transported from Mt Eden prison to Kaikohe for the trial. The police had the folios in their possession for eight hours and could have made them available to the prosecutor. There was a pointed silence while the judge pondered this revelation. Although he ignored the submission, he noted the point made. The trial proceeded with the police producing the first of their twenty-five witnesses.

The strategy adopted by WAC was to subject each witness to intense and protracted cross-examination. The first witness was the police photographer, who was questioned by Harawira for two hours. The line of questioning aimed to get an admission that the police operation at Waitangi was a 'set-up' designed to target and arrest particular activists. To this end there was a tent with a display board of photographs of known activists who were to be arrested, brought to the tent and checked against the photographs. When the witness was asked to verify that that was the purpose of the display board, the prosecutor signalled him with his hand not to answer the question. Harawira turned immediately to the judge and called on him to dismiss the case on the grounds that the prosecutor instructing the witness in the box was a travesty of justice. The judge was momentarily nonplussed by this turn of events and made no comment, whereupon Arthur Harawira, who had been silent while his brother conducted the defence interjected, in a booming voice, 'If you can't give us a judgment, get off the bench and get us a judge who can'. There was stunned silence at this open challenge to the authority of the judge. No one would have been surprised had Harawira been held in contempt of court. However, Judge Paul, known for his fairness, maintained his composure and the trial continued.

After a hearing of twenty days spread over several weeks, when only ten of the twenty-five police witnesses had been heard, Judge Paul dismissed the case on the grounds that the police evidence did not come close to the prescriptions he had of riotous behaviour. Chanting 'Shame!' and raising fists did not constitute a riot.[28] But despite that dismissal, the public perception remained that the protest at Waitangi was violent, because of the power of the mass media to distort and define reality for its consumers. This is one of the roadblocks in the way of the activists and the general Maori agenda for social transformation. The media buttress the social structure by defining reality in a way that maintains the structural relationship of Pakeha dominance and Maori subjection. The use of that power against the activists could easily be turned against any of the conservatives of Maori society should they engage openly in the practice of social transformation.

Liberation Theology

The cause espoused by WAC received support from an unexpected quarter, a member of the Anglican Church. Dr Richard Pelly of St John's Theological College wrote to the Christian Conference of Asia for a grant of $5,000 to support the WAC defendants and their families. Pelly argued that the the arrest and imprisonment of WAC members was politically motivated, as evidenced by the spurious and shifting nature of the charges. He contended that the New Zealand Government was incapable of dealing constructively with the issues raised by WAC because it was weak and unimaginative. The Government increasingly relied on police to bolster and assert its authority. It was a misuse of state power to force a celebration on those who were opposed to it. The Komiti Tumuaki (Maori Executive Committee) of the Auckland Diocese endorsed the view that the protest was peaceful and the arrests were politically motivated.

The mounting protest activity at Waitangi and escalated police response to see the celebrations through, caused disquiet in the National Council of Churches as well. The churches were becoming uncomfortable over their involvement in the celebrations. Although their part was small, being rostered to bless the occasion, they felt embarrassed at having to bless a celebration the Maori people saw as an injustice. Pakeha activist groups also expressed their misgivings over Waitangi by sending a telegram to the Governor-General, Sir David Beattie, urging him to reconsider his participation in the celebration.[29] These were straws in the wind that signalled a growing political consciousness in the general community over the Treaty, a development triggered by Maori activist groups such as Tamatoa and WAC who dared to travel the lonely road of political dissent.

In 1982 WAC marched from Auckland to Waitangi. In order to draw attention to their cause, 150 members of WAC attempted to cross the Auckland Harbour Bridge but were forced by police batons to abandon this plan. This was an escalation in police response to Maori activists. Whereas the Bastion Point protesters were treated gently or with minimal use of force, WAC was given no such indulgence. The hard line taken by the police was a corollary of the 1981 Springbok tour protests, when hundreds of demonstrators were batoned by the police, and a portent of rough treatment in the future for activists at Waitangi.

As the policing tactics escalated, so did the tactics of the activists. For the 1982 protest in the Treaty House grounds, WAC was strengthened by reinforcements. Over 300 demonstrators, including Pakeha activists, were kept at bay by a line of policemen fifty metres from the ceremony. As they heckled, missiles were thrown, including an egg which hit the Governor-General, and several home-made smoke bombs. There were twenty-seven arrests as a consequence of these actions.[30] The nuclear protest yacht *Pacific Peacemaker*, moored off Waitangi, was boarded by police and five hecklers were arrested.[31] During the ceremony it was the turn of the Catholic Church to give the blessing. Archbishop Williams conducted the service but replaced the usual prayer with his own version delivered in both English and Maori, as an indication of the changing stance of the churches. Taking note of the stand of the National Council of Churches the previous year, the Education, Justice and Development Commission of the Catholic Church decided to conduct an in-depth inquiry into Waitangi Day as a Catholic contribution to a 'corporate reflection' by the whole Christian Church.[32] The police for their part worried over the use of incendiary devices and pondered changing tactics by adopting more stringent measures to control what they termed the 'lunatic fringe'.

The following year there was a further shift in church opinion as Waitangi Day drew near. The Presbyterian Assembly and the Methodist Conference urged their congregations to repent for Waitangi Day.[33] But despite the growing consciousness of the churches, Waitangi Day, which had been beamed annually as a media spectacle by television into the living rooms of the nation, was bigger than ever. There were 4,000 people in attendance.[34] The policing action, as portended the previous year, was also greater. This time the police had riot helmets and long batons to protect the Governor. The grounds of the Treaty House were cordoned off, and spectators searched before being allowed in. But the biggest change was a pre-emptive strike by the police when ninety-nine protesters were arrested in a military-style operation. Over fifty protesters were arrested before getting near the Treaty House, down by the Waitangi Bridge. The rest were arrested at the Treaty House. Those arrested, including innocent members of the public, were bundled into police vans and held for several hours before being released. Among those held were John Minto and Dick Cuthbert of HART (Halt All Racist Tours), and Dr

Oliver Sutherland of ACORD (Auckland Committee on Racism and Discrimination). A month later the Auckland District Law Society issued a report stating the police had no power to arrest peaceful protesters in anticipation that a breach of the peace would occur.[35] It was a timely warning to politicians to stop the country drifting towards a police state. The National Council of Churches issued its own warning to the Minister of Lands, Jonathan Elworthy, by proposing a moratorium on Waitangi Day observances in 1984.[36] The Minister referred the matter to the Waitangi Trust Board for consideration. This crack in the Government's position could not have been made by WAC alone. The Maori, as a minority of 12 per cent in a population of three million, cannot achieve justice or resolve their grievances without Pakeha support. For this reason, Pakeha are as much a part of the process of social transformation in the post-colonial era as radical and activist Maori.

Te Hikoi ki Waitangi

The Waitangi Action Committee did not rest on its achievements but continued to expand its base of support. In October 1983 WAC convened a national hui at Waahi Marae, the home of Dame Te Atairangi-kaahu, the ariki of the Kingitanga. There it pulled off a political coup by bringing together the oldest Maori political movements in the country, Kotahitanga and the Kingitanga. The coalition came together for the purpose of a hikoi, a peaceful walk to Waitangi. The aim was to demonstrate a Maori unity of purpose to stop the Waitangi celebrations in 1984 by sheer weight of numbers. The veteran land protester Eva Rickard was elected president of the Hikoi, and Titewhai Harawira, a long-time Maori rights campaigner, its secretary. Early in December a planning meeting was held at Tauranga, attended by Kotahitanga delegates from all parts of the country. On 20 January a letter was sent to Queen Elizabeth, notifying her of the Hikoi and appealing for her support as the descendant of Queen Victoria, with whom the Treaty of Waitangi had been made. She was informed of how Maori efforts to present petitions on their grievances to her and to Prince Charles when they were in New Zealand were frustrated by the Government. A similar letter was sent to the Governor-General, Sir David Beattie, requesting that as the Queen's representative in New Zealand, he support Maori efforts to gain justice and equality.[37]

On 28 January, Kotahitanga contingents from Taitokerau, Tainui, Kahungunu, Tairawhiti, Tamaki and Poneke assembled and were welcomed at Turangawaewae Marae. There the Hikoi was given the seal of approval by the Kahui Ariki when the kaumatua Henare Tuwhangai said, 'Ka tautoko au i tenei hikoi inaianei' (I support this Hikoi now). The Hikoi leaders were taken into Mahinarangi and were received by the ariki Te Atairangikaahu, who encouraged them by saying, 'Mehemea he painga mo te iwi, mahia' (If there is good in it for the people, do it).[38] Fortified by Te Atairangikaahu's approval and a blessing from an ecumenical service, the Hikoi set off for Waitangi 300 kilometres away.

The political significance of the Hikoi lay in its deep, spiritual sense of unity. Like the land march in the previous decade, it brought together a wide spectrum of people under a common cause, to stop the celebration of a treaty that had been dishonoured by the coloniser. The Hikoi included members of Mana Motuhake, the Labour and National Parties, the Maori Council and Maori Women's Welfare League, land marchers, protesters from Bastion Point, radicals, activists, feminists, students, Maori clerics, and Pakeha supporters from ACORD, CARE and HART. When the Hikoi stopped overnight at Takaparawha (Bastion Point), Pakeha in these latter organisations served in the menial role of kanohi wera, the hot faces, tending the fire, cooking food, serving on tables and washing dishes. Pakeha assisting a revolutionary movement as auxiliaries is fundamental to the radical practice of social transformation. Liberation from Pakeha dominance is not a gift conferred on the Maori by the oppressor. The Maori have to lead their own liberation struggle, a task Pakeha are free to join as auxiliaries. Freire[39] makes a pertinent comment on this point:

> It is only the oppressed who, by freeing themselves, can free their oppressors. The latter, as an oppressive class, can free neither others nor themselves. It is therefore essential that the oppressed wage the struggle to resolve the contradiction in which they are caught. That contradiction will be resolved by the appearance of the new man who is neither oppressor nor oppressed — man in the process of liberation.

The overnight stay on Bastion Point, hosted by Joe Hawke and the people of Ngati Whatua, was also an act of defiance of the state. Despite the ruling of the court and the eviction of the protesters in 1978, the Hikoi stood by the slogan expressed by grafitti around Auckland that 'Bastion Point Is Maori Land'. The presence of the Hikoi under the mana whenua of Ngati Whatua was a symbolic statement of ownership, and indicated that the field of battle had not been conceded to the Crown.

Although the state presented a hard, uncompromising exterior to activists, as it did in the 1981 Springbok tour and to protesters at Waitangi, politicians and power-brokers are not immune to populist movements. Where previous Governors-General had subscribed unthinkingly to the ideology of one people, Sir David Beattie moved away from that position in 1981. In his address to the crowd at Waitangi he said, 'We are not one people, despite Hobson's oft-quoted words, nor should we try to be.' As a liberal thinker who took note of the obvious contradictions in the relationship between Maori and Pakeha, the Governor was even capable of stepping outside an historically defined role as well. The Prime Minister had ostracised the WAC activists as outcasts, but Sir David did not bow to the Government line.

After considering the letter from the Hikoi, feelers were put out to the leaders. On the last night of the Hikoi at Waiomio Marae, Eva Rickard and Pumi Taituha returned from a meeting with Sir David to announce that the Governor was prepared to meet a deputation of 100 representatives from the Hikoi and to receive their petition. The offer was discussed and rejected as being divisive. The Hikoi had walked 300 kilometres together through heat and dust in a spirit of unity. It was going to stay together and meet the Governor as a united body.

On the morning of Waitangi Day the Hikoi walked along the foreshore at Paihia. While they were doing so, the 'Tainui express' arrived at Opua with a group of elders. They were ferried across the bay, disembarked, and allowed by the police to cross the Waitangi Bridge and proceed up to the Treaty House. But the main body of the Hikoi was stopped by the police for over half an hour. In the meantime the Governor-General waited to receive the Hikoi while its leaders negotiated with the police. Eventually the Hikoi was allowed to proceed into Bledisloe Park, where it was restricted by police to an open space below the Treaty House. The police refused to allow the Hikoi into the Treaty House grounds because they feared it would not withdraw after meeting the Governor-General. Thus did the police prevent an historic meeting between the representative of the Queen and over 3,000 of her loyal subjects. Although the Hikoi dispersed without achieving the goal of stopping the celebration, another step towards liberation from Pakeha authority had been taken. Its political effects were to become manifest later.

The Conservatives

While the activists struggled to rouse the nation's conscience over the Treaty of Waitangi, the conservative leaders were busy with their own programmes for social change. In 1977 Kara Puketapu was appointed Secretary of Maori Affairs. Puketapu was a career public servant who rose to the rank of Assistant State Services Commissioner. As soon as he took up his new post, Puketapu introduced measures to empower Maori people as Ngata had done before him. More Maori were recruited into the department, while three with good service records were promoted to district officer status. From a series of consultative meetings Puketapu instituted with Maori people in different districts, he generated policies arising out of their needs. These were endorsed at 'Hui Whakatauira', annual conferences held in the legislative chamber of Parliament Buildings with 100 leaders drawn from all districts.

The ideology underlying the new community programmes of the Department of Maori Affairs was 'Tu Tangata', standing tall like a man in shaping the 'stance of the people'.[40] The organisation for the implementation of the programme was designated 'kokiri', meaning to advance into the twenty-first century. Kokiri community management groups were established at the district level to determine priorities and tasks for community action. Wellington City with its Maori population of 60,000 was divided into three kokiri units, while Auckland with its larger Maori population had seven. These management groups identified education, employment, vocational training and language learning as their main priorities for community action.[41]

The annual Hui Whakatauira, under Puketapu's administration, generated some of the best programmes in the history of the Department of Maori Affairs since the time of Ngata. These included rapu mahi, a job-search programme for the unemployed, women's wananga (women's workshops), business wananga, and kokiri skills centres which gave basic training in such things as motor mechanics, panel beating, garment making, rebuilding furniture, and Maori arts and crafts. Some of the major programmes that were to contribute to the growing cultural renaissance came out of recommendations from the 1981 Hui Whakatauira. One of these was the 'Matua Whangai' (foster parenting) programme designed to take young Maori out of the care of social welfare institutions and place them back within the care of their own tribal groups.[42] This was the beginning of the department's policy of recognising and negotiating with tribal authorities.

Kohanga Reo

The jewel in the crown of the Department of Maori Affairs' achievements was the kohanga reo (language nest), which provided the world with a model language-recovery programme. Knowledge of kohanga reo has spread around the Pacific rim as far afield as Vancouver. Television documentaries have been made of kohanga reo for showing to other speech communities, such as the Welsh and Gaels, whose language survival has been threatened by English.

Despite reversal in the 1970s of the colonial policy of suppressing the Maori language by its inclusion in the education system, the language continued to retreat. Research by Benton indicated that Maori, as a consequence of Pakeha domination, was dying out.[43] Benton's survey of who speaks Maori in New Zealand was based on a sample of 33,638 subjects in selected towns and cities. The data substantiated his dire prediction of imminent death of the Maori language unless something revolutionary was done about it. At the time of the survey in the seventies, 50 per cent of the Maori population was under fifteen years of age. Only 15 per cent of this age group could speak Maori. The age group above forty-five, which constituted only 12 per cent of the population, accounted for 38 per cent of the Maori speakers.[44] Since this was the age bracket that was being phased out by death at a time when there was insufficient replacement in the lower age groups, Benton's conclusion of language death was the only one that could be drawn from the data.

The elders at the 1981 Hui Whakatauira faced the challenge posed by Benton to rescue the Maori language by proposing the concept of kohanga reo, run by kuia, koro and mature women who were native speakers of Maori. In effect, the kohanga reo was to be a pre-school conducted entirely in the Maori language. The aim was to make every Maori child bilingual by the age of five, because 'Without the Maori language there can be no Maori culture, and the survival of a unique Maori identity; this is the spiritual force behind the creation of Te Kohanga Reo.'[45] Once the first pilot scheme established in 1981 at Pukeatua Kokiri in Wainuiomata proved the feasibility of the concept of kohanga reo, the idea was extended to other districts. Every new kohanga reo received an establishment grant from the department of $5,000. But for the programme to be viable, management teams had to take a koha of $25 as a weekly contribution from the parents.

Despite the cost of sending children to kohanga reo, the movement flourished as mothers up and down the country who were deprived of their language wanted a better deal for their children. By November 1983 there were 188 kohanga reo in operation, of which only thirty-four were licensed and qualified for the $18 per child subsidy from the Department of Social Welfare. To rationalise this new development, the Kohanga Reo Trust was established. One of its first tasks was to draw up a draft syllabus to be referred to the Consultative Committee on Child Care for official approval and recognition of kohanga reo for the purposes of state funding. These developments encouraged more growth so that by 1988, the number of kohanga had increased to 521.[46]

Ostensibly kohanga reo aimed to nurture Maori language among pre-school children. But there were other spin-off effects as mothers too, strove to learn the language in order to provide reinforcement at home. The mothers also became politically active as they grappled with bureaucracy for resources. Symptomatic of this politicisation was the attendance of 1,000 people at Turangawaewae Marae in January 1984 for the Kohanga Reo Conference. Kohanga reo is as much a political movement as it is a language-recovery programme and as such is an element in its own right of the modern Maori renaissance.

After two years in a kohanga, mothers are faced with the problem of where to send their children for primary schooling. There are only twelve bilingual schools in New Zealand where some instruction is conducted in Maori. There are approximately forty bilingual units within regular primary schools, nowhere near enough to cater for the needs of new entrants from kohanga reo. Parents unable to find such schools within reach put pressure on existing schools to make such provision, or decided to keep their children back in the kohanga until they were six, the age when it becomes compulsory for them to enrol for primary school.

School for Cultural Reproduction

The concern of kohanga reo mothers and Maori educationists over the need for continuity of Maori language provision in primary and secondary schools was expressed at the Maori Educational Development Conference in 1984.[47] There were reservations about state-controlled bilingual schools because it was felt that the dynamism of the kohanga reo stemmed from community control. For this reason alternative schools controlled by the community were thought to be necessary to ensure continuity in kohanga reo philosophy and method of language maintenance.[48] Maori parents claimed that within three weeks of a child arriving at a regular primary school, they exhibited negative attitudes towards Maori by suppressing it or losing it altogether. A small group of committed parents who were concerned with language maintenance of kohanga reo children into primary schooling launched kura kaupapa Maori. There are seven such schools in existence: at Hone Waititi Marae (Henderson), Waipareira (Kelston), Maungawhau (Mt Eden), Mataatua (Mangere), Otara, Manurewa and Ruamata (Rotorua). Two others are in the planning and setting up stage at Christchurch and Palmerston North. Kura kaupapa Maori are schools based on total immersion in Maori language. The establishment of such schools grew out of the realisation that regular schools functioned to reproduce Pakeha culture at the expense of Maori culture. The rationale for replacing bilingualism with total immersion is the threat of Maori language death. The pressing need is to rescue the language from oblivion by reproducing authentic native speakers, and kura kaupapa Maori was seen as the only solution. Kura kaupapa Maori are also symptomatic of the desire among Maori people to take control of the education of their own children.

The Maori Educational Development Conference also marked a turning point in the radical potential of the Maori to transform the education system and divert it from its historic role of eliminating Maori culture. For two decades after the Hunn Report, Maori leaders and educators co-operated with the authorities in trying to close the education gap, without questioning the structural role of the system in cultural reproduction. They adopted reformist strategies of raising money for the Maori Education Foundation, establishing Maori education advancement committees, and enthusiastic establishment of play centres. Several hundred Maori men and women entered the teaching profession in the post-war years under the Maori quota system before it was abolished in 1969. These teachers stepped up the Maori content in their social studies teaching and initiated cultural visits to marae. The Maori presence in the teaching profession was reflected in three resolutions in the 1971 Report of the National Advisory Committee on Maori Education (NACME).[49]

1. That cultural differences need to be understood, accepted and respected by children and teachers.
2. That the school curriculum must find a place for the understanding of Maoritanga, including Maori language.
3. That in order to achieve the goal of equality of opportunity, special measures need to be taken.

The Maori Battalion en route through Faenza, Italy, in 1944. The battalion rekindled the fighting spirit of a warrior race, who on their return home sought equality in towns and cities.
Alexander Turnbull Library

Mira Szaszy (née Petricevich) addressing the inaugural meeting of the Maori Women's Welfare League in Wellington, 1951. On her right is Whina Cooper, the first president of the league.
Alexander Turnbull Library

Te Arikinui Te Atairangikaahu addressing a hui in front of Te Tokanga-nui-a-noho meeting house at Te Kuiti in 1969.

Inset: *Donna Awatere and Ripeka Evans, the new wave of activists who were members of Nga Tamatoa in 1971 and prominent leaders in the 1981 protests against sporting contacts with South Africa.*
Gil Hanly

The Maori land march, 1975, in front of Parliament Buildings, Wellington.
John M. Miller

The clearing of Bastion Point by 600 police on 25 May 1978.
New Zealand Herald

Leaders of the 1984 Hikoi to Waitangi, Eva Rickard (centre) and Titewhai Harawira (right), conferring with the leader of the land march in the previous decade, Whina Cooper.
Gil Hanly

The activists defy the state again and reoccupy Bastion Point in 1982.
Gil Hanly

Activists take to the streets in the 1980s to protest against the hypocrisy of celebrating a broken covenant as the birth of a nation.
Gil Hanly

Matiu Rata, former Minister of Maori Affairs, founder of the Mana Motuhake Party and leader of the Muriwhenua Incorporation, with Waerete Norman and Jerry Ihimaera.
Gil Hanly

September 1984, Koro Wetere, Minister of Maori Affairs, listening to the hui at Turangawaewae Marae demanding retrospective power for the Waitangi Tribunal.
Gil Hanly

Display of solidarity by Kotahitanga, January 1984, in front of Te Puea, the first meeting house of an urban marae in the metropolis of Auckland.
Gil Hanly

Foundation members of the Waitangi Tribunal, Paul Temm QC, Sir Graham Latimer and Judge Eddie Durie, after a sitting of the tribunal at Orakei Marae, 1986.
Gil Hanly

The new growth: kohanga reo infants in front of the splendidly carved house Tumutumu-whenua, Orakei Marae, Auckland.
Gil Hanly

These resolutions by NACME enabled the Minister of Education to put in place the reforms advocated by Tamatoa for teaching Maori language in primary schools. In addition, by 1973 all seven teachers' colleges had established courses in Maori studies. To support the programme at the primary level, the Department of Education appointed thirty itinerant teachers of Maori. By 1971, Maori was being taught in 171 of New Zealand's 397 secondary schools. At the primary level, ITM staff had to be expanded to forty to service the 250 schools offering Maori studies to 50,000 pupils. Although these reforms were a welcome reversal of the former policy of language and cultural exclusion, they made little impression on the education gap. There was only a 10 per cent reduction of those who left school without qualifications, from 85 per cent to 75 per cent. There was something more fundamental at work in the system that was producing this constant negative result.

Bernard Gadd's paper 'Ethnic Bias in School Certificate' shifted the debate on Maori underachievement in education from the reformist strategy to one of attacking institutionalised racism.[50] Nairn defined institutional racism as the perpetuation by organisations, institutions or agencies of policies and practices that operate to the advantage of the powerful group and to the disadvantage of particular racial or cultural groups.[51] According to Gadd, ethnic bias in favour of Pakeha is implicit in the assumptions underlying the School Certificate examination. The vehicle for testing candidates for the examination is middle-class English, which is the assumed norm. No allowance is made for ethnic heterogeneity and language usage. Nairn goes on to say that racism is about outcomes of our policies and practices, and the regular predictable outcome, according to Gadd, is an education gap in favour of the Pakeha of 23.1 per cent. Gadd demonstrated the correlation between social class and ethnicity in examination success by tabulating the School Certificate English pass rates for sixty-eight secondary schools in metropolitan Auckland. At the top were twenty schools attended by the children of the élite with pass rates ranging from 60 per cent to 90 per cent for an examination in which only 50 per cent pass overall. At the bottom were schools with predominantly Maori and Pacific Island students, with pass rates ranging from 15 per cent to 29 per cent. (See Appendix 2.)

Attempts by Maori leaders to have their language and culture included in schools as a means of closing the education gap, while appearing to be gaining ground, were in fact, according to Simon,[52] subverted by Pakeha teachers. Simon provided empirical evidence demonstrating use of the ideology of 'one people' to delay or block the introduction of Maori programmes. When questioned why they were not implementing Maori programmes in their schools, teachers resorted to claiming 'We are all New Zealanders', 'We are all one people', 'I think of people as individuals', and that the inclusion of Maoritanga 'smacks of separatism'. Alternatively, Maori programmes were sabotaged by offering them as a club option in competition with other appealing activities such as sport, art or cooking. Maori language was also downgraded in school organisation by bracketing it with non-prestigious subjects such as typing, technical drawing and art, thus making it difficult for children in academic streams to take the subject.

Most of the 300 delegates who attended the Maori Educational Development Conference were teachers of Maori language. Many of them had mixed feelings towards the education system, which they felt actually manufactured Maori failure. Their feelings were encapsulated in a paper by Maiki Marks, a mature woman who entered teaching on the one-year training scheme for Maori language teachers. Commenting on the frustrations of being a Maori language teacher in a Pakeha-dominated school, Marks wrote:

> The frustrations of being a Maori language teacher are the same as being a Maori in our education system . . . I was not given a Maori language class. I was given a class of shattered youngsters to care for . . . The Maori language teacher every day faces the victims of the system . . . I see these girls coming into high school with their selves battered and bruised after eight years in the system . . . They have little confidence. Their behaviour often reflects their inner pain and confusion. And all the school does is to yell at them, to punish them, to expel them . . . The frustrations of being a Maori language teacher are summed up in the feeling that the education system has invited you to be a mourner at the tangihanga of your culture, your language, your self.[53]

In the workshops of the conference, other Maori language teachers expressed disillusionment with their role in education to the extent of considering resigning from an inherently flawed system. They felt that they had taught their students well because their marks in on-course assessment indicated the students were capable of passing School Certificate. But when the results came out, some students who were expected to pass failed. The explanation was found in a paper by Hughes who argued that over a ten-year period School Certificate marks were scaled in a manner that gave pass rates of over 80 per cent to students taking academic subjects and pass rates of around 40 per cent to students taking non-academic subjects.[54] The rationale for the different pass rates was that students who took academic subjects were bright and therefore should have higher pass rates than the conventional 50 per cent pass-fail ratio. The inverse of that reasoning is that students who take non-academic subjects are not so bright and therefore are less capable of achieving a 50 per cent pass rate. As a consequence of the desire not to penalise students taking academic subjects, a complicated formula of statistical manipulation of marks was introduced which increased the pass rate for academic subjects. But in order to maintain the 50 per cent pass rate overall, the increase was at the expense of non-academic subjects. Maori language in many schools is often listed with the non-academic subjects. Delegates to the conference were incensed by the revelation that Latin and French had pass rates of 86 per cent and 81 per cent while Maori was at the bottom with 41 per cent in 1982. In 1980, the Maori pass-rate fell as low as 39 per cent. (See Appendix 3.)

This derogation of the Maori language in the subject hierarchy pass rate of the School Certificate examination reflected the structural relationship of Pakeha domination and Maori subjection. The placement of Maori language at the bottom of the hierarchy not only confirmed the structural relationship but fuelled suspicion that the education system functioned to maintain it. This is the source of the radical potential of the Maori to transform the education system. That potential was expressed in a resolution calling for the dismantling of the subject hierarchy pass rate under threat of parents boycotting School Certificate. Another resolution declared that the existing system of education had failed Maori people and co-operating with it to introduce modifications had not helped the situation. For this reason Maori people were exhorted to take over the education of their own children by establishing alternative schools modelled on the principles underlying kohanga reo.

Radical and Conservative Convergence

Although Maori radicals are the cutting edge of social change, the conservatives are the slow grinding edge. Basically both radicals and conservatives pursued the same objectives of justice, resolution of Maori grievances under the Treaty of Waitangi, recognition of rangatiratanga and mana whenua, and an equal say with the Pakeha in the future of the country. The only difference between radicals and conservatives is the methods used by the radicals. But as the renaissance progressed through the decade of the eighties, there was a convergence of effort that was to have a profound effect on Pakeha dominance.

In February and May 1981 the Mana Motuhake Party held a large hui on Waitaha Marae and Hirangi Marae at Taupo. In June a candidate selection hui was held at Omeka Marae, one of the Ratana strongholds near Matamata. The state of the party at the time of the hui was 100 branches throughout the country, and a membership of 15,000, including children. The four candidates selected to contest the 1981 election were Matiu Rata, Northern Maori; Eva Rickard, Western Maori; Albert Tahana, Eastern Maori; and Amster Reedy, Southern Maori. Although none of these candidates was successful, they all polled higher than the National Party and Social Credit candidates. Labour had always held the Maori seats by substantial majorities against the conservative parties. The appearance of a new party to the left displacing the others from second place in all four electorates was clearly a matter of concern to Labour. The Mana Motuhake manifesto articulated the Maori agenda for social change that was being pursued by radicals and conservatives alike. The party sought ratification of the Treaty of Waitangi, unity in search of justice, recognition of mana whenua, self-determination in all matters affecting Maori people, retention of Maori language and customs, and the transformation of all the country's social and political institutions to include biculturalism.[55]

The rather benign Mana Motuhake manifesto as a statement of an agenda for social change was brought into sharper focus by Donna Awatere's publication of 'Maori Sovereignty' in the feminist magazine *Broadsheet* in June 1982. For Awatere,[56] Maori sovereignty sought nothing less than acknowledgement that New Zealand is Maori land, and she seeks return of that land. In Awatere's view, notions of Maori sovereignty range from the conservative claim for biculturalism to the radical overthrow of monoculturalism. In following this agenda, Awatere asserts, the Maori have no choice, because it is not a matter of sovereignty or nothing. Without sovereignty the Maori would be dead as a nation.

Appeal to Waitangi Tribunal

In the meantime, while the activists were conducting their frontal assault on racism, monocultural power and control, a long-running battle was being fought behind the scenes by conservative leaders to protect Maori land and fishery resources and to have those resources wrongly expropriated by the Crown returned to Maori ownership.

Because of Judge Prendergast's declaration in 1877 of the Treaty of Waitangi as a 'simple nullity', Maori experience of recourse to law for a settlement of their grievances was one of defeat. But gradually the foment of activism in the seventies refocused on the law and its mechanisms of the court as a way out of the impasse.

In June 1977 the Waitangi Tribunal heard its first two cases. The claim of Joe Hawke of a right under the Treaty to take shellfish, irrespective of the method, in this case the use of scuba gear, was, in the opinion of the tribunal, not well founded. Accordingly the tribunal made no recommendation to Parliament. The second case, brought by Ted Kirkwood on behalf of the Waikato tribes opposing the siting of the proposed Auckland thermal power station at Waiau Pa on the Manukau Harbour, was much more substantial. The basis of the objection was the proposal to take 560 hectares of mudflats for cooling ponds. To a technocrat, mudflats might have no intrinsic worth, but to a Maori they are a source of food and life itself. In a *tour de force* presentation of oral evidence concerning traditional use of the Manukau fishery, the species of shellfish harvested, their locality, the pelagic species that came into the harbour, their seasons, spawning grounds, and the methods of taking them, Kirkwood convinced the tribunal that his rights would be prejudiced by the power project. But the tribunal was relieved of having to make a recommendation to Parliament when the Electricity Department decided not to proceed with the project. The inconclusive nature of the hearings gave credence to Maori suspicions that the tribunal was no more than a token gesture.

Although nothing substantial came out of the first hearings of the Waitangi Tribunal, they were not entirely profitless. David Williams of the Law School at Auckland University submitted a memorandum to the Minister of Maori Affairs that was critical of the tribunal's procedures. He argued that the adoption of court procedures and the adversary style of hearing was not obligatory. A tribunal was free to use a more informal approach in hearing evidence, that was more culturally appropriate to Maori claimants. He also criticised the use of the ballroom of the Intercontinental Hotel as a venue for the tribunal because it was culturally alienating and inappropriate. Williams recommended that future sittings of the tribunal be held on marae, and that marae protocol of mihi, whaikorero and karakia be adopted. Although three years were to pass before the next claim was filed, the Williams memorandum was to have a profound effect on the future of the tribunal.

The Maori Affairs Bill

For the next three years the thrust of Maori leaders turned temporarily away from fisheries to land. The stimulus was the Maori Affairs Bill introduced into the House in 1978. The Bill was a document of 251 pages attempting to rationalise more than a century of accumulated legislation and amendments on Maori land and Maori affairs. The Maori Council responded to the Bill by organising three national seminars on it. At the seminar in Rotorua on 30 March the following year, students and activists from Auckland proposed scrapping the Bill, instead of making submissions on what history had proved to be a bad deal. The legislation had been so inimical to Maori interests that it defied improvement by submissions proposing amendments. The activists proposed that a Bill based on Maori philosophy and values pertaining to land be written and submitted as an alternative to put to Government. This was the course advocated by their forebears almost a century before, in the Maori Parliament.

The conservative leaders of the council responded with a dual strategy. They decided to proceed by preparing submissions on the Bill, but set up a special committee as well to redraft legislation incorporating Maori traditional values more cognisant with customary title rights.[57] The Maori Council made history by having the Maori Affairs select committee hear its submissions on Poho o Rawiri Marae in Gisborne. But the legislation was so convoluted that only ten pages were covered in a day-long sitting. There was a further hearing in Parliament, but again little progress was made. But in November, during an informal meeting with the executive of the Maori Council, the Minister of Maori Affairs, Ben Couch, asked what was to be done with the Bill. Latimer advised him to 'drop it'. The Minister was so debilitated by influenza at the time, and full of drugs prescribed for him by his Opposition colleague Dr Gregory, that he put up no resistance. He simply said, 'All right then', and that is how, after a century of trying, when such a thing was proposed by the Maori Parliament, the Maori was delegated the right to prepare the basis for a Bill. But, as predicted, the right was granted ninety years too late, when there was hardly any land left for its application.

The Maori Council Legislative Review Committee drew up a *Discussion Paper on Future Maori Development Legislation*. This document, sometimes referred to as the 'brown paper', basically summarised the agenda that had motivated Maori politics for more than a century. The paper proclaimed tangata whenua status as the rationale for Maori self-determination. It advocated recognition of biculturalism and the restructuring of laws and institutions to incorporate the claims of tangata whenua. The paper laid down the principle in Maori society of the group being paramount over the individual. It also advocated, as a fundamental principle for future legislation, the retention of Maori land as the basis of Maori identity.[58] By the time the Minister received the paper, he was restored to health and had regained his equilibrium. He rejected the paper as being dominated by the philosophy of Mana Motuhake, and asked the Maori Council for another, one that he could get through the House.

The Maori Council produced a second paper, entitled *Kaupapa*, in March 1982. Although this was a watered-down version of the original, it made the same claim that had been made for a hundred years. The new law should support the retention, use and management of Maori land by the tribe. At a time when claims for Maori sovereignty were being made, the document is notable for the statement in its preamble which was to have a profound effect on Pakeha thinking about the Treaty of Waitangi. It offered a compromise to the Government as a way out of guilt over a broken covenant. The document stated:[59]

> We believe the Treaty of Waitangi between the Crown and the Maori people is the origin and basis of British sovereignty and constitutional government in New Zealand. We also believe the Crown extends its protection over the Maori people and guarantees them their assets.

This acknowledgement of the constitutional right of Government to rule as emanating from the Treaty was neatly balanced by the reminder of the Crown and Government's fiduciary responsibilities to the Maori. The Kaupapa was promulgated in February 1983 and became the base on which the new Maori Affairs Bill was drawn up. The Bill appeared in serial form but was never completed. Part I came out late in 1983, and Part II early in 1984. The Maori Council was asked to comment on these piecemeal Bills before August. Hearing dates of the Maori Affairs Select Committee were fixed for July, but the process was halted by a snap election which swept Labour back into power.

CHAPTER 12

Ma te Ture te Ture e Patu

The Motunui Outfall

The fact that the Waitangi Tribunal was not tested by having to make recommendations to Government on the first two cases to come before it, tended to confirm the Maori view that it was a non-event. One man who did not give up on the tribunal was Aila Taylor of Taranaki, who lodged a claim on behalf of Te Atiawa in May 1981. A more specific claim was lodged in March the following year. Taylor claimed that the discharge of untreated sewage and industrial waste through the Motunui outfall from the Synfuels plant would pollute traditional fisheries reefs known as Taunga Te Puna, Titi Rangi and Orapa.[1] Taylor had lost the preliminary planning hearings and in desperation he turned to the Waitangi Tribunal as a last resort.

The Atiawa claim was heard on Manukorihi Marae at New Plymouth. This time Maori protocol was observed, and the hearings conducted in an informal manner. The tribunal took the view that on their home territory, Maori people would be better able to express their feelings and make their concerns known.[2] Another important change was the appointment of a culturally sensitive judge in Edward Durie as chairman of the tribunal.

Traditional evidence concerning the names of fishery reefs and the hapu boundary divisions along a 56-kilometre stretch of coastline was adduced by tribal witnesses. Evidence of ancient customs relating to rotational harvesting, conservation of habitat, avoidance of pollution by human waste, protection of fisheries by rahui, taboos concerning opening shellfish below high water mark, and prohibitions on menstruating women from engaging in harvesting shellfish was presented to the tribunal.[3] One witness objected to spiritual as well as physical contamination of fisheries resources. Treatment of human waste to 'purify' it before discharging it into the sea was unacceptable, because such a practice affected the 'life force' of all living things.

The findings of the tribunal marked a watershed in Maori-Pakeha relations. The tribunal was unequivocal in ruling that the Atiawa fisheries would be prejudicially affected by the Motunui outfall. Under the Treaty of Waitangi the Crown was obliged 'to protect the Maori people in the use of their fishing grounds and to protect them from the consequences of the settlement and development of the land'.[4] Accordingly, proposals for the Motunui outfall should be discontinued. Not sensing the winds of change, the Government overrode the tribunal because the water right for the Motunui outfall was secure and had Cabinet approval. One editorial saw the rebuff to the Waitangi Tribunal as offending conservative Maori leaders, and as casting 'petrol' among the 'radical sparks' of Maoridom.[5] Another editorial dubbed the Government's inept handling of a big issue 'monumental crassness'.[6] They were right. A hui at Manukorihi Marae advocated resort to direct action such as disbanding Maori councils, boycotting the royal tour, enlisting support from the Federation of Labour through industrial action, and calling on the four Maori members of Parliament to resign. But a further hui at Parihaka a fortnight later ruled out militant action. It decided to continue negotiation through proper channels with the Government, and failing that, to resort to the United Nations.[7] Three days later a deputation from Te Atiawa met with the Prime Minister to work out an agreement.

For once, the Maori had the initiative. The findings of the tribunal had beenly widely reported in the press and the issues clearly stated. There was considerable sympathy for the Maori position because pollution of fisheries and environmental degradation are matters of national concern. One editorial went so far as to criticise the Government for failing to honour the Treaty as the moral basis by which two races share one country.[8] This public acknowledgement of the moral high ground on which the Treaty stands gave the Waitangi Tribunal a form of power not envisaged by the architects of the legislation that brought it into being. They had not anticipated the power of the Treaty to influence events outside the century in which it was framed. Beside the moral influence of the Treaty and public sympathy for the Maori position, a report commissioned by the Ministry of Energy backed the interim solution suggested by the Waitangi Tribunal of using the existing Waitara outfall.[9] In response to the shift in public sympathy, the Government modified its position. It introduced the Synthetic Fuels Plant (Water Right) Bill into the House to apply for a water right at Waitara. In the meantime, the long-term solution of a new regional outfall, to cost $17 million, was left in abeyance.

Guardians of the Manukau

At the time that Aila Taylor was battling to protect the kaimoana of Taranaki, Nganeko Minhinnick, a leader of Ngati Te Ata on the south-west shores of the Manukau Harbour, opened up another battle-front before the Planning Tribunal for the recognition of Maori spiritual values relating to water. For almost a century the Tainui tribes, centred today on nine marae around the periphery of the Manukau Harbour, watched with political impotence the development of the harbour to the detriment of their fisheries. Some developments by harbour boards, such as wharves, they accepted with equanimity. Others, by private enterprise and local bodies, such as enclosures, reclamations, freezing works, sewage treatment plant, Auckland Airport and the New Zealand Steel mill, they viewed with silent misgiving.

Minhinnick, a humble woman of noble descent, was thrown into the cauldron of cultural politics by her people to fight for their concerns when they elected her to the Auckland District Maori Council in 1970. She had no tertiary education and lacked confidence, so the brief she carried on behalf of her elders sat uneasily on her shoulders. In the national forum of the Maori Council she was too diffident even to speak. It was not until the mid-seventies, after seeing the district council fight the Auckland Regional Authority to get the community at Ihumatao connected to the sewage system, and help the Whatapaka Marae fight the Auckland Thermal Number One power station, that she was politicised and enabled to embrace her role as leader. Thereafter she sat on the district council's planning subcommittee, which produced a Maori Planning Kit booklet, and got the whole of Chapter 10 of the Auckland Regional Scheme devoted to Maori concerns. The fact that the district council succeeded in using the Town and Country Planning Act to gain Maori representation on the planning committee of the ARA in 1979 was also an indication to Minhinnick that monocultural Pakeha power structures were not immune to Maori pressure. They were capable of being modified to incorporate Maori values and the concept of biculturalism. Having learned the techniques of negotiating and dealing with metropolitan society within the Auckland District Maori Council, Minihinnick returned to her tribal base. From there she launched her own attacks on the power structures of Government, to become one of the potent Maori leaders on the national scene in negotiating social transformation.

Before the Tainui elder Ted Kirkwood died, he expressed concern to his people around the Manukau that although the Auckland

Thermal Number One power project had been dropped, he feared that the thrust of metropolitan society to continue development on the harbour would come back to torment them. To counter further development, the tribes formalised their traditional view of themselves as the kaitiaki, the guardians of the Manukau, by adopting the name Te Puaha ki Manukau. Minhinnick was the voice of the guardians. In 1981 she appeared before Judge Turner of the Planning Tribunal, appealing against the granting of a water right to New Zealand Steel to take water from the Waikato River in order to pipe ironsand slurry to the mill at Glenbrook and discharge the water into the Manukau Harbour. Before stating her objections, Minhinnick commented on the institutions and procedures which forced Maori people to engage in an unequal contest in a foreign process of litigation:

> We as a people, have become involved in procedures which are foreign to our way of life. To put forward our view, we have had to undergo a whole learning process, trying to understand planning applications, rights for intakes, rights for discharge, rights of objection and appeal, water and soil legislation, planning legislation only to be told that despite all these procedures, there is no provision for spiritual and cultural matters Maori to be taken into account.[10]

The basis of Minhinnick's objection was essentially spiritual. The Waikato as an ecosystem has its own mauri, so has the Manukau. Minhinnick likened the mixing of the waters of these two systems, each with their own taniwha, or denizen spirits, to sacrilege. The Planning Tribunal ruled that the Water and Soil Conservation Act did not allow purely metaphysical concerns to be taken into account, and dismissed the appeal. At the time, Judge Turner adhered to the monocultural belief that he was required to apply 'rational, scientific and managerial techniques in the management of the natural environment'. He simply saw the purpose of planning as being to achieve an orderly, coherent system of land use.

The pragmatic views of Judge Turner were echoed in another decision of the Planning Tribunal on the Manukau Harbour by Judge Sheppard in March 1983. On that occasion the Auckland District Maori Council, acting on behalf of the guardians of the Manukau, appealed against the Manukau Harbour Maritime Planning Authority granting the Liquigas consortium permission to build a wharf terminal for an LPG tanker on the Papakura arm of the harbour. The basis of the objection was Article 2 of the Treaty of Waitangi, which guaranteed undisturbed possession of lands, forests and fisheries. Evidence of environmental degradation was advanced on behalf of the appellants.

The leaders of the tribal communities in their lifetime had noticed that, as a consequence of development, run-off from surrounding farmlands, pollution by industry, particularly from New Zealand Steel, the periodic shifts of shellfish beds had become more frequent and unpredictable, and when they did find them, they noted that some species did not grow to takeable size. This they put down to eutrophication of the harbour. Environmental degradation had reached a point where they feared imminent collapse of the life-sustaining power of the harbour. Consequently they did not want any further development at all. This statement was made knowing full well the appeal would not be sustained. But at least the Maori point of view had been made clear, so that the tribunal's decision would be made with full knowledge of Maori opposition.

Notwithstanding the Treaty of Waitangi Act 1975, which established the Waitangi Tribunal to hear complaints such as the one before him, Judge Sheppard followed legal precedent that the Treaty was not part of the municipal law of New Zealand, effectively ruling it out as a basis of objection. Furthermore, he noted in the judgment of Turner in *Re the Bed of the Wanganui River*, that the title to all land passed by agreement of the Maori to the Crown upon signing the Treaty. Although the appellant suggested the Crown's title to the bed of the Manukau Harbour could be the subject of a future claim before the High Court, and the judge admitted he could adduce no evidence as to how the harbour became vested in the Crown, he assumed the Crown achieved its title by lawful means consistent with the principles of the Treaty of Waitangi. Despite his concluding remark that he did not know if the fisheries of the harbour had been alienated by the tribes, and that it may be a question to be resolved by the Waitangi Tribunal, Judge Sheppard ruled in favour of the Maritime Planning Authority's granting of consent to the wharf terminal.[11]

In due course, taking note of the Waitangi Tribunal's ruling on the Motunui outfall, the Auckland District Maori Council advised Minhinnick to lodge a claim with the tribunal. The success of the Atiawa claim roused Maori interest in the Waitangi Tribunal. Over the next two years the tribunal heard claims on the Manukau Harbour, the Kaituna River, Waiheke Island, Orakei, and the Maori language, before it was dissolved in 1985, to be reconstituted and enlarged the following year.

The Manukau claim brought by Minhinnnick on behalf of the Huakina Development Trust was the most comprehensive one to come before the Waitangi Tribunal. It encompassed a number of issues including the confiscation of 58,475 hectares of tribal lands during the Land Wars of the last century, ranging southwards from Mangere, through to Pukekohe, Patumahoe, Tuakau, Waiuku and Pokeno; loss of mudflat fisheries to Auckland Airport, the Mangere sewage treatment plant, and the LPG wharf terminal; degradation of the harbour by farming and industrial development as cited in the earlier planning hearings; mining of iron sands by New Zealand Steel at Maioro, an ancient urupa of the Waikato tribes; the mixing of the waters of the Waikato and the Manukau by the slurry pipeline of New Zealand Steel; and the compulsory acquisition of 1,490 hectares at the north head of the Waikato River under the Public Works Act in 1932 for sand dune reclamation, and eventual planting of the Waiuku State Forest in 1935. Although many of the issues raised in evidence were outside the time-frame of 1975 and therefore the jurisdiction of the tribunal, the hearings served to place them on record. The report of the tribunal laid bare for public scrutiny the history of colonial oppression and injustice extending from the last century right into modern times.[12]

Waitangi Tribunal Transformed

Even as historical evidence outside the jurisdiction of the Waitangi Tribunal was being put to it in the hearings of the Manukau claim at Ihumatao Marae, moves were being made by conservative leaders to strengthen the tribunal and extend its jurisdiction back in time. The political initiative gained by the Hikoi in February was followed up in September 1984 by a national hui to discuss the Treaty of Waitangi at Turangawaewae Marae. This hui, involving a thousand people, was convened by Te Runanga Whakawhanaunga i Nga Haahi. In the workshop on the Waitangi Tribunal, the resource person gave the background history leading up to the tribunal's establishment, including the failure of its architect, Matiu Rata, to gain support from his colleagues to make it retrospective to 1900. It was put to the workshop that in the nine years since the tribunal came into being, events such as the land march, the occupation of disputed lands at Bastion Point and Raglan, protest marches and the Hikoi to Waitangi had raised the level of national consciousness to such an extent that perhaps the public would now accept a recommendation to make the tribunal retrospective to 1900. But just as a motion to that effect was put to the workshop, the chairman, Turoa Royal, asked forlornly where such a motion left the issue of the Thames and Coromandel goldfields. The resource person replied, 'Turoa, since your goldfield claim occurred in 1867, and if you want to take it to the tribunal, then you had better move an amendment to the motion to make it retrospective to 1840.' The amendment was moved, put and passed unanimously. Thus it was quite serendipitously that the motion for retrospective power was arrived at. The general assembly of the hui recommended to the Government that the Waitangi Tribunal be given retrospective powers to 1840 to hear grievances, and that adequate resources be made available to the tribunal to ensure that grievances were fully researched.[13]

The resolution of the hui at Turangawaewae was taken on board immediately by a Labour Government still flush from its stunning victory in the snap election. Before the House rose at the end of the year, it introduced a Bill to amend the Treaty of Waitangi Act. That the Government moved with such alacrity was due to the need to keep faith with its Maori voters and to prevent them from deserting the fold to Mana Motuhake. The Treaty of Waitangi Amendment Act 1985 was passed in December in the last session before the Christmas recess. Section 3(1)(a) of the Act amended Section 6 of the principal Act to extend the jurisdiction of the tribunal to hear claims retrospective to 1840. The tribunal was also strengthened by an increase in membership to seven. Considering the potential of the tribunal to uncover the past, and the history of colonial violence and injustice perpetrated by the Government itself, the question must be asked why the Government did it. One reason has already been suggested: the need to do something substantive in Maori policy or face the potential loss of electoral advantage in the four Maori seats. But considering the pain that would be inflicted on the nation by uncovering the truth of its nasty past, was such an advantage worth it? One can only speculate on the Government's motives. One possible reason is that the Labour Party had been too long in the political wilderness. By the time it came back to power, it had lost contact with the colonising ethos of its forebears and forgotten that the intractable problem of the Maori as the tangata whenua had been dealt with not by conceding to Maori proposals but by the assertion of power by successive governments. Whatever the reason, the change cast New Zealand firmly into the post-colonial era in which resort to ideology to sustain Pakeha dominance is now untenable.

Within months of the Waitangi Tribunal being made retrospective to 1840, huge land claims against the Crown were lodged by the Ngai Tahu, Tainui and Atiawa tribes. As the claims rose quickly to 120, it became obvious that at the clearance rate of four or five cases a year, it would take thirty years to deal with the backlog. In 1987 the two research workers of the tribunal had to be augmented by the addition of four researchers and a senior research officer. A year later, when the claims had risen to 150, the tribunal was strengthened again by an increase of members to sixteen.[14] It was also given greater flexibility by the power given to the chairman to appoint alternative chairmen, and allowing small claims to be heard by a minimum of three members. This empowerment of the Waitangi Tribunal gave the Maori people a more effective mechanism for resolving grievances. Consequently, the activist movements suspended resort to direct action, as the tribes moved to avail themselves of the tribunal and other legal avenues that opened up in the decade of the eighties.

The Search for Economic Power

The Maori renaissance has advanced on a broader front than just cultural recovery, politics and settlement of grievances. It encompasses a wide field of human endeavour, including economic power. Although there are a few Maori millionaires, their success has been largely an individual achievement, which has tended to alienate them from their people. Successful millionaires like Sir Graham Latimer, who works for the advancement of Maori people and sometimes has had to guarantee bank loans for the Maori Council pending payment of the government grant, are unusual. Another is Stan Keepa, a property developer who helped build an urban marae in Auckland and gave financial support to the Auckland District Maori Council. While individual success of this kind is admired, group success is desired as well.

The Maori ideal, harking back to the economic success of tribes in the 1850s, is achievement of wealth for the good of the community through co-operative enterprise. Only tribes with a remnant land base have attained this ideal through the establishment of incorporations and 438 trusts under the Maori Welfare Act. Some of them, like the Mangatu, Puketapu, Morikaunui, Mawhera, and Paranihi ki Waitotara Incorporations, and the Te Arawa and Whakatohea Trust Boards, are multimillion-dollar enterprises. But these enterprises, being located in tribal territories, serve only tribal interests. The bulk of the Maori population, living in the multitribal situation of urban centres, does not have that kind of financial power. Consequently, leaders in a pan-Maori organisation such as Graham Latimer of the

Maori Council have felt the need for a secure financial base to help advance the Maori cause. Another who shared the same vision was the Secretary of Maori Affairs, Kara Puketapu.

One of Puketapu's programmes, which aimed at closing the economic gap between Maori and Pakeha, was a series of business wananga designed to encourage individual Maori into business. Up to 1983, 400 people had attended these business seminars. That year, the Maori Trustee, Puketapu, provided loans to finance ninety-six people into business.[15] Although this was a start, it was too slow. The recession was hitting the Maori harder than anyone else. The age group between fifteen and nineteen had the highest unemployment rate in the country. For females unemployment was 41.3 per cent, and for males it was 27.3 per cent compared with the non-Maori rate of 12.5 per cent and 8.5 per cent respectively.[16]

Maori International

Puketapu had a broad vision to speed up the process of closing the economic gap by establishing a Maori economic base to relieve unemployment. He aimed to harness, through a pan-Maori enterprise, the financial potential of all the people. To this end, in 1983 he commissioned Richard Hovis, an American consultant, to look at business opportunities for Maori people. The outcome was the Hovis Report, *Maoritanga and the American Retail Marketplace*. The most startling proposal in the report was the concept of 'Maori International', a Maori-owned corporation to create and market proprietary products for export, using marae centres as manufacturing hubs. But the 'start-up' for Maori International, from which it would branch out into tourism, forestry and hotels, was predicated on taking over an existing production facility. The report painted a seductive scenario of taking a showcase of 'quality products' to the United States on 'show and tell' meetings to buyers who would take orders for prestigious department stores such as Bloomingdales in New York, Marshall Fields in Chicago, Nieman Marcus in Dallas, and so on.[17]

Puketapu resigned from his post in 1983 to launch Maori International Limited, with a share issue of $3.5 million, 30 per cent coming from public subscription, and 70 per cent from Maori International Holdings. The dollar shares in the latter company, whose sole purpose was to invest in MIL, were to come from Maori individuals, whanau, trusts, incorporations, kohanga reo, clubs, Maori Women's Welfare League and other Maori organisations. The board of directors of MIL consisted of eminent Maori leaders such as Sir Graham Latimer, Sir Henare Ngata, Sir Hepi Te Heuheu, Hori Forbes, Stan Newton and John Bennett. Each took out $100 shares and guaranteed a loan of $95,000 from the Maori Trustee to cover establishment costs of MIL.

The draft prospectus for MIL, which was issued in January 1984, planned to take over and lease from the Government the Maori Arts and Crafts Institute as its 'start-up' base and first venture into tourism. The institute consisted of buildings and sixty hectares of land valued at $3 million, and sixty staff. Its annual turnover ran at $1.3 million. Negotiations with the Government for the hand-over of the institute were facilitated by Puketapu and Latimer, who were both on the institute's management board. Latimer was in a particularly favourable position as chairman of the board, and a confidant of Ben Couch, Minister of Maori Affairs, and the Prime Minister, Sir Robert Muldoon. This planned devolution of a government-owned facility to a Maori organisation anticipated devolution that was to take place five years later under a Labour government. But it was an idea ahead of its time. Also, the politics were badly managed. The Arawa tribes, in whose territory the facility is located, were not properly consulted. They opposed the takeover, bringing adverse publicity to MIL, to the extent that the Government could not go ahead with the deal. In the meantime, confidence in MIL waned, as share subscriptions fell well short of a revised target of $2.5 million. Initially, only $75,000 was realised, indicating shortage of cash, lack of confidence and bad public relations by MIL. Despite the poor start, MIL traded, beginning with tourist visits to marae and marketing high-quality Maori craft work. By 1986 it had cleared its establishment debts and declared a modest profit. It survived the sharemarket crash in 1987, and made sufficient progress to declare a profit of $77,873 in 1989.

Although MIL was a registered public company, the economic initiatives in Maori Affairs taken by Puketapu to get it started were continued by his former deputy, Dr Tamati Reedy, when he became Secretary of Maori Affairs. In June 1984 the Department of Maori Affairs tested one of the ideas in the Hovis Report by taking a cultural exhibition and trade showcase of Maori art and craft work to Honolulu. The department's involvement in economic programmes was given further impetus by the Hui Taumata, the Maori Economic Summit Development Conference, in October 1984. The hui recommended the establishment of a Maori Economic Development Commission to implement economic development strategies for Maori people, including the establishment of a Maori Development Commission and the creation of a Maori Development Bank.[18] The following year a ministerial review committee of the Department of Maori Affairs also urged the establishment of a Maori Development Corporation. But it argued the structure of the department was inappropriate for engaging in economic activities.[19] Unfortunately, the advice was not heeded. The 'show and tell' exhibition in Honolulu had established a Hawaiian connection with American entrepreneurs that was to have fatal consequences for the department.

The Maori Loans Affair

In 1986 the desire expressed at the Hui Taumata to have a Maori bank was taken by Dr Tamati Reedy, Secretary of Maori Affairs, as a mandate for him to negotiate with Hawaiian middlemen to obtain an offshore loan of $600 million. Such an amount, offered at the discount rate of 6 per cent, at a time when interest rates were above 15 per cent from banks and finance companies, and as high as 39 per cent from loan-sharks, would have enabled Maori people to make a quantum leap forward economically into the twenty-first century. In the preliminary negotiations for the loan, Reedy signed a letter of intent to pay the middlemen a finders fee of 3.5 per cent, double the normal amount.[20] An offshore loan of this magnitude needed both Treasury and Cabinet approval. Reedy had neither, but continued to negotiate, hoping to pull off a financial coup that would enable Maori people to break the bond of dependency on Government. A row broke out over the matter in Parliament, when Winston Peters, the Member for Tauranga, disclosed Reedy's letter and claimed that the Cabinet knew nothing about the loan. The matter was investigated by Dr Roderick Deane of the State Services Commission, who reported to Government that Treasury had made it clear to Reedy that neither he nor Treasury had authority from Cabinet to borrow.[21] Despite the fact that the state system of checks and balances had prevented the Secretary of Maori Affairs from entering into a potential financial swindle, the matter did not end there. The so-called 'Maori Loans Affair' took on a life of its own.

The media rose to the bait of the Maori Loans Affair like hungry sharks. Newspapers fostered speculation whether the likely source of the loan was Arab money or 'Marcos Millions'.[22] The *New Zealand Herald* drew a parallel with an 'earlier scandal' that 'blotted the career' of Sir Apirana Ngata.[23] Like the village gossip rejoicing in scandal, the

Auckland Star ran stories about 'Key Maori Loans Man Who Ran Broke Companies', and 'New Zealand Loan Emissaries Are Two Former Bankrupts'. An editorial in the *New Zealand Herald* warned that Maoridom had a 'Taniwha by the Tail'.[25]

Maori people were shell-shocked by the unprecedented level of Maori bashing in the media, as headline followed headline over a loan that never happened. 'Maori Affairs In For Shakeup Come What May' wrote the *Herald*. 'Report On Loan Is Whitewash Say Nat MPs'.[27] The *Herald* claimed 'Maori Leaders Knew Of Loans Affair'.[28] 'Maori Loan Row Not Finished With Yet' claimed the *Herald*. 'Inquiry Only Way Out' said the *Star*.[30] Although the Deane Report had revealed there was no impropriety on the part of the Secretary of Maori Affairs, and the loan had not proceeded, the press persisted. It had the Maori on the rack and was not about to let its victim go. Even when the Speaker of the House ruled in a breach of privilege case that the Minister of Maori Affairs had not misled the House on the loan, and 'closed the lid' on the Peters-Wetere case,[31] the press continued. Seven months later, almost a year after the original story, the *Herald* ran the headline 'Second Maori Loan Affair Looming'.[32] The *Star* also wrote about 'a second Maori loans affair'.[33] Nothing came of this latter claim. The preoccupation of the press with a loan that never occurred is explicable on two grounds. Firstly, newspapers promote news in a sensational manner for economic reasons, to maintain their share of the market. Secondly, and more seriously for Maori people, is the role of the media in reflecting the social reality of Pakeha dominance and Maori subjection. Achievement of financial power by Maori people posed a serious challenge to that relationship. Maori-bashing in the media was a potent reminder of that structural bondage of a race under the tutelage of Pakeha hegemony.

Tamaki Maori Development Authority

While Maori International and the Department of Maori Affairs sought economic independence for Maori people through schemes on a grand scale, other leaders at the parochial level worked on a more modest scale to relieve unemployment by taking advantage of government funding for work schemes and Access training programmes. One of these was the Tamaki Maori Development Authority (TMDA), which had its genesis in a series of meetings in 1982 of Maori people in Auckland involved in the Labour Department's Temporary Employment Programme, and the later Project Employment

Programme. The underlying aim of the TMDA was to transform the existing government, social and economic structures dealing with unemployment by humanising them.[34] But what the TMDA sought above all, was to be recognised as a provider of training for the unemployed so as to qualify for direct funding from Government in the same way as local bodies. But it was not until 1984, when the Oruamo Community Development Society transferred its programme out of the Auckland Regional Authority to the TMDA, that it was established on a firm footing.

The founder of TMDA, Bert McLean, made his presence felt at the Hui Taumata by making such forthright submissions that government recognition soon followed. In 1985 Government named TMDA as one of three Maori authorities in the country to participate in and manage an Access programme. The Maccess, or Maori version of the programme, had its funds fed into the scheme through the Department of Maori Affairs. The TMDA training and employment programme employed six administrators overseeing twenty-six community-based tutors and 200 trainees in block courses of twelve weeks. As part of its programme to provide quality training, TMDA established its own Tamaki Technical Training Institute in 1988. The first courses taught were electrical and mechanical engineering.

Although TMDA was successful in the organisation of the Maccess programme, McLean and Colin Reeder, secretary of the management board, were not satisfied. The continuity of their programme depended on a continuous flow of government money amounting to $3.6 million per annum. That money could dry up at the whim of a capricious government. The ideal for the TMDA was to generate its own income and become independent of Government. To this end, grant money surplus to training requirements, instead of being returned to the Department of Maori Affairs, was invested in projects identified by a Projects Development Committee. To manage these investments, TMDA formed a separate company, the Tamaki Corporation of New Zealand Limited. But the company was registered in the names of McLean and Reeder. The grand aim of TMDA, with the Corporation as the vehicle, was to 'position' Maori whereby economic opportunities could be exploited and 'translated into jobs'.[35] The Tamaki Corporation had investments in a tourist travel company, a fishing vessel, marine farming, finance, and a hotel. The rationale for the Tamaki Corporation was the translation of investments into jobs. The only flaw in the plan was the registration of the company in the names of the two principals of the TMDA.

This excursion of the TMDA into business investments brought it under the scrutiny of the Assistant Secretary of Maori Affairs, Neville Baker, who disapproved of the 'shuffling of funds', especially public money granted for specific purposes, without consultation. The department demanded a return of $1 million,[36] despite the audit report finding that the amount involved could not be specified. Although the asset base of the Tamaki Corporation could account for the amount demanded, it was unlikely that the cash-flow from investments would cover it. In any case, according to McLean, several thousands of dollars had flowed back from the corporation to the TMDA. The future of TMDA at the time of writing was uncertain, as the department cut off its financial support for the authority and initiated legal proceedings to recover the amount claimed. The principals of TMDA filed a counter-claim against the department for defamation.

Black Power

One of the ironies of Maori economic development is the success of Tatau Te Iwi Trust, which was founded by one of the most feared and despised groups in the community, the Auckland chapter of the Black Power gang. When Abe Wharewaka, the present leader of the gang, joined in 1977, there were forty or so members in the group. Since then numbers have grown to 250. As a young man Wharewaka had been in and out of borstal and then prison for petty burglary and assaults. He joined the Black Power movement with his brothers at the age of thirty-five, after attending a national convention of 450 members because he was impressed by the organisation and its network of contacts. The national president, Ray Harris, had laid down rules for membership, including banning the swastika on gang regalia. Wharewaka saw advantage for his own family within an organisation of 'staunch' members who gave each other mutual support. At first the gang was concerned only in maintaining its territory against intimidatory raids by rival gangs. In one such raid, a shotgun was discharged at the Black Power pub, the Trident Hotel in Onehunga. After one retaliatory raid, Wharewaka, who had not been in gaol for twenty years, got an eighteen-month sentence. He spent the time in solitary confinement where he did some reading, thinking about the future and going into business.

On his release, Wharewaka started a labour hire pool, doing contract work for construction companies. He leased a factory in Panmure where the trust's tools were stored and where the men could fraternise after work over a beer. Gradually, the trust accumulated capital, taking 30 per cent of the contract price, plus $10 a week in membership fees. In addition, there were the profits from the sale of liquor. In 1982 the trust bought a plot of industrial land at East Tamaki for $39,000. It borrowed money for materials and with voluntary labour built the 'factory' as its headquarters. The word factory is a misnomer, for it is a well-appointed nightclub complete with bar, cubicles and pool tables. In 1983 the trust affiliated with the Auckland District Maori Council at the suggestion of Prime Minister Muldoon. This move was taken to enable the trust to refinance its mortgage of $28,500 through the Housing Corporation. Somehow the press got hold of the information and made a sensational story out of a government department lending to a gang. In due course the trust's operation expanded, buying additional land and extending the factory. Since banks would not lend money to the trust, it had to be borrowed from loan sharks at 39 per cent with penalty rates of 49 per cent for late payment.

In 1986, Wharewaka imported from Los Angeles eighteen used Harley Davidson motorcycles for his men and a stretched limousine for himself. Although the machines were landed at half the cost of new ones, their arrival drew considerable negative publicity in the media. Only the *Te Karere* television newsreader smiled with pleasure at the arrival of these symbols of Wharewaka's success as entrepreneur and chief of the Black Power. But the success was shaky. Crippling interest rates, combined with two police raids and fines of $10,000, almost destroyed the trust. In 1987 the trust applied successfully to the Liquor Licensing Commission for a liquor licence, enabling it to stabilise its position.

The trust also operated two work schemes for its members. The Maori Access scheme catered for twenty-four trainees, sixteen of them in building and related trades and eight in *Te Iwi*, the Maori newspaper started by Wharewaka. Under the general Access scheme with the Labour Department, there were forty trainees, twenty-four in building and sixteen in office administration. In addition the trust had a $1.2 million contract building houses for the Housing Corporation.

Recourse to Law

The winds of change, brought about by the transformation of the Waitangi Tribunal into a more effective instrument for dealing with Maori grievances, were also evident in the courts of the land. The prevailing view of the Treaty of Waitangi as a 'simple nullity', laid down by Chief Justice Prendergast in 1877, was considerably modified in the decade of the eighties. The straw in the wind was the judgment by Justice A. Williamson in the High Court at Christchurch in 1986. The case involved Tom Te Weehi, who had been convicted in the District Court of contravening the regulations under the Fisheries Act for the taking of shellfish. In his appeal against the conviction for taking undersize shellfish, Te Weehi argued that he was exercising a customary right guaranteed by the Treaty, to take shellfish for home consumption. Judge Williamson ruled under Section 88 of the Fisheries Act, which states that nothing in the Act shall affect any Maori fishing rights, that Te Weehi was exempt from certain requirements of the fishing laws, and therefore had not committed an offence.[37]

Fight Against the State Owned Enterprises Act

The direction taken by Judge Williamson, of recognising Treaty rights when they are incorporated in laws such as the Fisheries Act, was confirmed in the Court of Appeal at Wellington in June 1987 over the transfer of Crown land to state-owned enterprises. When the State Owned Enterprises Act came into force in December 1986, Maori people belatedly became agitated over its implications for their land claims against the Crown before the Waitangi Tribunal. The Act authorised the formation of profit-making state owned corporations to replace the former government departments. As part of the establishment of the SOEs, they were to be possessed of an estate in the form of Crown lands. The deadline set for the hand-over of Crown lands to the SOEs was May 1987. The implication for Maori people was the danger of the land being sold on to a third party, who would receive a title in fee simple guaranteed by the Crown, irrespective of how ill-gotten the land was in the first place. Since there is no more secure title to land than one held from the Crown, such lands would effectively be put out of Maori reach forever.

The Maori Council sought an injunction in the High Court to stop the transfer of Crown land, pending a change in the legislation to enable land to be recovered from the Crown should the Waitangi Tribunal rule in favour of a claimant. Concern over the SOE Act was voiced at a hui convened by the Maori Council at Turangawaewae Marae. One delegate postulated a conspiracy theory that the move was the last 'grab' by the Crown on Maori land. Another likened it to the 'ultimate confiscation' for which the Labour Government was responsible. The hui called for unity of the people to fight the SOE Act. Suggestions for fighting the measure included mounting a presence at the court hearing of the Maori Council's injunction, demanding an extension of time on the transfer of Crown land beyond the deadline of 4 May, and a concerted lobby by tribal runanga, trust boards, district councils and other Maori authorities on members of Parliament, the Prime Minister, Cabinet, the Attorney-General, and the Governor-General. Failing that, the hui would take the 'broken' Treaty of Waitangi to the International Court of Justice.[38]

The Maori concern was much wider than just the 1.2 million hectares of confiscated lands. It also encompassed Maori land grants to the Crown for reserves, schools, post offices, hospitals and other purposes, and lands taken under the Public Works Act for roads, lighthouses, dams, defence and so on. Government restructuring of the economy entailed the closure of many of these facilities, and the former owners of the lands, on which redundant facilities stood, wanted them back. Claims on Crown land lodged with the tribunal were still subject to claim under Section 27 of the SOE Act. But the problem lay with tribes that had not lodged a claim before the transfer of land occurred, and tribes that did not even know they had a right to claim on land where facilities were redundant. It was on behalf of these tribes that the Maori Council took out a general injunction against the transfer of Crown land, to enable them to do their research and file their claims. The injunction cited the Maori Council as the first applicant and Sir Graham Latimer as the second. The first respondent was the Attorney-General and the second the Ministers of Finance, Energy, Lands and Forests. This change in Latimer, from his conservative accommodation to Pakeha power to an assertive attack on the Government, was remarkable. It is an example of Freire's contention that even brokers for metropolitan society can be reclaimed and empowered by the revolutionary practice of the people.

The legal point on which the Maori Council injunction rested was the Treaty. Section 9 of the SOE Act stated that nothing in the Act shall permit the Crown to act in a manner that is inconsistent with the principles of the Treaty of Waitangi. The inclusion of the Treaty in the SOE Act, as well as Maori fishing rights in the Fisheries Act, gave leverage in the courts to Maori leaders that was not available to their predecessors. As a consequence of the injunction, various matters were dealt with first by the court in chambers. The Crown was directed to make available to the applicants schedules of land to be transferred to SOEs. The applicants were asked to give notice of three cases to illustrate their claim. At stake in this battle were assets held by the Crown worth $11.8 billion. It was up to the Maori to determine their share and fight for it.

Late in April the Maori Council notified the court of three cases. They were the Otakou Block in the South Island, where promised reserves were not made; Woodhill State Forest, where land had been taken near Muriwai in 1934 under the Public Works Act for sand dune reclamation, and subsequently planted in forest; and the Ngai Tama Block at Taranaki of 1,600 hectares, which was confiscated along with Atiawa lands, even though Ngai Tama was not involved in the Taranaki land war. The court delivered its verdict on 29 June. Five judges were unanimous that the Treaty of Waitangi, given effect by Section 9 of the State Owned Enterprises Act, prevented the Crown from transferring land to SOEs without entering into proper arrangements to protect Maori claims.[39]

It was an historic judgment, vindicating Maori faith in the Treaty of Waitangi after more than a century of recourse to it as their Magna Carta. In the judgment of Justice P. Cooke, the inclusion of the principles of the Treaty of Waitangi in Section 9 of the State Owned Enterprises Act had the effect of a constitutional guarantee within the field covered by the Act. In relation to land held by the Crown, he said, it should never again be possible to put aside a Maori grievance. Similarly, Judge Bisson concluded that the advent of legislation invoking the principles of the Treaty of Waitangi meant that the Treaty could no longer be treated as a 'simple nullity'. This judgment pitched New Zealand firmly into the post-colonial era, from which there is no retreat. It was the beginning of decolonisation of New Zealand in the sense of dismantling hegemonic domination of the Maori by the Pakeha. No government can ever again rule Maori people while at the same time dishonouring the Treaty, for the honour of the Crown itself is at stake.

Defining Principles of the Treaty

In his judgment on the State Owned Enterprises case brought by the Maori Council, Justice Cooke observed that the phrase 'the principles of the Treaty of Waitangi' had come into common use in recent years, especially since it was incorporated in a number of statutes.[40] These ranged from the the Treaty of Waitangi Act 1975, to the State Owned Enterprises Act 1986, the Environment Act 1986 and the Conservation Act 1987. This was a remarkable elevation in the status of the Treaty in a few years from a 'simple nullity' to the level of a constitutional instrument in the renegotiation of the relationship between Maori and Pakeha in modern times. This change vindicated Maori belief in the Treaty, their patience in persisting with it, and the fortitude of contemporary activists who continued the struggle against Pakeha domination. But the change would not have occurred without a responsive government and Pakeha supporters within bureaucratic systems who could see advantages for their concerns accruing from the incorporation of the Treaty in their statutes. The Conservation and Environment Acts are cases in point.

Judge Bisson concurred with his colleague Justice Cooke on the incorporation of the principles of the Treaty in statutes as a mark of respect that Parliament now had for the Treaty. He noted that although Parliament placed great weight on the principles of the Treaty, it did not define them in any of the statutes.[41] Both Justice Cooke and Judge Bisson commented on the key role of the Waitangi Tribunal in determining the principles of the Treaty arising out of the various cases brought before it. The only other attempt to define the principles was in the Maori Affairs Bill, which was so long in gestation that it has been overtaken by other events. The blueprint for the principles in the Bill were derived originally from the Kaupapa of the Maori Council. The Bill recognised the Treaty of Waitangi as the symbol of the special relationship between the Maori people and the Crown. It affirmed the exchange of sovereignty for the guarantee of protection of rangatiratanga. Rangatiratanga meant custody over matters significant to cultural identity, particularly land held in trust for future generations.[42]

The more specific and continuous determinations of the principles of the Treaty are those extrapolated by the Waitangi Tribunal from its hearings on Maori claims. In the Motunui case, the first principle laid down was the obligation of the Crown to protect the Maori interest in its fisheries from the consequence of development on land. In the Manukau Report, the tribunal laid down a number of principles. The tribunal, being aware of the discrepancies between the English translation and the Maori version of the Treaty, followed McNair's ruling on bilingual treaties. It laid down the principle that it was bound in its determinations to adhere to both texts since neither was superior to the other. Furthermore, both texts should be construed in the sense that they would be naturally understood by the Maori. The tribunal also argued that mana was equivalent to sovereignty. Since mana and rangatiratanga are inseparable, under the guarantee of rangatiratanga, 'the Maori retained his mana without denying that of the Queen'. In the same case the Tribunal also defined the Manukau Harbour, and even a river, as a taonga, a treasured possession, promised protection by Article 2 of the Treaty.[43] The tribunal also differed from the view of Judge Turner in the Planning Tribunal decision, on the appeal by Nganeko Minhinnick against the water right given to New Zealand Steel, that metaphysical concerns were outside the purview of the Water and Soil Conservation Act. The Waitangi Tribunal stated: 'We find the metaphysical concern is relevant to the provisions of the Treaty of Waitangi and that the failure to provide for it is inconsistent with the principles of the Treaty.'[44]

This finding of the tribunal had considerable influence in the case brought by the Huakina Development Trust in the High Court against the Waikato Valley Authority for granting a water right to discharge dairy effluent into the Waikato River. In this case, Minhinnick argued, as she had done previously before the Planning Tribunal, that pollution of the river would detrimentally affect a valuable tribal resource which provided the tribes with both physical and spiritual sustenance. Judge J. Chilwell, who presided over the case, took note of the findings of the Waitangi Tribunal and its recommendation that legislation ought to be amended to take account of Maori spiritual values. He acknowledged the expertise of the tribunal in its interpretation of Maori values in relation to the Treaty of Waitangi, and wondered whether the Planning Tribunal had availed itself of the provisions of the Treaty in the interpretation of the Water and Soil Conservation Act. Judge Chilwell ruled that a proper interpretation of Section 24(4) of the Water and Soil Conservation Act, which provides for an objection on the grounds of prejudice to the interests of an individual or group, cannot exclude Maori spiritual and cultural values if the evidence establishes spiritual, cultural, and traditional relationships with natural water held by a particular and significant group of Maori people.[45] Chilwell's judgment was a watershed in the modification of monocultural interpretation of law, to take account of the two main streams of New Zealand culture which have their founding charter in the Treaty of Waitangi.

The Waitangi Tribunal's decision in the Manukau case, that the harbour was a treasured possession which warranted protection under the principles of the Treaty, was directly applicable to the Kaituna claim brought by the tribes of the Arawa confederation. In this case, the tribunal recommended abandonment of the proposal to build a pipeline from the Rotorua waste-water treatment plant to discharge effluent into the Kaituna River. The Ngati Pikiao, on the upper reaches of the Kaituna, derived certain taonga, including fish, shell-fish, eels and freshwater crayfish, from the river. For these people, mixing effluent with water from which they derived food was spiritually and culturally unacceptable.[46]

In the Maori language claim brought before the Waitangi Tribunal in June 1985, by Huirangi Waikerepuru and Nga Kaiwhakapumau i te Reo, the tribunal had to determine whether language came under the definition of taonga which the Crown was obliged to protect under the Treaty. In this case, the tribunal laid down the principle that the word taonga covered both tangible and intangible matters. Language was essential to culture and was defined as a treasured possession. Having decided that language was a taonga, the tribunal then laid down a principle concerning the meaning of the word guarantee in the Treaty. The tribunal decided that guarantee meant 'more than merely leaving Maori people unhindered in their enjoyment of their language and culture'; it also required 'active steps' to be taken by the guarantor to ensure that the Maori people have and retain 'the full exclusive and undisturbed possession of their language and culture'.[47]

The principles of the Treaty, identified by the Waitangi Tribunal in its various reports, received support from the Commissioner for the Environment, Helen Hughes. The commissioner grouped the principles under three main themes of partnership, rangatiratanga and active protection. In the Crown's Resource Management and Local Government Reform programme, the commissioner recommended that implementation of the Treaty principles required a change in the existing power equation between the Treaty partners to give the tangata whenua an increased share in actual decision-making power at both central and regional levels.[48] This recommendation, coming from the commissioner after almost 150 years of Maori pursuit of that ideal, is an indication that the unequal power relations between Maori and Pakeha which derived from colonisation are not immutable.

The Fight for Air Waves

In 1973 a number of Maori organisations, including the Auckland District Maori Council, Te Whare Wananga Maori Committee (Auckland), Te Reo Maori (Victoria University), Manaaki Society (Victoria University), Nga Tamatoa (Victoria University), and Te Reo Irirangi Maori, made submissions to the Committee on Broadcasting on the need for a Maori radio station. Programmes catering for Maori needs were so few and scattered at different times on the national network, that one had to be a dedicated listener to follow them. A Maori news bulletin was heard only on Sunday evenings. There was a Maori half-hour on Wednesday evenings, a quarter-hour of Maori music on Friday, and a twenty-minute current affairs programme by Selwyn Muru on Saturday mornings.[49] These meagre offerings of less than an hour and a half per week, compared with the hundreds of hours of Pakeha broadcasting from the national network and commercial stations, were a direct reflection of monocultural dominance and Maori subjection. The Broadcasting Committee was so impressed by the proposals from Maori groups that it looked forward to a more varied future for radio. The idea of a Maori-Polynesian radio station domiciled in Auckland to cater for the population of 49,000 Maori and 40,000 Pacific Islanders appealed to the committee. But the committee agonised over the commercial viability of a Maori radio station and felt government support would be necessary because there was no room for four profitable commercial stations in Auckland. This timidity delayed the establishment of a Maori radio station. By the time moves were made in 1975 to convert one of the existing Radio New Zealand stations in Auckland, it was too late. The Labour Government lost the election and the incoming National Government negated the proposal on the excuse of financial stringency.

A whole decade passed before the battle for the expression of Maori culture through the medium of the air waves was renewed. One of the consequences of the 1984 Hui Taumata was the establishment of a Maori Economic Development Commission to report to the Minister of Maori Affairs on a number of matters pertinent to the development of the Maori. One of the committees of the commission was a Maori Broadcasting Committee. The chairman of the committee, Toby Curtis, criticised the performance of Radio New Zealand for providing less than 0.5 per cent of air time for Maori programmes in fifty years of broadcasting. The committee recommended to the Minister of Broadcasting the establishment of a Radio Aotearoa Network, commencing in Auckland and extending later to the major cities of Wellington and Christchurch. Future development would take in populous Maori areas such as Rotorua, Hastings, Whangarei, Wanganui and Ruatoria. Aspirations for Radio Aotearoa included bilingual broadcasting in Maori and English to reflect the bicultural nature of New Zealand society, programming reflecting Maori culture, and community involvement through access radio. The committee also wanted to provide a service that was uniquely New Zealand, because none of the existing stations offered anything indigenous for vistors to the country.[50]

While the Maori Broadcasting Committee was laying its plans, a private initiative to establish a Maori station in Wellington was launched by Nga Kaiwhakapumau i te Reo. This society, whose concern was maintaining Maori language, saw broadcasting as a means of promoting use of Maori, encouraging the young to learn it and thereby securing the future of the language. The society's station Te Upoko o te Ika acquired a non-commercial licence and began broadcasting continuous bilingual programmes early in 1988. While 50 per cent of salaries for staff came from the Maori Access scheme, the rest of the finance to run the station was raised by the society.

It was not until late in 1988 that Radio Aotearoa ran a pilot station in Auckland for six weeks. It captured Maori listeners in the metropolis and others at the limits of its range, a radius of 130 kilometres or so. Radio Aotearoa began transmitting eight hours a day in June 1989, with plans to extend transmissions once the initial programme format was consolidated.

The Maori Bid for the Third Television Channel

The desire to express Maori identity and culture through the medium of broadcasting did not stop there. A visible Maori presence was also wanted in television. With this in mind, the Maori Council founded the Aotearoa Broadcasting Trust. In 1985 the trust made application to the Broadcasting Commission under the name of Aotearoa Broadcasting Systems (ABS) for a warrant for the third television channel. ABS argued it was the only applicant that offered a real alternative to the other contenders and was capable of delivering a long-awaited 'fair deal' for tangata whenua. It also presented itself as posing the least threat to the revenue of the two existing channels run by the Broadcasting Corporation of New Zealand.[51]

In a submission to the Royal Commission on Broadcasting at the Hoani Waititi Marae in October 1985, Professor Whatarangi Winiata, the architect of the ABS bid for the warrant, reminded the commission of the Crown's obligations under the Treaty of Waitangi. Winiata criticised current institutional arrangements, by implication television, for failing to meet the cultural requirements of Maori people and their taonga. He alluded to the case before the Waitangi Tribunal that one of the taonga subsumed by the Treaty, and therefore guaranteed protection, was the Maori language. Furthermore, Winiata reminded the commission that Section 3 of the Broadcasting Act 1976 obliged authorities monitoring the performance of the broadcasting system to ensure it reflected and developed New Zealand's identity and culture. With respect to Maori culture, that obligation was neglected, because, said Winiata:

> It is accurate to describe BCNZ as Pakeha. The same description could be used of most other broadcasting organisations in Aotearoa. Minute by minute, hour by hour, day by day, and decade by decade the non-Maori culture of New Zealand has dominated the environment and activities of broadcasting.[52]

In support of his contention that the structural relationship of Pakeha dominance and Maori subjection needed to be changed, Winiata cited the *Directory of the New Zealand Government Departments and Agencies of State*. In 1984 the directory listed 454 positions. Only ten of those positions were held by Maori, four of which were in the Department of Maori Affairs.

ABS lacked the financial power to compete with the other seven applicants for the third channel. Instead it had to rely on its membership to give credence to its application. The ABS trust was supported by the Maori Council, Maori Women's Welfare League, the Kohanga Reo Trust, and the New Zealand University Students' Association. All told, it had a financial membership of 2,000. This membership, combined with ABS being the least threatening competitor for advertising revenue, persuaded BCNZ to support the ABS application. A deal was struck between ABS and BCNZ. Should ABS succeed in winning the warrant, then BCNZ would provide initial capital investment of $46.6 million. This was to be followed in the first three years with grants of $27.4 million and thereafter a 15 per cent share of advertising revenue worth $47.1 million, if ABS did not generate enough revenue to meet overhead costs. This was a remarkable offer, considering that up to that time BCNZ spent only $1 million of its turnover of $120 million on Maori content in its programmes.[53] In September 1985, Ian Cross, Chief Executive of BCNZ, wrote to ABS saying that all that remained was to draw up a contract. The contract was not consummated. In May 1986 BCNZ withdrew the offer on the grounds that as the cost of hearings for the warrant escalated, ABS had to ask for financial support from BCNZ. The expectation of tribal funding had not materialised, nor was there sign of Government commitment. Only a major change in Government policy would enable ABS to proceed, for that, rather than BCNZ, was where ABS should get its primary funding.

The principals of ABS were disappointed by the withdrawal of BCNZ support and likened it to the original betrayal of the Treaty. They felt they had gone close to pulling off a remarkable coup that would have provided employment and an economic base, as well as an outlet for the expression of Maori culture. But it was not all loss. The ABS application exposed the deficiency of Maori content in the applications of the other contenders for the third channel. This they made good at subsequent hearings by including Maori programming in their applications far in excess of what BCNZ offered at the time. Therefore, irrespective of which contender got the warrant, the Maori stood to gain more time on television. Subsequently BCNZ improved its performance for Maori people by extending the Maori news programme *Te Karere* from five to ten minutes. A Maori Programmes Department was established in 1987, which began with one person and grew to a staff of twenty. The department inherited the weekly fifteen-minute *Koha* programme. Its first new programme was *Nga Take Maori*, a twelve-part bilingual current affairs programme of twenty-four minutes duration. The department's major offering was the hour-long *Waka Huia* programme, which had thirty-eight programmes per annum in the series. At the time of writing, the milestone of 100 programmes was reached. For mothers and little children, there is the daily ten-minute kohanga reo programme. The Maori Programmes Department also has under its wing the fifteen-minute *Tangata Pasifika* programme.

Another gain for the Maori was the appointment of Ripeka Evans as cultural assistant to the head of television, Julian Mounter. Evans, in co-operation with the Department of Maori Affairs, instituted the one-year Kimihia television training scheme for Maori recruits. Almost two-thirds of the trainees found jobs somewhere in the industry.

The catalyst for this Maori breakthrough into television is attributable to two factors: the ABS challenge for the third channel, which exposed the paucity of a Maori presence in television, and the advent of Julian Mounter. As an Englishman and an outsider, Mounter saw immediately the dearth of Maori people on television. For instance, the original five-minute *Te Karere* news programme, pioneered and fronted by Derek Fox and Whai Ngata, had no researchers or back-up staff. Nor did it have its own camera team. To close the gap, Mounter had a Maori newsreader appointed to the main section of television and put resources into Maori programmes. Through these developments the Maori struggle for liberation from Pakeha domination moved another step forward.

The Fight for Maori Fisheries

The battle with the Crown over resources on land was extended out to sea in 1986. Despite the expropriation of fisheries around the waters of the New Zealand coastline by the Crown, the Maori regarded the fisheries as their property, guaranteed by the Treaty of Waitangi. Government control of the fisheries up to the 1960s was relatively benign. It issued licences to commercial fishermen and imposed quotas and regulations on size for the taking of shellfish. But in 1964 the Government established a Fishing Industry Board to promote expansion of the industry. Rigid licensing restrictions on the number of fishing boats were removed. In the late 1960s foreign vessels fished in the New Zealand area, exploiting both deep-water and inshore fisheries. Then in 1977 Parliament passed the Territorial Sea and Exclusive Economic Zone Act. With total government control over waters in its 200-mile exclusive economic zone, foreign vessels had to be licensed to fish the area and were encouraged to enter into joint ventures with New Zealand companies.[54] At first, catches increased and then declined as the sustainable yield was passed. For instance, snapper landings peaked to 18,000 tonnes in 1978, then declined to half that in 1983. This pattern was replicated with crayfish and other species.[55] Measures were introduced in the Fisheries Act 1983 to reform the fishing industry so that it could be switched from taking 'maximum yields to maximum sustainable yields'.[56]

Although Maori smarted under fisheries regulations and looked with a jaundiced eye at commercial intrusion into their fisheries, there was little they could do about the matter except make their misgivings known to the Government. The regulations were made tolerable only by the 'permit' system for taking kaimoana for hui and special functions on marae. But even this remaining vestige of their Treaty rights was subject to limitations as to nominating the species and exact quantity of shellfish a hui needed, and the time and place from where they would be taken. Tom Te Weehi's individual challenge to that system was the first success in the assertion of Maori fishing rights. It was soon surpassed by an even bigger challenge by the Muriwhenua Runanga in its claim to the Waitangi Tribunal.

The Muriwhenua Claim

The Muriwhenua claim was triggered by the Government's introduction under the Fisheries Act 1983 of the Quota Management System (QMS), which was an attempt to reduce stress on the fisheries and maintain them at a sustainable level. New Zealand waters in the 200-mile exclusive economic zone were divided by the Ministry of Agriculture and Fisheries (MAF) into seven fishing management zones. Within each zone MAF issued Individual Transferable Quota (ITQ) in an attempt to control the total allowable catch of species under stress, such as snapper and crayfish. The QMS system was to be progressively applied to other species. Once MAF issued quota to individuals or companies, they could fish it themselves, lease it out, or sell the quota to a third party. In practice, big companies got the lion's share of quota. Small or individual part-time fishermen were phased out.[57] The number of fishermen was virtually halved, as 1,500 to 1,800 were not given quota. In Northland, 300 of the 600 fishermen were phased out.[58] This restructuring of the fishing industry resulted in the concentration of ITQs in eighteen companies that have 75 per cent of the total allowable catch.

In the Far North, the Rarawa, Aupouri, Ngati Kuri, Ngai Takoto and Ngati Kahu tribes were incensed that breadwinners who supplemented their livelihood from the land by part-time fishing were not given quota. In 1985 these tribes, under various tribal authorities and incorporations, collectively known as Muriwhenua, filed a claim with the Waitangi Tribunal that the ITQ regime effectively created a property right in the sea from which they were excluded, thus contravening the principles of Article 2 of the Treaty of Waitangi.[59] At the three sittings of the tribunal in the North between November 1986 and January–March 1987, the people of Muriwhenua adduced evidence of long-standing involvement in fishing their coastal waters as far out as thirty-two kilometres. Witnesses giving evidence cited landmark co-ordinates for traditional fishing grounds of particular species well out to sea. Sometimes two tribes fished the same grounds using different landmarks. The tribes considered these fishing grounds their property, which at no time in their history did they relinquish to the Crown.

Before the tribunal completed its deliberations on the Muriwhenua claim, MAF signalled its intention to issue quota for jack mackerel and squid in waters of the Far North. At the end of September 1987 the Muriwhenua claimants and the Maori Council sought an interim ruling from the chairman of the Waitangi Tribunal on its findings in the Muriwhenua case to back an injunction in the High Court to stop the issue of quota. The chairman of the tribunal, Judge Durie, ruled that the area of seas referred to in the claim was owned and that it was property in the same way that land was. If the Crown wished to develop the sea in a commercial way, it had to acquire the right from the traditional user.[60] On the strength of that judgment, the Maori Council and the Runanga of Muriwhenua filed the injunction in the High Court to stop the issue of quota in Muriwhenua waters. The matter was heard in chambers late on the same day. Justice J. Greig concurred with the tribunal's interim finding that the Quota Management System contravened the rights of the Muriwhenua people. Those rights were guaranteed under Section 88(2) of the Fisheries Act, which said 'Nothing in this Act shall affect any Maori fishing right'. He ordered an interim stop to any further inroads under the quota system in Muriwhenua waters until their rights and the obligations of the Crown were resolved.[61] Although the plaintiffs wanted the injunction to apply to the whole of the New Zealand coastline, Justice Greig's concluding remark indicated that the injunction was limited in scope to that part of the fisheries management zone encompassed by Muriwhenua waters around Northland.

The Maori Fisheries Claim

As a consequence of the success of the Muriwhenua claim against the Quota Management System, a much more comprehensive injunction to suspend the ITQ regime over all tribal fisheries was lodged in the High Court on 30 October 1987 by the Maori Council, Tainui Trust Board, the Ngai Tahu Trust Board and other tribes. After reading the evidence put to the Waitangi Tribunal in the Muriwhenua claim, Judge Greig was satisfied that prior to 1840 there was a strong case for a highly developed and controlled Maori fishery over the whole coast of New Zealand. The logic of the evidence in the Muriwhenua claim indicated that the coastline was divided into zones under the authority and control of the hapu and tribes of each district. The rights of the people of Muriwhenua to the fisheries around their tribal waters had been proved before the Waitangi Tribunal. But in the case of the general injunction, the judge issued a caveat. Although Section 88(2) of the Fisheries Act protected Maori fishing rights, those rights were subject to proof of their existence, scope and extent. This meant that although Judge Greig could find no evidence of Maori surrendering their fishing rights guaranteed by the Treaty of Waitangi, they were still subject to proof in a court of law. Despite the caveat, Judge Greig concluded that the ITQ system breached the Fisheries Act, and was therefore wrong. He ordered an interim stop to the system until Maori rights to the fisheries were fully and finally resolved.[62] As a consequence of this judgment, both the Government and its Maori Treaty partner were advised to negotiate over Maori fishing rights, define what those rights were, and to see how best they could be recognised. To this end a joint working party of four Government members and four Maori members was established. The working party was given until 30 June 1988 to resolve the issue.

The Maori negotiators in the fisheries working party claimed 100 per cent ownership of the fisheries, despite the fact that the Crown had control of them for more than a century. But to soften the claim, which was being made from a position of weakness, they conceded a willingness to share 50 per cent with their Treaty partner. However, as a fall-back position should it be necessary to go back to court to prove ownership, all tribes were advised to research traditional use of their fisheries under customary law. As the deadline of 30 June approached, the working party was as divided as when they started. The government negotiators would concede only 29 per cent of the fisheries to the tribes. This share consisted of the whole of the inshore fishery, comprising 19 per cent of the total fishery, and 12.5 per cent of the deep-water fishery, comprising 10 per cent of the total fishery. The Maori members refused the offer because it locked Maori into the minority position. As a consequence of these irreconcilable positions, the working party issued two separate reports and then dissolved itself.

Rather than face a return to court, the Minister of State Owned Enterprises, Richard Prebble, and the Minister of Fisheries, Colin Moyle, stepped back into direct negotiations with the Maori members of the working party. As a result of these negotiations a deal was struck. The ministers made an offer of 50 per cent of the fisheries to be handed over to Maori at the rate of 2.5 per cent per annum over a twenty-year period. The Maori Fisheries Bill introduced into the House in September 1988 was designed to give effect to that formula. Although the Maori leaders were satisfied with the basic settlement, they objected to what they dubbed the 'Idi Amin' clauses in the Bill.[64] These were Sections 17 and 21 of the Bill which would have put a stop to Maori fishing claims before the courts, and a twenty-year moratorium on fishery claims to the Waitangi Tribunal. As a fall-back position, in case Maori leaders did not succeed in getting the objectionable clauses removed, thirty-eight tribes led by eminent persons such as Sir Charles Bennett, Sir Hepi Te Heuheu and Sir James Henare filed their claims back in the High Court. In the meantime, the Government came under extreme pressure from the fishing industry, which threatened to undermine government control by refusing to file quota documentation and withhold resource rentals.[65] In October, the Government dropped the original Bill altogether and unilaterally introduced a new plan conceding 10 per cent of the fishery over a four-year period and leaving the courts to determine the question of ownership over the other 90 per cent.

Attacking Institutionalised Racism

For 150 years the Maori has struggled against cultural invasion brought on by the onslaught of colonisation, and its consequences of social, economic and political subjection. That subjection is still evident today in all the social indices of education, employment, income, housing and health, which demonstrate how much the Maori are disadvantaged in relation to their Pakeha countrymen (see Appendix 4). With the end of Te Kooti's guerrilla campaign in 1872, the Maori adopted non-violent methods of dealing with Pakeha dominance. The consequence of giving up armed struggle as a means of achieving rapid social change by revolution is commitment to change by evolution. The problem with evolutionary change is the glacial pace at which it occurs. In a hundred years of dealing with Pakeha dominance, the Maori has demonstrated infinite patience with Pakeha reluctance to relinquish and share power with the people they colonised.

Although the Maori have quickened the pace of evolutionary change since they became urbanised in the last twenty-five years, some of the transformations they have achieved have been helped by Pakeha support. This support has come about because the Pakeha are now more remote in time from their colonising forebears. Some Pakeha, once they discover the truth of an unjust social order, engage in transforming action themselves, because 'to speak a true word is to transform the world'.[66] In 1960 there was Roland O'Regan, who waged the 'No Maoris No Tour' campaign against an all-white rugby team going to South Africa. In the 1970s there was Dr Oliver Sutherland, who queried the fairness of a monocultural judicial system to Maori offenders who appeared in court without legal representation. In a nice study of sentencing of offenders in the Nelson Magistrate's Court between 1970 and 1972, Sutherland exposed a discrepancy in the sentencing of Maori and Pakeha offenders. The reason was that

Maori appeared more often than not without legal representation. In 1973 he demonstrated that when Maori had legal counsel, the sentencing pattern changed. Imprisonment of Maori went down from 34 per cent to 19 per cent. Sentence to probation fell from 17 per cent to 5 per cent, and there was a corresponding rise of fines instead of the other sentences from 38 per cent to 60 per cent.

When he was transferred to Auckland, Sutherland formed ACORD, a group dedicated to combatting racial discrimination. Members included Dr Ross Galbreath, Mitzi Nairn, Ray Nairn and Jane Kelsey, a lecturer in the Law School at Auckland University. ACORD mounted a systematic, unremitting, and uncompromising attack on institutionalised racism. In one of its papers, ACORD defined racism as:

> the domination and oppression of one ethnic group by another. If such domination is part of the established ways of the society it is institutional racism. Institutional racism is insidious; it is not necessarily carried out by bigots, it need not involve obvious discrimination, and it need not be based on explicit distinctions between people of different racial origin. Even if you do not discriminate against other ethnic groups on an individual level you will still be part of the process and reality of institutional racism . . . New Zealand society is institutionally racist; one group, the Pakeha, holds the power (it controls the decision-making and the means for enforcing compliance with those decisions) . . .
>
> We Pakeha decide how everyone should live, what everyone should learn, and by what criteria people shall be judged and so on . . . The Pakeha understanding of democracy is summed up in the phrase 'majority rule'. Of course, consensus is often sought, but when opinion is often divided we fall back on the vote and the majority has its way.[68]

In 1975 ACORD attacked the discriminatory practices of team-policing of hotels frequented by Polynesians. Then followed a campaign for bilingual interpreters in Auckland hospitals; an inquiry in 1978 into the abuse of largely Maori children in social welfare homes; the use of electric shock treatment on Maori inmates in psychiatric institutions as punishment under the guise of therapy; a call for affirmative action in education; critiques of social welfare in the 1978 'Who Gets the Benefits', and of judges' 'blunders on the bench', the latter being a summation of gratuitous remarks to Maori and Polynesian offenders by judges who were being unwittingly racist; a report, 'The Backside of Justice', on the conditions under which defendants were held in custody at the Auckland Magistrate's Court, and a stunning exposé in 1983 of racist portrayal of the Maori in the souvenir industry.

ACORD blazed the trail for Pakeha in addressing the problem of institutional racism at a time when it was an unpopular cause, and Pakeha bridled at the slightest suggestion that they were racist.

The pioneering efforts of ACORD in addressing institutional racism from outside the institutions they scrutinised was followed up by the work of a Women Against Racism Action Group working within a government bureaucracy. In 1984 the group of nine women in WARAG, of whom the most senior was Tanya Cumberland, produced a report on institutional racism in the Auckland district office of the Department of Social Welfare. The report found from a survey of 68 per cent of a staff of 1,308 in the Tamaki-makau-rau (Auckland) region of the Department of Social Welfare, that Pakeha outnumbered Maori fifteen to one wheras the national ratio is nine to one. English was the dominant language spoken by 99 per cent of the staff. Only 3 per cent spoke Samoan and 2 per cent New Zealand Maori. This imbalance in ethnic composition of staff meant that those delivering service did not match the client group. For instance, only 22 per cent of inmates in residential institutions were Pakeha, against 62 per cent Maori and 16 per cent of Pacific Island origin. But 71 per cent of the staff were Pakeha, only 22 per cent Maori and 5 per cent Pacific Islanders. From this bias against cultural matching of consumers and helpers, the report concluded that the Department of Social Welfare was guilty of institutional racism in staffing. Its recruitment procedures, selection, training and promotion of staff were found to be culturally biased in favour of Pakeha personnel. The report recommended that the department take steps to eliminate institutional racism by incorporating anti-racism courses in its staff-training programmes. It also advocated that the department become bicultural by handing over power and resources to the Maori to enable their vision to be realised of how social welfare should be implemented.[69]

The New Dawn

John Grant, the Director-General of Social Welfare, was shocked by the tenor of the WARAG report. The women of WARAG were ordered not to hold any more meetings during working hours. Tanya Cumberland was admonished for trying to force the pace of change on the department. But after more sober reflection, and consultation with the Minister of Social Welfare, Anne Hercus, a Ministerial Advisory Committee on a Maori Perspective for the Department of Social Welfare was appointed. The chairman of the committee was John

Rangihau, who had retired from the post of advisor to Kara Puketapu, the Secretary of Maori Affairs. Rangihau, who had been a public servant all his life, intimated now that he was beyond the power of bureaucrats that he would not fudge the issues raised in the WARAG report by doing a 'white-wash job'. He would uncover the reality of welfare for Maori people. To this end, Rangihau took the committee to marae around the country to hear directly from the people.

For a bureaucrat such as John Grant, who was normally ensconced in a glass tower in the capital city and therefore insulated from the people who were recipients of his department's services, the tour of marae was a shattering experience. 'Like a litany of sound . . . recited with the fury of a tempest on every marae, and from marae to marae came the cries': DSW 'nurtures dependence and self-hatred rather than independence and self-love', 'removes power from people to look after themselves', 'views clients as irresponsible and somehow deserving of their poverty, powerlessness, and deprivation', 'violence done to tribal structures, violence done to cultural values', 'white males at the top and middle', 'Pakeha control of Maori', and 'rendered children and parents helpless at a great cost to racial, tribal, and personal integrity'.[70] In that vein the litany went on until the end of the tour.

The committee's findings reinforced those of the WARAG report. It concluded that institutional racism existed within the department, 'as it does generally through our national institutional structures'.[71] The roots of Maori dependency were traced to the history of colonisation. That history, combined with the way the department functioned, had made Maori people dependent on the welfare system, and principal consumers of its services. The most consistent call the committee heard around marae was for Maori people to be given the resources to control their own programmes. The committee believed that in reporting on a Maori perspective for the Department of Social Welfare, it was in fact reporting on needs which impact on all government departments.

In keeping with the title of the report, *Puao-Te-Ata-Tu*, the recommendations of the committee heralded a new dawn. It recommended to Government as a policy objective 'To attack all forms of cultural racism in New Zealand that result in the values and lifestyles of the dominant group being regarded as superior to those of other groups, especially Maori.' The corollary of this policy would mean 'incorporating the values, cultures and beliefs of the Maori people in all policies developed for the future of New Zealand'. To this end the committee exhorted the Government to 'attack and eliminate deprivation and alienation by allocating an equitable share of resources, sharing power and authority over the use of resources, and ensuring that legislation which recognises social, cultural and economic values of all cultural groups' is introduced.[72]

The recommendations in the *Puao-Te-Ata-Tu* report became influential as a charter in the development of government policies for the delivery of equity to Maori people. It also influenced decision-making at the parochial level. The Auckland College of Education, for instance, which had adopted a race-gender equity policy, took note of the report in the implementation of its programme. In 1987 the School of Social Work in the college inverted normal recruitment procedures. The head of the school persuaded the college council to allocate twenty of the forty places for trainees to Maori recruits, ten to Pacific Island people and ten to Pakeha. Although some members of the council felt uncomfortable with such a radical change, the rationale of matching delivery of service to consumers laid down by an official government report was hard to deny. But social transformations of this kind are fraught with difficulties. Expanding the Maori dimension in the training programme meant that the delivery of training by mainly Pakeha lecturers did not match the needs of students. In a situation of financial stringency, where there were no resources for the appointment of extra Maori staff, there was dissonance. The experience in the School of Social Work indicated that transforming the deeply entrenched relationship of Pakeha dominance was going to take some time to work through.

White Backlash

Implementing the principles of equity and biculturalism with the Treaty of Waitangi as the charter for doing so, increased racial tension as Maori competed with new vigour for power and resources to promote their half of the bicultural equation. Maori assertiveness arising out of the cultural renaissance, mounting land claims before the Waitangi Tribunal, the successful injunctions in the High Court over fisheries and the State Owned Enterprises Act engendered Pakeha anxiety and feelings of insecurity.

The overriding concern of Pakeha people was over Maori land claims before the Waitangi Tribunal. Pakeha landowners feared dispossession by the claims, even though they were against the Crown and the tribunal had no power to make awards. Although the Commissioner for the Environment observed that only twenty-one of the fifty-nine recommendations of the tribunal had been partially or fully implemented,[73] the fact that Maori were winning some battles was enough to cause anxiety. Suddenly, through the judgments of the tribunal, the world as Pakeha understood it was not what it seemed. The settlement of the issue of Bastion Point under the Muldoon Government, for instance, was found wanting, as the tribunal recommended more comprehensive reparations to Ngati Whatua.

Late in November 1987 the Waitangi Tribunal found in the Orakei claim that the Native Lands Act 1865, which enabled tribal ownership of land on the application of one member of the tribe to be extinguished without the consent of the remainder of the tribe, to be inconsistent with the principles of the Treaty. The vesting of the land in thirteen 'owners' to the exclusion of the majority also contradicted the principles of the Treaty. Statutes such as the Native Land Court Act 1894 were used wrongly to negate the Orakei Native Reserves Act 1882, thereby facilitating the making of orders to partition the Orakei Block and pave the way for its alienation. Furthermore, the Crown was at fault in not acting on the 1908 recommendations of the Stout-Ngata Commission when it could have taken steps to restore most of the land to the people of Orakei. Instead of securing the endowment of the tribe, the Crown breached its fiduciary obligations under the Treaty by its planned acquisition of the land in 1914.

The tribunal was unequivocal. The Crown was found culpable of wrongdoing. To put matters right, the tribunal recommended restoration of title to the Ngati Whatua of Orakei Maori Trust Board, of 67.25 hectares of land held as public parks and reserves. The control and management of the parks, to which the public would still have access, would be vested in a reserves board consisting of Ngati Whatua and Auckland City Council representatives. In effect, this recommendation was a restoration of mana whenua which had been trammelled by the Crown. The land on which the Orakei Marae was built 'for all the tribes' was also to be vested in the trust board. The debt of $200,000 imposed on the Ngati Whatua Trust Board by the Muldoon Government's settlement was to be wiped. The trust board was given an extra three hectares of land for future development and a payment of $3 million to inaugurate programmes for the rehabilitation of the tribe.[74]

Government acceptance of the Waitangi Tribunal's recommendations for the settlement of the Orakei claim met with a mixed reception. The mayor of Auckland City, Dame Cath Tizard, welcomed the

settlement. She hoped it was a turning point in race relations.[75] The
editor of the *New Zealand Herald* wrote that 'many people will wonder
just where Maori land claims are going to stop'.[76] The Opposition
spokesman on Maori Affairs, Winston Peters, said the Government
could face claims mounting to hundreds of millions of dollars as a
result of the decision. Government ministers thought their decision to
return land at Bastion Point to Maori ownership 'captured the true
spirit of partnership as espoused in the Treaty of Waitangi'.[77]

The Leader of the Opposition, Jim Bolger, sensing political advantage, homed in on the Treaty of Waitangi and the tribunal in a press
conference. Commenting on the Bastion Point decision, he said the
claims were 'starting to gnaw away at New Zealanders'.[78] Two months
later he fuelled the fire by questioning the impartiality of the tribunal
with its predominantly Maori membership. He played on people's
fears by saying they did not know whether their land was theirs. He
claimed the rewriting of 'the bones of history' was 'destroying the soul
of this nation'.[79] The situation was aggravated by a bold headline,
misquoted and attributed to a Landcorp official, that the 'Treaty Bill
Could Force Out Farmer'.[80] But the most outlandish statement of all
to 'scrap the Treaty' and substitute another pact came from Ralph
Maxwell, the Under-Secretary for Agriculture and Fisheries.[81] In the
end, attacks on the integrity of the tribunal impelled Judge Durie to
speak out in March 1989 when new members were appointed. He said
the accusation of bias was unkind because it was racist. The tribunal
with its membership increased to seventeen was well balanced with
eight Pakeha and eight Maori members with himself as chairman.[82]

Some semblance of sanity was restored to the debate on the tribunal
by the Commissioner for the Environment, who said that the Government had been remiss in the past in not acknowledging the validity or
otherwise of grievances investigated by the tribunal. The Government
should have informed the public why some form of redress was
required. The commissioner recommended that the Treaty Issues
Unit in the Department of Maori Affairs be given the resources to do
the job of co-ordinating interdepartmental responses to the work and
recommendations of the tribunal.[83] A Treasury paper to the Government also helped allay fears by reinforcing the value of the Treaty in
setting down basic principles applicable to all tribes in the settlement
of their grievances.[84]

The debate on the Maori fisheries claim was equally as rancorous
as that over land claims. Commercial fishermen, sensing a threat to
their monopoly of the industry from the Maori claim, pledged to fight

it.[85] They sought a variation in the court order suspending the ITQ regime.[86] Then they sought government intervention to settle the issue out of court. When the Government arrived at the twenty-year formula for the return of 50 per cent of the fisheries to Maori at the rate of 2.5 per cent per annum, media treatment of the issue simply reinforced Pakeha prejudices and myths of hand-outs to Maori. A bold headline saying 'Bill Gives Tribes Half New Zealand Fishery' was a distortion of the issue.[88] The operative word 'gives' should have been 'returns', which would have put the matter in its proper context in terms of the judgment by Justice Greig that he could find no evidence of the Maori having surrendered their property right in the fisheries. Sensational headlines, such as 'Tuna War Clouds Gather' between Far North Maori tribes and an Auckland company,[89] and 'Fishing Chief Claims Rage Breaking Out',[90] did not help the Maori cause. In the latter instance, a fishing industry leader, Peter Talley, accused Maori leaders of opportunism, saying their fishing claim would lead to racial problems.[91]

Although the Maori fisheries claim was against the Government, the leaders in the industry joined the fight to protect their monopoly. They threatened to withhold resource rental payments and not to fill in returns on quota documents if they were excluded from the consultations on the Maori Fisheries Bill.[92] In a play for public sympathy, the industry claimed it was edging closer to recession. Big fishing companies intimated that they were struggling financially with high fuel costs and resource rentals.[93] Because the Maori claim was allegedly causing uncertainty to the industry, Fletcher Fishing Ltd threatened to pull out of a $200 million investment in fishing.[94] The Leader of the Opposition, Jim Bolger, again sensing political opportunity, said the Fisheries Bill giving Maori control over half of New Zealand's fisheries would be repealed if National came to power.[95]

The Government succumbed to pressure from the industry and the way the Maori claim was portrayed in the press. It was an election loser. The Maori Fisheries Bill was withdrawn and replaced with another offer in November 1988 giving Maori 10 per cent of the quota and shifting the responsibility of deciding ownership of the remaining 90 per cent of the fisheries back to court.

Abolition of Maori Affairs

The fuss created in Parliament and the media over the so-called Maori Loans Affair was also perceived by Maori as white backlash.[96] But the pain for the Maori did not stop there. The Government established a commission of inquiry into the affair because the Deane Report had been done hurriedly in only eight days. Of particular interest, in view of the criticism by the Opposition spokesman on Maori Affairs, Winston Peters, was the part played in it by the Minister of Maori Affairs, Koro Wetere, and staff in his department. The commission reported in June 1987. It found that Puketapu's economic and community development programmes, especially the involvement and influence of iwi in decision-making, resulted in higher levels of community expectation. After he left, the department outran its capacity to co-ordinate the programmes, which had moved away from traditional bureaucratic concerns of land administration, including court and trust operations, and welfare as an appendage from the postwar years. Once the vision and dynamism of Puketapu was lost to the department, it faltered. There was no clear departmental kaupapa for inexperienced middle-level managers to follow. Consequently, cohesion and control were not maintained. These faults were attributed to leadership that was deficient in vision, cohesion, dynamism, and in some cases administrative competence. Strengthening of top management was recommended because there was no logical replacement for Dr Reedy.

The commission was concerned over the Government's policy of devolution of the functions of different departments under the restructuring programme for State Owned Enterprises, and its implications for Maori Affairs. It recommended a policy of partnership in Maori development by a progressive transfer of responsibilities for government programmes to iwi authorities, and the establishment of a new Ministry of Maori Development to undertake policy development, advocate Maori interests, and serve the needs of both Maori and Government. These recommendations sealed the fate of the department.[97]

In April 1988 the Minister of Maori Affairs circulated among Maori people a bilingual discussion entitled *Partnership Perspectives*. The paper portended the Government's intention to phase out the Department of Maori Affairs. Existing department programmes such as land, housing and welfare were to be transferred to mainstream departments and agencies. The department was to be replaced by a slimmed-down Ministry of Maori Policy with only sixty staff. The ministry's sole function would be to advise the Government on Maori policy.[98] Unlike its predecessor, it would not deliver services to the Maori people. They now had to take their chances with monocultural departments, ostensibly committed by government decree to the principles of the Treaty of Waitangi, biculturalism and delivering equity to Maori people. The new ideology of partnership between Government and Maori was to be implemented by devolution of some resources and government programmes to iwi authorities. Koro Wetere and Dr Reedy had the task of meeting tribes on their marae to pursuade them to accept the proposals in *Partnership Perspectives*.

Sir Graham Latimer, president of the Maori Council, called on the people to oppose the disestablishment of the department instead of sitting around like 'stunned mullet'.[99] He said despite its faults, the department had acted as a buffer between the Government and Maoridom.

Over 400 people who met with the minister at Orakei Marae in Auckland opposed the Government's plan. Instead they wanted the department restructured.[100] The bulk of the submissions received on the policy proposals opposed the closure of the department. These the minister brushed off lightly, saying, 'There may not have been total acceptance of the proposals in *He Tirohanga Rangapu*, but there is no argument that Maori people themselves want a greater say in their own destiny.'[101] This *non sequitur* imputed that the course unilaterally decided upon by Government was in fact giving them a greater say.

Kaupapa for Nationhood in the Twenty-first Century

The saving grace in the Government's policy statement, called *Partnership Response*,[102] is the affirmation of Government objectives. These include honouring the principles of the Treaty of Waitangi; eliminating the gaps that exist between the educational, personal, social, economic and cultural well-being of Maori people and the general population; promoting economic development and self-sufficiency for Maori people; dealing quickly and justly with grievances under the Treaty of Waitangi; allocating resources to Maori language and culture to enable the development of a unique New Zealand identity; promoting Maori participation in decision-making in the machinery of government and encouraging Maori participation in the political process. These goals the Maori have pursued for 150 years, but were consistently thwarted by the necrotic process of colonisation and Pakeha control. This official statement of policy from Government has at least provided Maori people with a charter for the fulfilment of their aspirations, and a document against which they can measure the performance of subsequent governments and their bureaucrats.

While the Government took measures through an Implementation Committee and an Iwi Transition Agency to action its plan for devolution and replacement of the Department of Maori Affairs by a Ministry of Maori Policy, Maori leaders laid their own plans. On 24 June 1989, Sir Hepi Te Heuheu, paramount chief of Tuwharetoa, convened an inter-tribal hui at Taupo where it was resolved to form a congress of tribes. Given the history of colonisation, and the bifurcated political response of the tribes through Kotahitanga and the Kauhanganui, unification was inevitable. Driven by the recovery of their stolen humanity, the affirmation of Maori identity, and the powerful ethos of the cultural renaissance, it was the obvious political response to a government that directed rather than listened to the people. For the Maori, the inheritors of a millenial culture, theirs is a struggle without end into the world of light. They know the sun has set on the empire that colonised them. They know too it will set on the coloniser even if it takes a thousand years. They will triumph in the end, because they are the tangata whenua.

EPILOGUE

The Maori struggle against an unjust social order took another step forward on 3 October 1989 when five judges in the Court of Appeal issued a unanimous decision in favour of Robert Te Kotahi Mahuta and the Tainui Trust Board against the Crown and its agent Coalcorp. The judgment declared that the Crown and Coalcorp should take no further action on selling land until measures were put in place for the protection of the Tainui land claim against the Crown before the Waitangi Tribunal. The judgment also ruled that the safeguards of the Treaty of Waitangi (State Enterprise Act) 1988 applied as well to the interests in land represented by the coal-mining licences in the Crown's agreement with Coalcorp issued in March 1988.

This judgment harked back to the claim made by Mahuta's ancestor Tawhiao to Grey in 1878 for the return of Waikato land confiscated in breach of the Treaty of Waitangi under the 1863 New Zealand Settlements Act. It also vindicated Tawhiao's declaration in 1894 that minerals including coal under tribal land was Maori property guaranteed by the Treaty.

The decision is congruent with the title of the final chapter of this book 'Ma te Ture te Ture e Patu', only the law can rule on the law. Where the Government has wavered on its commitment to honour the principles of the Treaty of Waitangi in relation to land and fisheries claims because of fear of electoral backlash or corporate power, the judiciary is under no such constraint. The judgment puts New Zealand firmly into the post-colonial era.

APPENDIX 1

The Treaty of Waitangi

English Version

Her Majesty Victoria, Queen of the United Kingdom of Great Britain and Ireland, regarding with Her Royal Favor the Native Chiefs and Tribes of New Zealand, and anxious to protect their just Rights and Property, and to secure to them the enjoyment of Peace and Good Order, has deemed it necessary, in consequence of the great number of Her Majesty's Subjects who have already settled in New Zealand, and the rapid extension of Emigration both from Europe and Australia which is still in progress, to constitute and appoint a functionary properly authorized to treat with the Aborigines of New Zealand for the recognition of Her Majesty's Sovereign authority over the whole or any part of those islands. Her Majesty, therefore, being desirous to establish a settled form of Civil Government with a view to avert the evil consequences which must result from the absence of the necessary Laws and Institutions alike to the Native population and to Her subjects, has been graciously pleased to empower and authorize me, William Hobson, a Captain in Her Majesty's Royal Navy, Consul, and Lieutenant-Governor of such parts of New Zealand as may be, or hereafter shall be, ceded to Her Majesty, to invite the confederated and independent Chiefs of New Zealand to concur in the following Articles and Conditions.

Article the First

The Chiefs of the Confederation of the United Tribes of New Zealand, and the separate and independent Chiefs who have not become members of the Confederation, cede to Her Majesty the Queen of England, absolutely and without reservation, all the rights and powers of Sovereignty which the said Confederation or Individual Chiefs respectively exercise or possess, or may be supposed to exercise or to possess, over their respective Territories as the sole Sovereigns thereof.

Article the Second

Her Majesty the Queen of England confirms and guarantees to the Chiefs and Tribes of New Zealand, and to the respective families and individuals thereof, the full, exclusive, and undisturbed possession of their Lands and Estates, Forests, Fisheries, and other properties which they may collectively or individually possess, so long as it is their wish and desire to retain the same in their possession; but the Chiefs of the United Tribes and the Individual Chiefs yield to Her Majesty the exclusive right of Pre-emption over such lands as the proprietors thereof may be disposed to alienate, at such prices as may be agreed upon between the respective Proprietors and persons appointed by Her Majesty to treat with them in that behalf.

Article the Third

In consideration thereof, Her Majesty the Queen of England extends to the Natives of New Zealand Her Royal protection, and imparts to them all the Rights and Privileges of British subjects.

W. Hobson
Lieutenant-Governor

Maori Version

Ko Wikitoria, te Kuini o Ingarani, i tana mahara atawai ki nga Rangatira me Nga Hapu o Nu Tirani, i tana hiahia hoki kia tohungia ki a ratou o ratou rangatiratanga, me to ratou wenua, a kia mau tonu hoki te Rongo ki a ratou me te ata noho hoki, kua wakaaro ia he mea tika kia tukua mai tetahi Rangatira hei kai wakarite ki nga tangata maori o Nu Tirani. Kia wakaaetia e nga Rangatira maori te Kawanatanga o te Kuini, ki nga wahi katoa o te wenua nei me nga motu. Na te mea hoki he tokomaha ke nga tangata o tona iwi kua noho ki tenei wenua, a e haere mai nei.

Na, ko te Kuini e hiahia ana kia wakaritea te Kawanatanga, kia kaua ai nga kino e puta mai ki te tangata maori ki te pakeha e noho ture kore ana.

Na, kua pai te Kuini kia tukua a hau, a Wiremu Hopihona, he Kapitana i te Roiara Nawa, hei Kawana mo nga wahi katoa o Nu Tirani, e tukua aianei a mua atu ki te Kuini; e mea atu ana ia ki nga Rangatira o te Wakaminenga o nga Hapu o Nu Tirani, me era Rangatira atu, enei ture ka korerotia nei.

Ko te Tuatahi

Ko nga Rangatira o te Wakaminenga, me nga Rangatira katoa hoki, kihai i uru ki taua Wakaminenga, ka tuku rawa atu ki te Kuini o Ingarani ake tonu atu te Kawanatanga katoa o o ratou wenua.

Ko te Tuarua

Ko te Kuini o Ingarani ka wakarite ka wakaae ki nga Rangatira, ki nga Hapu, ki nga tangata katoa o Nu Tirani, te tino Rangatiratanga o o ratou wenua o ratou kainga me o ratou taonga katoa. Otiia ko nga Rangatira o te Wakaminenga, me nga Rangatira katoa atu, ka tuku ki te Kuini te hokonga o era wahi wenua e pai ai te tangata nona te wenua, ki te ritenga o te utu e wakaritea ai e ratou ko te kai hoko e meatia nei e te Kuini hei kai hoko mona.

Ko te Tuatoru

Hei wakaritenga mai hoki tenei mo te wakaaetanga ki te Kawanatanga o te Kuini. Ka tiakina e te Kuini o Ingarani nga tangata maori katoa o Nu Tirani. Ka tukua ki a ratou nga tikanga katoa rite tahi ki ana mea ki nga tangata o Ingarani.

(Signed) William Hobson
Consul and Lieutenant-Governor

APPENDIX 2

Table of School Certificate Pass Rates
in Auckland Secondary Schools

Position	School	English %	Maths %
1	*St Cuthberts College (Epsom)	92.5	88.2
2	*Diocesan School for Girls (Epsom)	84.4	79.3
3	*Baradene College (Remuera)	81.5	84
4	Epsom Girls' Grammar	77.8	76
5	Auckland Grammar (Mt Eden)	76.5	79.8
6	MacLeans College (Bucklands Beach)	75.1	79.4
7	*King's College (Otahuhu)	74.8	83.6
8	*Carmel College (Milford)	73.3	82.5
9	*Auckland Metropolitan (Mt Eden)	72	30.8
10	Westlake Girls' High (Takapuna)	71.7	74.5
11	Rangitoto College (Mairangi Bay)	69.2	72.3
12	Edgewater College (Pakuranga)	67.8	71.4
13	Mt Roskill Grammar	66.3	57.5
14	Lynfield College	64.9	68.1
15	*St Kentigern's (Pakuranga)	64.3	75.8
16	*Rosmini College (Takapuna)	63.7	67.9
17	Pakuranga College	62.2	63.5
18	Takapuna Grammar School	60.7	70.2
19	Howick College	60.5	78
20	Green Bay High School	60	56.6
21	*St Mary's College (Ponsonby)	58.7	65.7
22	Glenfield College	56.7	70.2
23	*Marcellin College (Mt Roskill)	56.6	61.2
24=	*St Dominic's College (Henderson)	56.2	61
24=	Papatoetoe High School	56.2	51.5
26	*Marist Sisters (Mt Albert)	56.1	61.4
27	Northcote College	56	66.3
28=	Westlake Boys' High (Takapuna)	55.6	77
28=	Selwyn College (Kohimarama)	55.6	62.6
30	*Sacred Heart (Glen Innes)	54.9	63.3
31	James Cook High (Manurewa)	54	65.4
32	Auckland Girls' Grammar (Newton)	53.2	56.4
33	*Corran School (Remuera)	52.5	32.1

*Private or church school

34	Massey High School	52.1	53.5
35	McAuley High School (Otahuhu)	51.9	39.5
36	*St Peters' College (Mt Eden)	51.3	57.4
37	*Dilworth College (Epsom)	51.1	70.6
38	Homai College (for the Blind)	50	
39=	Avondale College	49.4	61.9
39=	Long Bay College	49.4	56.2
41	Rosehill College (Papakura)	49.2	64.3
42	Glendowie College	48.7	66.3
43	Manurewa High School	47.2	45.3
44	Waitakere College (Henderson)	46	60.3
45	*Liston College (Henderson)	43.9	66.1
46	*Kristin School (Albany)	43.7	75
47	Birkdale College	43.5	48
48	Kelston Boys' High	43	62.9
49	Onehunga High School	42.8	53.2
50	Rutherford High School (Te Atatu)	40.6	52.7
51	Aorere College (Papatoetoe)	40.4	59.2
52	Tamaki College	40.2	22.2
53	Penrose High School	40.1	58
54	Henderson Girls' High	38.1	49.1
55	Kelston Girls' High	38.1	44.2
56	*Seventh Day Adventist (Mangere)	37.8	53.6
57	Mt Albert Grammar	37.2	52.2
58	Papakura High School	36.6	54.5
59	Otahuhu College	36.1	42.9
60	*De La Salle College (Mangere)	36	53
61	*Queen Victoria School (Parnell)	34.1	34.6
62	*St Paul's College (Ponsonby)	30.2	49.4
63	Seddon High School (Western Springs)	29.9	34.5
64	Mangere College	23.7	45.8
65	Nga Tapuwae College (Mangere)	24.2	50.7
66	Tangaroa College (East Tamaki)	18.5	23.4
67	Hillary College (Otara)	16.6	31.2
68	*Hato Petera College (Northcote)	15.1	56.9

APPENDIX 3

School Certificate Pass Rates by Subject Grouping 1974–82

	1974	1975	1976	1977	1978	1979	1980	1981	1982
Latin	64.6	70.2	73.8	81.4	84.0	87.1	87.0	85.7	86.9
French	56.4	64.0	66.9	75.9	75.8	77.4	77.6	79.2	81.6
Other Foreign Languages	58.4	62.3	68.5	77.0	77.2	74.5	75.7	79.0	81.1
Physical Science	57.2	61.0	66.6	68.8	72.8	70.4	75.7	79.0	30.3
Music	55.1	62.3	66.0	63.3	65.9	65.9	66.9	70.9	69.5
Shorthand/Typing	50.9	49.9	53.6	61.8	61.1	65.9	64.9	61.5	64.8
Bookkeeping	48.4	48.8	50.2	60.4	59.4	60.5	62.2	60.5	62.5
History	55.6	56.3	56.3	57.4	57.5	60.5	57.2	59.0	62.9
Mathematics	52.5	54.3	55.7	55.3	54.8	58.3	52.5	57.0	57.5
Science	51.5	47.2	51.1	52.4	53.4	53.4	51.4	58.2	58.8
English	55.2	55.8	52.8	51.2	50.8	53.0	51.1	50.8	50.6
Geography	53.3	53.8	55.8	50.8	49.9	51.0	50.2	52.6	52.1
Technical Drawing	47.6	48.2	48.1	49.5	48.9	49.3	49.7	54.0	45.9
Art	53.5	57.1	53.4	55.9	53.6	54.6	49.5	51.5	50.1
Economics	46.0	46.4	46.8	49.2	49.2	48.9	49.2	53.5	55.1
Clothing and Textiles	47.7	50.3	49.3	52.2	52.3	51.5	48.9	38.5	37.2
Agriculture	46.3	46.4	45.2	48.5	42.8	43.3	47.9	44.1	45.4
Biological Science	48.6	52.1	50.5	48.7	45.8	47.0	45.6	44.5	45.4
Typewriting	44.9	43.8	44.2	44.9	45.7	44.6	43.7	43.6	43.5
Engineering	47.1	45.5	46.4	46.8	45.5	46.4	42.7	41.5	42.4
Woodwork	47.9	47.6	47.1	47.9	45.4	44.1	41.1	39.1	38.9
Home Economics	45.8	46.4	43.5	45.1	46.8	44.3	39.7	38.6	37.8
Maori	49.4	47.0	43.6	44.5	43.4	43.9	39.1	39.9	41.9
Total Pass Rate	52.3	52.8	53.1	52.9	52.6	52.3	51.7	53.9	54.3

Sources: 1974 Department of Education, 1975; 1975 Department of Education, 1976b; 1976 Department of Education, 1977; 1977 Department of Education, 1978; 1978 Department of Education, 1979; 1979 Department of Education, 1980a; 1980 Department of Education, 1980b.

APPENDIX 4

Social Profile of the Maori

	Maori	Non-Maori
Population*	404,185	2,857,598
Seats in Parliament	4	93
Life Expectancy* at birth (years)		
Male	63.8	70.8
Female	68.5	76.9
Tertiary Education	18.6%	38.8%
White-collar Occupation	33.1%	64.4%
Employers (hiring others)	1.2%	4.5%
Employers (including self-employed)	3.7%	10.5%
Median Income (NZ$) all sources of income included, i.e., welfare payments		
per person	10,287	11,889
per household	26,053	27,500
Home Ownership	48.9%	64.8%
Unemployment Rate		
Male	12.1%	4.7%
Female	15.9%	7.3%
Prison Inmates* (male)	2.7%	.2%

* Denotes data for the country as a whole, including Pacific Island people. The other statistics are derived from the 1986 census for the new Auckland City and do not include Pacific Island people.

Acknowledgement: Ratana Walker, Auckland City Council

GLOSSARY

ahi	fire
ahi ka	burning (domestic) fire, signifying continuous occupation of land
aho	line, lineage
ahurewa	sacred place, platform, high level
aitanga	tribal prefix, descendants of
aitua	misfortune
ana	cave, den
aomarama	world of life and light
ara	path, track, road
ariki	paramount chief, lord
ariki tapairu	female ariki
atua	god
aukati	closed boundary
hahunga	exhumation of bones
haka	war dance
hakari	feast
hakuturi	birds, insects and forest fairies
hanga	build, make
hangi	earth oven
hapa	pass over
hapu	sub-tribe, descendants, pregnant
hara	sin, wrong, offence
hau	vital essence
hauhau	common name for Paimarire cult
heke (nga)	migration
heketua	latrine, privy
hiki	lift
hikoi	peaceful walk
hoko	sell
hongi	greet, press noses
hui	assembly, gathering, meeting
ihi	power, authority, rank
iho whenua	centre portion of navel cord, connection to the land
inanga	whitebait, *Galaxias maculatus*
ira	life principle
iwi	tribe, bone
kaimoana	seafood
kainga	home, place of residence

kanohi	eye, face
kaitiaki	keeper, guard, guardian, minder
karakia	prayer, incantation
karanga	call, ritual high-pitched call of welcome by women
kaumatua	male elder
kaupapa	plan, principle, philosophy
kauta	outdoor cooking shelter
kawakawa	shrub, *Macropiper excelsum*
kawanatanga	governor, governance
kina	sea urchin, *Evechinus*
kingitanga	kingship, King Movement
kirihipi	sheepskin, parchment
kokiri	rush forward, charge
kore	no, not, absence, lack of anything
korero	talk, speech, history, story
kotahitanga	unification
kowhaiwhai	painted rafter decorations
kuia	female elder
kumara	sweet potato, *Ipomoea batatas*
kupapa	Maori who fought on side of the Crown
mahi	work
maire	house of instruction in sacred lore
makutu	spell, sorcery
mana	authority, power, prestige, psychic force
mangai	mouth
manuhiri	visitors, guests
manuka	tea tree
maori	normal, natural
marae	courtyard in front of meeting house
matakite	seer, second sight
mate	sick, illness, ailing, dead
matou	we, us
matua	parent
mauri	life force
mere	short flat weapon, club
mihi	greet, formal speech of welcome
moa	extinct flightless bird
mokai	servant, pet
moko	tattoo
mokopuna	grandchild
morehu	survivors
motuhake	discrete, separate, independent
motu	island, sever, cut
mua	front, past
muri	behind, rear, future
muru	plunder, wipe out, punish
nehera	ancient times, past

nga, ngai, ngati	tribal prefixes, descendants of
nga	the (plural)
noa	common, without sanctity or tapu
ohaki	last testament, farewell message
ohu	co-operative work goup
pa	barrier, fortification
paepae	beam across the front of a house
pahua	invasion
pai marire	good and peaceful
Pakeha	white man, European, related to pakepakeha and pakehakeha, imaginary beings with fair skins
pakeke	elder
papa	flat hard rock, slab or board
papakainga	residence, village settlement
papatipu	land under customary title
parekereke	seedling bed
patu	club, beat, kill, defeat
paua	univalve mollusc, *Haliotis* spp.
pipi	shellfish, *Paphies australis*
pito	navel, umbilical cord
po	night, dark, place of departed spirits
poi	flax ball on string used in posture dances
poroporoaki	eulogy, farewell to the dead
potae	hat, also symbol for crown
potiki	youngest child
pou	pillar, post
pouihi	carved pillar depicting person of rank
pounamu	greenstone, jade
poupou	carved posts inside meeting house
poutokomanawa	central pillar of a house
pouwhenua	carved standard symbol of land ownership
puhi	plumes, virgin chieftainess
pupuri	hold, retain
rahui	prohibition, closed season
raiona	transliteration of lion
rangatira	chief
rangatiratanga	chieftainship
rapu	seek, search
raupatu	conquer, overcome
rino	iron
roa	long, distant
rohe	boundary
runanga	council, assembly
taiaha	longstaff weapon
taihoa	wait, delay
takahi	trample
take	cause, reason, *casus belli*

tangata	man, human, person
tangi(hanga)	cry, weep, funeral
taonga	treasure, possession, gift
tapairu	first born female in a family of rank
tapatapa	to name, claim ownership by naming
tapu	sacred, prohibited, unclean
tarai	fashion, carve out
tatau	door
taua	war party
tauiwi	strange tribe, foreigner
taunaha	to bespeak, to claim
taurekareka	slave
te	the (singular)
teina	junior
tiki	carving of human form
tikanga	custom, rules
tinana	body
tohi	purification rite
tohunga	priest, expert, shaman, sorcerer
tonu	continue, persist
totara	*Podocarpus totara*, forest tree
totohe	to press forward, challenge
tuahu	altar, place of worship
tuakana	senior
tui	parson bird, *Prosthemadera novaeseelandiae*
tukemata	eyebrow
tukutuku	decorative wall panels in meeting house
tumuaki	leader, head
turangawaewae	standing in the tribe
ture	law, rule
tutua	commoner
uku	clay
urupa	burial ground, cemetery
ururu whenua	rites for entry into alien land
utu	payment, compensation, revenge
waerea	incantation, chant, to ward off evil spirits
waewae tapu	strangers, sacred feet
wahaika	weapon, club of bone or wood
wahi	place, location, area
wai	water
waiata	song, chant
wairua	spirit
waka	vessel, canoe
wananga	lore, occult knowledge, learning
wehi	awesome, fear
wera	hot, burn
wero	challenge

whai	chase, pursue
whaikorero	speech in reply to formal welcome
whakairo	carve
whakanoa	to remove tapu, to make common
whakapapa	genealogy
whakapohane	derisive baring of buttocks
whanau	birth, offspring, extended family
whangai	feed, adopt
whare maire	house of black arts and magic
wharepuni	dwelling, house, meeting house
wharenui	big house, meeting house
whare wananga	house of learning
whawhai	fight, war
whenua	land, afterbirth, earth, country
whetu	star
whiwhi	obtain
wiwi	indefinite place

REFERENCES

Chapter 1

1 D. R. Simmons, *Whakairo*, p. 17.
2 Sir Peter Buck, *The Coming of the Maori*, p. 434.
3 Sir George Grey, *Nga Mahi a Nga Tupuna*, p. 1.
4 Sir George Grey, *Polynesian Mythology*, p. 9.
5 Sir George Grey, *Nga Mahi a Nga Tupuna*, p. 5.
6 Sir Peter Buck, op. cit., pp. 449–53.
7 Anthony Alpers, *Maori Myths*, p. 237.
8 Sir George Grey, op. cit., p. 17.
9 Ibid., p. 12.
10 Ibid., p. 16.

Chapter 2

1 Janet Davidson, *The Prehistory of New Zealand*, p. 22.
2 G. S. Parsonson, 'The Settlement of Oceania', in *Polynesian Navigation*, edited by J. Golson, p. 37.
3 W. Kyselka, *An Ocean in Mind*, p. 124.
4 S. P. Smith, *Hawaiki*, p. 7.
5 Elsdon Best, *The Maori As He Was*, p. 33.
6 Sir Peter Buck, *Vikings of the Sunrise*, introduction.
7 Andrew Sharp, *Ancient Voyagers in the Pacific*, pp. 1–15.
8 G. S. Parsonson, op. cit., p. 59.
9 David Lewis, *We the Navigators*, pp. 45–223.
10 Sir George Grey, *Nga Mahi a Nga Tupuna*, p. 114.
11 Roger C. Green, *A Review of the Prehistoric Sequence in the Auckland Province*, p. 12.
12 Roger Duff, *The Moa-Hunter Period of Maori Culture*, p. 33.
13 Ibid., p. 365.
14 Sir Peter Buck, *The Coming of the Maori*, p. 19.
15 Sir George Grey, op. cit., p. 58.
16 Sir Peter Buck, op. cit., p. 20.
17 John Grace, *Tuwharetoa*, p. 140.
18 Roger Duff, *The Moa-Hunter Period of Maori Culture*, pp. 284–5.
19 Sir Peter Buck, op. cit., pp. 20–21.
20 Roger Duff, op. cit., introduction XI.
21 Ibid., pp. 32–80.
22 Ibid., pp. 83–137.
23 Ibid., pp. 161–96.

24 Janet Davidson, op. cit., p. 63.
25 Roger Duff, op. cit., pp. 198–230.
26 Janet Davidson, op. cit., p. 23.
27 P. Houghton, *The First New Zealanders*, p. 95.
28 N. J. Pricket, 'Prehistoric Occupation in the Moikau Valley, Palliser Bay', p. 43.
29 Janet Davidson, op. cit., p. 40.
30 D. G. Sutton, 'The Archaeology of Belief', pp. 10–11.
31 D. R. Simmons, op. cit., p. 207.
32 J. Golson, 'Archaeology, Tradition and Myth in New Zealand Prehistory', p. 381.
33 D. R. Simmons, op. cit., p. 205.
34 Sir Peter Buck, op. cit., p. 10.
35 Ibid., p. 9.
36 Elsdon Best, *Tuhoe*, p. 12.
37 D. R. Simmons, op. cit., pp. 63–100.
38 Elsdon Best, op. cit., p. 1.
39 Ibid., p. 13.
40 A. C. Lyall, *Whakatohea*, p. 12.
41 S. P. Smith, *Tales of the Taranaki Coast*, pp. 18–43.
42 D. R. Simmons, op. cit. p. 21.
43 S. P. Smith, op. cit., p. 50.
44 Ibid., p. 54.
45 Ibid., p. 56.
46 Sir Peter Buck, op. cit., p. 5.
47 D. R. Simmons op. cit., pp. 15–59.
48 Ibid., p. 32.
49 Sir Peter Buck, op. cit., p. 37.
50 S. P. Smith, *Hawaiki*, pp. 20–218.
51 Sir Peter Buck, op. cit., p. 7.
52 J. Davidson, op. cit., p. 23.
53 Sir Peter Buck, op. cit., p. 40.
54 Ibid., p. 40.
55 S. P. Smith, op. cit., pp. 89–90.
56 D. R. Simmons, op. cit., p. 56.
57 John Shaw, *A Tramp to the Diggings*, pp. 35–36.
58 S. P. Smith, *Hawaiki*, p. 219.
59 Elsdon Best, *The Maori As He Was*, p. 24.
60 Elsdon Best, *Tuhoe*, pp. 12–13.
61 Sir Peter Buck, op. cit., pp. 10–11.
62 Roger Duff, op. cit., pp. 14–15.
63 Sir Peter Buck, op. cit., p. 13.
64 Roger Duff, op. cit., p. 18.
65 Ibid., p. 153.
66 D. Sutton, 'A Culture History of the Chatham Islands', pp. 67–92.
67 M. Shirres, 'The Relationship of the Moriori Language to the Maori Language', unpublished paper, University of Auckland, 1977, p. 13.

68 D. Sutton, op. cit., p. 88.
69 D. Sutton, 'The Whence of the Moriori', pp. 10–11.
70 J. Larrain, *The Concept of Ideology*, p. 46.
71 Janet Davidson, op. cit., 184.

Chapter 3

1 D. Staffford, *Te Arawa*, pp. 1–14.
2 S. P. Smith, *History and Traditions of the Maoris of the West Coast*, pp. 86–87.
3 D. R. Simmons, *The Great New Zealand Myth*, p. 271.
4 Elsdon Best, *Tuhoe*, p. 13.
5 J. Grace, *Tuwharetoa*, pp. 194–205.
6 L. G. Kelly, *Tainui*, pp. 34–46.
7 D. M. Stafford, *Te Arawa*, pp. 20–57.
8 J. Grace, op. cit. pp. 133–55.
9 A. C. Lyall, *Whakatohea*, p. 21.
10 Elsdon Best, op. cit., p. 25.
11 D. R. Simmons, op. cit., p. 321.
12 Sir George Grey, *Nga Mahi a Nga Tupuna*, p. 59.
13 J. H. Mitchell, *Takitimu*, p. 30.
14 Sir George Grey, op. cit., p. 93.
15 Ibid., p. 59.
16 J. Grace, op. cit., p. 44.
17 D. R. Simmons, op. cit., p. 32.
18 J. Grace, op. cit., pp. 75–79.
19 Ibid., pp. 78–79.
20 Ibid., pp. 49–50.
21 Sir Peter Buck, *The Coming of the Maori*, p. 56.
22 J. Grace, op. cit., pp. 58–68.
23 J. H. Mitchell, op. cit., pp. 40–44.
24 Sir Peter Buck, op. cit., p. 53.
25 S. P. Smith, op. cit., pp. 101–02.
26 D. R. Simmons, op. cit., p. 317.
27 Sir Peter Buck, op. cit., p. 55.
28 S. P. Smith, op. cit., pp. 156–64.
29 A. C. Lyall, op. cit., pp. 20–21.
30 Pine Harrison, 'The Traditions of the Ngati Porou Tribe', unpublished paper, p. 4.
31 J. H. Mitchell, op. cit., pp. 22–24.
32 D. R. Simmons, op. cit., p. 318.
33 Florence Keene, *Tai Tokerau*, pp. 59–60.
34 J. H. Mitchell, op. cit., p. 59.
35 D. R. Simmons, op. cit., p. 321.
36 D. M. Stafford, op. cit., pp. 56–105.
37 J. Grace, op. cit., pp. 129–39.
38 J. H. Mitchell, op. cit., pp. 73–148.

39 L. G. Kelly, op. cit., pp. 83–250.
40 Ibid., pp. 300–48.
41 Pine Harrison, op. cit., pp. 4–11.
42 Elsdon Best, op. cit., pp. 210–400.
43 Ibid., pp. 387–94.
44 A. C. Lyall, op. cit., pp. 5–138.

Chapter 4

1 Elsdon Best, *The Maori As He Was*, p. 95.
  Raymond Firth, *Economics the New Zealand Maori*, p. 111.
2 Sir Peter Buck, *The Coming Of The Maori*, p. 333.
  Raymond Firth, op. cit., pp. 112–14.
  Elsdon Best, op. cit., p.96.
3 Sir Peter Buck, op. cit., pp. 333–4.
  Raymond Firth, op. cit, p. 114.
4 Sir Peter Buck, op. cit., pp. 336–7.
  Raymond Firth, op. cit., p. 115.
5 Sir Peter Buck, op. cit., pp. 337–8.
  Raymond Firth, op. cit., p. 106.
6 Elsdon Best, op. cit., p. 80.
  Sir Peter Buck, op. cit., p. 474–7.
7 Raymond Firth, op. cit., pp. 246–53.
8 Ibid., pp. 258–62.
9 Ibid., pp. 254–8, pp. 279–81.
10 Ibid., pp. 412–17.
11 A. P. Vayda, *Maori Warfare*, pp. 80–83.
12 Anne Salmond, *Hui*, pp. 115–77.
13 Roger Oppenheim, *Maori Death Customs*, p. 101–18.
14 Raymond Firth, op. cit., p. 328.
15 Ibid., p. 132.

Chapter 5

1 Sir Keith Sinclair, *A History of New Zealand*, p. 34.
2 Waitangi Tribunal, *Muriwhenua Fishing Report*, pp. 58–59.
3 Tony Simpson, *Te Riri Pakeha*, p. 15.
4 Waitangi Tribunal, *Muriwhenua Fishing Report*, p. 58.
5 P. Houghton, *The First New Zealanders*, pp. 130–48.
6 'The History of Ngati Whatua', 1981 unpublished research paper
  commissioned by Ani Pihema with senior students Maori Studies Dept.,
  University of Auckland.
7 Elsdon Best, *The Maori As He Was*, p. 136.
8 P. Houghton, op. cit., p. 135.
9 Judith Binney, 'Christianity and the Maoris to 1840', pp. 153–4.
10 David Stannard, *Before the Horror*, pp. 1–48.
11 A. Saunders, *History of New Zealand 1642–1861*, p. 83–84.
12 Judith Binney, *A Legacy of Guilt*, p. 49.

13 Judith Binney, 'Christianity and the Maoris to 1840', p. 146.
14 Judith Binney, *A Legacy of Guilt*, pp. 56–60
15 S. P. Smith, *Maori Wars of the Nineteenth Century*, p. 183.
16 S. P. Smith, op. cit., p. 184.
17 Ibid., p. 18.
18 Elsdon Best, *The Pa Maori*, pp. 367–9.
19 Sir Keith Sinclair, op. cit., p. 15.
20 S. P. Smith, op. cit., p. 442.
21 Judith Binney, 'Christianity and the Maoris to 1840', p. 148.
22 A. Saunders, op. cit., pp. 94–98.
23 S. P. Smith, op. cit., p. 443–4.
24 Ibid., p. 473.
25 Bronwyn Elsmore, *Like Them That Dream*, pp. 15–16.
26 Paulo Freire, p. 129.
27 J. M. Barrington and T. H. Beaglehole, *Maori Schools in a Changing Society*, p. 13.
28 Bronwyn Elsmore, op. cit., p. 24.
29 Ibid., pp. 24–25.
30 Ibid., p. 14.
31 Ibid., p. 34.
32 M. King, *Whina*, p. 153.
33 John Grace, *Tuwharetoa*, p. 424.
34 *Facsimiles of the Declaration of Independence and the Treaty of Waitangi*, p. 3.
35 Sir Keith Sinclair, op. cit., p. 56.
36 Ruth Ross, *The Treaty on the Ground*, pp. 16–30.
37 Claudia Orange, *The Treaty of Waitangi*, p. 40.
38 Ruth Ross, op. cit., p. 20.
39 Chief Justice Martin, quoted in Ruth Ross, op. cit., p. 20.
40 Claudia Orange, op. cit., p. 41.
41 Loc. cit.
42 L. T. Buick, *The Treaty of Waitangi*, p. 128.
43 Ibid., p. 142.
44 W. Colenso, *The Signing of the Treaty of Waitangi*, p. 30.
45 Ibid., p. 32–33.
46 L. T. Buick, op. cit., p. 218.
47 Ruth Ross, op. cit., p. 27.
48 L. T. Buick, op. cit., p. 225.

Chapter 6

1 James Belich, *The New Zealand Wars*, p. 21.
2 Claudia Orange, *The Treaty of Waitangi*, p. 92.
3 G. W. Rusden, *Aureretanga*, p. 11.
4 Marais, *The Colonisation of New Zealand*, p. 118.
5 Raymond Firth, *Economics of the New Zealand Maori*, p. 449.
6 Waitangi Tribunal, *Muriwhenua Fishing Report*, p. 82.
7 Tony Simpson, *Te Riri Pakeha*, p. 96.

8 Harry Evison, *Ngai Tahu Land Rights*, p. 16.

9 Prue Toft, 'Modern Maori Enterprise', pp. 70–75.

10 Raymond Firth, op. cit., p. 448.

11 Lady Martin, *Our Maoris*, p. 76.

12 W. Swainson, *Auckland the Capital of New Zealand and the Country Adjacent*, p. 143.

13 Alfred Saunders, *History of New Zealand 1642-1861*, pp. 186–203.

14 Ibid., p. 227.

15 James Belich, op. cit., pp. 58–64.

16 Ibid., p. 66.

17 Harry Evison, op. cit., pp. 17–32.

18 Ibid., p. 21.

19 *AJHR* 1858 C No. 3 p. 12.

20 Ibid., pp. 9–10.

21 Ibid., p. 11.

22 Ibid., p12.

23 Harry Evison, op. cit., p. 26.

24 *AJHR* 1858, C No. 3 p. 20.

25 Ibid., p. 34.

26 *AJHR* 1858 E No. 4 p. 3.

27 Marais, op. cit., p. 296.

28 *AJHR* 1860 C No. 4 pp. 2-3.

29 *AJHR* 1858 C No. 5 p. 3.

30 Alfred Saunders, op. cit., p. 275.

31 Harold Miller, *Race Conflict in New Zealand*, p. 7.

32 Alan Ward, *A Show of Justice*, p. 95.

33 John Grace, *Tuwharetoa*, p. 445.

34 J. E. Gorst, *The Maori King*, p. 61.

35 Pei Te Hurinui Jones, *King Potatau*, p. 223.

36 Harold Miller, op. cit., p. 221.

37 Ibid., pp. 19–30.

38 Ibid., p. 33.

39 James Belich, op. cit., p. 92.

40 *AJHR* 1860 E No. 9 p. 24.

41 G. W. Rusden, op. cit., p. 21.

42 Ibid., p. 22.

43 Harold Miller, op. cit., p. 35.

Chapter 7

1 *AJHR* 1858 E No. 5 pp. 2–3.

2 Sir Keith Sinclair, *Origins of the Maori Wars*, p. 88.

3 Harold Miller, *Race Conflict in New Zealand*, p. 81.

4 Alan Ward, *A Show of Justice*, p. 136.

5 John Gorst, *The Maori King*, p. 213.

6 Alan Ward, op. cit., p. 133.

7 John Gorst, op. cit., p. 229.

8 Ibid., p. 234.
9 Sir Keith Sinclair, op. cit., p. 245.
10 *AJHR* 1863 Vol. 2 E No. 2 pp. 2–10.
11 James Belich, *The New Zealand Wars*, p. 119.
12 Loc. cit.
13 Harold Miller, op. cit., p. 71.
14 John Gorst, op. cit., p. 378.
15 Harold Miller, op. cit., p. 108.
16 Ibid., op. cit., p. 105.
17 *AJHR* 1863 A No. 8 p. 2.
18 Ibid., p. 1.
19 *AJHR* A No. 8A p. 1.
20 Ibid., p. 6-8.
21 James Belich, op. cit., p. 138.
22 Alfred Saunders, *History of New Zealand*, vol. 1 p. 93.
23 Alfred Saunders, op. cit. p. 113.
24 James Belich, op. cit., p. 144.
25 Ibid., p. 154.
26 Harold Miller, op. cit., p. 112.
27 James Belich, op. cit., p. 161.
28 Alfred Saunders, op. cit., p. 116.
29 John Grace, *Tuwharetoa*, p. 419.
30 *AJHR* 1864 E No. 2 p. 16.
31 Ibid., p. 18.
32 James Cowan, *The New Zealand Wars*, vol. 1 pp. 368–9.
33 Ibid., p. 391.
34 James Belich, op. cit., p. 172.
35 Ibid., pp. 178–88.
36 Alfred Saunders, op. cit., p. 119.
37 R. J. Walker, *The Canons of Maori Warfare*, p. 11
38 James Belich, op. cit., p. 82
39 R. J. Walker, op. cit., p. 11.
40 James Belich, op. cit., p. 188.
41 Alfred Saunders, op. cit., p. 122.
42 G. W. Rusden, *Aureretanga*, p. 40.
43 Michael King, *Te Puea*, p. 28–29.
44 D. P. Lyons, 'An Analysis of Three Prophet Movements', p. 56.
45 W. Greenwood, *The Upraised Hand*, pp. 1–80.
46 Tony Simpson, *Te Riri Pakeha*, pp. 179–182.
47 John Grace, op. cit., p. 417.
48 Ibid., p. 420.
49 James Belich, op. cit., p. 244.
50 Alfred Saunders, *A History of New Zealand*, vol. 2, p. 255.
51 James Belich, op. cit., p. 255.
52 W. H. Ross, *Te Kooti*, p. 30.
53 James Belich, op. cit., pp. 221–5.
54 Ibid., p. 225

55 W. H. Ross, op. cit., p. 56.
56 Judith Binney, *Mihaia*, pp. 9–10
57 James Belich, *I Shall Not Die*, pp. 242–6.

Chapter 8

1   Royal Commission Report, *The Maori Land Court*, p. 10.
2   B. Murton, 'Changing Patterns of Land Ownership in Poverty Bay', pp. 167–8.
3   Royal Commission Report, op. cit. p. 11.
4   *AJHR* 1884 vol. 2 G2. pp. 2–3.
5   M. P. K. Sorrenson, 'Land Purchase Methods and Their Effects on Maori Population', p. 187.
6   Ibid., p. 187.
7   Ibid., p. 190.
8   R. Heerdegen, 'Land for the Landless', p. 35.
9   J. K. Hunn, *Report on the Department of Maori Affairs*, p. 64.
10 *Report of Commission of Inquiry into Maori Reserved Land*, pp. 248–89, and p. 24.
11 Waitangi Tribunal, *Muriwhenua Fishing Report*, pp. 77–83.
12 Ibid., p. 83.
13 Ibid., p. 85.
14 Alan Ward, *A Show of Justice*, p. 98.
15 *AJHR* 1860 E No. 7. pp. 4–5.
16 Ibid., pp. 2–7.
17 S. F. McClean, 'Maori Representation', p. 5.
18 Ibid., p. 4.
19 NZPD 1867 vol. 1 Part 1 p. 460.
20 W. R. Hawkins, 'The Hon Duncan McIntyre as Minister of Maori Affairs', pp. 159–61.
21 J. M. Barrington, 'A Historical Review of Policies and Provisions', p. 28.
22 *AJHR* 1967 A No. 3. p. 1.
23 R. J. Walker, 'Educational Replanning for a Multicultural Society', p. 228.
24 Bruce Biggs, 'The Maori Language Past and Present', pp. 74–75.
25 Richard Benton, *Who Speaks Maori in New Zealand*, pp. 1–23.
    The Legal Status of the Maori Language, p. 1.
    The Maori Language in the Nineteen Seventies, p. 13.
26 Alan Ward, *A Show of Justice*, p. 101.
27 *AJHR* 1860 E No. 9 p. 21.
28 *AJHR* 1870 A No. 21 p. 13.
29 Alan Ward, op. cit., p. 210.
30 *AJHR* 1867 vol. 1 A No. 10 p. 4.
31 Ibid., p. 8.
32 *AJHR* 1869 vol. 1 A No. 22 pp. 3–4.
33 *AJHR* 1871 vol. 1 A No. 2A p. 28.
34 Paulo Freire, *Pedagogy of the Oppressed*, p. 21.
35 Paulo Freire, op. cit., p. 35.

36 *Te Wananga*, 1876 No. 19 Book 3, p. 237.
37 *Te Wananga*, 1876 No. 3 p. 22.
38 *Te Wananga*, 1876 No. 13 Book 3, p. 168.
39 *Te Wananga*, 1876 No. 19 Book 3, p. 234.
40 *Te Wananga*, 1877 No. 12, p. 111.
41 *Te Wananga*, 1876 No. 34, p. 364.
42 *Te Wananga*, 1877 No. 12, p. 111.
43 Claudia Orange, *The Treaty of Waitangi*, p. 192.
44 *AJHR* 1879 Session 2 G8 pp. 28–35.
45   Claudia Orange, op. cit., p. 194.
46 *AJHR* 1876 vol. 2 G-4 p. 2.
47 *AJHR* 1878 vol. 2 G3 p. 20.
48 Dick Scott, *Ask That Mountain*, p. 31.
49 *AJHR* 1881 G7 pp. 6–8.
50 Hazel Riseborough, *Days of Darkness*, p. 68.
51 *AJHR* 1881 G7 pp. 7–8.
52 Dick Scott, op. cit., p. 81.
53 Dick Scott, op. cit., p. 138.
54 Hazel Riseborough, op. cit., p. 164–5.
55 Ibid., p. 168.
56 Dick Scott, op. cit., p. 138.

Chapter 9

 1 *AJHR* 1883 A6 pp. 1–3.
 2 Loc. cit.
 3 G. W. Rusden, *Aureretanga*, p. 165.
 4 Ibid., p. 168.
 5 *Te Paki o Matariki*, 6:10:1892.
 6 Loc. cit.
 7 Report of the Assembly of Kotahitanga, pp. 14–15.
 8 *Maori Parliament 1892*, p. 10.
 9 Ibid., pp. 1–8.
10 Ibid., p. 26.
11 Ibid., pp. 72–73.
12 *Maori Parliament 1895*, p. 26.
13 John A. Williams, *Politics of the New Zealand Maori*, p. 56.
14 *Maori Parliament 1895*, p. 22
15 Michael King, *Te Puea*, p. 29.
16 *Te Paki o Matariki*, 1892, No. 6.
17 *Te Paki o Matariki*, July 1893.
18 Loc. cit.
19 Loc. cit.
20 *Te Paki o Matariki*, August 1895
21 *Maori Parliament 1895*, pp. 10–14.
22 *Te Paki o Matariki*, 24:12:1897
23 *Te Manukura 1923*, p. 33.

24 Sir Hugh Kawharu, *Maori Land Tenure*, p. 24.
25 *Report of the Royal Commission on the Maori Land Court 1980*, p. 12.
26 *New Zealand Year Book 1977*, p. 68.
27 Eric Ramsden, *Sir Apirana Ngata and Maori Culture*, p. 36.
28 *New Zealand Year Book 1977*, p. 68.
29 J. K. Hunn, *Report on Department of Maori Affairs*, p. 20.
30 Sir Peter Buck 'He Poroporoaki — A Farewell Message', *Sir Apirana Ngata Memorial Tribute*, p. 61.
31 Graham Butterworth, *Sir Apirana Ngata*, p. 6.
32 J. F. Cody, *Man of Two Worlds*, p. 26.
33 *Pipiwharauroa 1901*, No. 42 p. 10.
34 Ibid., No. 43 p. 13.
35 Ibid., No. 35 p. 3.
36 Loc. cit.
37 *Pipiwharauroa 1901*, No. 38 p. 2.
38 Graham Butterworth, op. cit., p. 10.
39 *Pipiwharauroa 1901*, No.39 p. 2.
40 Ibid., 1902 No. 48 p. 3.
41 Ibid., 1902 No. 49 p. 6
42 Graham Butterworth, op. cit., p. 11.
43 *Pipiwharauroa 1902*, No. 50 p. 6.
44 J. F. Cody, op. cit., p. 45.
45 *Pipiwharauroa 1902*, No. 52 p. 11.
46 Ibid., 1903 No. 64 p. 5.
47 Michael King, op. cit., p. 32.
48 John A. Williams, op. cit., pp. 123–4.
49 Sir Hugh Kawharu, op. cit., p. 25.
50 *Pipiwharauroa 1905*, No. 90 p. 2.
51 Ibid., 1903 No. 70 p. 2.
52 Ibid., 1904 No. 73 p. 10.
53 Norman Smith, *The Maori People and Us*, p. 197.
54 *Pipiwharauroa 1905*, No. 91 pp. 2–3.
55 Ibid., No. 92 pp. 1–2.
56 Graham Butterworth, op. cit., p. 11.
57 *Pipiwharauroa 1905*, No. 93 p. 2.
58 Ibid., 1906 No. 97 pp. 3–4.
59 Ibid., No. 98 p. 98.
60 Graham Butterworth, op. cit., p. 12.
61 Sir Hugh Kawharu, op. cit., p. 26.
62 *Pipiwharauroa 1909*, No. 139 p. 3.
63 Ibid., 1907 No. 107 p. 8
64 Prof. I. L. G. Sutherland, 'Crusade Through Parliament', *Sir Apirana Ngata Memorial Tribute*, p. 26.
65 Graham Butterworth, op. cit., p. 13.
66 Dick Scott, *Ask That Mountain*, p. 196.
67 Ibid., p. 197.
68 Paulo Freire, *Pedagogy of the Oppressed*, p. 126.

69 J. F. Cody, op. cit., p. 46.

70 Ibid., p. 65.

71 J. B. Condliffe, *Te Rangihiroa*, p. 113.

72 J. F. Cody, op. cit., p. 119.

73 Michael King, op. cit., p. 92.

74 J. A. Williams, op. cit., p. 94.

75 Judith Binney, *Mihaia*, pp. 18–68.

76 Ibid., p. 53.

77 Alan Ward, *A Show of Justice*, p. 283.

78 Judith Binney, op. cit., p. 61.

79 Ibid., p. 132.

80 J. M. Henderson, *Ratana*, pp. 1–71.

81 Ibid., p. 57.

82 *Te Whetu Marama 1932*, p. 11.

83 Ibid., p. 9.

Chapter 10

1 J. K. Hunn, *Report on the Department of Maori Affairs*, p. 19.

2 J. Larrain, *The Concept of Ideology*, p. 47.

3 Graham Butterworth, *Sir Apirana Ngata*, p. 13.

4 S. F. McClean, 'Maori Representation', p. 67.

5 Sir Peter Buck, 'He Poroporoaki — A Farewell Message', p. 66.

6 N. J. Pricket, 'The Archaeologist's Guide to the Maori Dwelling', p. 119.

7 Douglas Sutton, 'The Archaeology of Belief', p. 19.

8 Janet Davidson, *The Prehistory of New Zealand*, p. 153.

9 David Simmons, *Whakairo*, p. 14.

10 R. J. Walker, 'The Genesis of the Meeting House as a Cultural Symbol', pp. 16–17.

11 T. Barrow, *Maori Wood Sculpture of New Zealand*, p. 70.

12 Sir Keith Sinclair, 'He Tikanga Pakeke', p. 85.

13 A. Taylor, *Maori Folk Art*, p. 30.

14 David Simmons, op. cit., p. 121.

15 Michael King, *Te Puea*, pp. 18–23.

16 Eric Ramsden, *Sir Apirana Ngata and Maori Culture*, pp. 45–46.

17 Michael King, op. cit., p. 117.

18 Ibid., p. 136

19 Ibid., p. 142.

20 *Te Wananga*, 1930 pp. 128–38.

21 *Te Toa Takitini*, 1923 No. 23 p. 2.

22 Ibid., 1926 No. 54 p. 317.

23 Lady Martin, *Our Maoris*, p. 175.

24 *Te Toa Takitini*, 1926 No. 57 p. 338.

25 Ibid., 1926 No. 61 p. 454.

26 Ibid., 1926 No. 62 p. 468.

27 Ibid., 1928 No. 81 p. 774.

28 J. M. Barrington and T. H. Beaglehole, *Maori Schools in a Changing Society*, p. 206.

29 *Report of the Young Maori Conference 1939*, p. 24.

30 Sir Apirana Ngata, 'Introduction to *Nga Moteatea*'.

31 Paulo Freire, *Pedagogy of the Oppressed*, p. 148.

32 I. L. G. Sutherland, 'Crusade Through Parliament', p. 34.

33 Sir Apirana Ngata, Preface, *Nga Moteatea*, Part 1.

34 Bruce Biggs, 'The Maori Language Past and Present', p. 75.

35 Graham Butterworth, op. cit., pp. 26–27.

36 Ibid., p. 28.

37 J. F. Cody, *Man of Two Worlds*, p. 58.

38 J. M. Henderson, *Ratana*, p. 89.

39 *Report of the Young Maori Conference 1939*, p. 1.

40 Ibid., p. 11.

41 *Puao-Te-Ata-Tu*, p. 16.

42 J. K. Hunn, *Report on the Department of Maori Affairs*, p. 19.

43 W. D. Rose, *The Maori in the New Zealand Economy*, p. 38.

44 Joan Metge, *A New Maori Migration*, p. 128.

45 Joan Metge, *The Maoris of New Zealand*, pp. 93–84.

46 R. J. Walker, 'The Politics of Voluntary Association', p. 167.

47 Loc. cit.

48 R. J. Walker, 'Maoris in a Metropolis', pp. 301–11.

49 Op. cit., p. 365

50 *Report of Young Maori Conference*, p. 27.

51 Michael King, *Te Puea*, p. 224.

52 Michael King, *Whina*, p. 172.

53 Ibid., p. 178.

54 R. J. Walker, op. cit., pp. 324–5.

55 Ibid., p. 326

56 J. K. Hunn, op. cit., p. 24.

57 NZMC Minutes, 29:6:62.

58 Ibid., 7:3:64.

59 Ibid., 26:7:62.

60 Ibid., 8:3:64.

61 Ibid., 26:9:64.

62 Loc. cit.

63 *Report of the Committee of Inquiry into Laws Affecting Maori Land and Powers
    of the Maori Land Court 1965*, pp. 8–9.

64 Loc. cit.

65 *Report on Conference on Recommended Changes in Maori Legislation*, 1966
    p. 1.

66 *Maori Education Foundation Report* 1966, p. 6.

67 Department of Social Welfare, *Juvenile Crime in New Zealand*, pp. 11–15.

68 *Report of the Young Leaders Conference* 1970, pp. 17–34.

69 Paulo Freire, op. cit., p. 60.

70 Ibid.

71 Sir Henry Ngata, 'The Treaty of Waitangi and Land: Parts of the Current
    Law in Contravention of the Treaty', pp. 49–57.

72 Michael King, *Whina*, p. 2–27.

73 F. D. Fenton, Chief Judge of the Native Land Court, *Important Judgments 1866-1879*, Judgement at Orakei, pp. 53–96.

74 Robert Stout and A. T. Ngata, 'Commission of Inquiry into Native Lands', *AJHR* 1908 vol. IV G-1P, p. 5.

75 Waitangi Tribunal, *Orakei Report* 1987, p. 4.

76 R. Kennedy, 'Commission of Inquiry into Lands at Orakei', *AJHR* 1939 vol. II G6, p. 35.

77 Justice J. Speight, *Bastion Point Judgment*, pp. 24–25.

Chapter 11

1 *Craccum*, AUSA newspaper, 6:5:71.

2 *Auckland Star*, 1:5:79.

3 *New Zealand Herald*, 3:5:79.

4 *Auckland Star*, 28:5:79.

5 R. J. Walker, 'Korero', *New Zealand Listener*, 4:8:79.

6 Kayleen Hazlehurst, *Racial Conflict and Resolution in New Zealand*, p. 11.

7 *Auckland Star*, 10:4:80.

8 *New Zealand Herald*, 10:4:80.

9 Ibid.

10 *Race Against Time*, p. 12.

11 *Auckland Star*, 5:5:80.

12 *New Zealand Herald*, 6:11:80.

13 Ibid., 2:9:80.

14 *New Zealand Herald*, 3:9:79.

15 Paulo Freire, *Pedagogy of the Oppressed*, p. 126.

16 *New Zealand Herald*, 4:9:79.

17 *Auckland Star*, 10:11:79.

18 Ibid., 7:11:79.

19 *New Zealand Herald*, 7:11:79.

20 *Auckland Star*, 14:11:79.

21 Ibid., 17:11:79.

22 *New Zealand Herald*, 20:11:79.

23 Ibid., 9:6:80.

24 Ibid., 7:2:81.

25 *Auckland Star*, 6:7:81

26 *New Zealand Herald*, 7:2:81.

27 *Auckland Star*, 10:2:81.

28 *New Zealand Herald*, 8:12:81.

29 Ibid., 4:2:81.

30 *Auckland Star*, 8:2:82.

31 *New Zealand Herald*, 8:2:82.

32 *Zealandia*, 7:2:82.

33 *Auckland Star*, 31:1:83.

34 *New Zealand Herald*, 7:2:83.

35 *Auckland Star*, 16:3:83.

36 Ibid., 12:7:83.

37 *Te Hikoi Ki Waitangi*, pp. 14–15.

38 Pat Hohepa and Atareta Poananga, 'The Road Back to Aotearoa', pp. 29–30.

39 Paulo Freire, *Pedagogy of the Oppressed*, p. 32–33

40 Kara Puketapu, 'Reform From Within', p. 4.

41 Department of Maori Affairs 1983 Annual Report, p. 10.

42 Ibid., p. 6.

43 Richard Benton, *Who Speaks Maori in New Zealand?*, p. 13.

44 Ibid., pp. 22–23.

45 Department of Maori Affairs 1983 Annual Report, p. 5.

46 Government Review of Kohanga Reo 1988, p. 19.

47 R. J. Walker, *Nga Tumanako*, Report of the Maori Educational Development Conference 1984, p. 16.

48 Ibid., pp. 16–17.

49 Maori Education: Report of the National Advisory Committee on Maori Education 1971.

50 R. J. Walker, op. cit., p. 27.

51 Mitzi Nairn, 'Racism as a Barrier in the Delivery of Health Care', p. 1.

52 Judith Simon, 'The Ideological Rationale for the Denial of Maoritanga', pp. 5–7.

53 Maiki Marks, 'The Frustrations of Being a Maori Language Teacher', p. 12.

54 David Hughes, 'The Examination System: The Cause of Unnecessary Failure', p. 30.

55 R. J. Walker, *Nga Kaupapa o Mana Motuhake*, The Manifesto of Mana Motuhake 1981, p. 4.

56 Donna Awatere, *Maori Sovereignty*, p. 10.

57 Looking Towards the 1980s: Submissions on the Maori Affairs Bill, NZMC, p. 4.

58 A Discussion Paper on Future Maori Development and Legislation, New Zealand Maori Council 1980, pp. 1–10.

59 *Kaupapa*, New Zealand Maori Council, p. 3.

Chapter 12

1 Waitangi Tribunal report *On an Application by Aila Taylor For and on Behalf of Te Atiawa Tribe in Relation to Fishing Grounds in the Waitara District* (Appendix).

2 Ibid., p. 9.

3 Ibid., pp. 12–13.

4 Ibid., p. 5.

5 *New Zealand Herald*, 29:3:83.

6 *Auckland Star*, 31:3:83.

7 Ibid., 18:4:83.

8 *New Zealand Herald*, 30:3:83.

9 Ibid., 8:4:83.

10 Nganeko Minhinnick, 1981 on behalf of Ngati Te Ata as Appellant, and Auckland Regional Authority acting as Auckland Regional Water Board as Respondent and New Zealand Steel Limited as Applicant, Before the

Planning Tribunal in the Matter of the Water and Soil Conservation Act 1967, p. 3.

11 *NZTPA Journal* vol. 9 Part 60.

12 Waitangi Tribunal, *Finding of the Waitangi Tribunal on the Manukau Claim 1985*, pp. 25–85.

13 Arapera Blank, Haare Williams and Manuka Henare, *He Korero Mo Waitangi 1985*, p. 4.

14 *New Zealand Herald*, 23:3:88.

15 *Report of the Department of Maori Affairs*, 1983 p. 9.

16 *Maori Economic Development Summit Conference 1984*, p. 5.

17 Richard Hovis, *Maoritanga and the American Retail Market Place*, pp. 125–44.

18 Report from the Maori Economic Development Conference, *He Kawenata*, pp. 2–3.

19 Report of the Ministerial Review Committee on the Department of Maori Affairs, 1985, Chairman R. Mahuta, p. 53.

20 *New Zealand Herald*, 18:12:86.

21 Ibid., 26:12:86.

22 Ibid., 18:12:86 and *Auckland Star*, 17:12:86.

23 *New Zealand Herald*, 18:12:86.

24 *Auckland Star*, 18:12:86 and 21:12:86.

25 *New Zealand Herald*, 18:12:86.

26 Ibid., 19:12:86.

27 *Auckland Star*, 18:12:86.

28 *New Zealand Herald*, 19:12:86.

29 Ibid., 10:2:87.

30 *Auckland Star*, 10:2:87.

31 Ibid., 11:12:87.

32 *New Zealand Herald*, 9:12:87.

33 *Auckland Star*, 11:12:87.

34 An Introduction to Tamaki Maori Development Authority, 1989, p. 11.

35 Ibid., p. 7.

36 *Auckland Star*, 11:6:89.

37 *Te Weehi v Regional Fisheries Officer* [1986] 1 *NZLR* 680.

38 *Nga Mamaetanga O Te Iwi Maori*, Report of the meeting at Turangawaewae 1987, p. 39.

39 *New Zealand Maori Council v Attorney General* [1987] 1 *NZLR* 641.

40 Judgment of Justice P. Cooke *Between the New Zealand Maori Council and Her Majesty's Attorney General CA 54/87*, p. 28.

41 New Zealand Maori Council v Attorney General CA/87 Judgment of J. Bisson 1987, p. 13.

42 *Kaupapa*, New Zealand Maori Council pp. 3–13

43 Waitangi Tribunal, *Finding of the Waitangi Tribunal on the Manukau Claim*, pp. 87–95.

44 Ibid., p. 78.

45 Huakina Development Trust v Waikato Valley Authority and R. P. and S. J.

Bowater, Judgment of J. Chilwell in the High Court of New Zealand,
Wellington Registry M 430/86.

46 Waitangi Tribunal, *Record of Hearing of Claim by Sir Charles Bennett and
Others Asking that the Nutrient Pipeline to the Kaituna River Not Proceed*
1985, pp. 6–15.

47 Waitangi Tribunal, *Finding of the Waitangi Tribunal Relating to Te Reo Maori
and a Claim Lodged by Huirangi Waikerepuru and Nga Kaiwhakapumau i te
Reo Incorporated Society* 1986, p. 29.

48 Commissioner for the Environment, *Environmental Management and the
Principles of the Treaty of Waitangi* 1988, pp. 1–3.

49 *The Broadcasting Future of New Zealand*, Report of the Committee on
Broadcasting 1973, p. 89.

50 *Report of the Maori Economic Development Commission on Broadcasting in
New Zealand* 1985, p. 30.

51 Application for Television Warrant by Aotearoa Broadcasting Systems
(NZMC files) 1985, p. 2.

52 Submission by Whatarangi Winiata on Behalf of Aotearoa Broadcasting
Systems (NZMC files) 1985, pp. 1–7.

53 Whatarangi Winiata, Background Note on the Agreement Between the
BCNZ and ABS (NZMC files).

54 George Habib, *Korero Piri Ki Tangaroa*, Department of Maori Affairs, 1983,
p. 6.

55 Ibid., p. 14.

56 Law Commission, *The Treaty of Waitangi and Maori Fisheries* 1989, p. 17.

57 W. Berryman, *Auckland Star*, 19:10:86.

58 Law Commission, op. cit., p. 17.

59 Waerete Norman, The Muriwhenua Claim, in *Waitangi*, edited by I. H.
Kawharu, pp. 183–5.

60 Waitangi Tribunal, Chairman's Comments in Chambers on Muriwhenua
Fisheries Claim 30 September 1987.

61 Reasons For the Order of Justice J Greig, pp. 2–8 (NZMC papers with
Luckie Hain Kennard & Slater, Wellington).

62 Ngai Tahu Maori Trust Board, New Zealand Maori Council and others v the
Attorney General (1987) in Waitangi Tribunal *Muriwhenua Report*, 1988, pp.
307–14.

63 *Reports of the Joint Working Group on Maori Fisheries*, pp. 1–6 and pp. 1–7.

64 *New Zealand Herald*, 28:9:88.

65 Ibid., 5:10:88.

66 Paulo Freire, op. cit., p. 60.

67 Oliver Sutherland, 'Justice and Race: A Monocultural System in a
Multicultural Society', Paper presented to the New Zealand Race Relations
Council Conference 1973, p. 4.

68 Auckland Committee on Racism and Discrimination, an undated paper
defining racism.

69 *Institutional Racism in the Department of Social Welfare Tamaki-Makau-Rau*
1984, pp. 7–40.

70 *Puao-Te-Ata-Tu*, p. 21.

71 Ibid., p. 24.
72 Ibid., p. 9.
73 Commissioner for the Environment, op. cit., p. 1.
74 Waitangi Tribunal, *Orakei Report* 1987, pp. 194–195.
75 *New Zealand Herald*, 27:11:87.
76 Loc. cit.
77 Ibid., 2:7:88.
78 Ibid., 4:12:87.
79 Ibid., 13:2:88.
80 Ibid., 21:1:88.
81 Ibid., 25:1:88.
82 Ibid., 14:3:89.
83 Commissioner for the Environment op. cit., pp. 2-3.
84 *New Zealand Herald*, 21:1:87.
85 Ibid., 15:4:88.
86 Ibid., 10:11:87.
87 Ibid., 27:11:87.
88 Ibid., 22:9:88.
89 Ibid., 2:12:88.
90 Ibid., 19:9:88.
91 Loc. cit.
92 Ibid., 5:10:88.
93 *New Zealand Herald*, 7:12:88.
94 *Auckland Star*, 14:7:88.
95 *New Zealand Herald*, 23:9:88.
96 See Introduction *Nga Mamaetanga o te Iwi Maori*, op. cit.
97 Report on Department of Maori Affairs, Mrs Bazely Deputy Chairperson State Services Commission, p. 8.
98 *He Tirohanga Rangapu: Partnership Perspectives*, 1988, Department of Maori Affairs, p. 9.
99 *New Zealand Herald*, 24:4:88.
100 Ibid., 28:7:88.
101 *Te Urupare Rangapu: Partnership Response* 1988, p. 1.
102 Ibid., p. 3.

BIBLIOGRAPHY

Appendices to the Journals of the House of Representatives, Auckland and Wellington, 1858–1939.

Alpers, Anthony, 1964, *Maori Myths*, Longman Paul, Auckland.

Awatere, Donna., 1984, 'Maori Sovereignty' *Broadsheet*, Auckland.

Barrington, J. M., 1970, 'A Historical Review of Policies and Provisions', in *Introduction to Maori Education*, edited by J. Ewing and J. Shallcrass, New Zealand University Press, Price Milburn, Wellington.

Barrington, J. M. and Beaglehole, T. H., 1974, *Maori Schools in a Changing Society*, New Zealand Council For Educational Research, Christchurch.

Barrow, T., 1969, *Maori Wood Sculpture of New Zealand*, A. H. & A. W. Reed, Wellington.

Belich, James, 1986, *The New Zealand Wars*, Auckland University Press, Auckland.

————, 1989, *I Shall Not Die*, Allen and Unwin Port/Nicholson Press, Wellington.

Benton, Richard, 1979, *Who Speaks Maori in New Zealand?*, New Zealand Council for Educational Research, Wellington.

————, 1979, *The Maori Language in the Nineteen Seventies*, New Zealand Council for Educational Research, Wellington.

————, 1979, *The Legal Status of the Maori Language*, New Zealand Council for Educational Research, Wellington.

Best, Elsdon, 1974, *The Maori As He Was*, Government Printer, Wellington.

————, 1925, *Tuhoe*, Polynesian Society, Avery & Sons, New Plymouth.

Biggs, Bruce, 1960, 'The Maori Language Past and Present', in *The Maori People in the Nineteen Sixties*, edited by Erik Schwimmer, Blackwood & Janet Paul, Auckland.

Binney, Judith, 1968, *The Legacy of Guilt*, University of Auckland, Oxford University Press.

————, 1969, 'Christianity and the Maoris to 1840', *New Zealand Journal of History* Vol. 3 No. 2.

————, 1979, *Mihaia*, Oxford University Press, Wellington.

———— and Chaplin, G., 1986, *Nga Morehu: The Survivors*, Oxford University Press, Auckland.

Blank, Arapera, Henare, M. and Williams, H., 1985, *He Korero Mo Waitangi*, He Tohu Aroha Ki Nga Tipuna, Te Runanga o Waitangi, Auckland.

Buck, Sir Peter, 1950, *The Coming of the Maori*, Maori Purposes Fund Board, Whitcombe & Tombs, Wellington.

————, 1951, 'He Poroporoaki — A Farewell Message', in *Sir Apirana Ngata Memorial Tribute*, Polynesian Society, Avery Press, New Plymouth.

————, 1985, *Vikings of the Sunrise*, Greenwood Press, Westport, Connecticut.

Buick, T. L., 1936, *The Treaty of Waitangi*, Thomas Avery & Sons, New Plymouth, Capper Press Reprint 1976, Christchurch.

Butterworth, Graham, 1968, *Sir Apirana Ngata*, A. H. & A. W. Reed, Wellington.

Cody, J. F., 1953, *Man of Two Worlds*, A. H. & A. W. Reed, Wellington.

Colenso, William, 1890, *The Authentic and Genuine History of the Signing of the Treaty of Waitangi*, Government Printers, Wellington.

Condliffe, J. B., 1971, *Te Rangihiroa*, Whitcombe & Tombs, Wellington.

Cowan, James, 1983, *The New Zealand Wars*, Vols 1 and 2, Government Printer, Wellington.

Davidson, Janet, 1984, *The Prehistory of New Zealand*, Longman Paul, Auckland.

Duff, Roger, 1977, *The Moa-Hunter Period of Maori Culture*, Government Printer, Wellington.

Elsmore, Bronwyn, 1985, *Like Them That Dream*, Tauranga Moana Press.

Evison, Harry C., 1987, *Ngai Tahu Land Rights*, Ngai Tahu Maori Trust Board, Christchurch.

Facsimiles of the Declaration of Independence and the Treaty of Waitangi, 1877, reprint Government Printer, 1976.

Fenton, F. D., *Important Judgments 1866–1879*, Chief Judge of the Native Land Court.

Firth, Raymond, 1959, *Economics of the New Zealand Maori*, Whitcombe & Tombs, Wellington.

Freire, Paulo, 1972, *Pedagogy of the Oppressed*, Penguin Books, Harmondsworth.

Gorst, Sir John E., 1864, *The Maori King*, Macmillan, London.

Grace, John, 1959, *Tuwharetoa*, A. H. & A. W. Reed, Wellington.

Green, Roger, 1970, *A Review of the Prehistoric Sequence in the Auckland Province*, 2nd ed. University Bookshop, Dunedin.

Greenwood, W., 1980, *The Upraised Hand*, Polynesian Society, University of Auckland.

Grey, Sir George, 1953, *Nga Mahi a Nga Tupuna*, Maori Purposes Fund Board, Wellington.

Habib, G., 1987, *Korero Piri Ki Tangaroa*, Maori Economic Development Commission and Department of Maori Affairs, Wellington.

————, 1987, Submission to the Waitangi Tribunal re the Muriwhenua Fisheries Claim, Kaitaia, Christchurch.

Harre, J., 1966, *Maori and Pakeha*, A. H. & A. W. Reed, Wellington.

Harrison, Pine, 'The Traditions of the Ngati Porou Tribe', unpublished paper.

Hazlehurst, K., 1988, *Racial Conflict and Resolution in New Zealand*, Peace Research Centre, Australian National University, Canberra.

Hawkins, W. R., 1975, 'The Hon Duncan McIntyre as Minister of Maori Affairs', MA thesis, University of Auckland.

Henderson, J. M., 1972, *Ratana*, Polynesian Society Memoir, A. H. & A. W. Reed, Wellington.

Heerdegen, R., 1967, 'Land for the Landless', *New Zealand Geographer*, Vol. 23 No. 1.

Hohepa, P. and Poananga, A., 1984, 'The Road Back to Aotearoa', in *Te Hikoi ki Waitangi*, Waitangi Action Committee.

Houghton, Philip, 1980, *The First New Zealanders*, Hodder & Stoughton, Auckland.

Hovis, R., 1983, 'Maoritanga and the The American Retail Market Place', Communications Research and Development Corporation, Georgetown Station, Washington DC.

Hughes, D., 1983, 'The Examination System: The Cause of Unnecessary Failure', *New Zealand Counselling & Guidance Journal*, Vol. 5 No. 1.

Jones, P. T. H., 1959, *King Potatau*, Polynesian Society, Wellington.

Kawharu, Ian Hugh, 1977, *Maori Land Tenure*, Oxford University Press.

Keene, Florence, 1975, *Tai Tokerau*, Whitcoulls, Auckland.

Kelly, Leslie G., 1949, *Tainui*, Polynesian Society, Wellington, Capper Press Reprint 1980, Christchurch.

King, Michael, 1977, *Te Puea*, Hodder & Stoughton, Auckland.

————, 1983, *Whina*, Hodder & Stoughton, Auckland.

Kyselka, W., 1987, *An Ocean in Mind*, University of Hawaii Press, Honolulu.

Larrain, J., 1979, *The Concept of Ideology*, Hutchison, London.

Lewis, David, 1972, *We The Navigators*, A. H. & A. W. Reed, Wellington.

Lyall, Alfred C., 1979, *Whakatohea*, A. H. & A. W. Reed, Wellington.

Lyons, D. P., 1975, 'An Analysis of Three Prophet Movements', in *Conflict and Compromise*, edited by I. H. Kawharu, A. H. & A. W. Reed, Wellington.

McClean, S. F., 1967, 'Maori Representation 1905–1948', MA thesis, University of Auckland.

————, 1988, *Te Urupare Rangapu*, Partnership Response, Department of Maori Affairs, Wellington.

Marais, J. S., 1927, *The Colonisation of New Zealand*, Oxford University Press.

Marks, Maiki, 1984, 'The Frustrations of Being a Maori Language Teacher', in *Nga Tumanako, Maori Educational Conference 1984*, NZMC & CCE, University of Auckland.

Martin, Lady, 1884, *Our Maoris*, E. & J. B. Young, New York.

Metge, J., 1964, *A New Maori Migration*, University of London, Athlone Press, Melbourne University Press.

————, 1967, *The Maoris of New Zealand*, Routledge & Kegan Paul, London.

Miller, Harold, 1966, *Race Conflict in New Zealand*, Blackwood & Janet Paul, Auckland.

Minhinnick, N., 1981, Before the Planning Tribunal in the matter of the Water and Soil Conservation Act 1967 Between Nganeko Minhinnick on behalf of Ngaati Te Ata and Auckland Regional Authority acting as Auckland Regional Water Board and New Zealand Steel Limited.

Mitchell, J. H., 1972, *Takitimu*, A. J. & A. W. Reed, Wellington.

Munz, P. (edit.), 1969, *The Feel of Truth*, A. H. & A. W. Reed, Wellington.

Murton, B., 1966, 'Changing Patterns of Land Ownership in Poverty Bay', *New Zealand Geographic*, Vol. 22.

Nairn, M., 1984, Racism as a Barrier in the Delivery of Health Care, Maori Health and Cultural Awareness Programme, CCE, University of Auckland.

New Zealand Depart. of Maori Affairs, 1988, *He Tirohanga Rangapu*, Partnership Perspectives, Department of Maori Affairs, Wellington.

New Zealand Maori Council, 1966, Report of Conference on Recommended

Changes in Maori Land Legislation, New Zealand Maori Council, and Extension Department, University of Auckland.

Ngata, A. T., 1959, *Nga Moteatea*, Polynesian Society, A. H. & A. W. Reed, Wellington.

Ngata, H., 1972, 'The Treaty of Waitangi and Land: Parts of The Current Law In Contravention Of The Treaty', in *The Treaty of Waitangi its Origins and Significance*, Extension Department, Victoria University, Wellington.

Norman, W., 1989, 'The Muriwhenua Claim', in *Waitangi*, edited by I. H. Kawharu, Oxford University Press, Auckland.

————, 1980, Looking towards the 1980s, Submissions on the Maori Affairs Bill, New Zealand Maori Council, Wellington.

————, 1980, A Discussion Paper on Future Maori Develpment and Legislation, Legislative Review Committee, New Zealand Maori Council, Wellington.

————, 1983, *Kaupapa*, New Zealand Maori Council, Wellington.

Oppenheim, Roger, 1973, *Maori Death Customs*, A. H. & A. W. Reed, Wellington.

Orange, Claudia, 1987, *The Treaty of Waitangi*, Allen & Unwin/Port Nicholson Press, Wellington.

Parsonson, G. S., 1963, 'The settlement of Oceania', in *Polynesian Navigation*, Polynesian Society, A. H. & A. W. Reed, Wellington.

Pohuhu, N., 1863, Manuscript, in *Te Wananga*, Maori Purposes Fund Board, Whitcombe & Tombs, Wellington.

Polynesian Society, 1951, *Sir Apirana Ngata Memorial Tribute*, Polynesian Society, Wellington.

Pricket, N. J., 1979, 'Prehistoric Occupation in the Moikau Valley, Palliser Bay', in *Prehistoric Man in Palliser Bay*, edited by B. F. Leach and H. M. Leach, National Museum of New Zealand, Bulletin 21.

————, 1982, 'An Archaeologist's Guide to the Maori Dwelling', *NZJA*.

Puketapu, K., 1982, 'Reform From Within', Department of Maori Affairs, Wellington.

————, 1982, Decisions, Tu Tangata Wananga Whakatauira, Department of Maori Affairs, Wellington.

Ramsden, Eric, 1948, *Sir Apirana Ngata and Maori Culture*, A. H. & A. W. Reed, Wellington.

Reports, 1892, Assembly of Kotahitanga.

————, 1892, *Maori Parliament*.

————, 1895, *Maori Parliament*.

————, 1939, *Young Maori Conference*, Auckland University College.

————, 1960, *Report on Department of Maori Affairs*, J. K. Hunn, Government Printer, Wellington.

————, 1963, *New Zealand Year Book*, Government Printer, Wellington.

————, 1965, *Report of the Committee of Inquiry into Laws Affecting Maori Land and Powers of the Maori Land Court*, I. Pritchard and H. T. Waetford.

————, 1966, Fifth Annual Report, *Maori Education Foundation*, Wellington.

————, 1970, *The Young Maori Leaders Conference*, University of Auckland.

————, 1971, National Advisory Committee on Maori Education.

————, 1973, *The Broadcasting Future for New Zealand*, Report of the Committee on Broadcasting.

————, 1973, *Juvenile Crime in New Zealand*, Department of Social Welfare, Government Printer, Wellington.

————, 1974, *Report of the Commission of Inquiry into Reserved Land*, Government Printer, Wellington.

————, 1977, *New Zealand Year Book 1977*, Government Printer, Wellington.

————, 1980, *The Maori Land Courts*, Report of the Royal Commission of Inquiry.

————, 1980, *Racial Harmony in New Zealand*, Human Rights Commission, Auckland.

————, 1982, *Race Against Time*, Race Relations Conciliator, Human Rights Commission, Wellington.

————, 1983, *Department of Maori Affairs Annual Report*, Wellington.

————, 1984, *Te Hikoi Ki Waitangi*, Waitangi Action Committee, Auckland.

————, 1984, *Maori Economic Development Summit Conference* Background Papers, Department of Maori Affairs, Wellington

————, 1984, *He Kawenata*, Department of Maori Affairs, Wellington.

————, 1985, *Report of the Maori Economic Development Commission on Maori Broadcasting in New Zealand*, Department of Maori Affairs.

————, 1985, *Institutionalised Racism in the Department of Social Welfare Tamaki-Makau-Rau.*

————, 1986, *Puao-Te Ata-Tu*, Report of the Ministerial Advisory Committee on a Maori Perspective for the Department of Social Welfare, Wellington.

————, 1988, *Joint Working Group on Maori Fisheries.*

————, 1988, *Environmental Management and the Principles of the Treaty of Waitangi*, Helen R. Hughes, Commissioner for the Environment, Wellington.

————, 1988, *Government Review of Kohanga Reo.*

————, 1989, *An Introduction to the Tamaki Maori Development Authority*, Auckland.

————, 1989, *The Treaty of Waitangi and Maori Fisheries*, Law Commission, Wellington.

Riseborough, Hazel, 1989, *Days of Darkness*, Allen & Unwin/Port Nicholson Press, Wellington.

Rose, W. D., 1967, *The Maori in the New Zealand Economy*, Department of Industry and Commerce, Wellington.

Ross, Ruth, 1972, 'The Treaty on the Ground', in *The Treaty of Waitangi, its Origins and Significance*, Department of University Extension, Victoria University, Wellington.

Ross, W. H., 1966, *Te Kooti Rikirangi*, Collins, Auckland.

Rusden, G. W., 1974, *Aureretanga*, Hakaprint, Cannon's Creek.

Salmond, Anne, 1976, *Hui*, 2nd ed., Reed Methuen, Auckland.

Saunders, Alfred, 1896, *History of New Zealand 1642–1861*, Vols 1 and 2, Whitcombe & Tombs Ltd, Wellington.

Schwimmer, E. (editor), 1968, *The Maori People in the Nineteen Sixties*, Blackwood & Janet Paul, Auckland.

Scott, Dick, 1975, *Ask That Mountain*, Heinemann/Southern Cross, Auckland.

Sharp, A., 1956, *Ancient Voyagers in the Pacific*, Polynesian Society, Avery Press, New Plymouth.

Shaw, John, 1852, *A Tramp to the Diggings*, Bentley, London.

Shirres, Michael, 1977, 'The Relationship of the Moriori language to the Maori language', unpublished paper, University of Auckland, p. 13.

Simmons, D. R., 1976, *The Great New Zealand Myth*, A. H. & A. W. Reed, Wellington.

————, 1985, *Whakairo*, Oxford University Press, Auckland.

Simon, Judith, 1984, 'The Ideological Rationale for the Denial of Maoritanga', in *Nga Tumanako*, Maori Educational Development Conference 1984, NZMC and CCE, University of Auckland.

Simpson, Tony, 1979, *Te Riri Pakeha*, Alister Taylor, Martinborough.

Sinclair, Keith, 1957, *Origins of the Maori Wars*, New Zealand University Press, Wellington.

————, 1959, *A History of New Zealand*, Penguin Books, Harmondsworth.

————, 1969, 'He Tikanga Pakeke', in *The Feel of Truth*, edited by P. Munz, A. H. & A. W. Reed, Wellington.

Smith, Norman, 1948, *The Maori People and Us*, Maori Purposes Fund Board, A. H. & A. W. Reed, Wellington.

Smith, S. Percy, 1904, *Hawaiki*, Whitcombe & Tombs, Wellington.

————, 1907, 'History and Traditions of the Taranaki Coast', in *Journal of the Polynesian Society*, Vol. XVI.

————, 1910, *Tales of the Taranaki Coast*, Polynesian Society, Thomas Avery, New Plymouth.

————, 1910, *Maori Wars of the Nineteenth Century*, Whitcombe & Tombs, Wellington.

Sorrenson, M. P. K., 1956, 'Land Purchase Methods and Their Effects on the Maori Population 1865–1901', *Journal of the Polynesian Society*, Vol. 65 No. 3.

Speight, G. E., 1978, *Bastion Point Judgment*, Department of Lands and Survey.

Stannard, David E., 1989, *Before the Horror*, University of Hawaii Press, Honolulu.

Stafford, D. M., 1967, *Te Arawa*, A. H. & A. W. Reed, Wellington.

Sutherland, I. L. G., 1951, 'Crusade Through Parliament', in *Sir Apirana Ngata Memorial Tribute*, Polynesian Society, Avery Press, New Plymouth.

Sutherland, O. R. W. and Others, 1973, 'Justice and Race: A Monocultural System in a Monocultural Society', Report to the New Zealand Race Relations Council Annual Conference.

Sutton, D., 1980, 'A Culture History of the Chatham Islands', in the *Journal of the Polynesian Society*, Vol. 89.

————, 1985, 'The Whence of the Moriori', in *The New Zealand Journal of History*, Vol. 19 No. 1.

————, 1989, 'The Archaeology of Belief', publication pending in *A Man and a Half*, edited by A. Pawley, University of Auckland.

Swainson, W., 1853, *Auckland the Capital of New Zealand and the Country Adjacent*, Smith Elder & Co., London.

Taylor, Alan, 1988, *Maori Folk Art*, Century Hutchinson, Auckland.

Toft, Prue, 1984, 'Modern Maori Enterprise', MA thesis, University of Auckland.

Turner, A. R., 1985, 'The Changing Basis of Decision-Making, Is Reason Sufficient?' *New Zealand Engineering*, April 1985.

Vayda, A. P., 1960, *Maori Warfare*, Polynesian Society, Avery Press, New Plymouth.

Waitangi Tribunal: Reports, 1978, *Claim by T. E. Kirkwood* on behalf of the Waikato sub-tribes served by Whatapaka.

————, 1983, Findings and Recommendations of the Waitangi Tribunal on the *Application by Aila Taylor for and on behalf of the Ati Awa Tribe* in Relation to Fishing Grounds in the Waitara District, Justice Department, Wellington.

————, 1984, Record of Hearing *Kaituna Claim* by Sir Charles Bennett and others, 1984.

————, 1985, Findings of the Waitangi Tribunal on the *Manukau Claim*.

————, 1986, Finding of the Waitangi Tribunal Relating to *Te Reo Maori Claim*, Lodged by Huirangi Waikerepuru and Nga Kaiwhakapumau i te Reo Incorporated Society, 1986.

————, 1987, *Orakei Report*.

————, 1987, Waitangi Tribunal Chairman's Comments in Chambers, Muriwhenua Fisheries Claim, 30 September 1987.

————, 1987, New Zealand Maori Council and Another v the Attorney-General reported in the Waitangi Tribunal *Muriwhenua Fishing Report* pp. 303-7.

————, 1988, *Muriwhenua Fishing Report*.

————, 1988, Ngai Tahu Maori Trust Board, and Others v Attorney-General [1987] reported in Waitangi Tribunal 1988.

Walker, R. J., 1970, 'Maoris in a Metropolis', PhD thesis, University of Auckland.

————, 1975, 'The Politics of Voluntary Association', in *Conflict and Compromise*, edited by I. H. Kawharu, A. H. & A. W. Reed, Wellington.

————, 1979, 'Korero', *New Zealand Listener*, 4:8:79.

————, 1980, 'Maori Adult Education', in *Towards a Learning Society*, edited by R. Boshier, Learning Press, Vancouver.

————, 1980, 'Educational Replanning for a Multicultural Society', in *Schools in New Zealand Society*, edited by G. H. Robinson and B. T. O'Rourke, Longman Paul, Auckland.

———— (edit), 1981, *Nga Kaupapa o Mana Motuhake*, Manifesto of Mana Motuhake.

———— (edit), 1984, *Nga Tumanako, Maori Educational Development Conference*, New Zealand Maori Council, and CCE, University of Auckland.

————, 1987, *Nga Mamae o te Iwi*, Report of the hui, at Tuurangawaewae, New Zealand Maori Council and Te Roopu Whakawhanaunga i Nga Haahi.

————, 1988, 'The Canons of Maori Warfare', unpublished paper read at the Stout Research Centre, Victoria University, Wellington.

————, 1989, 'The Genesis of the Meeting House as a Cultural Symbol', paper read to Staff Seminar, Anthropology Department, University of Auckland.

Ward, Alan, 1973, *A Show of Justice*, Auckland University Press.

Williams, J. A., 1969, *Politics of the New Zealand Maori*, Auckland University Press.

Auckland Star.
Craccum.
New Zealand Herald.
Pipiwharauroa.
Te Manukura.
Te Paki o Matariki.
Te Toa Takitini.
Te Wananga 1876–1877, Henare Tomoana, printed by Henare Hira, Napier.
Te Wananga 1929, Vol. 1 No. 2. Maori Purposes Fund Board, Wellington.
Te Wananga 1930.
Te Whetu Marama, 16:4:1932.

INDEX

Aborigines Protection Society, 120, 125, 143–4
Activists, modern Maori, 209–36
Activists, Pakeha, 220–1, 233–4, 235, 277–81
Agriculture, Maori, development of, 29, 32–3, 100
Akaroa, 97
Amos, Phil, 211
Aotea, 35–6, 44–5, 48, 52
Aotearoa Broadcasting Systems, 270–2
Arawa, 44–6, 47, 50
Arawa people, 48, 55; claim to lake beds, 191; and Kaituna River claim, 267–8; and MIL, 257
Archaic period of Maori culture, 33, 38
Artifacts, 30–1
Assimilation, 146–8, 151–2, 172, 198–9
Auckland: establishment of, 99–100, 216; growth of, 110; Maori migration to, 198, 202
Auckland City Council, and Orakei Block, 216, 282
Auckland College of Education, 281
Auckland Committee on Racism and Discrimination (ACORD), 220, 278–9
Auckland District Law Society, 234
Auckland District Maori Council, 223, 250, 251, 262
Auckland Regional Authority, 250
Auckland Thermal Number One power station. *See* Waiau Pa
Auckland University Students' Association, 221
Awarau, Mangu, 220, 229
Awatere, Donna, 244

Baker, Neville, 261

Ballance, John, 165
Banks Peninsula, purchase of, 108
Bastion Point, 215–9, 235
Beattie, David, 229, 234, 236
Belich, James, 127
Belshaw, H., 196
Bennett, F. A., 192
Best, Elsdon, 25, 40, 194
Bisson, Judge, 265–6
Black Power, 261–2
Black Women, 220
Bolger, Jim, 283, 284
Broadcasting Committee, 269
Broadcasting Corporation of New Zealand (BCNZ), 271–2
Brother-in-law relationship, 18, 21, 49, 69
Browne, Thomas Gore, 113–6
Bryce, John, 158–9
Buck, Peter (Te Rangihiroa), 25, 36, 39, 40, 179–81, 194
Busby, James, 88–9

Cameron, General, 120, 122–4, 126–8
Cannibalism, 72
Canoes. *See* Waka
Canterbury Block, purchase of, 106
Carey, General, 126
Carroll, James, 172, 175, 177, 179
Carroll, Turi, 205, 206
Carving, art of, 176–7, 178–9; revival of art of, 189–91
Catholic Church. *See* Roman Catholic Church
Chatham Islands, 40, 41–2, 132
Chilwell, J., 267
Christianity, Maori conversion to, 86
Church groups, Maori, 199
Churches: and Maori bishops, 191–3; and Waitangi protests, 232–4
Classic period of Maori culture, 33, 38

Colenso, William, 95–6
Commissioner for the Environment, 268
Conservation Act (1987), 265
Cook, James, 78, 79
Cooke, P., 265–6
Cooper, Whina, 202, 212, 214–5, 229
Couch, Ben, 246–7, 257
Crime, juvenile, of Maori, 208
Cultural continuity, 199–200
Cultural renaissance, Maori, 186–94
Culture clubs, Maori, 199
Cumberland, Tanya, 279
Curtis, Toby, 269
Customary rights, at law, 263, 276
Customs, Maori, 63–77
Cuthbert, Dick, 233

Dalton, Ben, 220, 224
Dannevirke Borough Council, 215
Dansey, Harry, 222
Deane report, 258
Department of Maori Affairs, 197; abolition of, 284–6; housing programmes, 202; and MIL, 256–7; Pakeha district officers of, 211; and Puketapu, 237–43; Treaty Issues Unit, 283. *See also* Native Affairs Department
Department of Social Welfare (DSW), 279–81
Deputations to England: of chiefs, 160–5; of Ratana, 183–4
Derby, Lord, 163–4
Diseases, contagious, introduction of, 80–1
District Maori councils, 204
Dog: creation myth of, 18; tax on, 182
Duff, Roger, 30, 33, 40
Durie, Edward, 248, 275, 283

Economy, Maori: in 1840s, 99–101; in 1980s, 255–62
Education, of Maori, 203, 208, 238–43. *See also* Language, Maori *and* Schools
Electoral revision and Maori seats, 145
Elworthy, Jonathan, 234
Environment Act (1986), 265
Evans, Ripeka, 272

Fenton, Francis, 136, 149
Fire, Maui and, 17–8
Fisheries: of the Arawa, 191; of Te Atiawa, 248–9; expropriation of, 142–4, 155, 273; and fishing industry, 273–7, 283–4; on Manukau, 245; and Maori Parliament, 167
Fisheries Act, and Treaty, 275
Fisheries regulations, 273
Fishing industry, 274, 277, 284
FitzRoy, Robert, 99, 102
Flax cultivation, to gain muskets, 83
Flour mills, of Maori, 101
Forest protection, 178
Fortifications, development of, 33, 37, 83. *See also* Gunfighter's pa
Fox, William, 125
Franchise qualifications, 111, 143
Freire, Paulo, 151, 180, 193, 209, 227, 235

Gadd, Bernard, 241
Gangs, urban, 208, 222, 261
Gardening. *See* Agriculture
Gate Pa, Battle of, 127–8
Glenbrook mill, 251
Golson, Jack, 33
Gordon, Arthur, 158
Gorst, John, 118
Government, responsible, ministers of, 117, 121, 124, 125, 144
Grant, John, 279–80
'Great Fleet' fallacy, 39, 45
Great flood myth, 14
Greer, Colonel, 128
Gregory, Bruce, 228, 246
Greig, J., 275
Grey, George, 103–10, 112, 155–6; and Land Wars, 117–25, 161
Gunfighter's pa, 83–4

Hahunga (exhumation), 75–6
Haka party incident, 221–5
Hakari (feast), 76–7
Hamilton, J. W., 108–9
Hanan, Ralph, 205
Hapu: definition of, 64; in recent times, 199–200
Harawira, Arthur, 229

Harawira, Hone, 224, 229–31
Harawira, Titewhai, 234
Harvesting rituals, 14
Hauhau rebellion, 130–4
Haumiatiketike, 12, 13
Hawaiki, 37–8, 47, 48, 55
Hawke, Joseph Parata, 214–6, 218,
    235, 245
He Taua, 220, 222–5
Health, Maori: and Maui Pomare,
    175, 179, 180–1
Heke, Hone: and Treaty, 95, 96; and
    Heke's war, 103–4, 160
Heke, Hone (MP), 168, 179
Heretaunga Block, 137
Herries, William, 183
Hikoi (1984), 234–6
Hinauri, 19
Hineahuone, 14
Hinenuitepo, 15, 18–9
Hinetiitama, 14–5
Hoani Waititi Marae, Te Atatu, 201,
    270
Hobson, William, 90, 94–5, 99
Hoko whenua, 136, 137
Holland, Harry, 184
Hongi Hika, 81–3
Horouta, 53
Horticulture. *See* Agriculture
House of Representatives. *See*
    Parliament
Housing Corporation, and Maori
    housing, 202
Housing estates. *See* State houses
Hovis Report, 256, 257
Huakina Development Trust, 252–3,
    267
Hughes, Helen, 268
Hui Taumata (Maori Economic
    Summit Conference, 1984), 257–8,
    260, 269
Hui Wakatauira, 237–8
Human Rights Commission, 225
Hunn Report, 203
Hunting and gathering, 28–9, 32
Hutt Valley, 105

Incorporations and trusts, Maori,
    255–6
Irawaru, 18

Iwi, definition of, 65
Iwi Transition Agency, 285–6
Iwikau, 96–7

Jackson, Syd, 220, 221
Jones, Pei Te Hurinui, 205

Kae, 20
Kaituna River claim, 267–8
Kauhanganui, 169–72, 287
Kaupapa, 247, 266, 286–7
Kawiti, 94, 103–4
Keepa, Stan, 255
Kemp, Tacy, 106
Kendall, Thomas, 81, 85
Kereopa Te Rau, 131
Kimberley, Lord, 160, 162–3
King Country, 126, 134, 137
King movement (Kingitanga), 112–3,
    114, 118–9, 122, 234–5
Kingi, Wiremu, 113–4, 160
Kirkwood, Ted, 245, 250–1
Kiwa, 53
Knowledge, Maui and, 17
Kohanga reo, 238–9
Kohere, Rewiti, 192
Kohimarama Conference, 114–5, 148,
    154. *See also* Runanga
Kokiri community management
    groups, 237
Kororareka, 87; flagstaff at, 103
Kotahitanga mo Te Aute, 173–4, 177,
    178, 234–5
Kotahitanga (of Waitangi) Movement,
    149, 152–3, 165, 170, 173, 287. *See
    also* Runanga
Kotuku, Hone, 152
Kumara, 28, 32–3, 79
Kupe, 34–7, 49
Kura kaupapa Maori, 240
Kurahaupo, 51–2

Labour Government, 254
Labour Party: and Rata, 227–8; and
    Ratana, 184–5, 228
Lakes, Maori claim to, 191
Land, Maori: alienation of, 1950s–80s
    212–9; bought by missionaries, 87;
    confiscation of, 120–2, 129, 131;
    consolidation of interests, 178;

designation of, 139, 206–7; under
   leasehold, 196, 206, 213–4, 253–4;
   and Maori Council, 206–7; and
   Maori Parliament, 167–8; maps of,
   140–1; and Native Land Court,
   135–8, 149–50; Ngata's development
   policy for, 177, 187, 198; at Orakei,
   215–9; purchase of, 98–110, 111,
   122, 176, 179, 187; in reserves *See*
   Reserves, Maori; and SOE Act,
   263–5, 281; taken by conquest, 72;
   territorial claims to, 47. *See also*
   Waitangi Tribunal *and* Whenua
Land commissioners, 106–10
Land councils, 176
Land march to Parliament (1975),
   214–5
Land rights movement, Maori, 207,
   212–9
Land Wars, 113
Language, Maori: claim before
   Waitangi Tribunal, 268; and
   kohanga reo, 238–9; neglect of, 176;
   Ngata's recovery programme for,
   193; in schools, 146–7, 174–5, 208,
   210–1, 239–43; in universities, 194
Latimer, Graham, 205, 224, 227,
   229–30, 255, 286; and MIL, 257;
   and transfer of Crown land, 264
Lewis, David, 26
Liquigas consortium wharf, 251–2
Liquor sales, and Maori, 182
Literacy, Maori, 85–6
Literature, Maori, 193, 194

Maccess programmes, 260, 262, 270
McDonnell, Colonel, 131–2
Mackay, James, 109
McLean, Bert, 260
McLean, Donald, 111, 115, 117, 144,
   152, 155–6
Mahuika, 17
Mahuta, 170, 175–6
Makeatutara, 16–7
Mamaari, 35
Mana Motuhake, 227–9, 244
Mana whenua, 45–6, 55–62
Manaia, 49, 51
Mangakahia, Hamiora, 166
Maning, Frederick, 149

Mantell, Walter, 106–8
Manukau City Council, 226
Manukau Harbour, 245, 250–3, 266
Manukorihi Marae, New Plymouth,
   248, 249
Maori Affairs Act (1953) and
   Amendment Act (1967), 139, 207,
   212
Maori Affairs Bill (1978–84), 246–7,
   266
Maori Affairs Department. *See*
   Department of Maori Affairs
Maori Arts and Crafts Institute, 257
Maori Battalion, 195, 197
Maori Broadcasting Committee,
   269–70
Maori committees, 204
Maori Community Centre, Auckland,
   200
Maori Council, 203–9, 214; and Maori
   Affairs Bill, 246–7; and Maori land,
   206–7; and SOE Act, 263–5; on
   Treaty, 211–2
Maori Economic Development
   Commission, 269
Maori Education Foundation, 203,
   240
Maori Educational Development
   Conference (1984), 239–40
Maori electorates, 149, 177, 185; and
   Labour Party, 195; and Mana
   Motuhake, 244
Maori Ethnological Research Board,
   194
Maori Fisheries Bill, 276–7, 284
Maori International Limited, 256–8
Maori Land Court, 207. *See also*
   Native Land Court
Maori loans affair, 258–9, 284–5
Maori (marae) councils, 171–2, 176,
   204
Maori-Pakeha relations, 186, 225,
   248–9, 266, 277–84
Maori Parliament, 161, 165–9, 173,
   227
Maori People's Liberation Movement
   of Aotearoa, 220
Maori Representation Act (1867),
   144–6
Maori Trustee, 138–9, 256

Maori Welfare Act, 255
Maori Women's Welfare League, 202–3, 206, 214, 223
Maori (word), 94
Marae, 174, 187; subsidies for building, 204–5; urban, 200–1
Marae councils. *See* Maori (marae) councils
Maranga Mai, 225–7
Marks, Maiki, 242
Marsden, Samuel, 81
Martin, William, 116
Mataatua, 44, 45, 47, 54, 59
Matakite o Aotearoa, 215
Matawhero, battle of, 133
Matua, Henare, 153
Matua Whangai (foster parenting), 237
Matukutakotako, 23
Maui, 15–9
Maui Nation, 33
Maungapohatu, 133, 182–3
Maxwell, Ralph, 283
Mead, Hirini, 227
Media. *See* News media
Meeting houses. *See* Wharepuni
Memorial of Rights, 214–5
Meremere, Battle of, 123
Military settlers, 121
Minhinnick, Nganeko, 250–3
Mining Act, and Treaty, 211
Ministry of Agriculture and Fisheries (MAF), 274
Ministry of Maori Policy, 285–6, 287
Minto, John, 233
Missionaries: arrival of, 81–2; and land purchases, 87; and Maori customs, 86–7; as peacemakers, 84–5; request for governor, 89; schools of, 85, 146
Moa, 29
Moa-hunters, 30–2, 33
MOOHR, 209–10
Moriori, 34, 39–42
Motunui outfall claim, 248–9, 266
Moturoa, battle of, 132
Mounter, Julian, 272
Moyle, Colin, 276
Muldoon, Robert, 230, 257, 262
Murchie, Elizabeth, 224
Murirangawhenua, 17

Muriwhenua, 47; claim to Waitangi Tribunal, 273–5
Muskets and musket wars, 81, 82–4, 85

Naming of children, 21
National Advisory Committee on Maori Education (NACME), 240–1
National Council of Churches, 232, 233, 234
National Government, and Maori Council, 205
Native Affairs Department, 117, 195. *See also* Department of Maori Affairs
Native Land Commission (1891), 171
Native Land Court, 135–8, 149–50, 153, 167; and Arawa Lakes Agreement, 191; boycott of, 168–9; and Orakei, 216. *See also* Maori Land Court
Native Land Purchase Board, 176
Native Rights Bill, 168
Native (word, use of), 196
New Zealand Company, 89–90, 99, 101, 111
New Zealand Constitution, 110–1
New Zealand Steel, 251, 252
News media: and fisheries claims, 284; and Maori loans affair, 258–9; and Maori politics, 222, 223, 228, 229–30; and Motunui outfall claim, 249
Nga Hau E Wha Marae, Christchurch and Pukekohe, 201
Nga Kaiwhakapumau i te Reo, 268, 270
Nga Tamatoa, 209, 210–2, 221
Ngai Tahu: farming, 100; loss of land, 106–10, *107*; origins, 51; and Treaty, 97
Ngai Tama Block, 265
Ngaiterangi, 126–9
Ngapuhi, 152, 154, 170; deputation of chiefs, 160–3; in musket wars, 82–4; origins, 54
Ngata, Apirana, 173–81, 187, 190–6
Ngata, Henare, 205, 206
Ngati Awa, 54, 60
Ngati Haua, 123; and Native Land Court, 149; at Orakau, 126

Ngati Kahu, 53
Ngati Kahungunu, 163; origins, 56–7
Ngati Koura, origins, 60
Ngati Mahuta, origins, 58
Ngati Maniapoto, 176; at Orakau, 126;
    origins, 57
Ngati Maru: and goldfield leases,
    213–4; in musket wars, 82; origins,
    57–8
Ngati Mutunga, 58
Ngati Paoa, in musket wars, 82
Ngati Porou, 177, 178; origins, 53,
    58–9
Ngati Raukawa: at Orakau, 125–6;
    origins, 58
Ngati Ruanuku, 115
Ngati Tama, origins, 51
Ngati Te Ata, 250
Ngati Toa, origins, 58
Ngati Wai Land Retention
    Committee, 213
Ngati Whatua, 54, 235; in musket
    wars, 83; and Orakei, 215–9, 282;
    and Tamaki, 99–100
Ngatoroirangi, 44, 46, 48–51
Northland tribes, 53–4
Nukutere, 53

Ohaeawai, Battle of, 103
Ohinemutu village road, 213
Orakau, Battle of, 125–6
Orakei Block, 216–9, 282–3
Orakei hui (1879), 154–5
O'Regan, Roland, 277
Otago Block: claim before Waitangi
    Tribunal, 265; purchase of, 106
Otara: housing estates, 198, 202;
    kinship networks in, 200

Pai Mariri (cult), 130
Paikea, 53
Pakeha (word), 94
Papahurihia (cult), 130
Papatuanuku, 11–4
Parihaka, 157–9, 161
Parliament, Maori representation in,
    143, 144–6, 149, 152–3, 167–8, 187.
    See also Maori electorates
Partnership Perspectives and
    Partnership Response, 285–6

Paterangi line, 124
Paul, H. R. H., 230–1
Pawa, 53
Pelly, Richard, 232
Pere, Wi, 168, 177
Peters, Waipu, 213
Peters, Winston, 213, 258, 283, 285
Petricevich, Mira. *See* Szaszy, Mira
Petroleum Act, and Treaty, 211
Pig, introduction of, 79
Planning Tribunal, 250–2
Playcentre movement, and the Maori,
    202–3
Police and Maori activists, 221, 224,
    232–3, 236
Polynesian navigation, 25–8
Polynesian settlers in NZ, 28, 47
Pomare, Maui, 175, 179, 180–1
Population, Maori: in Classic period,
    47; after European contact, 80–1,
    172, 196; after WWII, 197
Population, Pakeha: in 1850s, 111
Potatau I (Te Wherowhero), 112–3
Potato, introduction of, 79
Potiki, 15
Poutapu, Piri, 189–90
Prebble, Richard, 276
Prendergast, James, 158
Pritchard-Waetford Report (1965) on
    Maori land, 206–7
Prophets, Maori, 129–30
Protectors of Aborigines, 105–6
Puao-Te-Ata-Tu, 280–1
Public Works Act: applied to Orakei,
    217; and Treaty, 211
Puhi, 54
Puketakauere, Battle of, 114
Puketapu, Kara, 237–43, 256–7, 285
Pupuri whenua, 136, 137

Quota Management System (QMS),
    274–5

Race Against Time, 225
Race Relations Conciliator, 225, 226
Racial Harmony in New Zealand, 225
Racism, institutional, 277–81
Radio Aotearoa Network, 269–70
Radio New Zealand, 269
Radio station, Maori, 268–70

Raglan Golf Course land, 213
Rangatira (chiefs), 65–6
Rangatiratanga, 266–7
Rangiaowhia, attack on, 124, 131
Rangihau, John, 279–80
Ranginui, 11–2
Rangiriri, Battle of, 123–4
Rangitihi, 55
Rata, 23
Rata, Matiu, 212, 227–8, 244
Ratana, Wiremu Tahupotiki, 181,
   183–5, 195–6
Ratana Church, 183, 192
Rating Act (1967): applied in rural
   areas, 212–3; and Treaty, 211
Reeder, Colin, 260
Reedy, Tamati, 257, 258, 285, 286
Rehua, 19
Reserves, Maori: 106–9, 150; Pakeha
   control of, 138–42; in Taranaki, 180
Resource Management and Local
   Government Reform programme,
   268
Rewa, 94
Rewi Maniapoto, 119, 120, 125
Richmond, James C., 113, 114, 143
Rickard, Eva, 234, 236, 244
Ringatu faith, 132–3
Ritual, correct performance of, 17
Rolleston, William, 146
Roman Catholic Church: and Maori
   bishops, 193; and Te Uunga Waka
   and Te Whaiora, 201; and Waitangi
   protests, 233
Rongomatane, 12, 13, 14
Ross, Ruth, 90–2
Royal, Rangi, 202
Royal, Turoa, 253–4
Rua Kenana, 181–3
Ruapekapeka, Battle of, 103–4
Ruatahuna, 134
Ruaumoko, 14
Rugby, 175
Runanga (Maori councils), 118–9,
   148–9, 152–5, 160; at Waiohiki,
   Pakowhai, Omahu and Orakei,
   153–5
Rupe, 19
Russell, Thomas, 120, 122

Savage, Michael Joseph, and Ratana,
   184–5
School Certificate, 241–3
School of Maori Arts, Rotorua,
   189–90
Schools: mission, 85, 146–7; native,
   147. *See also* Education, Maori *and*
   Language, Maori
Secret ballot and Maori voters, 145,
   196
Seddon, Richard John, 171, 172, 175
Selwyn, George Augustus, 116, 192
Sentencing discrepancies, 277–8
Sharp, Andrew, 25–6
Sharples, Pita, 222–3
Sheep farming, 109
Sheppard, D., 251–2
Shipping, coastal, of Maori, 100–1
Simmons, David, 37, 47
Skinner, H. D., 40, 194
Smith, S. Percy, 25, 36, 39–40
Smoked heads, 83
Spain, William, 99
Sports clubs, Maori, 199
Springbok tour protests, 232–3, 236
State houses, 198
State Owned Enterprises Act (1986):
   and Maori claims, 263–5; and
   Treaty principles, 265
Stirling, Dick, 224
Stout, Robert, 179
Street kids, 208
Subsidies, for marae building, 204–5
Sutherland, Oliver, 234, 277–8
Sutton, D., 41
Szaszy, Mira, 202

Tahu, 51
Tainui, 44, 46, 47, 50
Tainui people, 46, 57–8, 163
Tainui Trust Board, 201
Taitokerau District Council, 229
Taituha, Pumi, 236
Taiwhanga, Hirini, 160, 162
Takamoana, Karaitiana, 149, 150, 152
Takitimu, 47–8, 51
Talley, Peter, 284
Tama Te Kapua, 44–5, 48, 50
Tamaki Corporation of New Zealand
   Ltd, 260–1

Tamaki Maori Development Authority (TMDA), 259–61
Tamaki Technical Training Institute, 260
Tamatea, 54
Tamihana, Wiremu, 111–2, 123–4, 143, 148
Tanemahuta, 12, 14–5
Tangaroa, 12, 13, 27–8
Tangihanga, 74–5; in urban context, 200
Tangotango, 22–3
Taonga: language as, 268; in Treaty terms, 267
Tapu, 67–9
Taranaki people, loss of land, 180
Taranaki war, 114–6, 119–20, 161
Taranga, 15–6
Tarawera River shingle island, 213
Tatai Hono Marae, Auckland, 201
Tataraimaka, 115, 119
Tatau Te Iwi Trust, 261–2
Taurekareka (slaves), 65, 66
Tawhaki, 21–2, 67
Tawhiao, 129, 134, 155–6; his deputation to England, 163–5; and Kauhanganui, 169–72
Taylor, Aila, 248
Te Aomarama, 12
Te Atairangikaahu, 234–5
Te Atiawa, and Motonui outfall claim, 248–9
Te Aute Association. *See* Kotahitanga mo Te Aute
Te Aute College, 173
Te Hau-ki-Turanga, Manutuke, 188–9
Te Heuheu, 97
Te Heuheu, Hepi, 287
Te Heuheu, Tureiti, 173
Te Hokioi, 209, 210
Te Ika a Maui, 17, 18
Te Iwi, 262
Te Kawau, Apihai, 83, 99, 216
Te Kooti Arikirangi Te Turuki, 132–5; his wharepuni, 189
Te Kore, 11–2
Te Ngutu o te Manu, Battle of, 131
Te Po, 12
Te Puaha ki Manukau, 251

Te Puea Herangi, 181; and Turangawaewae, 190; and Waikato compensation, 201–2
Te Puea Marae, Mangere, 201
Te Ranga, battle of, 128–9
Te Rangihaeata, 105
Te Rangikaheke, Wiremu Maihi, 15, 18, 152
Te Rata, 165
Te Rauparaha, 87; arrest of, 105; and Treaty, 96; and Wairau, 101–2
Te Rauparaha, Tamihana, 148
Te Roopu o te Matakite, 214–5
Te Ua Haumene, 130
Te Upoko o te Ika, 270
Te Uunga Waka Maori Centre, Auckland, 201
Te Waharoa, Taingakawa, 171
Te Weehi, Tom, 263, 273
Te Whaiora Marae, 201
Te Wheoro, Wiremu, 150–1, 163
Te Wherowhero: and Grey, 105; as Maori king, 112–3; and Treaty, 97
Te Whiti, 86, 157–9
Te Wiata, Inia, 190
Teachers, Maori, 197, 240; of Maori language, 210–1, 241
Television, Maori, 270–3
'Tenths'. *See* Reserves, Maori
Thames and Coromandel goldfield leases, 213–4, 253–4
Thierry, Charles de, 88
Thornton, John, 173, 175
Tia, 50
Tinirau, 19–20
Tiramorehu, 108
Tiriti o Waitangi Marae, 152, 161, 165
Titokowaru, 131–4, 135
Tizard, Cath, 282–3
Tohu, 159
Tohunga, 66–7, 69
Tohunga suppression, 174, 181
Toi, 34, 36
Tokomaru, 51, 52
Tomoana, Henare, 153, 166–7, 170
Toroa, 59
Town and Country Planning Acts, 213, 250; and Treaty, 211–2
Townships, Maori, 138, 139

Trade, Maori-Pakeha, 78–9, 83, 100, 102

Treasury, 258

Treaty of Waitangi: Acts in contravention of, 143, 211–3; celebrations and protests, 211, 221, 229–36; and deputations to England, 160–5; drafting and signing of, 90–7; effect of, 98–9; and fisheries, 142–4, 274–7; hui on (1984), 253–4; in Land Wars, 114–6; moral ground of, 249; principles of, in modern legislation, 264–8, 281–4, 286–7; ratification petition, 195–6; and WAC, 221

Treaty of Waitangi Amendment Act (1985), 254

Tree-cutting rituals, 14, 23

Tribal assemblies. *See* Runanga

Tribal boundaries, 55–62; map of, *61*

Tribal committees, 203–4

Tribal incorporations and trusts, 255–6

Tribal migrations, 44–62

Tribalism, rise of, 33–7, 42–3

Tuhaere, Paora, 148, 150, 154–5, 164

Tuhoe people, 60, 62, 125, 133; and Rua, 181–3

Tuhuruhuru, 20–1

Tumatauenga, 12, 13

Turangawaewae, 70; marae as, 187

Turangawaewae, Ngaruawahia, 190–1, 235

Turi, 35–6, 37, 45, 52

Turner, Judge, 251, 267

Tutua (commoners), 65, 66

Tuwharetoa people, 46, 47, 48, 51; origins of, 55–6

Uenuku, 44, 45

Uepohatu, 33, 53. *See also* Maui Nation

Unemployed, training of, 260–1

Unification of tribes. *See* Kotahitanga

United Tribes of NZ, 88–9, 96

Urban migration, Maori, 197–9, 208

Urewera, 133, 134, 182–3

Utu: myth of, 20; principle of, 69–70

Volkner, Carl, 131

Voluntary associations, Maori, 199

Von Tempsky, Gustavus, 131

Wahawaha, Ropata, 133–4

Wahieroa, 21, 23

Waiau Pa power station proposal, 245, 251

Waikato people, 176; and King Movement, 112–3, 119; land confiscations, 129, 156, 201; and land sales, 137–8; and Te Puea Marae, 201; and Waiau Pa station, 245; and World War I, 181

Waikato River, and Waitangi Tribunal, 251, 267

Waikato war, 120–6, 161

Waikerepuru, Huirangi, 268

Waimate Plains, survey of, 157–8

Waipatu Marae, Heretaunga, 165–6

Wairau affray, 101–2

Wairau Bar, 30–1

Waitangi Action Committee (WAC), 220–1, 229–36

Waitangi Day, 211, 233, 236

Waitangi Treaty. *See* Treaty of Waitangi

Waitangi Tribunal, 212, 244–5, 248–9, 252–5; and fisheries claims, 273–7, 283–4; and other courts of law, 262–8; and Pakeha fears, 281–4; retrospective powers of, 253–5

Waitara purchase, 113–4, 119–20

Waitoa, Rota, 192

Waiuku State Forest, 253

Waka: construction of, 24–5; cultural symbolism of, 28, 38–9, 42–3; names of, 54–5; as social grouping, 65; traditions of, 44–55. *See also* individual canoe names

Waka Nene, Tamati, 95, 104, 105

Wakefield, Arthur, 101–2

Wakefield, Edward Gibbon, 89

Wakefield, William, 89–90

Wardens, Maori, 203–4

Warfare: development of, 33; model for conduct of, 20–1, 128; tribal, 55–62, 71–2

Waring, Marilyn, 226

Waste land, 98–9

Water and Soil Conservation Act, and
    Treaty, 267
Welcome, the, 73–4
Welfare officers, Maori, 197
Wellington, Merv, 226
Wero, 73
Wetere, Koro, 285, 286
Whakatau Potiki, 20–1
Whakatohea, 62, 131
Whaling, 78
Whanau: definition of, 63; in recent
    times, 199–200
Wharepuni: development of, 32,
    188–91; in 1880s, 176–7; in urban
    marae, 201
Wharewaka, Abe, 261–2
Whenua, 70–1
Whitaker, Frederick, 120, 162

Whitmore, Colonel, 132, 133, 134
Williams, Archbishop, 233
Williams, David, 245
Williams, Henry, 84
Williamson, A., 263
Winiata, Whatarangi, 270–1
Women Against Racism Action Group
    (WARAG), 279–80
Women, Maori, in 20th century,
    201–3
Woodhill State Forest, 265
World War I: and Maori volunteers,
    181; and Tuhoe, 182
World War II, and Maori, 196, 197

Young Maori Conference, 196
Young Maori Leaders Conference,
    208–9